Trauma, Meaning, and Spirituality

Trauma, Meaning, and Spirituality

Translating Research Into Clinical Practice

Crystal L. Park, Joseph M. Currier,
J. Irene Harris, and Jeanne M. Slattery

American Psychological Association • Washington, DC

Published by
American Psychological Association
750 First Street, NE
Washington, DC 20002
www.apa.org

To order
APA Order Department
P.O. Box 92984
Washington, DC 20090-2984
Tel: (800) 374-2721; Direct: (202) 336-5510
Fax: (202) 336-5502; TDD/TTY: (202) 336-6123
Online: www.apa.org/pubs/books
E-mail: order@apa.org

In the U.K., Europe, Africa, and the Middle East, copies may be ordered from
American Psychological Association
3 Henrietta Street
Covent Garden, London
WC2E 8LU England

Typeset in Goudy by Circle Graphics, Inc., Columbia, MD

Printer: Bang Printing, Brainerd, MN
Cover Designer: Mercury Publishing Services, Rockville, MD

The opinions and statements published are the responsibility of the authors, and such opinions and statements do not necessarily represent the policies of the American Psychological Association.

Library of Congress Cataloging-in-Publication Data

Names: Park, Crystal L., author. | Currier, Joseph M., author. | Harris, J. Irene, author. | Slattery, Jeanne M., author. | American Psychological Association, publisher.
Title: Trauma, meaning, and spirituality : translating research into clinical practice / Crystal L. Park, Joseph M. Currier, J. Irene Harris, Jeanne M. Slattery.
Description: First edition. | Washington, DC : American Psychological Association, [2017] | Includes bibliographical references and index.
Identifiers: LCCN 2016019614 | ISBN 9781433823251 | ISBN 143382325X
Subjects: | MESH: Trauma and Stressor Related Disorders—psychology | Spirituality | Models, Psychological | Counseling—methods
Classification: LCC RC552.T7 | NLM WM 172.5 | DDC 616.85/210628—dc23
LC record available at https://lccn.loc.gov/2016019614

British Library Cataloguing-in-Publication Data
A CIP record is available from the British Library.

Printed in the United States of America
First Edition

http://dx.doi.org/10.1037/15961-000

CONTENTS

Trauma, Meaning, and Spirituality

1

THE INTERSECTION OF RELIGION/ SPIRITUALITY AND TRAUMA

Keya Banks grew up in rural North Dakota in an intact, Presbyterian family, the daughter of a physician and a homemaker.[1] Her family was financially secure and respected in the community, and through her elementary and high school years, she had strong social support in her peer group and was academically successful. She regularly participated in youth group mission trips with her church, engaging in activities such as building houses after natural disasters. Before she went to college, her most stressful experience was watching her family deal with her sister's Addison's disease. She was concerned about her sister and quite involved in her care. Months of testing were necessary to arrive at a diagnosis, and the family's lifestyle changed dramatically to help her sister return to health. Ms. Banks's faith group valued occupations that provided help and care for others, so she went to college

---

[1]The details of the case studies in this volume have been changed to preserve the anonymity of the individuals involved.

http://dx.doi.org/10.1037/15961-001
Trauma, Meaning, and Spirituality: Translating Research Into Clinical Practice, by C. L. Park, J. M. Currier, J. I. Harris, and J. M. Slattery

3

considering a career in biological sciences, possibly to become a nutritionist or a physician, like her father. For her, a career in this area felt like the most effective way she could pursue a religious mission to help and serve others.

However, in her first week of school, at a fraternity party to welcome first-year students, she was given punch that had been laced with hypnotics and was subsequently sexually assaulted. Having grown up in a secure community and environment, it had never occurred to her that anyone would deliberately harm her; she felt betrayed by her college community and by God. She felt that she had been doing everything she could to do what she thought was right, and interpreted the predestination beliefs of her church to mean that God had planned for this assault to happen to her. Her faith was severely challenged, and her acute trauma reaction was sufficiently disabling that she left college midway through her first semester, certain that she would not return to the same college, if she returned to school at all.

This case illustrates the sudden and severe nature of trauma and the sweeping impact it can have in key life domains. Importantly, for Ms. Banks, as for many who experience trauma, among the most damaged domains was her spiritual life.

OUR AIMS IN WRITING THIS BOOK

Given the pervasive roles of spirituality and religiousness in many individuals' responses to traumatic events and in their efforts to cope with them, attending to the ways in which religion and spirituality impede or foster resilience in trauma survivors and the ways that trauma may shape people's subsequent religious or spiritual lives will advance our understanding of human adaptation to trauma and our ability to help those who are suffering. It is our shared conviction that attending to the conjoint influences of spirituality and trauma is essential to a full understanding of human behavior and is highly relevant to clinicians working with clients who have a history of trauma.

The authors of this book include leading theorists and researchers in psychology of religion as well as active clinicians working with trauma survivors in both clinical and research settings. All the authors have backgrounds in clinical or counseling psychology, and this book is intended for mental health professionals from these and other disciplines who similarly focus on trauma survivors in their practice and research. Importantly, the authors collectively span a range of religious and spiritual backgrounds as well as current beliefs and practices (e.g., Roman Catholic and Evangelical Christian to agnostic and Buddhist or yogic spiritualities). We feel it is important to disclose the diversity of our perspectives to emphasize that, regardless of readers' personal backgrounds and current spiritual lives, this book can be quite relevant to their values and clinical approach; we attempted not to privilege any particular spiritual or religious backgrounds, beliefs, and practices. In fact, for each of the authors, research findings and clinical experiences have demonstrated the importance of individuals' spiritual lives in the process of making meaning of and recovering from traumatic experiences. All the authors have also been struck by the lack of scientific literature necessary to effectively address spiritual concerns in trauma survivors and have dedicated much of their careers to addressing this need.

OVERVIEW: THEORY AND RESEARCH ON TRAUMA AND SPIRITUALITY

Research on trauma and its aftermath has been increasing in volume and scope in recent decades (Friedman, Keane, & Resick, 2007). This proliferating interest has been spurred in part by the recent wars in which the United States has been involved, as well as official recognition of posttraumatic stress disorder (PTSD) following the challenges of many Vietnam veterans (American Psychiatric Association, 1980), and in part by a general increase in cultural awareness of the toll taken by many types of trauma (Friedman et al., 2007). However, researchers have only relatively recently begun to focus on spirituality in the context of trauma (Y. Y. Chen & Koenig, 2006a). Theory and research in this area primarily have focused on the ways in which religion or spirituality may serve as coping or resilience factors when people confront traumatic events (e.g., Fallot & Heckman, 2005; Peres, Moreira-Almeida, Nasello, & Koenig, 2007). A smaller amount of theory and research has outlined the effects of traumatic and highly stressful events on people's spiritual lives (e.g., P. Kennedy & Drebing, 2002; Uecker, 2008).

In tandem with the increased research focus on trauma, clinicians have increasingly focused on developing effective assessment and clinical interventions following trauma and its aftermath (e.g., van der Kolk, 2007), yet the spiritual aspects of trauma and recovery are rarely considered in clinical practice. Most mainstream approaches to treating trauma exposure and diagnosed PTSD, including the work of Resick (2001), Foa and Rothbaum (1998), Briere and Scott (2006), and Ehlers and Clark (e.g., Michael, Ehlers, Halligan, & Clark, 2005), make almost no mention of spiritual or religious issues. Such omission may suggest that these issues are unimportant to clinical practice with people who have histories of trauma. Briere and Scott, for example, mentioned spirituality only once. Numerous books are available regarding spiritual and religious issues in counseling and therapy, many with an explicit Christian focus (e.g., McMinn & Campbell, 2007; Worthington, Johnson, Hook, & Aten, 2013). These books, however, make minimal reference specifically to trauma. For example, Pargament's (2007) book, *Spiritually Integrated Psychotherapy*, mentions the word *trauma* 18 times in 384 pages. However, along with a growing appreciation by mental health professionals regarding the critical role of religion and spirituality in many people's lives, the intersection of spirituality and trauma appears to be garnering more attention. For example, Walker, Courtois, and Aten (2015) recently published an edited book, *Spiritually Oriented Psychotherapy for Trauma*, which brings together these two themes.

This relative lack of attention to the spirituality–trauma interface may be, at least in part, because psychologists tend to be far less religious than the average American (Delaney, Miller, & Bisonó, 2007). For example, survey responses of a sample of members of the American Psychological Association were compared with responses from the general U.S. population. Psychologists were much less religious than was the general population. The vast majority, however, regarded religion as beneficial (82%) rather than harmful (7%) to mental health (see Table 1.1). Although recent data have suggested that fewer Americans identify with a specific religious affiliation (termed the *religious nones*), most of these people still report believing in God or a higher power and endorse some aspects of spirituality (Pew Research Center, 2015). Still, the composition of religiousness in Americans is changing, which may have implications for both therapists and the clients they serve.

Although researchers have been slow to attend to the links of religion and spirituality with trauma and most approaches to clinical intervention still ignore religious and spiritual issues, we take the position that religiousness and spirituality should indeed be considered in the context of trauma because they are often closely intertwined in human experience. We now know that trauma often forces individuals to face the uncertainty and instability underlying human existence and reconsider their sense of identity as well as their deepest beliefs regarding control, responsibility, justice, trust, guilt, suffering, and forgiveness (S. Smith, 2004). These confrontations frequently tap into individuals' most profound dimensions of spirituality, regardless of whether they are explicitly framed as such. Further, research has made it clear that individuals often turn to religious and spiritual strategies to cope with their traumas (e.g., Y. Y. Chen & Koenig, 2006b).

DEFINING RELIGIOUSNESS AND SPIRITUALITY

In spite of the extensive efforts of many theorists and researchers over the past few decades to develop satisfactory definitions of *religiousness* and *spirituality* (Oman, 2013), such definitions remain elusive. Any proposed definitions of religiousness and spirituality (and any distinctions drawn between

TABLE 1.1

Survey Responses (in Percentages) Regarding Spirituality and
Religion in Members of the American Psychological Association (APA)
Compared With the General U.S. Population

Questions and responses	APA, 2003	U.S.
How important is *religion* in your life?		
Very important	21	55
Fairly important	31	30
Not very important	48	15
During the past year, how often did you participate in religious worship at a church, mosque, synagogue, feast day, etc.?		
Never or rarely	55	40
Once or twice a month	22	13
Once a week or more	23	47
Belief in God		
God really exists	32	64
Some doubts but believe in God	19	20
Some belief, higher power	25	10
Don't believe in God, don't know	25	5
What do you personally believe about the effects of religion, in general, on mental health? Do you think that being religious is most likely to be:		
Harmful to mental health	7	
Irrelevant to mental health	11	
Beneficial to mental health	82	
How often do you inquire about or assess your clients' religion or spirituality?		
Never/rarely	14	
Sometimes	35	
Often	37	
Always	14	
How often are spiritual or religious issues relevant in the treatment that you provide?		
Never/rarely	17	
Sometimes	57	
Often	23	
Always	3	

Note. From "Religiosity and Spirituality Among Psychologists: A Survey of Clinician Members of the American Psychological Association," by H. D. Delaney, W. R. Miller, and A. M. Bisonó, 2007, *Professional Psychology: Research and Practice, 38,* p. 540. Copyright 2007 by the American Psychological Association.

them) generate vigorous dissent (see L. H. Martin, 2015; Paloutzian & Park, 2015), leading others to try once again. In this book, we follow the lead of a recent proposal by Pargament and his colleagues in their *APA Handbook of Psychology, Religion, and Spirituality* (Pargament, 2013; Pargament, Mahoney, Exline, Jones, & Shafranske, 2013). They defined *spirituality* as "the search for the sacred," with *sacred* referring not only to God or higher power but also to "other aspects of life that are perceived to be manifestations of the divine or imbued with divine-like qualities, such as transcendence, immanence, boundlessness and ultimacy" (Pargament, Mahoney, et al., 2013, p. 7). In contrast, they defined *religion* as "the search for significance that occurs within the context of established institutions that are designed to facilitate spirituality," with that significance referring to a multiplicity of goals that may be "psychological (e.g., anxiety reduction, meaning, impulse control), social (e.g., belonging, identity, dominance), and physical (e.g., longevity, evolutionary adaptation, death), as well as those that are spiritual" (Pargament, Mahoney, et al., 2013, p. 15).

Pargament, Mahoney, et al. (2013) noted,

> Religion occurs within the larger context of established institutions and traditions directed toward the pursuit of a broader array of destinations or significant goals than spirituality. Religion serves the important function of facilitating spirituality itself, but it serves other functions as well. When they are, they also fall beneath the spiritual umbrella. (pp. 15–16)

Similarly, Oman (2013) noted that a new, more restricted meaning of religion emerged near the end of the 20th century, by which *religion* connotes the organized and institutional components of faith traditions, in contrast to the more inward and personal sides, which are often now referred to as *spirituality*. Thus, there are both complementary and polarizing distinctions between religion and spirituality (Zinnbauer & Pargament, 2005). Here, we take the more complementary perspective, with religion and spirituality as overlapping (but not identical) constructs.

S. Smith (2004) noted that as the United States has been changing toward a more religiously pluralistic society, the concepts of religion and spirituality have become more polarized in the public consciousness (Hill & Pargament, 2003). Although their definitions imply different connotations, Hill and Pargament (2003) asserted that religion and spirituality contain more integrated themes than separate ones. They stated that polarizing these concepts such that religion is considered inflexible and dogmatic whereas spirituality is considered freeing and enlightening does a disservice to both concepts. Religion and spirituality contain overarching and intertwined themes. Both originate from needs to acknowledge and uphold that which is considered sacred. Both are means by which human beings strive to understand, cope with, and perhaps transcend their daily lives. In this book, for purposes of consistency, we largely rely on the term *spirituality* when speaking about these constructs in general discussions of theory and research. However, when distinctions between them become important to our discussion or when we describe the faith experiences of traumatized clients, we draw distinctions between religion and spirituality.

DEFINING TRAUMA AND ITS IMPACTS

The American Psychiatric Association's definition of trauma is often used as an official definition in research on this topic. The latest edition of the *Diagnostic and Statistical Manual of Mental Disorders* (fifth ed.; DSM–5; American Psychiatric Association, 2013) describes *trauma* as exposure to actual or threatened death, serious injury, or sexual violence, involving direct exposure, witnessing (in person or indirectly), by learning that a close relative or close friend was exposed to trauma, or experiencing repeated or extreme indirect exposure to aversive details of the event(s), usually in the course of professional duties, as with first responders. This exposure must be direct and does not include exposure through electronic media, television, movies, or pictures. The *DSM–5* also explicitly excludes death of a family member or friend from natural causes from their definition of trauma—although many people perceive these experiences as traumatic. The official definition excludes major medical events such as cancer diagnosis or treatment (Kangas, 2013), though these types of events certainly can generate similar changes in emotion, cognition, and behavior as those observed following events that meet the *DSM–5* definition of trauma. The *International Classification of Diseases* (10th rev.; World Health Organization, 2016) does not explicitly define *trauma* but does note that PTSD can arise from stressful events or situations "of exceptionally threatening or catastrophic nature, which is likely to cause pervasive distress in almost anyone" (World Health Organization, 2016, F43.1).

Some have argued that the parameters of the *DSM–5*'s definition too narrowly describe what qualifies as trauma (e.g., Brewin, Lanius, Novac, Schnyder, & Galea, 2009). For example, Briere (2013) suggested that trauma may also include "threats to psychological integrity, including major losses, events that were very upsetting but did not include fear of death or injury, and early and severe childhood neglect" (para. 4). An interesting study of the utility of the *DSM–IV–TR* (American Psychiatric Association, 2000) criteria compared undergraduates who reported exposure to a traumatic event that was consistent with the *DSM* definition with those who reported exposure to a traumatic event that was inconsistent with the definition. Surprisingly, the latter group reported significantly greater PTSD symptom severity than did those who reported an official trauma (Gold, Marx, Soler-Baillo, & Sloan, 2005). In addition, significantly more people in the *DSM* trauma-incongruent group met criteria for PTSD diagnosis than did those in the *DSM* trauma-congruent group. Nearly two thirds of the *DSM* trauma-incongruent group identified the death or illness of a loved one as their traumatic experience, which would not qualify as a bona fide trauma in the *DSM* definition. Similar findings have been reported for a sample of 860 Australian adults (Van Hooff, McFarlane, Baur, Abraham, & Barnes, 2009).

Beyond disagreement about what qualifies as trauma, research has erased any doubt that exposure to these types of events is common. Epidemiological studies in the United States using *DSM–IV–TR* criteria for defining a traumatic event (which were somewhat broader than more recent *DSM–5* criteria) produced lifetime prevalence rates ranging from 51% to 90% (for reviews, see P. Frazier, 2012; F. H. Norris & Slone, 2007). Although varying definitions of trauma may generate different prevalence rates, it appears that 25% of the general U.S. population will indeed encounter at least one such event before early adulthood, and the remainder will likely experience such an event by middle adulthood (F. H. Norris & Slone, 2007). In addition, exposure rates are greater among certain subgroups (e.g., urban poor, military veterans), and other findings have further suggested that most people who encounter a trauma of some sort will have repeated exposures over the lifespan, rather than an isolated experience (F. H. Norris & Slone, 2007). Hence, exposure rates will undoubtedly be higher in communities that lack the economic resources and infrastructure for deterring violence and maintaining social order (i.e., cultural groups where affiliation with conventional forms of religiousness are perhaps the most common in the United States and throughout the world).

Research has also documented that exposure to trauma can lead to a variety of negative sequelae, including anxiety, depression, interpersonal difficulties, and posttraumatic stress (e.g., Bonanno, Brewin, Kaniasty, & La Greca, 2010). Exposure to a traumatic event can also lead to symptoms consistent with a formal diagnosis of PTSD; when compared with other psychiatric conditions that form the basis of mental health care, exposure is in fact part of the definition of this disorder (American Psychiatric Association, 2013). However, the prevalence of PTSD in the general population is much lower than would be predicted by trauma exposure alone: Although the conditional risk of PTSD is greater for certain types of traumas, it appears that, on average, about 8% develop this condition after confronting a trauma (Kessler, Sonnega, Bromet, Hughes, & Nelson, 1995; Vieweg et al., 2006). Given the rather exclusive nature of defining trauma at present, prevalence of PTSD conducted using these new criteria is not expected to change much when new epidemiological reports become available (e.g., P. S. Calhoun et al., 2012). The discrepancy between the high incidence of trauma exposure and the relatively low prevalence of PTSD suggests that traumatic events lead to psychiatric illness relatively infrequently (Breslau et al., 1998). However, many individuals experience sub-threshold levels of posttraumatic symptoms; clinical levels of depression, anxiety, or substance abuse; or considerable distress. Further, trajectories of distress and recovery following trauma exposures vary, a point we take up in Chapter 11.

WHY CONSIDER SPIRITUALITY AND TRAUMA TOGETHER?

From the existential terror and shattering of normalcy that might follow exposure to trauma to the various ways in which survivors might draw on spiritual traditions in coping with these experiences, there are many reasons to consider spirituality in the context of trauma. The noted discrepancy between the high incidence of trauma exposure and the relatively low prevalence of PTSD may also reflect people's natural resilience, and an important part of that resilience may lie in considering survivors' spiritual resources. In addition, as we discuss throughout this book, trauma can change spirituality (either positively or negatively). Further, spirituality can either increase or decrease survivors' stress and distress or help resolve trauma (Slattery & Park, 2015). Issues of meaning in life (i.e., coherence, purpose, and mattering; George & Park, 2014)—and its restoration following severe challenges to it (i.e., meaning making)—are pervasive throughout processes of distress and recovery. Consider the interplay of spirituality, trauma, and meaning as we continue our discussion of the case study that began the chapter.

Ms. Banks had difficulty accessing therapy services from her rural town. The nearest source of mental health services was a 2-hour drive, but her family pulled together to support her as they supported her sister was she ill. On hearing her fears that God had deliberately caused this assault, her therapist recommended further consultation with the family's clergy. The minister met with Ms. Banks frequently during the course of her therapy, helping her to draw different spiritual meanings from this event than she did in her initial appraisals. The minister clarified that God would not have made that young man rape her and that God was compassionately present in her suffering and would hold the rapist accountable for his actions. The minister also said that although God loved Ms. Banks and would never want her to be raped, part of being Christian involves experiencing adversity, as Jesus did, and finding ways to use what we learn, responding to adversity in ways that will help others. The minister also supported Ms. Banks in her therapy, encouraging her not to avoid difficult issues with her therapist and to have confidence that no one who truly knew and cared for her would blame her for the assault.

With support from her family, therapist, and clergy, Ms. Banks made several decisions about how she might best use this experience to be helpful to others. She felt that it was important that her rapist be stopped from hurting someone else. She and her family met with an attorney and examined several options; she eventually decided that the best recourse would be to file a complaint with the college against the perpetrator. This led to a series of hearings within the college's internal justice system, and eventually the young man was expelled from school. Ms. Banks elected not to pursue further legal action, primarily because she did not want to endure lengthy court processes or the potentially demeaning cross-examinations she would likely face. However, it was difficult for Ms. Banks to imagine having the courage to take these steps without the strength of her faith and relational support from her spiritual community.

As Ms. Banks moved forward in her recovery, she learned of a resource group for sexual assault survivors in the nearest city, a 2-hour drive away. Although she remained fearful of leaving her rural community, and the time commitment was arduous given her lengthy commute, she began volunteering there, first organizing educational materials, then working as a member of a speakers' bureau to provide education to prevent sexual assaults, and finally working on a crisis hotline for sexual assault survivors. After working on the hotline, she told her family and minister that she felt she had experienced a "calling." When she spoke with others in acute distress after surviving sexual assault, she could see where she had been months ago and, at the same time, could see how far she had come in her recovery. She realized that the way she wanted to make meaning of her experience was to work in a counseling profession so that she could help others recover from sexual assault. She decided to pursue a degree in human services. She also chose a small college close to home this time, not only so that she had access to support from her spiritual community but also so that she could be available to her family and friends when they needed support from her.

For Ms. Banks, religious and spiritual meanings regarding her trauma and recovery were integral to both her distress and her subsequent resilience. Her initial perception that God may have somehow predestined this attack threatened the meaning system she had used to order and understand her life up to that time, forcing her to explore new approaches to making meaning of her experiences. In her efforts to develop a new, more mature meaning system, she also changed her career plans and her relationships with her family to become an advocate and instrument of healing and restoration for others who might encounter similar traumas.

This case illustrates many points of intersection between spirituality and trauma. Ms. Banks's family and community were steeped in religious traditions and an ethos that strongly shaped her beliefs (e.g., in the benevolence of others and the safety of the world) as well as her life goals (to serve others in the service of God). These types of links between religion and global meaning are delineated in Chapter 3 and highlighted throughout the book. Ms. Banks's initial way of understanding her assault, in large part based on her relatively under-developed religious worldview, was that this was somehow God's plan for her. The meaning she assigned to the assault, therefore, violated her beliefs in a secure and loving relationship with God and caused her great emotional and spiritual distress.

Essential to Ms. Banks's healing was her reappraisal of the meaning of the assault in a way more consistent with her deep-seated religious beliefs and the orthodox teachings of her faith tradition. As she made meaning of her traumatic experience, she was able to restore her sense of being loved by God and seeing God as not being the culprit in the assault. Further, she was able to align her sense of suffering with the trials and tribulations of Jesus and to use her experience of adversity and recovery in a positive way: to serve others who were suffering as well.

ORGANIZATION OF THIS BOOK

This book first provides conceptual frames and then applies them to assessment, treatment, and ethical issues. Case material is provided to illustrate applications of how clients' spirituality may impede or facilitate their making of meaning following trauma. The first three chapters provide the foundational conceptual material on which the book is based.

- Chapter 1 provides definitions and background material used throughout the book.
- Chapter 2 presents the conceptual framework of the meaning-making model, a comprehensive framework describing how meaning manifests in day-to-day life as well as in encounters with traumatic events. Importantly, this model distinguishes meaning-making processes and products of that process (meaning made).
- Chapter 3 discusses in greater depth the meaning-making process in terms of the reciprocal interplay between spirituality and trauma. The mutual influences of spirituality and trauma are detailed, focusing both on how spirituality influences responses to trauma and how trauma can also influence spirituality in transformative ways.

Subsequent chapters delve more deeply into trauma and its treatment, describing how current approaches have not adequately considered religious and spiritual issues and how the concerns of many trauma survivors can be more comprehensively understood using the reciprocal meaning-making model. Subsequent chapters then incorporate the reciprocal meaning-making model to detail the therapist's role in treatment and describe implications for assessment and case conceptualization.

- Chapter 4 outlines the contemporary approaches to understanding and treating PTSD, noting that trauma sequelae are often the specified presenting problem in therapy, but that trauma also is an important issue for many clients presenting with other issues as well.

- Chapter 5 identifies clinical issues that may arise according to this reciprocal meaning-making model. In particular, this chapter highlights how one's spiritual life can affect appraisal and coping with trauma and vice versa.
- Chapter 6 provides an overview of strategies for assessing spirituality and relates these to the reciprocal meaning-making model. Specific suggestions and examples of assessment approaches and instruments are included; the book's Appendix contains validated measures.
- Chapter 7 describes three treatment objectives through the lens of a reciprocal meaning-making model: building the therapeutic alliance, resolving discrepancies in meaning, and creating new meaning in life.
- Chapter 8 explores transactional issues between therapist, client, and God. The reciprocal model is used to consider issues of secondary or vicarious trauma and other occupational hazards for therapists working with this population, as well as changes in meaning experienced by both therapist and client and how they can influence treatment.
- Chapter 9 focuses on the past, examining how trauma can disrupt a person's global meaning system and how recovery often entails creating a new sense of one's place in the world and shifts in one's relationships with other people, and possibly with God. We describe how therapists can help clients turn to, strengthen, and develop new spiritual coping strategies in the treatment process.
- Chapter 10 focuses on the present, including resolving spiritual struggles and increasing spiritual well-being. Both implicit and explicit approaches to integrating spirituality into treatment are presented and elaborated.
- Chapter 11 describes the roles that spirituality and meaning making may play in preventing problems and maximizing trauma-related recovery and possible growth. In addition, we identify interventions that could be helpful in facilitating resilient trajectories in the aftermath of stress and trauma.
- Chapter 12 focuses on broader ethical issues for addressing spirituality with trauma survivors, particularly through the lens of the reciprocal meaning-making model.
- Chapter 13 summarizes the current state of knowledge regarding trauma, spirituality, and the reciprocal meaning-making model and suggests future directions for research and for the development of more efficacious interventions that attend to spiritual issues in the context of trauma.

2

THE CENTRALITY OF MEANING IN HUMAN LIVES

People understand and navigate their lives through their systems of meaning. These meaning systems inform how people understand themselves, their lives, and the larger world. They also direct their personal aims and projects and, through them, their general sense of well-being and life satisfaction (e.g., Emmons, 1999). *Meaning systems* comprise people's fundamental beliefs—about themselves, the universe, and their sense of meaning and purpose—as well as their unique hierarchies of goals and values.

People also rely on their meaning systems to interpret and label the specific situations they encounter in life (e.g., appraisals of threat, harm, loss, controllability), and these interpretations then shape the emotional and behavioral consequences of these encounters (Lazarus & Folkman, 1984; Park, 2010). *Global meaning* influences people's appraisals of ordinary experiences as well as traumas and other highly stressful events. *Situational meaning* encompasses the meanings assigned to these experiences, the potential

http://dx.doi.org/10.1037/15961-002
Trauma, Meaning, and Spirituality: Translating Research Into Clinical Practice, by C. L. Park, J. M. Currier, J. I. Harris, and J. M. Slattery

discrepancies between global and appraised meaning, the processes involved in reconciling those discrepancies (termed *meaning making*), and the changes resulting from these reconciliation processes (termed *meaning made*). See Figure 2.1 for a depiction of this process.

This chapter explicates the various aspects of global and situational meaning, also highlighting the ways in which spirituality pervasively influences many people's global beliefs and goals and the meanings they make in particular situations. We draw on the case of Ms. Kim throughout this chapter to illustrate the interplay of global and situational meanings in both the etiology of trauma-related distress and its resolution.

INTRODUCTION TO MS. KIM

Yong Kim presented to a university counseling center as a senior animal sciences major with a long-standing career plan to become a veterinarian and work in pharmacy research. However, several cultural circumstances slowed her social development in college. Ms. Kim immigrated to the United States from South Korea when she was 15, and she had very different cultural values and communication patterns than those of her peers at a southern Gulf state college. In addition, she was one of only three women in a cohort of 50 animal science majors; many of the male students felt that veterinary studies were inappropriate for women, sometimes harassing the female students in the class. Competition to get into graduate study for veterinary science was also

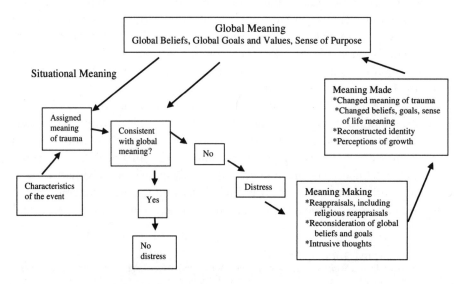

Figure 2.1. The reciprocal meaning-making model.

daunting for Ms. Kim and her classmates. With this combination of social barriers, Ms. Kim spent most of her time outside of class studying, with the only consistent exception being weekly attendance at Catholic Mass with a small all-Korean congregation. According to Ms. Kim, she valued these services for tapping into her connection with God, her connection with the Korean community, and the purpose of her demanding planned vocation (developing medicines to heal others).

Although Ms. Kim was quite successful academically, she had almost no friends at school. However, she met another Korean American student, Mr. Park, while singing in the college choir during her senior year. Both of them appreciated opportunities to speak their native language, enjoy Korean food together, and be free from the fairly constant struggle to communicate using American social norms instead of their own. Nonetheless, when the warm relationship with this young man developed into a romantic attraction for both, Ms. Kim became deeply troubled and ambivalent about their relationship.

That is, she reported intrusive memories about her grandfather when she allowed Mr. Park to touch her in a caring or affectionate manner, as well as nightmares, episodes of panic, and overwhelming feelings of fear and guilt related to childhood experiences that she barely had language to express in either Korean or English. It was quite difficult for Ms. Kim to ask for help from the counseling center. She would have preferred to seek support from her family, but she did not feel that members of her family would support her decision even to discuss her concerns. It took several sessions with her therapist before she could honestly express the source of her ambivalence about her relationship with Mr. Park.

As a child growing up in Korea, her grandfather had lived with the family and had consistently sexually abused Ms. Kim from the time she was 5 years old until he was too disabled by cancer to continue doing so. As the eldest living member of the family, her grandfather's wishes and decisions were not to be questioned, and Ms. Kim had never told her parents because she feared that she would be severely punished for doing so. As her relationship with Mr. Park became closer, sexual feelings and impulses often led to reexperiencing symptomatology (e.g., flashbacks) and bouts of insomnia. Furthermore, she was afraid that the topic of marriage may come up and, although her parents were pressuring her to marry, her global beliefs about sexuality and marriage were that only virgins could marry. She was fearful of disappointing both her parents and boyfriend; her sense of guilt disturbed her ability to sleep and her emotional well-being, her concentration when she attempted to study, and her tolerance for interacting with peers in study groups. She described situational beliefs about herself regarding these symptoms by saying, "I am a fallen woman; I do not deserve to marry or have children." She was considering ending her relationship with Mr. Park to assuage her guilt.

Despite these barriers, Ms. Kim was willing to explore with her therapist situational meanings related to her history of sexual abuse and was soon able to identify different situational meanings from the perspectives of both Korean and American cultures. Korean values of obedience to elders and silence about sex left her unable to address the abuse in an adaptive manner, though the incest violated Korean and Catholic values on chastity. Initially, when Ms. Kim considered acknowledging that she may not be to blame for the abuse, she experienced a spiritual crisis—if she did not deserve this treatment from her grandfather, how could God have allowed this to happen to her? She began to doubt the existence of God and, with that, all of her previous life goals. If serving God through serving others was irrelevant, why was she working through a difficult animal science program and hoping to develop medications when she could make more money doing something much easier?

At the same time, her Catholic congregation was one of few ties she had with the Korean community, and she did not want to leave that community. Her therapist recognized her concern as a struggle with theodicy and encouraged her to consult with her parish priest. Ms. Kim did not want her priest to know about her history, but she nonetheless took advantage of an opportunity to go to confession with a visiting priest to address her apparent choice of either feeling horribly guilty or altogether abandoning her faith. The Korean priest was aware of the cultural dynamics of Ms. Kim's abuse and was able to assure her of two core meanings: (a) being obedient to her grandfather was not a sin and (b) when humans sin, their sins hurt others in ways that God would never want or choose. The priest went on to explain that Ms. Kim's grandfather had been entrusted by both God and his culture to teach younger people what was good and right, and his violation of this trust by abusing her was a reprehensible sin on his behalf. Instead of assigning her penance, the priest asked her to pray for help in understanding in a more profound way how much Jesus experiences anguish when she and others are exploited and abused by persons in authority.

With the help of the priest's perspective, she was able to work toward letting go of her guilt without losing her faith. As she looked back on the abuse using the new lenses she had acquired in the course of treatment, she realized that she had also been viewing her abusive past from an adult American perspective, in which women are perceived as being more autonomous and responsible for their behavior. This belief had contributed to her view of herself as condemnable for failing to seek help and resist her grandfather. As she reconsidered her past and developed a revised narrative of herself as a young Korean girl when the abuse occurred, she came to realize that it was her fierce concern for her parents' feelings and her family's reputation that compelled her decision to keep silent about the abuse. Her tolerance of the abuse, rather than being an abhorrent choice, was actually a heroic effort to honor and care for her family.

GLOBAL MEANING

Global meaning has three essential elements: overarching beliefs, goals, and a subjective sense of meaning and purpose (Park & Folkman, 1997). As this case illustrates, these elements inform individuals' meaning systems in fundamental ways, providing the frameworks through which individuals interpret, evaluate, and respond to their experiences. For many, spirituality serves as the foundation of their meaning systems throughout the life course—underpinning their beliefs, identity, goals, and values, providing a sense of purpose, and serving as a primary lens through which they perceive and interpret their world (McIntosh, 1995; Ozorak, 2005).

Surprisingly little is known about how global meaning systems develop and evolve over time. Extensive research is currently available on a few specific beliefs (e.g., theory of mind; Henry, Phillips, Ruffman, & Bailey, 2013); aside from these limited and narrow lines of research, we know little about global meaning formation. Social–cognitive models assume that global beliefs are formed largely by one's personal experiences. For example, Kelly (1969) detailed how, throughout life, people act as naive personal scientists, testing their implicit hypotheses in interactions with their surroundings to construct and refine their beliefs. However, as illustrated by Ms. Kim's reappraisal of her role in the sexual abuse from a Western cultural perspective, even direct experiences are subject to extensive interpretation imposed by one's social environment (including parents, siblings, and peers), institutions (e.g., education and religion), and the broader cultural milieu (e.g., mass media; Braswell, Rosengren, & Berenbaum, 2012; Koltko-Rivera, 2004). In addition, one's personality and cognitive capacities may influence global belief formation in critical ways (Koltko-Rivera, 2004; Ozorak, 2005). Few theories have been offered as to how global goal systems or subjective sense of meaning in life develop.

Ms. Kim's case illustrates the formation of a global meaning system as a complex interaction of cultural, developmental, and familial influences along with personal experiences. For example, Ms. Kim was caught between two worlds as a first generation immigrant to the United States and often struggled to maintain fidelity to her family as well as to acculturate into her new society. Her sense of her identity, values, and goals derived both from being a member of a traditional Catholic Korean family and from her experience of American culture, which provided messages that simultaneously complemented and contradicted her Korean upbringing. Culture may be an important framework for global meaning making; consider, for example, differences in the meanings of betrayal by a family member in collectivist versus individualist cultures, or the role of dominant religions in a culture's values and respect for or condemnation of survivors of sexual trauma. One's position as a cultural minority or privileged group likely also affects perceptions of self and others and influences meaning-making processes.

Developmentally, Ms. Kim's understanding of her faith changed dramatically from the time the abuse started at age 5 to her adult efforts to initiate recovery from unresolved posttraumatic stress disorder (PTSD) symptomatology. In addition, Ms. Kim's faith included strong values of caring for family; her value of chastity was in fact part of a constellation of beliefs about maintaining a lifestyle that supports strong family relationships. Having a family member force her to violate behavioral expectations related to values about caring for family created a challenge for global meaning; Ms. Kim's multicultural background increased the challenge as well as the repertoire of meaning resources available to address these trauma-related concerns.

Global Beliefs

Global beliefs (also called *assumptive worlds*, *schemas*, *personal theories*, or *worldviews*; see Koltko-Rivera, 2004, for a review) are broad assumptions about the self, others, and the larger world. These beliefs concern benevolence, fairness, the nature of humanity, personal control, luck, randomness, and vulnerability, as well as how and why events occur (Janoff-Bulman, 1992; Koltko-Rivera, 2004). Global beliefs also include people's core views of themselves that form their sense of personal identity (Leary & Tangney, 2003). Every individual is unique in his or her specific constellations of beliefs, resulting from a lifetime of continuous exposure to a flow of direct and received experiences along with one's unavoidable interpretation and reinterpretation of them (Christiansen, 2000; Leary & Tangney, 2003).

For many people, their spirituality, including their beliefs about God or of the Divine as loving and benevolent, wrathful, or distant, informs their core beliefs about the nature of people (e.g., inherently good, made in God's image, sinful) and this world (e.g., the coming apocalypse, the illusory nature of reality) and, often, the next (e.g., heaven, reincarnation; Slattery & Park, 2015). Spirituality also forms the core of many people's identities in terms of how they understand themselves as religious or spiritual beings (e.g., as unworthy of God's love, as being chosen by God rather than vice versa; Pargament, 1997; Slattery & Park, 2011b), as well as their social identification with a religious group (Ysseldyk, Matheson, & Anisman, 2010). Religious identity can also provide a source of self-esteem and moral superiority (Sedikides & Gebauer, 2010). As such, it is important to note both that one's religious upbringing or denomination would constitute only one factor in determining any particular individual's beliefs and also that there is considerable variation in beliefs, values, goals, and behaviors even within a particular religious group. Another important aspect of individuals' spirituality is their beliefs regarding their relationship with God. Table 2.1 describes some of the global beliefs associated with religions prominent in the world today.

Religious identities and beliefs interact with varying aspects of cognitive, social, and personal development over the lifespan. Individuals' capacities for understanding and forming the depth of beliefs within their own and others' religious reference groups may change dramatically as their meaning systems mature (Fowler, 1981). Psychospiritual development is also likely an important factor in this development, determining subsequent flexibility or capacity for tolerating complexity in religious aspects of global beliefs. Table 2.2 outlines what clinicians might encounter in working with traumatized persons at different levels of psychospiritual development.

Religious and spiritual beliefs can inform and influence other global beliefs in profound ways, such as beliefs regarding fairness, control, coherence, benevolence of the world and other people, and vulnerability (Koltko-Rivera, 2006–2007). A large body of research has documented links between religiousness and beliefs regarding control through both direct and primary means and through secondary means, such as through intercessory prayer (Rothbaum, Weisz, & Snyder, 1982; M. J. Young & Morris, 2004). Some forms of conventional religiousness explicitly encourage a surrender of control to God or powerful others (Exline, 2002). Clinically, the helpfulness of this type of self-surrender in recovering from PTSD or other trauma-related concerns depends on a number of contextual concerns.

For example, when considering Ms. Kim's challenges in reconciling her abusive past, she was encouraged as a Korean to hand over personal control to her grandfather. Although sanctioned by her culture, this self-surrender limited her capacity for safety from further abuse. However, engaging more deeply in her Catholic faith provided both the primary (e.g., trusting in God's love and justice) and secondary (e.g., routine of Mass, praying the Rosary, consulting with the priest in confession) means for managing difficult thoughts and emotions and somehow resolving discrepancies between her global and situational meaning as her affection for Mr. Park deepened.

The concept of theodicy is gaining research attention and appears to hold great promise for understanding how people may come to withstand life's difficulties, even from traumatic events. Broadly defined, *theodicy* refers to explanations for human suffering or the "philosophical/theological attempts to reconcile the presence of evil and suffering in the world with the idea of an all-powerful and good creator God" (Hall & Johnson, 2001, p. 5). Individuals often struggle to hold simultaneously the following three propositions in the

TABLE 2.1

A Brief Summary of Global Beliefs Held by Major Religious Groups

	Buddhism	Christianity	Hinduism	Islam	Judaism
God	No supreme being, although some sects believe in various deities. The Buddha is human, but the ultimate example of an enlightened consciousness.	One God who is a Trinity of Father, Son, and Holy Spirit. God is personal, involved, eternal, loving, and perfect. Jesus is the human manifestation of God, who came to Earth to save people from sin.	One supreme reality (Brahman) that takes the form of many gods and goddesses. Everyone is part of Brahman, like drops of water in the sea. Sometimes seen as loving, but more often as impersonal and uninvolved.	Allah is the almighty, creator and sustainer of the universe. He is believed to be involved in every moment of one's life.	One God (Yahweh), who is seen as both merciful and compassionate and as powerful and just. He is seen by some as personal with human emotions but by others as more impersonal and remote.
Afterlife	For most people, rebirths continue until they obtain enlightenment.	Entry into heaven depends on faith for some Christian groups and taking the sacraments and performing good works for others.	For most people, rebirths continue until they obtain enlightenment.	Those who believe and do righteous deeds will be greatly rewarded in the afterlife, whereas those who disbelieve and do bad deeds will be severely punished.	The here and now are emphasized over an afterlife. Getting to Heaven, however, depends on moral behavior and is possible for Jews and non-Jews.
Purpose of life	To end unnecessary suffering and gain enlightenment and release from the cycle of rebirths.	To end separation from God through faith in Christ and, for some, sacraments and good works.	To gain enlightenment and release from ignorance and illusion, gaining either a better rebirth or release from the cycle of rebirths.	Life is only a test and preparation for an eternal one. This concept encourages people to lead good lives on earth because they know the fate that awaits them if they ignore the commands and warnings of Allah.	To obey God's commandments and live ethically. Focus is on this life rather than an afterlife.

Nature of humans and life	Everything, including people, changes. Evil (and goodness) derive from karma earned in this and previous lives.	People are born with original sin inherited from Adam and Eve and have a tendency toward evil. People must fight against evil and suffering, especially against their own sinful nature.	Life is full of distress that is temporarily masked by earthly pleasures. However, the human soul is identical with supreme Brahman, who is above and apart from this world.	People were created with equal inclinations for good and bad. They can choose either right or wrong and are rewarded or punished accordingly.	People have the ability to choose between good and evil.
Causes of evil and suffering	Suffering (a) is inevitable, (b) is increased by attachment (an unwillingness to accept that everything changes), and (c) can be decreased by ending attachment.	Suffering—and evil—are not caused by God but by Satan, the fall from grace, and alienation from God. Humans do not cause evil, but spread it when they fail to fight it.	Evil is a natural part of life. Suffering is deserved, a product of karma from this or earlier lives.	Suffering is a test from Allah to separate believers from nonbelievers.	Suffering is a normal part of life, but difficult for humans to understand because of our limited nature.
Redemption	Attachment is ended through personal effort by following the Noble Eightfold Path: Right View, Right Intention, Right Speech, Right Action, Right Livelihood, Right Effort, Right Mindfulness, and Right Contemplation. Following these lead to mental and behavioral self-control and loving kindness.	There are various views of this, including being saved by faith, through sacred rituals, good works, grace, or some combination of these. Redemption can be permanent or temporary depending on the specific religion.	Moksha, the ultimate release from the world, can only be obtained by transcending physical and social limitations. Ending rebirths—or earning a better rebirth—occurs through practice of the Four Yogas (i.e., knowledge, loving worship, altruistic action, and meditation).	Through sin, people turn away from God and through repentance return to the path of God. Repentance is a means to purify oneself and return to an original sinless state, thus reaching redemption. Through Allah's mercy and grace, sins are disregarded and repentance accepted.	Faith, grace, and beliefs are less important than ethical action.

(continues)

TABLE 2.1
A Brief Summary of Global Beliefs Held by Major Religious Groups *(Continued)*

	Buddhism	Christianity	Hinduism	Islam	Judaism
Forgiving and forgiveness	Forgiveness is not sought from a supreme being. Karma is a natural consequence of one's actions; redemption occurs by changing one's behavior.	It is impossible to save oneself through wisdom or action alone; instead, Jesus died to symbolically cleanse and remove sins. Jesus urged turning the other cheek and loving one's enemies.	Forgiveness does not come from sacrifice or good deeds, but from spiritual enlightenment.	Forgiveness is granted only by Allah under certain conditions and especially when one returns to Him and repents and pledges not to return to the same sinning acts. However, the act of forgiving itself is valued.	People should seek forgiveness from God and those whom they have offended. God forgives people, but the Mosaic Law can bring people into line with God's wishes. Forgiving is seen as a pious act.
Time orientation	Time is fundamentally unreal. The past and future are constructs of the human mind. We can only live in the present moment (which is always changing). Apparent beginnings and endings of the self are illusory.	Often the focus is more on afterlife than here and now. In Western societies, time is linear and translates into emphasis on hurry and time pressure.	Respectful of past, but also has a relaxed attitude about time due to views of time as cyclic and eternal. Apparent beginnings and endings of the self are illusory.	One's allotted time on earth is unpredictable and should be valued and used well.	Here and now are emphasized over an afterlife.

	Buddhism	Christianity	Hinduism	Islam	Judaism
Sex and sexuality	Some urge avoiding bodily pleasure, others urge non-attachment to bodily pleasure (i.e., appreciating sex without needing it). The Five Precepts specifically preclude sexual misconduct, which includes sexual violence, manipulation, and deceit.	Most Christians believe that sex within a marriage is good, but liberal and conservative Christians diverge in their focus on either the Golden Rule (acceptance of nonexploitive sexuality) or biblical passages that appear to exclude homosexuality, for example.	Sexuality is seen as a way of expressing and fostering intimacy. Does not exclude or judge any part of human nature, including birth control, sterilization, masturbation, homosexuality, polygamy, or pornography.	Sex should be confined to marriage, is believed to build intimacy between partners, and should be mutually satisfying. Modesty in men's and women's clothing and behavior are ways to prevent sexual misbehavior.	Sex should be confined to a marriage but is a divine gift that fosters intimacy between two people. Like other biological urges, when uncontrolled, sex can lead people astray.
Spiritual practices	Meditation, mindfulness, mantras, and following the Eightfold Path and the Five Precepts. Study of the Dharma and the Buddha's life.	Prayer, Bible study, baptism, Eucharist, church on Sundays and religious holidays.	The Four Yogas, meditation, worship (puja), devotion to a god or goddess, pilgrimage to holy cities, living according to one's dharma (purpose or role).	Following the Five Pillars (profession of faith, ritual prayer, almsgiving, fasting during Ramadan, pilgrimage to Mecca), attending mosque services on Fridays, ablution before prayer, avoiding alcohol and pork. Holidays related to the pilgrimage and fast of Ramadan.	Studying the Bible and Talmud. Circumcision at birth, bar/bat mitzvah at adulthood. Synagogue services on Saturdays. Avoiding pork and other nonkosher foods. Holidays related to historical events.

Note. This table presents a general overview of various religious traditions and does not, therefore, address the contradictions and tensions within a given religion, differences between fundamentalist and more liberal branches of denominations or groups, and variations among individuals belonging to a single religion. From *Spiritually Oriented Interventions for Counseling and Psychotherapy* (pp. 17–21), by J. D. Aten, M. R. McMinn, and E. L. Worthington, Jr., (Eds.), 2011, Washington, DC: American Psychological Association. Copyright 2011 by the American Psychological Association.

TABLE 2.2
Fowler's (1981) Theory of Psychospiritual Development and Implications for Trauma

Stage	Approximate developmental period	Meaning-making mechanisms	Other attributes	Implications if traumatized at this stage	Implications for treatment
Pre-stage I: Undifferentiated faith	Infancy	Pre-language perceptions of caregivers/world	Sets stage for subsequent concepts of higher powers	Impaired ability to trust higher powers or view world as safe. Impaired ability to move past view of self as central	May have difficulty with therapeutic alliance and using language to make or change meanings related to trauma
Stage I: Intuitive—projective faith	Age 2 or 3 to onset of concrete operations	Early language. Assimilates parts of cultural and religious myths. Uses fantasy or imagination, little access to logic	First symbolized concepts of good and evil. Can only consider own perspective	May develop rigid, angry, or dangerous concept of higher power or world. May view self as unlovable or flawed in some fundamental manner	Spiritual and moral cognitions may be rigidly categorical or judgmental of self and others
Stage II: Mythic—literal faith	Age 7 or 8, or onset of concrete operations through adolescence or onset of formal operations	Uses logic. Makes spiritual meanings through narrative (cultural stories)	Expects a just world—good will be rewarded, evil will be punished	Faith may be shattered when the world is not just. May blame self for trauma to maintain faith	May struggle with need to blame self or others for trauma; forgiveness can be difficult

Stage	Age of onset	Characteristics		
Stage III: Synthetic—conventional faith	Most late adolescents and adults	Begins to create personal narrative / Higher power constructed as a possible relationship / Meaning bound to symbols	Can conceive perspectives of self and other / Uncritical focus on others' expectations (parents and clergy)	Sense of guilt if own behavior differs from community / Threatened by and sometimes judgmental of alternative belief and value systems / May experience anxiety when exploring new spiritual meanings of trauma, unless within and condoned by spiritual leaders and/or tradition
Stage IV: Individuative—reflective faith	May start in early adulthood or middle age	Reliance on logic / Can work with meaning outside of symbols / Maintains categorical ideas of right and wrong	Capable of critical evaluation of group beliefs and values / Increased religious doubts, may grieve loss of Stage III faith	May rely too much on own experience to draw spiritual conclusions / Greater flexibility in exploring new meanings, but may have difficulty incorporating emotion into spiritual meaning making
Stage 5: Conjunctive faith	Rarely seen before middle age, most adults do not reach this stage	Sees limits of logic; seeks meaning through paradox and dialectical realities / Right and wrong no longer categorical	Nondefensive of own perspective / Sees all faiths parts of truth or attempting similar aims / Values on justice and inclusion	May struggle with own role, contrasting spiritual vision for the world with one's own needs for safety and resources / Value on others' perspectives may carry risk of attempts to prematurely foreclose to forgiveness
Stage 6: Universalizing faith	Rarely seen	Views the world as universal community; sees the sacred in all others / Selflessly serves goals of compassion and justice	Can be imperfect in spiritual functioning / Can tend to subvert authorities (government, religious)	Most in this stage have a history of significant hardship, if not trauma / Unknown

aftermath of a trauma or critical life event: God is all powerful, God is all good, and evil exists in the world. Given the need to maintain these three seemingly contradictory realities, survivors may expend great cognitive effort to maintain beliefs that these three statements are logically compatible in the aftermath of traumas like sexual abuse. Such considerations are not abstractions when a survivor confronts a personal tragedy or trauma; theodicies can provide a needed sense of cohesion and stability in the fabric of one's meaning system.

Efforts to solve the dilemma of apparent belief contradictions lead to a variety of theodicy beliefs. Hall and Johnson (2001) noted that one influential Christian viewpoint holds that goodness can occur only in a world where evil also exists, particularly those virtues that an individual comes to embody and practice through encounters with evil and suffering. Those virtues include patience, mercy, forgiveness, endurance, faith, courage, and compassion (Hall & Johnson). From this perspective, one can come to see one's trauma or tragedy as an opportunity to grow through suffering (e.g., to build one's soul, to become more Christ-like, to grow in agape love; Hall & Johnson). Another solution may be to view suffering as necessary for reaching future aims, such as the ultimate goal of salvation (Baumeister, 1991). One recent measure of theodicies, the Views of Suffering Scale, assesses a variety of different theodicies for Christian traditions as well as other prominent religious groups in the United States, including those of karma, randomness, and views of suffering as retribution and as soul building, along with beliefs that God has limited knowledge and that God suffers along with the sufferers (Hale-Smith, Park, & Edmondson, 2012; see Appendix). Future research linking theodicies with responses to traumatic events may shed light on how these types of global beliefs influence meaning-making processes.

Although spirituality exerts positive influences on global beliefs, spirituality can certainly negatively influence beliefs in terms of specific content. For example, some religious cognitions, such as ideological extremism, as well as beliefs about an angry, uncaring, or punitive God, can have destructive implications for personal and social functioning in the context of stress or trauma (see Exline & Rose, 2013, and Moghaddam, Warren, & Love, 2013). Although a sense of secondary control (through God's intercession) is often helpful, especially in low-control situations, such surrendering of personal control poses the risk of religious fatalism, by which people abdicate responsibility to take direct actions to alleviate problems (e.g., Franklin, Schlundt, & Wallston, 2008; Norenzayan & Lee, 2010). For example, when Ms. Kim began to reconstrue responsibility for her abuse, initially changing the idea that she was responsible for the abuse, many of her religious beliefs, such as that God failed to protect an innocent person, posed barriers to recovery. However, the priest's reframing of her global beliefs in a way that allowed her to hold her grandfather responsible became critical in her recovery.

Global Goals

Global goals refer to people's motivation for living, choice of goals, standards for judging behavior, and basis for self-esteem, those higher order ideals, states, or objects that people work toward attaining or maintaining over the course of their lives (Karoly, 1999; Klinger, 2012). Broadly defined, global goals might be viewed as internal representations of ultimate concerns (Emmons, 2005), one's desired long-term processes, events, or outcomes (Austin & Vancouver, 1996). Goals encompass desired future states and, perhaps especially important in the context of dealing with trauma, states that one already possesses and desires to maintain (Karoly, 1999; Klinger, 1998). Global goals commonly include the domains of relationships, work, health, wealth, knowledge, and achievement (Emmons, 2003).

Spirituality is central to the life purposes of many people and can inform their ultimate goals in manifold ways. Ultimate goals may include connecting to what one regards as being sacred in the universe; living a life full of benevolence, forgiveness, or altruism; achieving enlightenment; finding salvation; knowing and experiencing God; or experiencing transcendence (Emmons, 1999; Pargament, Magyar-Russell, & Murray-Swank, 2005). Other goals can be derived from these superordinate ones, such as having peace of mind, working for peace and justice in the world, devoting oneself to one's family, or creating a strong sense of community with other believers or in the community in which one resides. Of course, negative goals, such as supremacy and destruction, are sometimes embraced in the name of religion as well (see Moghaddam et al., 2013). Hence, in the same way that religion might encourage different types of self-surrender, there is also a duality with respect to the role of faith in shaping global goals.

Some goals are explicitly spiritual in nature (e.g., to serve God). However, all goals may become connected to what people hold as sacred through the process of sanctification (e.g., Mahoney et al., 2005). *Sanctification* involves assigning spiritual significance and character to otherwise secular objects or goals (Mahoney et al., 1999). Hence, any goal can take on spiritual value if the individual associates it with his or her notions of the sacred (Pargament, Magyar-Russell, et al., 2005). Ms. Kim, for example, had apparently sanctified both sexual values and relationship goals; she viewed opportunities to marry and bear children as sacred privileges to be earned through a chaste and pious lifestyle. Her career goal related to medical research was also related to a sanctified goal of helping others; this sanctified career choice was threatened when her faith was shaken with the emergence of posttraumatic symptomatology.

Values, or individuals' broad preferences about the worth of ultimate goals and the appropriate courses of action to achieve those goals, are a key part of the goal element of global meaning. Values serve as guidelines to determine worth, importance, or correctness of one's goals and the means of achieving them (Baumeister, 1991; Schwartz & Bilsky, 1990). Religion and spirituality are extremely potent sources of values, supplying a framework for determining what is right and good to be pursued and, conversely, what is wrong and bad and to be avoided (Baumeister, 1991). Ms. Kim's concern about premarital sex is an example of the latter. Religions are in an unusually esteemed position to determine or establish criteria of right and wrong and good and bad (Saroglou & Cohen, 2013). For instance, divine will is often considered to be the ultimate arbiter of right and wrong, and human desires that are inconsistent with the understood will of God are typically to be overridden (Baumeister, 1991; Emmons, 1999). For many, perceptions of God's will sets the standards against which people judge their own and others' behavior (Einolf, 2011). These kinds of judgments about right and wrong are likely to remain categorical and rigid until the individual's level of psychospiritual development allows for more flexible judgments (Fowler, 1981).

Sense of Meaning and Purpose

The emotional aspect of global meaning refers to the experience of a sense of meaning or purpose in life or as being connected to something greater than oneself (Klinger, 2012; Peterson, Park, & Seligman, 2005). Those who characterize their lives as high in meaning believe that their lives are purposeful, comprehensible, and significant (Steger & Frazier, 2005). When one's global beliefs and goals are functioning well, the world is meaningful, generating perceptions of one's behaviors as consistent with core values and as representing progress toward desired future goals (Baumeister, 1991; McGregor & Little, 1998; Park, Edmondson, & Hale-Smith, 2013). Religion and spirituality can enhance a sense of meaning in life (e.g., Steger & Frazier, 2005; Tomer & Eliason, 2000), which may be partly due to the consistent emphasis in many faith traditions on their ability to provide a sense of significance and even transcendence (Hood, Hill, & Spilka, 2009). Engagement in specific spiritual behaviors and religious rituals, such as Ms. Kim's participation in weekly Mass, also enhances many people's sense of meaning in life via predictable practices that attempt to cultivate closeness with God (Steger & Frazier, 2005).

Ms. Kim's global beliefs, goals, and sense of meaning in life came primarily from her first Korean Catholic culture. She was raised with cultural beliefs about the importance of traditional family roles, as well as expectations regarding the need for ambitious educational and career goals. She initially made meaning of this heritage by assuming traditional and expected roles in her family of origin (parents and grandparents) and pursuing culturally consistent educational and vocational goals. However, as she progressed in her new life in the United States, her global beliefs about appropriate roles in her relationship with Mr. Park (e.g., that she must be a virgin bride) were in conflict with beliefs about appropriate roles in her family of origin (i.e., to be an obedient granddaughter and protector of her family's reputation), thereby setting the stage for a significant conflict in values as her relationship with Mr. Park deepened.

SITUATIONAL MEANING

Situational meaning refers to how global meaning, in the context of a particular situation, influences one's reaction to that situation. Specifically, situational meaning includes the appraised meaning of the situation, detection of violations between that appraised meaning and global meaning, meaning-making processes, and meaning made from the situation. As we discuss, spirituality can be a pervasive influence on all aspects of situational meaning.

Appraised Meaning of Events

People appraise or assign meanings to situations that they encounter in life to understand their value and significance (Lazarus & Folkman, 1984). These appraised meanings are to some extent determined by the specific details of a given particular situation, but are largely informed and shaped by individuals' global meaning systems. For example, those with a strong sense that stressful situations are amenable to change may try to understand an event in terms of which aspects can be modified, whereas someone who believes that events are distributed fairly might seek to understand what prior mistake or offense he or she committed to deserve the present adversity.

Aspects of individuals' spiritual meaning systems can strongly influence their appraised meanings of specific situations. Religious beliefs provide many alternative possibilities for interpreting an event. For example, notions that there is a larger plan for one's life, events are not random, or personal growth can arise from struggle can inform the specific meaning of an event in adaptive ways. Some individuals may believe that God would not harm them or visit more adversity on them than they could handle at any one time, whereas others may believe that God is somehow trying to teach or communicate something important through the event (Furnham & Brown, 1992).

Studies from people facing many types of stressful experiences demonstrate the influences of global spiritual meaning on the appraised meanings people assign to specific events. For example, in a study of students dealing with a particularly severe hurricane season (including Hurricanes Katrina and Rita), higher general religiousness was positively associated with interpreting hurricane-related events as a loss by Christian participants, but as a benefit by Jewish participants. For both groups, general religiousness and positive God images were related positively to perceptions that God was in control (Newton & McIntosh, 2009). Religious beliefs are also commonly implicated in how people understand the afterlife and respond to bereavement (Benore & Park, 2004; Carone & Barone, 2001). For example, some people believe that the deceased loved one continues to exist, that they will be reunited with the deceased after death, and even that they can continue to interact with the deceased in the present, albeit in a different way, whereas others believe that there is no afterlife or that it is unpleasant or even painful (Flannelly, Ellison, Galek, & Koenig, 2008).

Causal attributions, people's understandings of why a given event occurred, are another important type of event appraisal that might be shaped by religious beliefs (Spilka, Hood, Hunsberger, & Gorsuch, 2003). Attributions can be naturalistic, religious, or both. For example, naturalistic explanations for the occurrence of cancer may involve exposure to carcinogens, previous injury, or genetics, whereas religious attributions can include God's efforts to teach, challenge, or punish the afflicted or to teach a lesson to others (Spilka et al., 2003). It is quite common for individuals to make naturalistic attributions for the immediate or proximal cause of the event but also invoke religious or metaphysical explanations for the more distal metaphysical cause (see Park & Folkman, 1997). Returning to our case example, Ms. Kim had attributed her abuse to her personal failure to seek help before entering therapy and, therefore, experienced substantial inappropriate guilt; the process of changing her attribution to her grandfather's violation of religious and cultural trusts quelled her self-condemnation and allowed her to recover.

Religious attributions are particularly likely to be made for aversive or harmful events (K. Gray & Wegner, 2010) and for those of high ambiguity and threat to personal meaning (Spilka et al., 2003). The likelihood that an individual will make religious or nonreligious attributions for particular experiences or encounters also depends, in large part, on the relative availability of global religious and naturalistic beliefs (K. Gray & Wegner, 2010; Spilka et al., 2003), as well as the extent to which the explanatory power of each type of attribution is congruent with global meaning (Spilka et al., 2003).

Violations

After appraising the initial meaning of an event, individuals determine the extent to which that meaning is congruent with their global views of the world and themselves and their desires and goals. Myriad events are simply assimilated into global meaning, requiring little perceptual distortion or cognitive reworking. However, some events require accommodation to make sense of them, given their strong discrepancy with global meaning (Janoff-Bulman, 1992). According to the meaning-making model, the magnitude of the resultant distress is proportional to the degree to which global meaning has been violated (Janoff-Bulman, 1992; Steger, Owens, & Park, 2015).

Confrontation with trauma may violate or even "shatter" global meaning systems. Such violations or discrepancies thus provide the impetus for initiating cognitive and emotional processing—meaning-making efforts—to rebuild meaning systems in a manner that in some way accounts for the reality and consequences of the trauma. Meaning making involves efforts to understand and conceptualize stressors in ways that are more consistent with a person's global meaning and to incorporate that understanding into the larger system of global meaning through processes of assimilation and accommodation (Park & Folkman, 1997).

People perceive discrepancies when they experience situations in which they identify violations of their global beliefs (e.g., that people are kind and benevolent, that the world is fair) and their goals (e.g., wanting to be in an intimate relationship but feeling dirty, unsafe, or undeserving of such a relationship). Discrepancies can also arise when global beliefs or goals conflict with one another (e.g., wanting to seek justice but also wanting to put a traumatic event in the past; Baumeister, 1991; Emmons, 2005; Park, 2005). For example, an assault may violate one's global beliefs that the world is fair, that others are benign, or that one has control over his or her life. Global goals are violated when an event is appraised as discrepant with what one wants. Thus, being sexually assaulted may also violate one's goals of staying healthy, safe, and intact.

Even as a child, Ms. Kim experienced the sexual assaults by her grandfather as a violation of her personhood, feeling unable to end them but knowing they were wrong. She continued to endure many instances of discrepancies between her desires and those of her environment, such as the harassment she experienced as an outsider in her academic studies due to both her gender and her major. Ms. Kim found it difficult to both remain silent about her history of abuse and to work toward developing a relationship with Mr. Park. Finally, when she began to relinquish self-blame for the abuse, she needed help to find ways to understand the abuse that would not violate her assumptions about a just God. In the context of violations in her meaning system occurring at a younger stage of psychosocial development, she needed assistance to consider multiple perspectives and multiple judgments about responsibility to resolve that violation.

Meaning Making

Mismatches between global and appraised meaning are distressing, and people are often highly motivated to alleviate this distress (M. A. Greenberg,

1995; Janoff-Bulman, 1992; Joseph & Linley, 2005). When experiencing situations discrepant with their global meaning, people may respond in many different ways, including avoidance, distorting the experience, or seeking help (as Ms. Kim opted to do). They may also attempt to solve directly or change the situation, often referred to as *problem-focused coping* (Aldwin, 2007); however, many problems, such as the traumatic experiences of Ms. Kim, cannot be directly solved and thus require meaning making—cognitive restructuring that reduces and resolves the meaning violations.

Meaning making refers to attempts to resolve global meaning violations by reaching a more acceptable appraisal of a distressing event to better incorporate it into one's existing global meaning system or changing one's global meaning to accommodate it (Park, 2010; Park & Folkman, 1997). Meaning-making processes can include both automatic processes (e.g., intrusive thoughts, dreams) and more deliberate efforts (Park, 2010). Although reappraised meaning can be either positively or negatively toned, the motivation to reduce distress leads to reappraising stressful situations in a more favorable light by giving them a more acceptable or benign meaning or one more consistent with global beliefs and goals. Reattributions are probably the most commonly studied change in situational meaning. The process of making meaning can be difficult and is often accompanied by increased anxiety, depression, rumination, and anger as well as decrements in functioning. However, when people are able to make meaning of stressful situations—through constructing more benign situational meanings (e.g., I have been transformed and grown as a result of this trauma) and restoring or even creating more positive global meanings—they typically experience better adjustment to stressful events (Keesee, Currier, & Neimeyer, 2008).

People make meaning in many different ways, attempting to change their appraised meaning of the stressor to make it less aversive or minimize its impact, or change their global beliefs and goals to accommodate the unwelcome experience. In terms of deliberate attempts at coping, people might search for more favorable or consistent understandings of the event and its implications for their beliefs about themselves and their lives. Meaning making may also entail reconsidering one's global beliefs and life goals (see Wrosch, Scheier, Miller, Schulz, & Carver, 2003) or questioning and revising their sense of meaning in life (Steger, 2009). Other meaning-making processes may be less effortful and experienced as intrusive or unbidden (see Park, 2010, for a review). For example, the emergence of Ms. Kim's flashbacks to being sexually abused as a child when she first sought treatment highlighted this more distressing type of meaning making.

Is meaning making helpful? Empirical findings are mixed: Some researchers have found meaning making following highly stressful events to co-occur with distress symptomatology, whereas others have reported that meaning making is related to improved adjustment (for a review, see Park, 2010). These inconsistencies regarding the effects of meaning making appear to be due to differences in when and how adjustment is assessed in the meaning-making process. This rebuilding process is assumed to lead to better adjustment, particularly if adequate meaning is found or created (Park, 2010). However, when people continue their efforts to assimilate or accommodate without success, these efforts can devolve into maladaptive rumination or even negative changes in beliefs, values, and goals (Segerstrom, Stanton, Alden, & Shortridge, 2003). That is, meaning making is helpful to the extent that it produces a satisfactory product (i.e., *meaning made*; Park, 2010). Therefore, distinguishing between the meaning-making process (the search for meaning) and meaning made (the products of a search for meaning) is important, because the former is associated with distress, whereas the latter is associated with more positive adjustment (Currier, Holland, & Neimeyer, 2006).

Meaning-making efforts often have a salient spiritual aspect. In fact, most types of religious coping with trauma and other stressful situations are efforts to make meaning. Pargament, Smith, Koenig, and Perez (1998) identified a range of religious meaning-making efforts and organized them within a framework of positive and negative coping. Religious meaning-making coping takes many forms, including benevolent religious reappraisal (using religion to redefine the stressor as benevolent and potentially beneficial, perhaps seeing in the stressor a "lesson" from God), reappraisal of God's powers (redefining God's ability to influence the stressful situation), seeking spiritual connection (thinking about how life is part of a larger spiritual force, a situational reappraisal), seeking religious direction (finding new global goals), or active religious surrender (doing what one can and then putting the rest in God's hands; see Pargament, Koenig, Tarakeshwar, & Hahn, 2004). Religious meaning-making coping, however, is not always positive. For example, people may reappraise stressful events as the work of a punitive or angry God (Pargament, 1997; C. H. Stein et al., 2009). These religious reappraisals of both one's global meaning and the meaning of the stressful event are fairly common and may facilitate adaptive or maladaptive changes in meaning that influence adjustment to stressful events (see Pargament, Falb, Ano, & Wachholtz, 2013).

Ms. Kim was able to avoid perceiving the conflict between cultural expectations that she obey her grandfather and protect her family and the cultural expectation that she be a virgin bride until her feelings for Mr. Park became serious and her global goals began to change. At that time, situational meanings related to the abuse from her grandfather emerged as violations; she could no longer ignore the fact that doing what was "right" based on one aspect of her meaning system was "wrong" in another part of the system. The resulting emotional pain and conflict forced Ms. Kim to seek professional help and work toward changing her global beliefs and appraisals of both herself and cultural expectations over the course of therapy sessions.

Her budding romantic relationship with Mr. Park brought the discrepancies between her views of herself, her worthiness and her own responsibility, her past experiences, and her future goals to a head. Through treatment, Ms. Kim was able to explore both her global beliefs and goals and her appraisals of her upbringing and the abuse. She reappraised the situation as one in which she could highlight her strengths and see herself as enduring the abuse as a sacrifice for her values at the time. From her adult perspective, she might wish she had not remained silent over the preceding years, but she was able to understand the abuse in a way that promoted a view of herself as strong and as upholding the collective values of her culture. In so doing, Ms. Kim gradually came to forgive herself and developed a sense of agency to work through her traumatic past in courageous ways. From her emerging Western perspective on her identity and life goals, Ms. Kim was also able to resolve much of the discrepancy she perceived between her responsibility for the childhood sexual abuse and her desires for a healthy adult romantic relationship. In therapy, she was invited to look at her self-judgments through multiple cultural and developmental lenses in the context of multiple cultures and alternative global belief systems, which proved to be a helpful route to creating more adaptive global and situational meanings.

Meaning Made

We distinguish between the process of *meaning making*, which involves ongoing and often difficult attempts to make sense or understand the event, the world, or the self differently and reformulate beliefs and goals to regain consistency among them, and *meaning made*, which refers to outcomes of these meaning-making processes. These outcomes include changes in appraisals of a stressful event (e.g., coming to see it as less damaging or perhaps even fortuitous), changes in global meaning (e.g., changing one's identity to embrace the experience), and stress-related growth (e.g., experiencing increased appreciation for life, stronger connections with family and friends, or greater awareness of one's strengths; Park, 2010; Park, Edmondson, Fenster, & Blank, 2008). Successfully making meaning of stressors can reduce a sense of discrepancy between appraised and global meanings and restore a sense that the world is meaningful, life is worthwhile, and the future is hopeful.

The eventual products or outcomes of meaning making are changes in appraised meaning of the stressful event and, sometimes, changes in global meaning. Because global beliefs tend to be relatively stable, people confronting crises are thought to be more likely to use assimilative processes, reappraising their perceptions of situations to fit their preexisting global meaning, than to change their global meaning (Pargament, 1997). However, traumas are often so discrepant with global meaning that no amount of reappraisal will restore a sense of congruence with one's preexisting global meaning. In these instances, individuals may reduce the discrepancy between their understanding of an event and their global meaning by changing their fundamental global beliefs or goals, including, perhaps, their understanding of themselves, others, and the world; their views of good and evil; the importance of forgiveness; their sense of meaning in life; and their relationships with family, community, and God (McCullough, Bono, & Root, 2005). For example, people may come to believe that they are unable to control or even comprehend everything that happens in their lives and may move toward approaching the world with less agency and more surrender. Alternatively, individuals may change or reprioritize their global goals, rededicating themselves to their family or community service. This process of accommodation can either be adaptive and growth promoting or maladaptive and even self-destructive, as can the assimilative process, depending on the specific outcomes of that process (Park, 2010).

As seen in Figure 2.1, individuals may make many distinct types of meaning through their meaning-making processes. Among the most commonly described meanings made are more acceptable causal understandings of the event (e.g., Janoff-Bulman & Frantz, 1997), reconstructed or transformed identities that integrate the stressful experience (Gillies & Neimeyer, 2006), transformed meanings of the stressor (e.g., Manne, Ostroff, Fox, Grana, & Winkel, 2009), changed global beliefs (e.g., Park, 2005), changed global goals (e.g., Thompson & Janigian, 1988), restored or changed sense of meaning in life (e.g., Janoff-Bulman & Frantz, 1997), and perceptions of growth or positive life changes, probably the most commonly assessed meaning made (e.g., L. Calhoun & Tedeschi, 2006).

Perceptions of growth are a type of meaning made that straddles the global–situational meaning divide. Perceived growth appears to arise from looking for positive aspects of negative events and identifying some redeeming features of the experience; these redeeming features may involve changes in both situational and global meaning (Park & Fenster, 2004). Some changes may be profound, such as reorienting one's life and rededicating oneself to reprioritized major goals, whereas others involve smaller changes, such as being more intimate with loved ones, handling stress more effectively, taking better care of oneself, seeing one's identity more clearly, feeling more appreciative of the everyday aspects of life, and having the courage to try new things (Park, 2009).

Ms. Kim experienced growth from her ability to resolve her past by acknowledging that her decisions about coping with the abuse made sense given the global and situational meanings she had constructed about her cultural and social roles. In fact, she could respect her desire to protect her family and use that underlying motivation to resolve her trauma-related guilt. This situational meaning allowed her to engage more fully in her relationship with Mr. Park and to give herself permission to move toward developing a greater capacity to function in her increasingly intimate and trusting relationship with him.

CONCLUSION

The meaning-making model provides a comprehensive framework for understanding how meaning serves as the basis of human functioning. Each individual has a unique set of global beliefs, goals, and sense of meaning and purpose in life; spirituality often is involved in global meaning in complex ways. This global meaning manifests in day-to-day life as well as in encounters with traumatic events, shaping the meanings individuals assign to them and the degree to which any particular event is distressing. People engage in meaning making to resolve the distress they experience following traumatic events, and this meaning making is often of a spiritual nature. In Chapter 3, we discuss the reciprocal interplay between spirituality and trauma in more detail, focusing especially on how spirituality influences the meanings one assigns to potentially traumatic events and how those meanings of traumatic events can also influence spirituality in transformative ways.

3

RECIPROCAL RELATIONSHIPS BETWEEN SPIRITUALITY AND TRAUMA

Traumatic events reveal the dark aspects of existence, including the presence of evil in the world, the random and unjust distribution of events, the vulnerability of human beings, our fundamental lack of control over our fate, and the reality of our ultimate demise (Garbarino & Bedard, 1996; Herman, 1992; Janoff-Bulman, 1992). Trauma also frequently confronts individuals with the undeniable uncertainty and instability inherent in our existence in the universe (Wilson & Moran, 1998). Thus, some writers have argued that trauma constitutes, first and foremost, an assault on one's spirituality, broadly defined (Garbarino & Bedard, 1996). From this view, trauma might be considered to be an essentially spiritual experience because it forces survivors to reexamine their previously held values and worldviews, and it can rattle their core sense of self and reality (Decker, 1993; Falsetti, Resick, & Davis, 2003; S. Smith, 2004). Trauma can violate one's sense of trust and

http://dx.doi.org/10.1037/15961-003

Trauma, Meaning, and Spirituality: Translating Research Into Clinical Practice, by C. L. Park, J. M. Currier, J. I. Harris, and J. M. Slattery

security in the world in profound ways (S. Smith, 2004), producing feelings of emptiness and abandonment, doubt, cynicism, guilt and shame, and betrayal, along with a sense of isolation, despair, and alienation in the social realm (S. Smith, 2004; Vis & Boynton, 2008). Although this view of trauma as primarily spiritual is not common among mental health professionals, spirituality is a core aspect of understanding and recovering from traumatic events for many survivors (Thielman, 2011).

The meaning-making model described in Chapter 2 applies well to these spiritual aspects of trauma. Throughout our discussion in Chapter 2, we referred to broad issues of meaning and touched on the role of spirituality in meaning-making processes. This chapter focuses more explicitly on the pervasive roles of spirituality in making meaning of trauma, as well as trauma's potentially long-lasting effects on individuals' spiritual lives. Specifically, we describe the meaning-making model as it pertains to relationships between spirituality and trauma in a reciprocal cycle (i.e., how spirituality influences individuals' responses to trauma and vice versa). Trauma and spirituality can interact in ways that may profoundly help or hinder the adjustment process for many survivors.

This reciprocal model illustrates how individuals' meaning systems, of which spirituality is commonly a central motivating and organizing factor, will influence the appraisal of a trauma. However, characteristics of the trauma will also influence the meaning ascribed to the particular experience (Park & Folkman, 1997). Thus, together, individuals' global meaning systems, including their understanding of themselves, God, and their relationship with God, as well as the specifics of the traumatic encounter, determine the meanings ascribed to the trauma and the magnitude and nature of the perceived gap between their global meaning and their understanding of this traumatic occurrence. The distress generated by this gap determines the amount and kinds of meaning making in which individuals will engage.

As noted in Chapter 2, this meaning making is often of a spiritual nature, and thus, survivors' subsequent meanings made often consist of new spiritual or religious understandings and motives. These spiritual meanings made will, in turn, constitute traumatized individuals' newly revised meaning systems, which will form the basis for meaning-making efforts when future stressful encounters occur. This reciprocal relationship is a lifelong process of understanding and responding to stressful situations in ways that may change one's global meaning at different points, supporting survivors in moving forward such that this new meaning will then shape subsequent understandings. To illustrate different elements of this recursive process of coming to terms with trauma, we draw on the cases of two siblings, Ralph and Jillian, who were exposed to a tragic natural disaster.

CASE STUDY: RALPH AND JILLIAN

The Richardson family lived in a typical, middle Tennessee Bible belt rural area and were members of a local Baptist church; both of the children and their parents attended worship and Sunday school classes weekly. Ralph was 11 and Jillian was 13 when a tornado destroyed their family home. Their father was paralyzed by falling wreckage, but the children and their mother were comparatively unscathed by the storm. Ralph and Jillian reacted very differently to this tragedy. Jillian rose to the challenge, taking on many adult responsibilities, such as caring for Ralph, cooking, and cleaning their temporary shelter, while her mother adapted to her new life role and attended to her husband's medical care. Jillian dropped out of many after-school activities to have time for these responsibilities and was certainly sad about her family's losses, especially her father's disabilities, but she still maintained good grades in school and friendships with her peers. Ralph, however, became sullen and withdrawn and started to fail in school. Jillian tried to be encouraging and helped to tutor Ralph, as did their mother, but none of their efforts seemed to help.

Eventually, the family sought help from the school guidance counselor, who had seen other students with similar sudden academic difficulties after the tornado. When talking with the whole family, the counselor asked Jillian what kept her going in the months after the tornado. Jillian replied,

> When I was able to get out of the storm cellar, and I saw the bits of our house all scattered around, and I saw how bad Dad was hurt . . . after I heard that Dad was going to live, I felt that God must love us very much. We are blessed to have each other—all of us—when so many people died in that storm. It's been hard, but I will do anything to help my family because I am so lucky to still have them.

The counselor asked Ralph the same question. Ralph acknowledged that he could not think about school since the storm and then tearfully continued:

> It's my fault. The night before the storm, Sparky [the family cat] bit me. It was my fault; I was playing too rough with him. But I was mad at him and when I prayed that night I told God I didn't want Sparky to bite me anymore. Sparky died in the storm, so he doesn't bite me anymore, but the storm also hurt Dad and lots of other people. I asked for it, and it killed all those people.

The spiritual meanings Ralph and Jillian assigned to the trauma affected their subsequent functioning very differently. Jillian focused on how she and her family were lucky or "blessed" to be spared the worse fates she had observed in her community; as a result, her appraisal of the trauma led to less distress than one might otherwise expect. Ralph's developmentally normal attributions for a child of his age, however, demonstrated the painful bargain many trauma survivors make when they attempt to make meaning of these types of events in a manner that assumes that they somehow have control over the occurrence of trauma. Although these appraisals allow them to avoid the terror of acknowledging how little control they have over their world, one of the trade-offs can be a pervasive sense of self-blame and high levels of often-disabling guilt. Unlike his sister, Ralph, therefore, needed to explore new ways of making meaning of the trauma to adjust more effectively to his family's new situation and to create more benign attributions about the tornado's occurrence.

This case highlights the powerful impact of trauma on individuals' global beliefs and goals. The tornado, an "act of God," arose suddenly and capriciously destroyed their home and seriously injured their father. Along with these physical losses, the tornado also violated Jillian's and Ralph's sense of safety, invulnerability, predictability, and controllability. However, Jillian and Ralph made very different situational meanings of the tornado and its aftermath, and these appraisals then had significant implications for their subsequent coping, the way they framed their spiritual roles and the world, and their adjustment to their altered life circumstances.

SPIRITUAL INFLUENCES IN RESPONDING TO TRAUMA

Survivors' spiritual meaning systems can powerfully shape both their interpretations of and efforts to cope with traumatic events, such that even siblings like Ralph and Jillian may have radically different reactions to the same situation. Spiritual meaning systems can determine the types of appraised meanings people assign to trauma, the extent to which this appraised meaning is discrepant from their global meaning, the types of resources and coping strategies they have available and on which they rely in the adjustment process, and ultimately, the meanings they make through their processing of the traumatic experience.

Appraisals

Individuals differ widely in their initial interpretation of potential traumas, such that some people will not appraise or experience that event as stressful enough to constitute a "trauma" for them, whereas others will perceive the event as highly traumatic (Bovin & Marx, 2011). Those who perceive the event as traumatic may vary widely in the extent of rupture or distress they experience (Peres, Moreira-Almeida, Nasello, & Koenig, 2007). Initial appraisals of trauma can be highly influenced by a person's unique spiritual meaning system. Spiritual beliefs, such as those regarding good and evil, responsibility, and one's own perceived invulnerability and deservedness, may influence appraisals of the trauma. Ralph, for example, framed the tornado as an event related to sin and guilt, whereas Jillian framed it as divine providence and made a downward comparison to perceive her family's outcome after the storm to be a blessing.

Some strains of spirituality may also inhibit malevolent or maladaptive appraisals. For example, having an extremely strong sense of God's love and protection may promote more benign appraisals and make appraisals of extreme threat or damage less likely. However, as noted in Chapter 2, some types of spirituality may increase one's likelihood of making distress-inducing appraisals in some circumstances. In the aforementioned study of students who had been strongly affected by the 2005 hurricanes along the U.S. Gulf Coast, for example, those who were more religious appraised the hurricanes as more threatening and as representing more of a loss and less of a challenge than did less religious students (Newton & McIntosh, 2009). Those who view such events as an indication of God's punishment or wrath have also been shown to be more likely to seek help for their spiritual distress in therapy (Exline, Yali, & Sanderson, 2000).

Spirituality may similarly influence individuals' appraisals of the reasons for potentially traumatic occurrences, thereby affecting the severity of their responses. For example, naturalistic explanations for a motor vehicle accident can include human inattention or error, alcohol use, or road conditions, but these explanations do not satisfactorily answer the question "Why me?" (Weeks & Lupfer, 2000). More distal, metaphysical explanations are often of a spiritual nature (K. Gray & Wegner, 2010). Such attributions can include understanding the event as God's efforts to challenge or punish or to teach a lesson to the afflicted person or to other people who learn about the event (Hale-Smith, Park, & Edmondson, 2012; Pargament & Hahn, 1986).

Research has also documented that the specific nature of appraisals of causation and responsibility for a stressful experience (e.g., "Did God intend to harm me? Why? Have I done something to anger Him?") strongly influence one's level of distress (Roesch & Ano, 2003). Attributions about an angry or vengeful God tend to be associated with higher levels of distress, whereas those about a loving or purposeful God tend to be associated with less distress (e.g., Park & Cohen, 1993). In this vein, appraising a potential trauma as resulting from the intentions of an angry or malevolent God will not only lead to greater distress but, if this understanding persists, may also reinforce negative global spiritual meanings. For example, Ralph viewed the tornado as God's way of answering his prayer, revealing a potential internalized image of a vengeful, angry God; Ralph then began to view the world around him as inherently dangerous and himself as unworthy. The reciprocal processes of reappraising both the trauma and his spiritual beliefs prior to therapy sessions created a spiral of increasing anxiety and dysfunction.

Violations

The mismatch between one's appraised meaning of a trauma and global meaning often implicates one's spiritual meaning framework; traumatic exposures can violate one's spiritual beliefs, spiritual aims, and fundamental sense of purpose in life. Trauma can be devastating when it violates deeply held spiritual global meanings, such as beliefs that God is a loving and protective parent, good people will not suffer, or human nature is primarily benevolent and good. These spiritual violations have been well described recently in the context of moral injury: "The distinct inner conflicts and psycho-spiritual consequences of exposure to or participation in traumatic events that violate deeply held moral values" (Foy & Drescher, 2015, pp. 235–236). *Moral injury*, which involves disruption in one's beliefs about "his/her own and others' capacity to behave ethically, brought about through witnessing, perpetrating, or failing to prevent immoral acts involving suffering and/or death of others," is highly distressing and strongly linked to posttraumatic stress disorder (PTSD) symptoms in combat veterans (Litz et al., 2009, p. 700). Although formal research on moral injury is just beginning, recent qualitative findings from clinical professionals (Drescher et al., 2011) and Vietnam veterans (Vargas, Hanson, Kraus, Drescher, & Foy, 2013) have indicated that spiritual problems were, in fact, a central concern for those who were struggling with chronic PTSD and other symptoms of being morally injured after their war-zone service.

Further, the strength and specific content of individuals' spiritual beliefs and goals can strongly determine the extent to which they appraise an event as violating their global meaning. More religious people may perceive traumatic events as more discrepant with their global meaning systems. Sudden and inexplicable aversive events may be particularly challenging to a devout survivor's positive global meaning (Park, 2005; Park & Cohen, 1993), especially among those survivors operating at a preconventional or conventional stage of spiritual development, who see the world more simply, rigidly, and dichotomously and as more centered on the self (Day, 2013). Given Ralph's age, it was not surprising that he framed both God's intentions and his own role in causing the tornado in black-and-white terms (see Table 2.2).

These violations have also been framed in terms of attachment theory (S. Smith, 2004): People's expectations that God will protect them in times of danger or difficulty are similar to a child's expectations of a parent (Hill & Pargament, 2003). Thus, perceptions of betrayal when people experience God as failing to prevent the traumatic event can be experienced as a profound and devastating breach of trust (S. Smith, 2004; Wilson & Moran, 1998).

This notion that spirituality—particularly more rigid or undifferentiated beliefs—can confer vulnerability has been supported by several studies. For example, a study of college students coping with the death of a significant other found that religiousness was related to higher levels of disruption of both global beliefs and goals (Park, 2005). Similarly, bereaved parents of infants who died from sudden infant death syndrome who rated religion as more important to them also reported engaging in more searching for meaning shortly after the death than did less religious parents (McIntosh, Silver, & Wortman, 1993), suggesting a positive link between religiousness and global meaning violation. These types of findings suggest that views of a benevolent universe or a protective, loving God are likely to be highly violated when individuals encounter trauma. In turn, such meaning violations about God could then lead to a spiral of questions about how this trauma could happen, and specifically happen to me, why God had not prevented it, and so on.

Aside from these studies, little research has examined this increased vulnerability that naively positive beliefs about the divine may confer, and it remains poorly understood. It may be that those with a strong, mature faith system and those with little faith will experience less violation and subsequent distress than those who have moderately strong faith, faith that sustains a benevolent worldview in ordinary circumstances but is not strong enough to withstand trauma (Park, Edmondson, & Mills, 2010).

Meaning Making

Finding a way forward after trauma can be painful and difficult. Depending on the type and nature of the event, trauma survivors might have to attend to a variety of practical matters, often including financial, legal, and interpersonal issues. These various secondary stressors often require problem solving and seeking information and support from others (M. J. Gray, Maguen, & Litz, 2007). In tandem with addressing these immediate concerns, trauma survivors might have to find ways to reduce discrepancies between their trauma appraisal and their global meaning. Trauma can have a long-term impact on the very core of one's emotional well-being (M. J. Gray et al., 2007), creating prolonged and complex distress and necessitating meaning making to recover a sense of wholeness and to reestablish a sense of comprehension and purpose in one's life.

Spirituality can be involved in many different aspects of individuals' meaning making as they strive to recover following trauma and adapt to a new reality. Spirituality may infuse individuals' characteristic styles of coping with stressful situations, making their use of spirituality in dealing with trauma much more likely (Roesch & Ano, 2003). Further, in dealing with extreme stressors, spirituality may become a primary coping resource, given its unique appropriateness for those situations in which people come face-to-face with their limits of certainty and control, leaving them feeling vulnerable, helpless, and confused (Newton & McIntosh, 2013; Park, 2016).

Spiritual beliefs and practices can provide a comprehensive cognitive framework in which to work through issues raised by trauma (Boehnlein, 2007). Religion and spirituality are often sources of comfort, meaning, and purpose when dealing with extremely difficult and traumatic life events (Y. Y. Chen & Koenig, 2006b). A coherent spiritual meaning system can help traumatized individuals interpret their experience in more benign ways and begin to integrate it into their life narrative. Building narratives based on healthy spiritual perspectives can facilitate individuals' integration of traumatic sensory and cognitive fragments in a more coherent narrative (Peres et al., 2007).

The religious and spiritual meaning-making coping strategies described in Chapter 2 are common responses to trauma (Harris et al., 2008; Park, 2016). For instance, traumatized individuals may try to find new ways to understand the trauma that allow them to assimilate it into their preexisting global meaning. They may try to see how they were responsible for the trauma, perhaps as punishment for some prior transgression. Trauma survivors often pray for guidance to better understand the trauma, turn to religious or spiritual texts to help them reframe their experience, or rely on fellow congregants for support and understanding. Many survivors reaffirm their faith, feeling that it provided them with the strength they needed to survive their trauma and to recover stability in their thoughts and emotions (Falsetti et al., 2003). Survivors may strive to understand how God is walking with them through their trials, bringing them closer together (K. Gray & Wegner, 2010). These types of spiritual coping strategies help individuals assimilate their experience into their global meaning in ways that do not interfere with or require changes in their global spiritual beliefs and goals, as Jillian did when she was able to focus on her family's spared resources and construe her experience of the tornado as a "blessing."

Other types of spiritual meaning making focus on accommodating the trauma by changing global spiritual meaning. For example, traumatized individuals may try to identify new sources of meaning and significance as they progress through the meaning-making process (Pargament, 1996). They may come to see themselves as sinful and deserving of punishment, as Ralph did in his immature attempts at theodicy related to his experience of the tornado. Ralph's concrete understanding of God did not allow him to blame, criticize, or experience anger at God (i.e., honestly engage in an accommodative approach), so he instead made meaning by blaming himself. Trauma survivors may change their understanding of how things happen, shifting their understanding of suffering and God's place in preventing or creating that suffering. They may also let go of some of their spiritual goals, perceiving them as no longer attainable.

Negative spiritual appraisals and coping strategies focusing on both assimilation and accommodation often follow trauma. Efforts to understand trauma from a spiritual standpoint may generate distressing emotions. Feeling abandoned or betrayed by God can lead to feelings of anger, despair, guilt, and shame. People sometimes create narratives in which the trauma is cast as an attempt by God to harm them, either through deliberate action, such as the punishment of an angry God or through passivity and neglect (Exline & Rose, 2013). Such negative appraisals may also spur negative changes in global meaning—for example, understanding the trauma as a punishment from God may lead to a shift toward viewing God as more angry and less loving than one previously did or as more capricious and less protective.

In their attempts to make meaning, people may struggle with many different aspects of the trauma and their implications (Walker, Courtois, & Aten, 2015). Spiritual struggles and distress are common in the aftermath of trauma (Exline & Rose, 2013), and traumatized individuals may experience strains or even ruptures in their sense of belonging in the world or in their relationship with God. Spiritual struggles that follow trauma may arise from the individual's preexisting negative spiritual meaning system or may result from meaning-making efforts following the trauma.

Negative spiritual coping efforts may limit people's ability to make meaning of trauma, impair their ability to manage their lives, and put them at greater risk of later problems. For example, one study that followed a sample of African American homicide survivors over 6 months found that higher levels of complicated grief predicted subsequent difficulties in the spiritual domain, suggesting that the violent loss of attachment associated with sudden and horrific loss undermined a sense of meaning and relationship with God and the spiritual community that followed (Burke & Neimeyer, 2014). It is also possible that individuals who have unhealthy or immature global spiritual meanings (like Ralph's beliefs about religion and a vengeful and vindictive God) may experience high levels of spiritual struggle and distress, even if the trauma does not change those fundamental global assumptions.

Meaning Made

As noted in Chapter 2, spirituality offers many avenues for reducing perceived discrepancies between the meaning of a trauma and one's global meaning, either through changing the meaning of the trauma or revising one's global meaning system via accommodative processes. These outcomes of meaning-making processes are critically important in recovery; until they occur to the satisfaction of the traumatized individual, he or she will continue to experience posttraumatic distress and seek relief from suffering. Meaning-making efforts persist until they result in changes in situational or global meaning that once again allow harmony between them (M. J. Gray et al., 2007).

Spirituality can facilitate changing the situational meaning of the trauma in ways that reduce discrepancies with global meaning. Benign spiritual beliefs can facilitate traumatized individuals' creation of more positive reattributions, such as seeing the trauma as bringing one closer to God. Narratives about the implications of the trauma for one's life going forward can also involve spirituality. For example, with time and perspective, people may come to see the trauma as a spiritual opportunity or as a time to pause and reevaluate their life's direction or cultivate a deeper connection with God.

As described in Chapter 2, it is common for those who are traumatized to change their global beliefs in coming to terms with trauma. For example, following trauma, survivors may feel they have less control over the things that happen to them or see the world as more unpredictable and random. They may view God differently, feel distanced from God, or see God as less powerful than before the trauma (Harper & Pargament, 2015; Kushner, 1981). Survivors may no longer believe in God or come to believe that they are unable to comprehend everything that happens in the world or God's reasoning for it. For example, Jillian and Ralph made very different global attributions about God following the tornado; Jillian focused on resources that were spared for her family and, therefore, went forward with global beliefs about God's love, protection, and blessings for her and her family. Ralph's focus on trying to resolve Sunday school teachings about a good and powerful God with a community catastrophe led him to blame himself to maintain an illusion of control over the universe.

Following exposure to trauma, individuals may have a different sense of self or identity that may include changes in their spiritual identity or nature. They may feel more worthy and in closer collaboration with God or they may embrace a more negative self-view, such as becoming overly preoccupied with their own sinful nature (see Exline & Rose, 2013). Their life goals and sense of direction may have shifted. Sometimes this purposeful commitment has an overtly spiritual tone, such as the rededication to religious commitments or the pledge to be more devout in spiritual practices or disciplines (Emmons, Colby, & Kaiser, 1998). For example, sometimes people who have experienced a trauma devote themselves to helping others or reducing the threat of trauma to others. Many organizations (e.g., Mothers Against Drunk Driving, the Komen Foundation) were indeed founded by people who were dealing with their own traumatic losses, and they are supported by many others also touched by tragic life events. People who dedicate themselves to alleviating the suffering of others or to changing the legal system or the culture create new life goals for themselves, the pursuit of which can bring a strong sense of purpose that eases their pain.

Spirituality and Changes in Appraised Meaning

In changing the meaning of a stressful situation, spirituality offers many possibilities for causal attributions and for highlighting other aspects of the situation. As noted in Chapter 2, people typically assign a causal understanding to a traumatic event fairly shortly after its occurrence. Through processes of meaning making, this attribution is often revised (C. G. Davis, Nolen-Hoeksema, & Larson, 1998). For example, people may initially be angry at God, feeling that God neglected to care for them or even deliberately and unjustly caused the traumatic event. Over time, however, they may come to see the trauma as the mysterious will of a loving or purposeful God, even if it is a God who is inscrutable and beyond human understanding (Spilka, Hood, Hunsberger, & Gorsuch, 2003). Spirituality offers many avenues for making these types of positive reattributions and is frequently invoked in the search for a more acceptable reason for an event's occurrence than what one may have originally thought. Like Jillian and Ralph, people can come to see the trauma as a spiritual opportunity, as the punishment of an angry God, or the product of human sinfulness (Pargament, 1997). Thus, spiritual explanations permit religious individuals to trust that every event, regardless of its overt appearance and painfulness, is part of God's plan (Baumeister, 1991).

Although religion commonly facilitates adaptive processes of meaning making, these reinterpretations are not always positive. For example, people sometimes come to believe that God harmed them, either through deliberate action or through passivity and neglect. These negative products of making meaning can then lead to mistrust, anger, hurt, and disappointment toward God or even doubt regarding God's existence (Exline & Rose, 2013).

Spiritual growth may also arise through making meaning from trauma (Harper & Pargament, 2015). Many religious traditions contend that spiritual growth occurs primarily through suffering (Aldwin, 2007). Thus, many individuals believe that, through suffering, they will develop character, become purified, and become closer to God or the Divine. Many religions also attempt to cultivate virtues such as compassion, which render people more attuned to the suffering of others (Exline, 2002). Further, experiencing trauma may increase compassion and empathy for others who suffer (Morris, Shakespeare-Finch, & Scott, 2012).

The trauma may have challenged the person's global meaning system to such an extent, and the reduction of violation through meaning making produced such altered understandings, however, that permanent changes have occurred in an individual's spiritual life. These meanings made constitute shifts in global spiritual meaning and are a critical part of recovery and adjustment following trauma. As such, these newly revised meaning systems are critically important to understand because they affect how individuals will perceive and deal with daily life and its attendant challenges and stressors, as well as any subsequent traumas they encounter. As demonstrated in the reciprocal meaning-making model, these new meanings then become the recovering individual's new spiritual life and, therefore, constitute that person's meaning system in his or her post-trauma reality (Park et al., 2010).

Forgiveness is another way of resolving global and situational discrepancies, particularly with regard to interpersonally mediated traumas (e.g., torture, assault, abuse at the hands of a trusted attachment figure; Worthington, Davis, et al., 2013). People's commitment to religion and spirituality, religious beliefs, and religious coping strategies influence how they perceive those offending against them, see themselves, relate to God, and conceptualize and experience the potential trauma (Worthington, Davis, et al., 2013). In turn, these perceptions and relationships may also affect their incorporation of and commitment to their religious and spiritual beliefs and practices. Higher levels of forgiveness have been associated with better psychological well-being in many studies (see Worthington, Davis, et al., 2013, for a review). For example, in a study of older adults, forgiveness—by God, of themselves, or of others—partially or completely mediated relationships between religion and both depressive symptoms and subjective well-being (Lawler-Row, 2010). Although religious people frequently value forgiveness, there is little evidence that they are more forgiving than nonreligious people when it comes to specific events (McCullough & Worthington, 1999). This discrepancy between beliefs and actions may be a source of distress for religious individuals because people may perceive their lack of forgiveness as a moral shortcoming (Wade, Johnson, & Meyer, 2008).

Worthington, Davis, and their colleagues (2013) described relational spirituality as it relates to forgiveness, in particular observing the unique relationships among (a) victim, (b) offender, (c) transgression, and (d) the sacred. This model is more like secular models of forgiveness that attend to the degree of relational damage to predict the depth of trauma. A client's perceptions of God and forgiveness can facilitate or complicate the healing process. Further, the ways that a survivor imbues a traumatic event with spiritual meaning (e.g., "God believes I deserved this," "My body and sexuality have been defiled") can affect the depth of trauma and a survivor's ability to forgive. Across time and exposures to traumas, people may experience changes in both forgiveness and unforgiveness (respectively, positive or loving feelings and grudge holding or vengeful feelings; Worthington, Davis, et al., 2013). Learning how to forgive a serious offense, such as child abuse or sexual assault, may provide a survivor with skills and spiritual development that potentiate future forgiveness. However, repeated trauma with unresolved forgiveness processes may create additive barriers to learning how to forgive (Worthington, Davis, et al., 2013).

One might further expect that the degree to which a trauma also has been imbued with spiritual meaning will lead to greater spiritual struggle and more difficulty forgiving in instances of meaning violations. Interpersonally mediated traumas may have multiple consequences for religious persons. For instance, people may have been offended against, perceive themselves as falling short of moral standards and expectations (e.g., "I must have been raped because I was asking for it"), and see themselves as abandoned by God or their higher power.

EFFECTS OF TRAUMA ON SUBSEQUENT SPIRITUAL LIFE

As these posttraumatic changes in global spiritual meaning stabilize, they come to constitute the new foundation for the survivor's spiritual life. This posttraumatic global spirituality—comprising new or changed beliefs, goals, and sense of meaning and purpose—can pervasively influence people's post-trauma adjustment, including their identity, relationships, and ability to manage their lives. Of course, the specific effects of individuals' posttraumatic global spirituality vary depending on the changes they made through the process of making meaning of their trauma.

Theoretical formulations abound in this vein: Some theorists have suggested that spirituality may increase after trauma (e.g., Decker, 1993), particularly when people use spirituality to help them recover (S. Smith, 2004). These theorists propose that one's global beliefs about oneself, God, and one's relationship with God often change as a result of making meaning of trauma. In particular, recovering from trauma may lead to greater reliance on religious and spiritual teachings, positive changes in one's view of God and the universe, and alterations in one's sense of relationship with a deity. In fact, Decker (1993) contended that meaning made of trauma necessarily involves spiritual change and transformation, leading traumatized individuals to a greater awareness of "existential truth."

Other theorists have suggested that spirituality may decline, particularly when the trauma strongly violates one's beliefs in God's benevolent or loving nature (e.g., Garbarino & Bedard, 1996; Lawson, Drebing, Berg, Vincellette, & Penk, 1998). Attempts to make meaning of trauma might lead to views of oneself as sinful or deserving of misfortune. People may lose their faith or connection to a particular religion (see Paloutzian, Murken, Streib, & Rößler-Namini, 2013, for a review). Trauma can also lead to losses in a sense of meaning, purposefulness, connection, and trust in a guiding force (Exline & Rose, 2013).

Still other theorists have posited that the effects of trauma exposure on spirituality are complex and vary depending on many personal and situational factors (Ben-Ezra et al., 2010; Drescher & Foy, 2008). Thus, trauma may lead some people to abandon their spiritual beliefs and values and others to embrace their faith even more strongly (e.g., Y. Y. Chen & Koenig, 2006b; Fontana & Rosenheck, 2004). Although research has only recently begun to rigorously examine changes in posttraumatic global spiritual meaning systems, findings suggest that these post-trauma changes are indeed complex and vary tremendously on the basis of many factors, including the type of trauma (e.g., Slattery, Park, & Snavely, 2014).

Some studies have demonstrated increases in spirituality following trauma. In particular, studies that directly ask participants whether they have experienced posttraumatic spiritual growth have consistently demonstrated that these perceptions are quite common (e.g., J. E. Kennedy, Davis, & Taylor, 1998; Yanez et al., 2009). For example, following cancer, survivors often report using more religious coping and increasing their religious commitment and their involvement in their community (e.g., Cole, Hopkins, Tisak, Steel, & Carr, 2008).

Research on religious conversion also implicates trauma as an impetus for increased faith. Periods of extreme stress and subsequent difficulties in making meaning from them often precede radical religious transformation (Spilka et al., 2003). Converts may search for and find alternative systems of global beliefs and goals that help them answer their difficult existential questions and solve life problems through their new denomination or religion (Zinnbauer & Pargament, 1998). However, this finding does not suggest that people experiencing trauma typically convert, just that many who convert do so after experiencing trauma.

In contrast, studies comparing traumatized and nontraumatized samples or groups varying in degree of trauma exposure have yielded a different picture, often finding that trauma exposure relates to lower levels of spirituality, variously assessed (see Slattery et al., 2014, for a review). For example, in a study of Mormon women, those who had experienced childhood sexual abuse had a more negative relationship with God and felt more detached and distant from God than did those who had not experienced abuse (Pritt, 1998). Studies using more rigorous study designs have demonstrated an even more complicated picture. For example, in a prospective study over 2 months that measured religiousness before and after traumatic events in college students, 7% of the sample experienced reliable increases in religiousness scores, whereas 11% experienced reliable decreases. The sample mean for religiousness for students who experienced a traumatic event during the study did not change but decreased in the group that did not experience a traumatic event (Perera & Frazier, 2013). Further, studies that have examined spiritual changes pre- to post-trauma have demonstrated that people's self-reports of change are not closely related to measured changes (e.g., Y. Y. Chen &

Koenig, 2006b; P. Frazier et al., 2009). That is, survivors seem motivated to report change, even when others observe little change and few changes are reported on objective measures pre- to postevent.

CLINICAL IMPLICATIONS OF POSTTRAUMATIC CHANGES IN SPIRITUALITY

Trauma survivors' newly revised spiritual meaning system influences many aspects of their lives. These changes made over time through a process of meaning making should ultimately help them to reduce discrepancies and thus reduce PTSD symptoms or other trauma-related distress (M. J. Gray et al., 2007). Such changes restore harmony between trauma survivors' perceptions of their experiences and their spiritual understanding, allowing resolution and recovery to occur.

However, the content of the new spiritual meaning system will have long-term implications extending far beyond this particular traumatic instance. In considering these other effects on a survivor's life, the more general literature on relations between spiritual meaning and well-being applies. Thus, losing faith or coming to a view of God as distant, capricious, or neglectful may lead to more general spiritual strains and struggles within themselves, with others, and with God (Exline & Rose, 2013). These struggles are strongly associated with poorer psychological and physical health (Aldwin, Park, Jeong, & Nath, 2014; Park & Slattery, 2013a). Thus, negative spiritual meanings made may give rise to many secondary problems, including problems with interpersonal relationships, parenting, work, and substance use (Exline & Rose, 2013).

Further, this newly revised spiritual meaning system will become the set of beliefs, goals, and core sense of life meaning that survivors possess as they encounter subsequent stressors. As Foy and Drescher (2015) noted, over-accommodation toward negative spiritual meaning might allow survivors to move on and recover, but at the cost of an important coping resource. Such a loss of positive spiritual meanings may, therefore, decrease an individual's resilience in coping with subsequent stressful or traumatic events.

However, individuals who recover from trauma with their spiritual meaning system relatively intact or who come to a more positive, albeit nuanced, reconstituted spiritual life may enjoy a happier and healthier day-to-day existence. Further, this positive spiritual meaning system may enhance their resilience as they encounter future stressful situations. If people encounter a subsequent trauma, this spiritual meaning may be protective or serve as a central appraisal and coping resource (Falsetti et al., 2003). Spiritual growth or positive spiritual meaning may also, therefore, have pervasive implications for survivors' well-being. These long-term impacts of changed spiritual meaning highlight the possible importance of attending to spiritual meaning systems in the course of treatment and resolving traumatic discrepancies in ways that promote positive spiritual beliefs, goals, and a sense of meaning and purpose.

CONCLUSION

The reciprocal meaning-making model provides a useful way for understanding and working with survivors of highly stressful and traumatic events by highlighting how spirituality may be involved in the processes of post-traumatic meaning making and how spirituality may also change as a result of this process. This model is also more broadly useful, however, in describing the complex and intertwined histories of experiences and meaning systems that accrue over the life course for all individuals, regardless of whether trauma-related issues are the focus of treatment. In subsequent chapters, this model serves as the basis for our discussion of assessment and treatment involving spiritual meaning in the context of trauma.

4

CURRENT TREATMENT APPROACHES TO TRAUMA AND POSTTRAUMATIC STRESS DISORDER

Trauma can be addressed in psychotherapy as an ancillary issue arising during the therapeutic process or as a presenting problem that represents the focus of treatment (as cases from the prior chapters exemplify). In these latter trauma-focused approaches, posttraumatic stress symptoms that meet criteria for a posttraumatic stress disorder (PTSD) diagnosis are frequently present, and interventions typically target the origins and consequences of the condition in the context of individual psychotherapy. However, PTSD symptoms can be a concern seen in other types of treatment as well (e.g., couple and family therapy, substance abuse treatment), and trauma can pervasively affect an individual's life across multiple domains (not just psychologically or spiritually).

The treatment of PTSD and other trauma-related concerns has received considerable research attention over the past half century, and several organizations have outlined clinical guidelines for working with traumatized

http://dx.doi.org/10.1037/15961-004
Trauma, Meaning, and Spirituality: Translating Research Into Clinical Practice, by C. L. Park, J. M. Currier, J. I. Harris, and J. M. Slattery

clients on the basis of this work (e.g., Foa, Keane, Friedman, & Cohen, 2009; Institute of Medicine, 2008). Because we specifically focus on addressing spirituality in trauma treatment, we do not restate these guidelines here or attempt to introduce a new model for treating PTSD. Instead, we encourage readers to consult the recommendations of the International Society for Traumatic Stress Studies for a comprehensive summary of the current knowledge base for working with this population (see Foa et al., 2009).

Before discussing how the reciprocal meaning-making model might enhance existing therapeutic approaches, it is imperative to contextualize this perspective within a general understanding of key clinical concerns and available evidence-based strategies for working with trauma survivors. Drawing on material from a case in which religion and/or spirituality was not a predominant focus in the meaning-making process, the two main goals of this chapter are to (a) provide an overview of general clinical concerns for treating traumatized persons and (b) introduce a phase-based model of recovery with specific attention to evidence-based therapies that address different tasks and objectives in the therapeutic process. Case material from the treatment of Mr. Denton will be used to illumine the present discussion as well as establish a foundation for upcoming chapters in which we will address clinical applications of a spiritually integrative approach.

INTRODUCTION TO MR. DENTON

Henry Denton was a 63-year-old African American man referred by his primary care physician to a clinic specializing in PTSD assessment and treatment. He was married for nearly 40 years and had two adult children and four grandchildren (ages 5–16 years) who resided in a nearby rural town. Mr. Denton had been drafted into the U.S. Marine Corps after graduating from high school, and he completed two combat deployments in Vietnam while the fighting was still quite intense in the late 1960s. The second of these tours entailed considerable exposure to potential traumas because Mr. Denton served as the point person on a covert "seek-and-destroy team" that provided reconnaissance and arms support to neighboring units during times of heavy fighting and mass casualties.

Following a period of "going crazy" for the first 2 years postmilitary service in which Mr. Denton drank heavily and experienced a range of trauma-related problems, he established a meaningful and productive life. Mr. Denton married his high school sweetheart shortly after returning from the war and then spent the next 4 decades working for the postal service and maintaining a moderately sized farm. Although Mr. Denton was not hostile toward God, he did not identify with a particular religious tradition at the time of the referral and had never explicitly drawn on religion or traditional spiritual frameworks for finding meaning or coping with difficulties in his life.

On entering treatment, Mr. Denton's primary complaints involved a debilitating reemergence of PTSD symptomatology over the prior year, secondary to several major role transitions and worsening of medical problems. That is, he had to retire from the postal service because of increasing mobility problems and chronic pain in his lower back. He had also recently completed radiation treatment for a "cancer scare" (Stage II prostate cancer) and was contending with uncontrolled hypertension and other cardiac problems. Given these concerns, Mr. Denton had to assume a reduced role on his farm and delegate most responsibilities to an adult son. This change in circumstances was quite a challenge for Mr. Denton because work had provided a deep sense of purpose and control in his life since returning from Vietnam. In addition, he reportedly turned to work for "getting space" away from people, relieving stress, and distracting himself from periodic distressing thoughts and feelings about his war-zone experiences.

Although he likely suffered from varying levels of PTSD symptomatology over the preceding decades, Mr. Denton reported being totally "haunted" and "going crazy again" at the time of the referral. He exceeded the clinical threshold on the Posttraumatic Stress Disorder Clinical Checklist for his combat experiences at the time of the referral (overall score = 78; Weathers & Ford, 1996). He was also consuming alcohol in increasingly larger amounts as a sleep aid and as a way to manage anxiety throughout most days. Mr. Denton denied having any intention or plan to harm himself; however, he was feeling quite hopeless and had begun to entertain the possibility of suicide if his situation did not improve in the near future.

Mr. Denton had an unremarkable history of mental health problems or trauma exposure prior to serving in Vietnam. Of the many possible traumas that occurred during his deployments, he initially indicated that his most distressing event entailed being stranded in a minefield during a firefight after a nearby unit had been ambushed and two of his close personal friends were killed within arm's reach. However, as Mr. Denton felt more trusting and comfortable in the therapeutic relationship, he disclosed another event that he had never shared and had planned to "leave off the table" in his treatment as well. On an occasion in which he was scouting an area where enemy troops were allegedly based, Mr. Denton killed a Vietcong soldier of similar age at close range. According to Mr. Denton, the two men stumbled onto one another from opposite sides at the crest of a small hill and initially "froze" for a few moments as they gazed into one another's eyes. When the other man broke from the unexpectedly long stare and motioned for his weapon, Mr. Denton quickly drew his machine gun and fired a round into the other man's chest. On inspecting the body, Mr. Denton found a picture of what appeared to be the man's wife and young child.

In addition to distressing nightmares about this event and frequent hallucination-like experiences of this man "visiting" him, Mr. Denton was also feeling guilty about taking this man's life and worried about how the wife and child had fared since the war. At some level, Mr. Denton believed that his health problems and worsening of PTSD symptoms were warranted because of taking this man's life and other unnamed decisions and actions that occurred during his deployments.

GENERAL CLINICAL CONCERNS

As highlighted in the opening chapter, epidemiological research has suggested that most persons in the United States will encounter a potential trauma at some point in their lives. In addition, depending on the type of events, research has suggested that 10% to 20% of this group will develop persistent alterations in cognitions, feelings, and behaviors (for a review of the epidemiology of trauma, see F. H. Norris & Slone, 2007). Research on PTSD in particular has suggested that multiple clinical presentations can emerge following exposure to traumatic events, including fear-based anxiety symptoms, dysphoria/anhedonia, aggressive/externalizing problems, guilt and shame, and negative appraisals about oneself, others, and the world (Friedman, Resick, Bryant, & Brewin, 2011). Several diagnostic frameworks have been offered over the years for capturing the challenges of traumatized persons such as Mr. Denton (e.g., soldier's heart, Da Costa's syndrome, traumatic neurosis, combat fatigue, gross stress reaction).

In the current nomenclature of the *Diagnostic and Statistical Manual of Mental Disorders* (fifth ed.; DSM–5; American Psychiatric Association, 2013), PTSD entails four interrelated but distinct diagnostic clusters based on experiences involving actual or threatened death, serious injury, or sexual violation (as Ms. Kim's case from Chapter 2 highlighted): (a) reexperienced symptoms (e.g., traumatic nightmares, intrusive recollections regarding the trauma), (b) emotional and/or physiological reactivity and arousal (e.g., sleep disturbance, irritability, hypervigilance, reckless or self-destructive behavior), (c) avoidance behaviors (e.g., avoiding conversations about the trauma, avoidance of specific activities, places, and/or people associated with the trauma), and (d) negative alterations in cognitions and mood (e.g., psychic numbing, estrangement from others, persistent and maladaptive sense of blame of self or others). With the recent reincorporation of this fourth domain into the PTSD diagnosis, clinicians should be especially mindful about possible spiritual struggles associated with PTSD and other trauma-related symptomatology. The nature of these spiritual struggles was introduced in Chapter 3 and is addressed in greater depth in the following chapters.

Before shifting into these spiritual concerns, several other concerns should be considered when working with persons suffering from PTSD or related difficulties. As a starting point, clinicians should recognize that symptomatology of a more chronic nature can present special treatment challenges. Consistent with general patterns of comorbidity for psychiatric diagnoses, many survivors who have suffered from severe PTSD over a long period contend with other mental health problems that could be equally or more distressing and in need of clinical attention (e.g., substance abuse, depression). Such co-occurring problems can both complicate treatment and exacerbate the course of PTSD. As the recent addition of reckless or self-destructive behavior in the *DSM–5* also underscores, many persons with PTSD also find themselves engaging in activities, situations, and scenarios that may replicate their trauma and endanger their safety (e.g., dangerous driving, lack of health care adherence).

As with Mr. Denton's health problems, research has also suggested that traumatized persons are at increased risk for developing a variety of medical illnesses (e.g., cardiovascular issues; for reviews, see Del Gaizo, Elhai, & Weaver, 2011; Pietrzak, Goldstein, Southwick, & Grant, 2011; Qureshi, Pyne, Magruder, Schulz, & Kunik, 2009) and even of dying of accidental or behavioral causes (e.g., motor vehicular events; Drescher, Rosen, Burling, & Foy, 2003). Although Mr. Denton was able to get his drinking under control soon after beginning treatment and maintained close relationships with his family, clinicians should also be mindful that many clients have likely attempted psychological treatments for trauma-related symptoms in the past, often with limited success. As a result, these clients have possibly accumulated a series of painful losses and disappointments due to challenges in negotiating the reality and consequences of their experiences (e.g., lack of occupational stability or success, divorce, estrangement from their children).

Clinicians should also be mindful of the many possible types of traumatic experiences that can occur and whether the client has experienced isolated or repeated traumas during his or her lifetime. Nearly every person has a breaking point, and it is axiomatic that the risk for PTSD and related problems increases with greater exposure to trauma. In this vein, it is helpful to distinguish between Type I and II traumas, with the former referring to isolated episodes (e.g., single assault, accidents, natural disasters, physical illness), such as in the case of Ralph and Jillian in Chapter 3, and the latter capturing complex and repeated exposure to the threat of violence (e.g., military combat, childhood abuse, genocide), as in the case of Ms. Kim in Chapter 2. Although research has not thoroughly examined whether a history of prior traumas or certain types of events significantly affects responses to treatment, exposure to Type II traumas—particularly during critical developmental periods and with respect to events of an interpersonal nature (e.g., torture, perpetration of abuse or harm from a trusted attachment figure)—is often associated with a higher probability of precipitating PTSD and other constellations of problems (Cloitre et al., 2009; Cloitre, Stovall-McClough, Zorbas, & Charuvastra, 2008; Herman, 1992; van der Kolk, Roth, Pelcovitz, Sunday, & Spinazzola, 2005).

Given the deep violation of trust that characterizes Type II traumas, these clients can also struggle to develop a therapeutic alliance. Further, they frequently present a range of trauma-related alterations in functioning that can warrant serious clinical attention along with the treatment for PTSD (e.g., emotional dysregulation, somatization and medical problems, instability in relationships, as well as issues with attention and consciousness, self-perception, and identity; Courtois, 2004). Research on PTSD treatments has largely focused on survivors of Type I traumas (Cloitre, 2009); however, several promising treatments have also been developed to specifically address Type II concerns as well (e.g., Paivio & Pascual-Leone, 2010).

All these clinical possibilities underscore the importance of receiving adequate training and conducting careful assessments before initiating treatment with traumatized persons like Mr. Denton. Engaging these clients in treatment also requires the clinician to evaluate the client's psychosocial resources, goals for treatment, and ability and willingness to commit to a specific course of treatment. Notably, many treatments have complementary but somewhat dissimilar goals, ranging from promoting healthier functioning in occupational, physical, or relational domains or reduction in substance abuse to directly addressing trauma-related problems. Even in cases of disabling PTSD symptoms like Mr. Denton's, traumatized clients can present with heterogeneous problems that necessitate flexible decision making about the nature and direction of treatment. Although the reduction of PTSD symptoms is an excellent first-line goal for many clients, other clients may have other pressing concerns or lack the resources to focus on these tasks at the start of treatment.

Consider the role of spirituality in shaping global meaning and cultural assumptions about trauma (as discussed in Chapters 2 and 3): Many non-Western survivors or persons from certain religious traditions might not view trauma from a traditional mental health standpoint and may require clinicians to facilitate treatment in a manner that honors the possible spiritual dimensions of their experiences. For example, although Mr. Denton did not present as particularly religious, African American and Latino/a people as groups typically maintain more religious worldviews compared with their Caucasian counterparts (Dunn & Horgas, 2004; Esser-Stuart & Lyons, 2002; Leblanc, Driscoll, & Pearlin, 2004; Pole, Gone, & Kulkarni, 2008; Taylor, Chatters, &

Jackson, 2007) and often expect that spiritual concerns will be considered as integral to their health care (Devlin, Roberts, Okaya, & Xiong, 2006).

HEALING FROM POSTTRAUMATIC STRESS DISORDER: PHASES OF RESTORATION

Clinicians should recognize that most persons with PTSD do not follow a linear course of recovery but rather ebb and flow in their symptomatology during the recovery process. Several models have been offered for conceptualizing phases of restoration for clients like Mr. Denton (e.g., Herman, 1992; van der Kolk, MacFarlane, & van der Hart, 1996). According to Herman (1992), recovery from PTSD entails a shift from unpredictable danger and powerlessness to safety and empowerment, from avoidance of the traumatic past to an acknowledgment and processing of one's painful experiences, and from isolation and meaninglessness to reconnection with others and the restoration of global meaning. Assuming such a phase-based perspective can allow for a respectful client-centered posture throughout treatment in which clinicians can be intentional in contextualizing their approach according to the specific concerns and needs of the client.

In addition to establishing a safe and trusting relationship and atmosphere in treatment, clinicians may focus on three sets of goals in this restorative process:

- promoting safety,
- processing traumatic memories and situational meanings, and
- restoring relationships and global meaning.

Attending to these goals can compel clinicians to incorporate multiple therapeutic interventions as they attempt to promote healing with their traumatized clients. In extreme cases, clinicians address these phases in a sequential manner. However, it is frequently preferable to focus on multiple therapeutic tasks at the same time or even to repeat certain interventions as the client moves toward restoration amid what can sometimes be a distressing and deconstructive journey.

Although there are differences of opinion about how best to address traumatic memories in treatment, it is assumed that persons with PTSD have the greatest probability of healing if they can find the courage to process directly their traumas to some degree with their clinician. Hence, depending on the severity of reexperiencing and other distress symptoms, it may be appropriate to focus on tasks associated with Phases 1 and 2 before shifting therapeutic conversations to existential and/or spiritual concerns in Phase 3. Table 4.1 outlines therapeutic objectives, possible clinical indicators and mechanisms, and treatment approaches of the phase-based recovery model.

TRAUMA, MEANING, AND SPIRITUALITY

TABLE 4.1
General Clinical Concerns of Phase-Based Model of Posttraumatic Stress Disorder Treatment

Concern	Phase 1	Phase 2	Phase 3
Therapeutic objective	To promote healthy self-care as well as emotional and physical safety	To adequately process the trauma memory and maladaptive appraisals about the event	To repair relationships with significant others and establish a functional meaning system
Clinical indicators	Ongoing abuse Domestic violence Unstable living situation Unhealthy social bonds Cutting and/or self-injury Risky sexual behaviors Serious substance misuse Self-destructive behaviors Suicidal thoughts and behaviors Psychiatric comorbidities Medical comorbidities Lack of coping skills	Client motivation and "buy-in" Adequate coping and resources Active reexperiencing of trauma Self-recrimination about the event Pervasive guilt and/or shame Over-accommodation of beliefs	Existential questioning Lack of purpose in life Diffuse values Meaninglessness Loneliness and isolation Sense of alienation Longing for intimacy Spiritual struggles
Possible mechanisms	Environmental changes Improved relationships Improved coping Emotion regulation Behavioral activation Acceptance Self-efficacy Agency	Habituation of anxiety Emotional processing Narrative integration Corrective emotional experience Improved relationships Behavioral activation Acceptance Self-efficacy Agency	Enhanced purpose Values clarification Improved intimacy Forgiveness Acceptance Self-efficacy Agency

Psychological treatments

Social advocacy
Case management
Medical referral
Psychotropic medication
Behavioral sleep therapy
Stress management
Mindfulness meditation
Breathing retraining
Relaxation exercises
Coping skills training
Activity scheduling
Supportive therapy

Cognitive restructuring
In vivo exposure
Imaginal exposure

Couples therapy
Family therapy
Spiritually integrative
approaches

Phase 1: Promoting Safety

For traumatized persons who are actively engaging in substance abuse or other self-destructive behaviors, promoting safety is the most urgent clinical need. Used in this context, "safety" could entail reducing drug and/or alcohol use, suicidality, self-injury, unsafe sex, and other risky behaviors. Beyond limiting these types of concerns, promoting safety could also signify letting go of harmful relationships (e.g., substance-abusing friends), learning new coping strategies, using community resources, pursuing a regular sleep cycle, more closely adhering to a physician's recommendations, or taking care of one's body and cultivating a healthy lifestyle.

In this initial phase, it is essential to routinely monitor suicidal thoughts and behaviors and to consider hospitalization when a client has become emotionally unsafe and is in danger of harming him- or herself. There is also an increased risk for both additional trauma exposures and psychological problems with the number of traumatic events experienced. As such, clinicians should be mindful that the more vulnerable an individual is from the start of treatment, the greater the probability that he or she will confront other traumas and experience long-term psychological and possible spiritual disturbances. It can, therefore, be imperative to address a client's physical safety and consequences of engaging in different therapeutic tasks before shifting into Phase 2 aims. In instances of physical danger (e.g., domestic violence), unsafe clients might have a strong need for case management and/or advocacy to obtain new housing or employment. Several psychotropic medications have also demonstrated modest efficacy in reducing PTSD and related symptoms (Friedman, Davidson, & Stein, 2009). Thus, just as Mr. Denton's physician implemented sertraline in conjunction with a referral for trauma-focused therapy, many emotionally unsafe clients could also gain a needed sense of control and grounding via an adjunctive medication.

Najavits's (2002) Seeking Safety (SS) is presently the most researched treatment for promoting stabilization and self-care among vulnerable clients with PTSD, substance abuse, and possible other comorbid problems. SS is a present-focused and problem-oriented model that attempts to reduce these distress symptoms and behaviors in a time-limited manner. In keeping with a meaning-making perspective, SS honors both the violation of global meaning that can accompany PTSD and other trauma-related concerns and the importance of spirituality as an adaptive resource for many survivors. For example, the overall treatment consists of 25 topics, each of which is framed as a positive ideal rather than a particular maladaptive feature of PTSD or substance abuse (e.g., "Asking for Help," "Compassion," "Taking Good Care of Yourself"). Treatment topics can be covered in any order, with each session structured to promote education, self-reflection, and a behavioral commitment of some sort.

Najavits (2002) developed SS to be highly flexible in that this treatment can be implemented in individual or group formats, in clinical and community settings, or as a stand-alone or adjunctive approach for all types of traumas and substances. In a qualitative review of 22 outcome studies for SS, Najavits and Hien (2013) found that the full model consistently yielded positive effects in reducing PTSD and substance abuse relative to those persons who did not receive the intervention. Although other results were more mixed, several studies found some benefit for implementing an abbreviated version of SS as well (Najavits & Hien, 2013).

Linehan's (1993a) dialectical behavior therapy (DBT) is another highly structured, problem-focused, cognitive–behavioral treatment with broad applications for promoting safety among traumatized persons. DBT was initially developed to address the concerns of chronically suicidal persons diagnosed with borderline personality disorder—a condition that is often comorbid with PTSD and that often results from repeated exposure to sexual abuse or other complex traumas during childhood. The core of DBT focuses on deficits in emotion regulation skills and incorporates insights and practices from several spiritual traditions (e.g., Buddhism) in negotiating a critical dialectic between acceptance and change in the restorative process. When applied in a traditional manner, implementing DBT with traumatized persons would entail a longer term course (e.g., 1–2 years) of individual psychotherapy combined with weekly skill-building groups for teaching strategies of mindfulness, emotion regulation, distress tolerance, and interpersonal effectiveness (Linehan, 1993b).

As with selecting SS topics or as in an adjunctive manner, a second approach to using DBT is to incorporate elements of the skill-building modules for fostering clients' emotional stability as they attempt to transition into Phase 2 tasks. Although there is insufficient evidence to suggest that DBT skills training should become a standard part of PTSD treatments, several studies have indicated that these strategies indeed promote stability and self-efficacy for clients who otherwise might not tolerate trauma-focused interventions at the time they seek help (for a review of this work, see Cahill, Rothbaum, Resick, & Follette, 2009).

Phase 2: Processing Traumatic Memories and Situational Meanings

Since Breuer and Freud's (2000) unanticipated discovery of the "talking cure" with a young woman struggling to overcome consequences of childhood sexual abuse, facilitating clients' engagement with emotionally challenging thoughts and emotions has been a critical aspect of most models of psychotherapy for trauma. In the context of treating PTSD in particular, this type of therapeutic "exposure" entails a variety of proposed mechanisms for alleviating symptoms. For instance, revisiting trauma can promote deconditioning of the memory and the extinction of conditioned anxiety reactions (often termed *habituation*). Intentionally engaging in the trauma-related material in a safe and supportive context can also provide a corrective emotional experience and help the client learn that remembering the trauma does not place him or her in imminent danger and, further, that it is possible to differentiate these events from other benign experiences in life. In so doing, the client may gain a sense of mastery from confronting his or her fears and find the necessary emotional distance for newer adaptive meanings to emerge. Hembree and Foa (2000) also proposed that exposure can enhance the narrative organization of the trauma story in profound ways. Promoting coherence in the "micronarrative" of the trauma might then position clients to reconcile the situational meanings of their experiences with aspects of their global meaning system as they progressively move into a posttrauma reality that will no longer be defined by PTSD.

Although researchers are just now beginning to clarify the mechanisms of these Phase 2 treatments, several models emphasizing this type of systematic processing of traumatic memories and situational meanings have demonstrated impressive reductions in PTSD across a large number of well-designed studies. The interested reader can refer to the following reviews for a synopsis of this work: Bisson and Andrew (2005); Bisson et al. (2007); Bradley, Greene, Russ, Dutra, and Westen (2005); Cahill et al. (2009); Cloitre (2009); Institute of Medicine (2008); Ponniah and Hollon (2009); Powers, Halpern, Ferenschak, Gillihan, and Foa (2010); and Resick, Monson, and Gutner (2007).

Among these therapeutic approaches, cognitive processing therapy (CPT; Resick & Schnicke, 1993) is a trauma-focused treatment that has consistently yielded benefits in improving PTSD related to several types of potential traumas (e.g., rape, childhood sexual abuse, military combat; for narrative summaries of this work, see Cahill et al., 2009; Cloitre, 2009; Ponniah & Hollon, 2009). CPT focuses on emotional processing of the memory through a written account of the trauma that the client reads aloud in session and reviews at home over the initial weeks of treatment. In keeping with a meaning-making perspective, this intervention draws on a social–cognitive understanding of PTSD that emphasizes the possible impact of trauma on aspects of a client's global meaning system and the necessary adjustments that must occur to adaptively reconcile situational meanings with prior beliefs and values. According to Resick and Schnicke (1993), traumatized persons become stuck in the recovery process when the trauma is not assimilated or when the event becomes too integrated and there is an over-accommodation of maladaptive global beliefs.

In contrast to many other approaches, CPT primarily emphasizes a survivor's situational meanings of the trauma and its consequences, including "manufactured emotions," such as shame, guilt, and anger, which are generated when higher order cognitive processes go awry. From a procedural standpoint, CPT predominantly uses cognitive restructuring exercises in which the client learns to better challenge unhelpful thoughts surrounding the trauma (e.g., self-blame). In particular, clients are first guided to challenge their assimilated beliefs and then to focus on revising possible overgeneralized beliefs stemming from the index event. These "stuck points" span five important content areas for traumatized persons who have over-accommodated their global beliefs as a way of making meaning of their experiences: safety, trust, power and control, esteem, and intimacy. The latter half of the CPT protocol addresses each of these domains in this same sequence.

Foa and colleagues' (Foa, Hembree, & Rothbaum, 2007; Foa & Rothbaum, 1998) prolonged exposure (PE) is another trauma-focused intervention that has arguably received the most empirical support to date. In a meta-analytic review of 13 randomized trials of PE versus a variety of no-treatment groups, Powers et al. (2010) documented large effects for PE in reducing PTSD and secondary problems (e.g., depression, general psychiatric distress) at post-treatment and follow-up assessments. PE emerged out of emotional processing theory (Foa & Kozak, 1986), which proposed that PTSD develops from a fear network of mental structures in memory (e.g., event stimuli, responses, and situational meanings) associated with the trauma. That fear network contributes to avoidance behaviors and limits adaptive meaning-making processes. Each of these mental structures might be activated by information linked with the trauma, which can subsequently trigger other dimensions of the fear network as well.

According to Foa and colleagues (Foa et al., 2007; Foa & Rothbaum, 1998), PE attempts to revise the fear network when the clinician cultivates two conditions in therapy: (a) activating these maladaptive structures in sessions and (b) providing information that is discrepant from the fear network in the safety of the therapeutic relationship and other nontraumatic situations. In so doing, PE also addresses two common global beliefs for traumatized persons that can hinder recovery from PTSD: "I am incompetent," and "The world is completely dangerous."

In addition to addressing safety tasks (e.g., psychoeducation about PTSD, breathing retraining), PE includes three basic components that are usually implemented over eight to 12 sessions: (a) confronting people, places, and possible activities that are reminiscent of the trauma that the client has been avoiding since the event (i.e., in vivo exposure); (b) repeatedly revisiting the central traumatic memory and engaging with painful emotional content both in sessions and listening to recordings of these exercises at home (i.e., imaginal exposure); and (c) working through the emotional content and situational meanings of the trauma through open-ended discussions following imaginal exposure exercises with the clinician (i.e., emotional processing).

Given the severity of Mr. Denton's posttraumatic symptoms, he verbalized a willingness to "try anything" at the time of the referral and consented to participate in PE on a weekly basis over the ensuing several months. The first two of these sessions focused on psychoeducation about PTSD from an emotional processing perspective, breathing retraining, and construction of a fear hierarchy and initial plan for in vivo exposure exercises. Of the many situations he had been avoiding, Mr. Denton was most upset by an increasing reliance on safety behaviors to manage his anxiety (e.g., always carrying a loaded handgun) along with a perceived inability to watch his grandsons play athletics for the local high school or accompany his wife to the grocery store and other outings in their small rural community.

Beginning in the third session, Mr. Denton began to revisit his memory of the extended firefight in the minefield. However, following little symptom improvement over the next 2 months, his therapist probed deeper into possible other traumas, at which point Mr. Denton reluctantly (and tearfully) disclosed the account of taking the life of the Vietcong soldier at close range. In addition to his ongoing practice of calm breathing and in vivo exposure interventions, Mr. Denton achieved considerable lessening of reexperiencing and anxiety symptoms once he had the courage to revisit systematically this painful memory in increasing depth over the next eight sessions. In so doing, he revised many guilt-laden meanings associated with the event and began to connect with deep sadness over the unfortunate meeting with the young man without interrupting these adaptive emotions or becoming emotionally overwhelmed when they emerged. Following each of the imaginal exposures, the therapist also devoted ample time to debriefing these exercises and exploring maladaptive meanings from the trauma narrative that Mr. Denton had constructed about himself with respect to his war-zone experiences (e.g., "I don't deserve to be alive," "I am not worthy of being loved," "I should have been the one who was killed").

Phase 3: Restoring Relationships and Global Meaning

Once clients have achieved safety and are no longer plagued by PTSD or other trauma-related sequelae (Phase 2), they might need support in restoring global meaning and repairing or reinvesting in relationships. Developing the capacities to care for oneself and work through a traumatic memory can certainly be meaningful accomplishments in themselves. For instance, clients may experience a newfound sense of agency, empowerment, or cohesiveness at this point in treatment. However, many clients will also confront relational and identity-specific concerns as they struggle to clarify the type of person they want to be and what they now want their life story to be about (i.e., develop new global goals). Although treatments for PTSD are often consistent with the meaning-making model, most of these approaches predominantly focus on alleviating distress and seldom emphasize the restoration of purpose and valued living that many trauma survivors desperately long for as well.

Even if a clinician thoughtfully implements interventions to eliminate posttraumatic nightmares, such as ending Mr. Denton's near nightly replaying of killing the Vietcong soldier through the systematic revisiting and processing of the event in PE sessions, many clients will go on to struggle with another equally pressing existential question: "What do I dream about now in my life?" (C. B. Eriksson, personal communication, August 15, 2012). Regarding the objectives of this phase, Herman (1992) eloquently wrote,

> Having come to terms with the traumatic past, the survivor faces the task of creating a future. She has mourned the old self that the trauma destroyed; now she must develop a new self. Her relationships have been tested and forever changed by the trauma; now she must develop new relationships. The old beliefs that gave meaning to her life have been challenged; now she must find anew a sustaining faith. (p. 196)

Now that the client has courageously appraised the reality of the trauma and possibly grieved its consequences (e.g., loss of innocence), he or she may also have to reexamine the quality of his or her relationships and dreams and reclaim or construct new aspects of global meaning that will allow for a deeper sense of fulfillment and purpose in the life chapters to come.

In considering these types of therapeutic objectives, it is important to recognize that trauma and PTSD not only affect the individual survivor but can also have ripple effects on other significant characters in his or her life story as well. For example, persons with PTSD often complain about becoming emotionally deadened and opt to distance themselves from intimate contact as a means of self-protection or out of concerns about injuring their loved one with dysregulated emotion or an unintended repetition of the event. For example, Mr. Denton opted never to disclose any details of his war-zone experiences with his wife and would seek solitude in times of stress on the basis of what he believed was a loving concern about what he might say or do in these moments. Although Mr. Denton had developed a strong bond with his wife, experiential avoidance robbed him of restorative interactions in his marriage, and both parties felt hurt and alienated from one another when his posttraumatic symptoms reemerged.

Partners of a traumatized person might also observe their loved one's inner turmoil in various ways and become the object of anger and hostility.

For example, in one of their early interviews, Mr. Denton's wife tearfully corroborated many of her husband's self-reported trauma-related issues, such as screaming out in distress during nightmares and often having a "short fuse" with her. In addition, partners might have their own trauma histories that can become activated as their loved one struggles with PTSD, such that both parties are challenged to reasonably appraise one another's intentions and attend to their partner's emotional needs. Any of these dynamics may place serious stress on one's partner and disturb the overall family system. Like the eradication of resources from the weakening of one's spiritual meaning system, the breakdown of relationships in one's family can also lead to relational distress and disrupt the foundation of otherwise loving and supportive bonds during the meaning-making process.

Research on couples therapy for trauma and PTSD is only just beginning (for a review, see Riggs, Monson, Glynn, & Canterino, 2009). However, several approaches have been proposed that might be helpful for addressing aims in Phase 3 (e.g., emotionally focused [Johnson, 2002], integrative behavioral [Erbes, Polusny, MacDermid, & Compton, 2008], cognitive–behavioral conjoint [Monson, Fredman, & Adair, 2008] therapies). In keeping with systems-oriented models, many of these therapies are not principally concerned with the alleviation of PTSD per se, but rather focus on repairing aspects of the couple's relationship (e.g., reducing couples distress and conflict, increasing support and relational satisfaction) and/or correcting other problematic family dynamics caused by the trauma and its sequelae (e.g., experiential avoidance).

Clinicians might also incorporate the partner in an adjunctive manner in individual therapy to garner support as the client progresses in his or her treatment and works to restore global meaning. For example, as PE sessions reached completion and Mr. Denton was able to discuss his traumatic past without becoming fragmented and emotionally overwhelmed, he drew on the therapist's guidance to share with his wife a "newspaper version" of his traumatic past and how war-zone experiences had affected his capacity for intimacy in their marriage over the years. To avoid secondarily traumatizing his wife, Mr. Denton worked closely with his therapist to develop a structured agenda for this conversation and role-played a trauma narrative in preparation for sharing these vulnerable details of his life. Contrary to his unrealistic fears of being misunderstood and abandoned, Mr. Denton's wife responded with compassion and regret that he had not confided in her earlier. As such, Mr. Denton was able to invite his wife to share how his struggles with PTSD had affected her sense of global meaning throughout their marriage; with the help of his therapist, Mr. Denton then drew on his newfound understandings about trauma to educate her about why certain activities and situations had been such a challenge for him over the past year in particular.

In addition to focusing on the quality of relationships with the partner or other major characters, clinicians might also have to address thematic issues about the client's life story at this point in treatment. Although research on these types of tasks is quite limited, indirect support for addressing existential and/or spiritual concerns in treatment is suggested in the growing literature on posttraumatic growth. As spiritual traditions have emphasized for millennia, *posttraumatic growth* (PTG) refers to the paradoxical tendency for many survivors to report a range of constructive intra- and interpersonal life changes as a result of struggling with trauma.

Tedeschi and Calhoun's (2004) model of PTG, in particular, involves a common shift toward existential concerns as PTSD or other trauma-related distress abates, which is characterized by a survivor's deliberate attempts to self-reflect and reconcile aspects of his or her global meaning system with the significance of the experience. Cross-sectional studies with survivors of physical assaults (Kleim & Ehlers, 2009), war captivity (Solomon & Dekel, 2007), and other potential traumas (McCaslin et al., 2009) have documented nonlinear links between PTG and PTSD, in which growth typically does not materialize without some degree of meaning violation or experience of overwhelming distress (such as with Mr. Denton's initial clinical presentation). In keeping with a phase-based model, these results suggest that many traumatized clients will initially be too preoccupied with their difficulties to obtain benefit from directly focusing on Phase 3 tasks. However, as treatment progresses, many clients can benefit from interventions that support them in taking behavioral action to live out these changes in beliefs, values, and relationships. Importantly, just as a strengthened relationship with one's partner may provide healing resources and decrease the likelihood of a relapse in PTSD, longitudinal research with newly diagnosed cancer patients (Tomich & Helgeson, 2012) and survivors of the 9/11 terrorist attacks (Butler et al., 2005) has similarly indicated that these types of perceived positive life changes have been associated with significant reductions in trauma-related distress over time.

Many clients will recognize a spiritual dimension in this process and discover that their faith tradition, community, or relationship with God provides a crucial foundation for restoring global meaning and reconnecting with significant others. However, other clients will not attempt to sanctify or endow their revised goals with spiritual meaning as they gain restoration of global meaning. For example, Mr. Denton focused on traditional secular values in revising his identity and sense of purpose after working through the causes and precipitants of PTSD, negotiating prostate cancer and other serious health problems, and coming to peace with his unanticipated retirement. As goals of Phases 1 and 2 were satisfactorily met, Mr. Denton, in fact, became increasingly self-reflective and existentially minded in therapeutic conversations. Given that he was no longer haunted by war-zone traumas, he was able to wrestle with redefining his hopes and dreams for the next chapter in his life story in an inspiring manner.

At this point in treatment, the therapist drew on several acceptance and commitment therapy (ACT) exercises for supporting Mr. Denton's desire for greater valued living (for a description of the ACT model for PTSD, see Walser & Westrup, 2007). In so doing, Mr. Denton came to reaffirm a life-long commitment to his family and was able to sacrifice occupational goals to spend more leisure time with his wife and play an active caregiving role in the day-to-day lives of his grandchildren—something that Mr. Denton's father had not modeled or provided for him. Although he opted to avoid large crowds and kept a small handgun in the glove compartment of his truck, Mr. Denton committed to doing his best to seize every opportunity to chauffeur, babysit, and attend his grandchildren's extracurricular activities. In addition, following much urging from his wife, he unexpectedly signed over the ownership and executive decision-making authority for his farm to the adult son who was also struggling to find a sense of purpose in life. In keeping with Eriksonian notions of generativity, now that Mr. Denton was not constricted by his traumatic past, he came to treasure the legacy of his family relationships and shifted his primary meaning project in life to creating positive memories and cultivating a satisfying future for the younger generations in his family.

CONCLUSION

Mr. Denton's case exemplifies the multifaceted and possibly sequential nature of therapeutic tasks and objectives in treating PTSD. The purpose of this chapter was to introduce general clinical concerns and intervention strategies for working with this population. Although Mr. Denton did not show signs of a spiritual struggle or draw on religion in developing a more adaptive meaning system, meaning making was a major part of his treatment. Regardless of the spiritual orientation of the client, clinicians should be prepared to support clients in their attempts to restore aspects of global meaning. As highlighted in this chapter, some treatments feature meaning making as part of the recovery process (e.g., Najavits, 2002; Resick & Schnicke, 1993). However, treatment models for PTSD seldom emphasize Phase 3 aims. Aside from referencing teachings about mindfulness and meditation strategies from Buddhism and other traditions, PTSD treatments also rarely mention how spirituality might protect clients from PTSD and/or contribute to recovery in many cases. At present, evidence-based treatments for PTSD often do not address the role of maladaptive spiritual responses to trauma and do not focus on how traumatic events can profoundly affect survivors' functioning in the spiritual domain. For example, although CPT explicitly focuses on meaning making and revision of schemas in the recovery process (Resick & Schnicke, 1993), clinicians should consult sources outside the manual to obtain knowledge for integrating spirituality into cognitive restructuring and other possible therapeutic strategies. With this overview of general clinical concerns for treating PTSD in mind, we next provide a conceptual framework for understanding different trajectories of spiritual meaning making for traumatized clients who might benefit from a more integrative treatment approach.

5

THE RECIPROCAL MEANING-MAKING MODEL: CLINICAL IMPLICATIONS

The reciprocal meaning-making model illuminates many clinical issues that might arise in treating trauma survivors for whom spirituality factors prominently in recovery. Although not every traumatized client will appraise his or her experiences in explicitly spiritual terms (as illustrated by Mr. Denton's case in the last chapter), this model assumes that spirituality can be both part of the problem and part of the solution in treating posttraumatic stress disorder (PTSD) and other trauma-related concerns. Spirituality does not automatically protect survivors from developing these types of difficulties or allow for the efficient restoration of global meaning when traumatic events occur. Rather, for religious and nonreligious persons alike, a reciprocal framework assumes that, for recovery, traumatized persons have to engage in a meaning-making process to reconcile the reality and consequences of the traumas with their previous beliefs, values, and goals.

http://dx.doi.org/10.1037/15961-005
Trauma, Meaning, and Spirituality: Translating Research Into Clinical Practice, by C. L. Park, J. M. Currier, J. I. Harris, and J. M. Slattery

Clinicians can, therefore, incorporate the reciprocal model into their work to better understand their clients and tailor their treatments accordingly. For example, clinicians can hear their clients' spiritual disconnects as they complain about feeling alienated from others, not perceiving a meaningful future, and holding negative beliefs about themselves, others, and possibly God. Clinicians can also help clients to draw on their spiritual beliefs and resources in viewing, reframing, and coping with traumatic experiences. We discuss several important issues that may emerge over the course of treatment in the next chapter.

This chapter summarizes clinical implications of the reciprocal meaning-making model using the following case example of a young woman whose religious faith both hindered and supported her healing following a history of complex trauma. In particular, building on material presented in Chapters 2 and 3, we discuss four possible categories of spiritual meanings that clinicians may apply to their therapeutic work in addressing concerns related to trauma and PTSD in the context of treatment.

INTRODUCTION TO MS. LOPEZ

Gabriela Lopez was a 21-year-old Latina who sought psychotherapy at a community-based clinic for severe depression (e.g., frequent crying, weight gain, hypersomnia, loneliness and social isolation, lack of purpose, hopelessness, thoughts of suicide) secondary to transferring to a large state university 2 months earlier. She was in the first year of her undergraduate studies and had spent the prior semester at a prestigious private university.

Ms. Lopez grew up in a large West Coast city and was primarily raised by her mother throughout childhood and adolescence. She had a rocky relationship with her mother at the time of treatment, which she attributed to her mother's long-term problems with bipolar disorder and addictions to alcohol and prescription medications. Ms. Lopez had no siblings, and her father had been only sporadically involved in her life since she was a young child. As a result, Ms. Lopez spent much of her life switching back and forth between the homes of extended family members.

Ms. Lopez presented with many resilience factors and had achieved much academic success, culminating in a competitive scholarship to a private university. Notwithstanding her strong work ethic and intellectual gifts, she had struggled to meet the grade requirements of her scholarship and expressed concerns about underachieving and "not living up to expectations" at this point in her life. With a combination of anger and sadness in her voice, Ms. Lopez inquired in the first session, "What is my life about anyways?" In addition, Ms. Lopez strongly identified with Roman Catholicism and spoke remorsefully about "wandering away" from God.

Once Ms. Lopez gained sufficient trust in her therapist, she also disclosed concerns about engaging in sexually risky behaviors. She was attracted to older men and had regularly taken part in unsafe sexual acts and sadomasochistic bondage scenarios in recent years. Also, Ms. Lopez disclosed that in the short time since she had located to the new city, she had engaged in unprotected sex with two acquaintances in public places for the "thrill of it." Ms. Lopez derived little pleasure from these encounters, felt disconnected from her partners, and felt even more emotionally and spiritually "empty" after the sex was over. Given the need to establish safety in this domain, early sessions explored the nature of these behaviors and focused on psychoeducation, self-care, and strategies for adaptive coping.

In these early sessions, Ms. Lopez also reported a high frequency of sexual behavior at her previous university and having been forced to have sex against her will by a friend of one of her regular partners. This sexual assault had been the major impetus for her decision to transfer to another university and get a "fresh start" in a new region of the country. As Ms. Lopez's depression lifted and she grew more emotionally stable, she also disclosed that she had been was sexually abused from age 9 to 14 by an uncle and two male cousins. Other than reaching out to her mother on multiple occasions to stop the abuse, Ms. Lopez had never mentioned this history to anyone because the perpetrators blamed her for initiating the sexual acts and threatened they would hurt her if she got them in trouble.

Although Ms. Lopez's trauma-related symptoms ebbed and flowed over the years, the recent rape had reactivated her other memories, and she again met criteria for PTSD. In fact, Ms. Lopez paradoxically felt more haunted by intrusive recollections about the abuse as she became less depressed and ceased engaging in risky sexual acts. For example, she now found herself feeling anxious much of the time, sleeping less than 3 hours a night multiple times per week, and becoming overwhelmed at the possibility of discussing her childhood traumas in any depth. Even when Ms. Lopez tried to piece together micronarratives about her abuse in early attempts to process her traumatic past in treatment (Phase 2 aims), she became panicky and displayed possible signs of dissociation (e.g., not remembering important aspects and events).

Despite achieving some safety in the early part of treatment, Ms. Lopez also felt "dead inside" and "totally at a loss" about how to develop satisfying relationships in her life. She had also constructed a maladaptive system of global beliefs about herself, others, and God that perpetuated a pervasive sense of alienation and meaninglessness (e.g., viewing herself as "dirty," "unlovable," "unforgivable"). Hence, even though Ms. Lopez was performing well at her new university and no longer engaging in reckless behaviors, she lacked hope about the future, and her emotional life consisted largely of shifting between not feeling anything (i.e., psychic numbness) and feeling deep shame about perceived moral failures and ongoing difficulties to live in accordance with her faith. As such, Ms. Lopez appraised herself as deserving of the abuse and altogether struggled to transform herself and her life in healthy directions.

SPIRITUAL MEANINGS MADE OF TRAUMA

Many factors influence the manner in which spirituality shapes responses to traumatic events and how these traumas recursively influence survivors' spiritual lives. When considering spiritual meaning-making processes for persons like Ms. Lopez, the products of these efforts can vary in their helpfulness for both global and situational meaning. Although many spiritual meanings can meet essential existential needs in dealing with trauma (e.g., sense of purpose, self-efficacy, worth as a person; Baumeister, 1991), they do not always translate into adaptive, prosocial coping and the establishment of a well-functioning meaning system. That is, too much integration of trauma in the meaning-making process is also possible, or, sometimes, a micronarrative of the traumatic event is fitted into an existing plot structure that was already contaminated by overly dark existential and/or emotional themes (e.g., fear, betrayal, shame). Many survivors may also draw on assimilative as well as accommodative strategies for incorporating their traumatic episodes into their global meaning as they work to create consistency and gain a sense of purpose and predictability for future chapters in their life story.

From a clinical standpoint, we can, therefore, delineate four general categories of clinical concerns that may emerge through the lens of a reciprocal model of conceptualizing the possible intersection of spirituality and meaning making in the context of trauma recovery: (a) adaptive assimilation, (b) maladaptive accommodation, (c) maladaptive assimilation, and (d) adaptive accommodation (see Table 5.1). However, as Ms. Lopez's journey from chronic spiritual problems to growth will illustrate, these categories are not mutually exclusive; survivors may transition between different spiritual meanings across different developmental periods and according to other transformative episodes in their life stories (both traumatic and nontraumatic).

Adaptive Assimilation: Spiritual Resilience After Trauma

People seek to conserve or hold onto their spiritual beliefs and values in the context of coping with stress and trauma (Pargament, 1997, 2007). In keeping with other research suggesting that resilience after traumas is typical

TABLE 5.1
Clinical Concerns Related to Trajectories in Spiritual Meaning Making

	Adaptive assimilation	Maladaptive accommodation	Maladaptive assimilation	Adaptive accommodation
Posttraumatic outcome	Spiritual resilience after trauma exposure	Emergence of struggles in the spiritual domains	Perpetuation or exacerbation of ongoing spiritual struggles	Perceived spiritual growth via struggles with trauma
Status of pre-trauma spiritual meaning system	Affirmation and possible strengthening of well-functioning spiritual meaning system	Previously adaptive meaning system threatened by trauma; conservation of spiritual beliefs, values, and goals not possible	Unhealthy resolution of prior spiritual struggle; affirmation and possible strengthening of unhealthy spiritual meaning system	Constructive transformation of spiritual meaning system after painful violation of spiritual beliefs/values and goals
Clinical severity	No symptomatology or acute distress that will abate efficiently over adjustment process	Worsening of functioning and possible onset of PTSD and/or related problems in psychological, relational, and/or spiritual domains	Ongoing problems in living; worsening of potentially chronic psychiatric symptomatology and struggles with spirituality or matters of faith	Improved functioning with possible distress symptoms of a moderate nature following recovery from PTSD or other forms of trauma-related distress
Therapeutic presentation	Unremarkable history of trauma exposure and psychiatric problems; availability of social support and resources for healthy coping	Possible lack of prior trauma exposure and psychiatric problems; lack of intra- and interpersonal resources to make meaning of trauma via spiritual meaning system	Previous trauma history and potentially significant history of unresolved difficulties in psychological, relational, and/or spiritual domains; lack of intra- and interpersonal resources to make meaning of trauma via spiritual meaning system	Possible sub-clinical trauma-related distress amid increased spiritual or existential mindedness; increased sense of connectedness, hope, and purpose about the future

(continues)

TABLE 5.1
Clinical Concerns Related to Trajectories in Spiritual Meaning Making   (Continued)

	Adaptive assimilation	Maladaptive accommodation	Maladaptive assimilation	Adaptive accommodation
Phase-based objectives	Provide emotional and spiritual support to maintain well-functioning global meaning system	Establish emotional and physical safety (Phase 1) Process trauma memory and situational meanings (as indicated; Phase 2)	Establish emotional and physical safety (Phase 1) Process trauma memory and situational meanings (as indicated; Phase 2)	Support healthy coping (Phase 1) Restore cultivation of well-functioning global meaning system and connectedness in relationships (Phase 3)
Therapeutic concerns	Psychoeducation and normalization of acute reactions Do not pathologize spiritual distress Affirm connection with available resources in spiritual and other life domains Support adaptive processing of distressing thoughts and emotions Processing of grief and related concerns	Promote healthy coping and necessary environmental changes Clarify nature of struggle and associated losses and therapeutic concerns Revisit the trauma and related spiritual meanings Challenge attempts to over-accommodate one's spiritual meaning system (i.e., de-convert or abandon faith too quickly) Support to persevere in struggle and reengage with existing resources	Promote healthy coping and necessary environmental changes Clarify nature of struggle and associated losses and therapeutic concerns Revisit the trauma and related spiritual meanings Reengage meaning making processes regarding maladaptive resolution recent and/or past exposures to traumatic events Cultivate new coping skills and relationships	Affirm relevant perceptions or signs of personal growth Stay focused on alleviating distress and promoting healthy functioning Support behavioral attempts to apply changes in spiritual meaning Do not instrumentalize matters of faith in the treatment

(e.g., Bonanno, 2004), it appears that survivors with a well-integrated spiritual meaning system most often assimilate traumatic events into existing beliefs, values, and goals in such a way that will at worst trigger only moderate and transitory disruption in their functioning. In such cases, spirituality appears to provide a highly versatile framework for grappling with challenging existential questions in an emotionally and intellectually satisfying way that can translate into an abiding sense of coherence, identity, and control during an otherwise confusing and chaotic period.

Although research is limited, results from several studies have suggested that the majority of survivors indeed do not experience a shattering of their spiritual meaning systems after traumas (e.g., Eriksson et al., 2015; Falsetti, Resick, & Davis, 2003; Seirmarco et al., 2012). For example, in a longitudinal study of 124 bereaved parents, those parents who considered religion to be more important to them were more likely to display better coping and to engage in assimilative strategies for cognitive processing and making meaning of their losses (McIntosh, Silver, & Wortman, 1993). In addition, when faced with an experimental task that could at least momentarily engender a sense of threat (e.g., Stroop task), research demonstrated that persons with a stronger religious devotion and belief in God displayed less reactivity in a brain system that figures prominently in self-regulation (i.e., anterior cingulate cortex; Inzlicht, McGregor, Hirsh, & Nash, 2009). So long as survivors do not overly disavow their emotional and spiritual needs, these types of findings suggest that the development of a functional spiritual meaning system may, in fact, afford adaptive ways to assimilate traumatic events in a manner that will not necessitate comprehensive reorganization of global beliefs, values, and goals.

Research has also suggested that spirituality can provide several pathways by which survivors may adaptively absorb trauma into their meaning systems. Although communities differ in their acknowledgment and adequacy of teachings on darker themes of human existence, all religions offer explanations for trauma and suffering in their sacred texts. Many religious persons will, therefore, have developed certain theodicies that may promote cognitive flexibility and better prepare them for wrestling with distressing existential realities in the meaning-making process. For example, survivors could be primed to view their suffering as a catalyst for personal growth, an opportunity to trust more deeply in God's providence, somehow perceive God's compassionate presence in their suffering, or believe that God is suffering along with them (Hale-Smith, Park, & Edmondson, 2012). All of these theodicies might shape the situational meanings of a trauma in a manner that fits more easily with pretrauma global meaning, such that survivors do not encounter a painful sense of violation or feel the need to engage in an arduous process of meaning making.

As highlighted briefly in Chapter 3, spiritual meaning systems can also promote adaptive assimilation by transforming the situational meaning through comforting appraisals that may help a survivor obtain a fuller perspective and, paradoxically, recognize constructive dimensions of the trauma (Spilka, Shaver, & Kirkpatrick, 1985). For example, religious persons may come to view the trauma as an unanticipated blessing in disguise or a test of their faith. In addition, they might believe that their day-to-day micronarratives of life are a mysterious but essential part of a bigger story or redemptive plan for the universe (e.g., Mr. O'Malley, Chapter 11). When confronted with their vulnerability and finitude, such a transcendent and forward-looking type of appraisal may help survivors relinquish the compulsion to figure out why the trauma occurred and limit counterfactual reasoning and other types of unhelpful rumination commonly associated with PTSD (El Leithy, Brown, & Robbins, 2006). Ongoing engagement in a healthy community or possession of a benevolent but realistic spiritual meaning system may similarly protect against encountering other traumatic episodes that may further overwhelm one's adaptive resources.

When an event is appraised as being discrepant with one's global beliefs and goals, spirituality may provide a vast repertoire of meaning-based coping strategies for supporting resilience and facilitating efficient restoration of global meaning. The common use of high levels of religious coping after stressful life events is well documented (e.g., Bjorck & Thurman, 2007). Reliance on constructive aspects of spirituality has been linked with better mental and physical health amid an array of life stressors (for a review, see Gall & Guirguis-Younger, 2013). Even in cases of severe or repetitive exposure such as Ms. Lopez's sexual abuse, survivors tend to draw on adaptive forms of religious coping rather than maladaptive ones (Fallot & Heckman, 2005) and to perceive spirituality as a source of comfort (Gall, 2006). Other studies with both clinical and nonclinical samples have similarly found that people tend to derive more comfort than strain from their faith systems amid stressful situations (e.g., Exline, Yali, & Sanderson, 2000).

Even in instances in which a trauma severely challenges one's global meaning, these findings suggest that spirituality may provide many intra- and interpersonal resources to help survivors persevere through transitory struggles and achieve a sense of coherence and stability. For example, spiritually oriented persons may draw closer to God, seek spiritual support from members of their community, draw on sacred writings from their tradition, participate in worship services and other community events, pray or meditate, or engage in other activities that promote positive emotions (e.g., joy, compassion) and prevent isolation and feelings of meaninglessness and helplessness (e.g., serving other people). By thus resolving a meaning crisis in a satisfying and efficient manner, exposure to trauma may then affirm or even strengthen survivors' confidence in their spiritual understandings and resources.

Although survivors in this first category will typically not require trauma-focused therapy (Phase 2), they might seek professional help for regaining safety and stability in the acute period (Phase 1) or working through obstacles to restoring global meaning (Phase 3). In keeping with recovery-oriented models that guide evidence-based treatments for PTSD (e.g., Foa, Hembree, & Rothbaum, 2007; Resick & Schnicke, 1993), clinicians should recognize that some perturbation in one's spiritual meaning system and trauma-related symptoms in the early adjustment period could be normative and quite adaptive. Hence, even resilient persons may present some distress for a protracted period as they digest the reality of the trauma and possible consequences for their lives (Bonanno, 2004). Research has also suggested that even resilient persons might simultaneously draw on both positive and negative forms of religious coping in this process (Pargament, 1997, 2007). As such, it is important to recognize that feeling disconnected from God or wrestling with tough existential questions in the aftermath of a traumatic event might not be indicative of a poorly functioning meaning system or predictive of later psychopathology (Park, 2010).

Like Mr. Denton's sadness over killing another young husband and father in Vietnam (see Chapter 4), adaptive assimilators could also experience appropriate grief that will fuel the meaning-making process in adaptive directions. In the same way that PTSD may develop from an overreliance on avoiding distressing thoughts and emotions (Foa & Kozak, 1986; Hembree & Foa, 2000; Resick & Schnicke, 1993), resilient survivors may need a therapist to normalize their situation and help them face and respond to their spiritual distress. When these persons do seek support, clinicians should initially assess for safety issues and explore ways to promote adaptive coping in psychological, social, and spiritual domains (Phase 1). PTSD might not interfere with the restoration of meaning for persons in this group, such that the systematic revisiting of the trauma episode will not be clinically indicated in many cases (Phase 2). Rather, many of these persons may restore their global meaning primarily by relying on their available resources and working through psychological and spiritual concerns as necessary in treatment.

Maladaptive Accommodation: Emergence of Spiritual Struggles

There is increasing recognition that efforts to make meaning of trauma in spiritual terms can also fail, causing some survivors to struggle with their meaning system in profound ways (e.g., Exline, 2002, 2013; Kusner & Pargament, 2012; Pargament, Murray-Swank, Magyar, & Ano, 2005; Park, Edmondson, & Hale-Smith, 2013). As with Ms. Lopez's increasing struggle to reconcile her abuse with a belief in a God who values her safety and worth, sometimes the discrepancy between trauma and global meaning is simply too immense and survivors are challenged to revise their most sacred beliefs, values, and goals in the recovery process. Conservational coping strategies may no longer be helpful in such cases, and a struggle to accommodate one's spiritual meaning system may ensue. Pargament, Murray-Swank, and colleagues (2005) broadly defined these types of spiritual struggles as "efforts to conserve or transform a spirituality that has been threatened or harmed" (p. 247). Herman (1992) described this predicament as follows:

> Trauma can violate people's faith in a natural or divine order and cast them into a state of existential crisis where they lose faith in an all-powerful and good God, recognize that their world is anything but safe and well-ordered, and begin to believe that they are bad and deserving of bad outcomes. (p. 51)

When compared with spiritually resilient persons, numerous factors can predict a spiritual struggle of this sort. Persons in this group might have had a far greater magnitude of exposure to traumas than adaptive assimilators (e.g., multiple interpersonal traumas), lacked maturity or strength in their pretrauma spiritual meaning system, or lacked recourse to crucial psychosocial resources for healing and adaptively working through the meaning violation. Trying to resolve these types of discrepancies in spiritual meaning can be complex and painful. In constructing harmony between global and situational meanings, survivors in this category may transform their spiritual meaning systems in ways that lead to a weakening of spirituality or disengagement from previously adaptive beliefs and/or behaviors in this domain.

Although research on maladaptive accommodation is limited, results of a recent study with two clinical samples of military veterans seeking treatment for PTSD indirectly supported these conjectures (Currier, Drescher, & Harris, 2014). Compared with demographically matched persons from the community (with respect to age, gender, ethnicity, and education), veterans from the Vietnam and Iraq/Afghanistan eras generally reported lower levels of adaptive reliance on spirituality (e.g., positive religious coping, daily spiritual experiences) while also endorsing more spiritual distress (e.g., negative religious coping, problems with forgiveness). Other descriptive work has also found that when survivors report a loss of faith or weakening of their spirituality, more severe PTSD symptoms tend to co-occur with these changes (Ben-Ezra et al., 2010; Dew et al., 2010; Falsetti et al., 2003; Seirmarco et al., 2012).

These findings indicate that when spiritual strugglers can no longer maintain a stable and satisfying faith system, they may also encounter additional trauma-related losses (e.g., lack of healthy coping strategies, supportive relationships, direction and/or purpose in life) that interfere with their capacity for healing. For example, as Ms. Lopez became more and more mistrustful and ambivalent about God's character after several years of being abused, she also lost a sense of connection and security from the only attachment figure she had perceived as trustworthy in her life. In turn, she felt compelled to stop practicing spiritual disciplines that had provided a sense of transcendence and inner peace and to stop participating in her church community.

A number of cross-sectional studies have also supported an association between spiritual struggles and poorer psychological functioning after traumas. Whether focusing on survivors of childhood abuse (Fallot & Heckman, 2005), intimate partner violence (Bradley, Schwartz, & Kaslow, 2005), military trauma (Currier et al., 2014; Ogden et al., 2011; Witvliet, Phipps, Feldman, & Beckham, 2004), natural disasters (B. W. Smith, Pargament, Brant, & Oliver, 2000) or ones perpetrated by human beings (Pargament, Smith, Koenig, & Perez, 1998), or more diverse sets of stressors (Harris et al., 2008), research has consistently documented that negative spiritual appraisals of traumas (e.g., as divine punishment) and related behaviors (e.g., passive or avoidance-based coping) predict greater risk of PTSD and other psychiatric problems. Further, recent longitudinal studies with trauma survivors of different ages also found that spiritual struggles predicted a more symptomatic course of PTSD over time (Harris et al., 2012; Wortmann, Park, & Edmondson, 2011). Overall, this emerging empirical literature suggests that just as spirituality and meaning may influence one's coping responses, spiritual struggles may exacerbate and even perpetuate trauma-related distress for persons in this second category. That is, just as spiritual struggles may cause distress in their own right, it is also probable that psychiatric symptoms may challenge one's spiritual meaning system in a way that could drive spiritual struggles and further complicate adjustment to trauma.

Given our current state of knowledge, clinicians should attend to several domains of spiritual struggles that may hamper posttraumatic adjustment in this manner (for reviews, see Exline, 2002, 2013; Pargament, Murray-Swank, et al., 2005). First, survivors can struggle with intrapersonal conflicts about their spirituality, including religious doubting and questioning key beliefs and practices of their tradition, difficulties attaining a certain standard of moral perfection, or problems with self-forgiveness or forgiving others for perceived acts of wrongdoing.

One of Ms. Lopez's long-term struggles in this domain was figuring out how not to dismiss adaptive anger toward her mother for overlooking the abuse while at the same time respecting the scriptural commandment to honor her parents (Exodus 20:12). In addition, Ms. Lopez had long wondered whether she was somehow responsible for not stopping the abuse, and she questioned whether she was deserving of divine forgiveness in light of her perpetrators' comments and her subsequent spirals into risky sexual relationships. These types of struggles highlight how many survivors may experience a constellation of guilt and shame from negotiating ambiguous situations in which certain actions (or lack thereof) in traumatic episodes can trigger or perpetuate a violation of one's most sacred beliefs and values. Like Mr. Denton's chronic guilt about being the one to pull the trigger first rather than allowing himself to be killed, Ms. Lopez's struggles with religious doubting, personal morality, and forgiveness made restoring global meaning in her treatment more complex.

Spiritual struggles can also occur in one's relationships with family and friends or within churches and other communities (Exline, 2002, 2013; Pargament, Murray-Swank, et al., 2005). Consistent with the examples of Job's friends offering maladaptive appraisals of his terrifying predicament (e.g., justifiable punishment for evil or prior wrongdoing, result of not being spiritually stronger or of turning away from God), trauma may challenge others' spiritual meaning systems. In turn, friends or loved ones might prematurely seek recourse to harmful or existentially unsatisfying understandings. As a way of resolving this secondary violation in meaning, these otherwise supportive persons may also withdraw from future interactions in a manner that leaves survivors feeling only more alone, alienated, and hopeless about repairing their faith. As with Job's interpersonal struggles, survivors could also be criticized for behavior related to their trauma or inability to heal and move forward in life. Indeed, research has suggested that many religious persons can be quite concerned with maintaining their reputation and not losing social standing in their communities (Krause, Ellison, & Wulff, 1998); as a result, they may hesitate to seek support even when those resources are available.

Some may opt to distance themselves from their communities as a way of protecting others from somehow being contaminated by their traumas. For instance, although Ms. Lopez lacked the necessary bonds in her outside relationships to engender these types of concerns, one of the barriers to processing her traumatic past in treatment was a fear of being judged and not wanting to affect her therapist's spirituality in negative ways. Just as Mr. Denton refrained from disclosing his most distressing memory as imaginal exposure work began, concerns about the security of the therapeutic relationship had to be addressed first as Ms. Lopez transitioned into Phase 2 aims in her treatment. We cover additional concerns for therapists working with trauma survivors in upcoming chapters.

A third type of spiritual struggle entails turmoil in one's relationship with God (Exline, 2002, 2013; Pargament, Murray-Swank, et al., 2005). Many people derive a sense of attachment security from their relationships with God or a higher power (for a review, see Granqvist & Kirkpatrick, 2013), and research has linked negative attitudes about God's character and powers with poorer mental health in general (e.g., Silton, Flannelly, Galek, & Ellison, 2014). When compared with intra- and interpersonal struggles, studies with other community samples have also suggested that divine struggles may contribute to distress in a pronounced way for many survivors (e.g., Ellison & Lee, 2010). Particularly in cases of PTSD, survivors may feel deeply betrayed by God and come to experience this relationship as quite troubling. Others may view God as distant and unresponsive in their crisis or appraise their suffering as a judgment for sinfulness or a punishment for a lack of devotion in this relationship. In any of these scenarios, attributing a trauma to God or questioning God's character and capability of ordering the universe after traumatic events may exacerbate one's anguish and interfere with other beliefs that could help restore a previously functional spiritual meaning system (e.g., feeling that one's life matters or that he or she is a person of worth, confidence that much of the world is a relatively safe place).

In a series of five studies on this topic, Exline, Park, Smyth, and Carey (2011) found that some anger toward God was normative but that more severe struggles in the divine domain were linked with depression and greater difficulties with meaning making. In addition, the rates of anger toward God were consistently higher for persons who had weaker religious commitments and were not affiliated with a specific religious group or tradition (Exline et al., 2011). In keeping with Ms. Lopez's disengagement from God, these latter results suggest that struggles with the divine may be a therapeutic concern for many persons in this second group.

In the same way that intimate relationships with other people may need to tolerate some degree of anger or periodic conflict, clinicians should also anticipate that religious clients will typically experience tension with God at different times in their lives. These situations appear to be harmful when a survivor is overly reluctant to acknowledge his or her struggles, does not persevere in working through a conflict, or opts to surrender altogether sacred beliefs, values, and goals far too quickly to create consistency in their global meaning system (Exline, Kaplan, & Grubbs, 2012). For instance, even though one may distance oneself from a relationship with God, some persons could find themselves feeling stuck and carrying "unfinished business" (L. S. Greenberg & Malcolm, 2002) that hinders subsequent psychological and spiritual development in the years following their trauma.

It is also important for clinicians to recognize that different types of spiritual struggles will rarely occur in isolation and may reinforce one another in many instances (Ellison & Lee, 2010). For example, as Ms. Lopez increasingly experienced mistrust and ambivalence toward God, she also stopped attending Mass and engaging in religious practices that had earlier provided comfort and security (e.g., prayer and reconciliation). As such, it may be important for clinicians to assess a full spectrum of spiritual struggles for maladaptive accommodators and to revisit these concerns in the context of treatment in a manner that reinvigorates the meaning-making process and supports the reworking of unhelpful spiritual meanings.

Maladaptive Assimilation: Chronicity of Spiritual Problems

Spirituality may not always support people in responding to trauma in constructive ways or promote an adaptive type of meaning making. Exposure to traumas may also not precipitate a new struggle for each client for whom problems with spirituality demand clinical attention. Rather than struggling to accommodate a functional spiritual meaning system, survivors in this category might have developed maladaptive spiritual beliefs and values earlier in life that increased their risk of making unhelpful and distressing appraisals of later traumas. In contrast to people who have made maladaptive accommodations, these survivors might not perceive a discrepancy between global and situational meaning or feel motivated to engage in meaning making at the time of treatment. Other individuals in this group might feel numb or hopeless about resolving their spiritual struggles and might no longer possess the motivation or resources to rebuild an adaptive meaning system.

Available longitudinal research has indicated that chronic spiritual problems can be quite detrimental to well-being. In a study of older medically ill patients, Pargament, Koenig, Tarakeshwar, and Hahn (2004) found that only those with high levels of spiritual problems at the start and end of the 2-year assessment interval displayed declines in their mental and physical health. A similar pattern emerged in Exline et al.'s (2011) work with cancer survivors; that is, those survivors who were spiritually discontent or hostile toward God throughout the entire study period yielded the greatest negative changes in their mental and physical health. Though maladaptive appraisals of this sort may not translate into comforting understandings of trauma, they can provide a needed sense of predictability, coherence, and stability that survivors might not desire to question or challenge at the time of treatment.

Research has also suggested that a history of previous trauma could be a key concern for many chronic spiritual strugglers. For example, in a review of 34 studies on changes in religiousness and spirituality among survivors of childhood abuse, Walker, Reid, O'Neill, and Brown (2009) found that the predominant pattern was for a considerable weakening in this domain (i.e., 14 studies reported negative changes from abuse vs. 12 that found both negative/positive changes and 8 that only noted positive changes). These changes were most frequently characterized by a diminished relationship and damaged view of God (e.g., wrathful, unfair, distant, not loving), particularly when a parent or spiritual authority was responsible for the abuse or if the abuse was justified by distorted interpretations of sacred texts (Walker et al., 2009).

From a reciprocal meaning-making lens, negative spiritual beliefs and values for persons in this group may stem from an overaccommodation of trauma or unhealthy resolution of an earlier crisis in spiritual meaning making. In turn, this maladaptive reorganization in global meaning could then thwart one's further spiritual development and constrict the capacity for engaging in positive spiritual coping or making adaptive appraisals of future traumatic episodes. For example, in another study of survivors of sexual abuse, Gall (2006) found that those who were older when the abuse occurred indicated that spirituality was more of a resource for them as adults. That is, older survivors possibly may have had more opportunity to internalize a more resilient spiritual meaning system than did their younger counterparts, and spirituality could, therefore, better provide comfort.

Notwithstanding these possibilities, the potential toll of severe and repeated exposures to trauma should not be overlooked by clinicians. In Ms. Lopez's case example, she recounted remarkable resilience in her spiritual history in therapeutic conversations. For instance, she maintained an active prayer life and conversational relationship with God, attended Mass and reconciliation on a regular basis (often by herself), and tried to collaborate with God to protect herself from more abuse. However, after feeling that her devotion was not being respected and requests for help were falling on deaf ears, her spiritual struggles intensified. She then grew increasingly ambivalent about matters of faith and was no longer able to view God or her fellow believers in a benevolent light.

In keeping with changes in self-perceptions and systems of meaning commonly observed in the context of interpersonally mediated traumas (Courtois, 2004; Herman, 1992), Ms. Lopez also internalized several unhelpful spiritual lessons as a child that affected her self-worth and manner of relating to others. Ms. Lopez somehow came to believe that she deserved this punishment for being "dirty" and tempting her abusers. Hence, although her abuse stopped in adolescence, she found herself living out these meanings and recreating dangerous sexual situations that confirmed her maladaptive beliefs about herself, others, and God. For example, after the rape had occurred, her sense of alienation from God, others, and herself intensified, and she could no longer meet the demands of her life on her own. An early turning point in treatment occurred when Ms. Lopez resolved to conduct an "abstinence experiment" for up to one year and attended confession at a local parish of her own volition. Although she was not yet ready to focus on Phase 2 aims with her therapist, she first disclosed certain details about her traumatic past with a priest and slowly began to open herself to new meanings about these experiences by reestablishing the previously important practice of reconciliation in her life.

Ms. Lopez's case exemplifies how repeated trauma exposures can push people beyond their breaking point, as discussed in Chapter 4. However, these types of events may not be the main cause of spiritual problems for survivors in this group. According to Pargament (1997, 2007), spiritual problems grow out of a larger "orienting system" or meaning system that includes an array of personal, social, and spiritual domains (e.g., personality, attitudes, lifestyle, emotions, relationships). Whether following trauma or not, survivors will be most vulnerable to chronic spiritual problems when they confront stressors that mobilize unhealthy or unresolved dimensions of their global meaning system. Research has suggested that certain dimensions of religiousness consistently overlap with health and unhealthy dimensions of personality (e.g., Saroglou, 2002). For example, people with vulnerability for anxiety (neuroticism) may lack confidence in their own resources and could struggle to feel secure in relationships with God and others, such that malevolent appraisals will be more probable after trauma.

The possible benefits of spirituality will also depend on the availability of resources to engage in activities that may promote an adaptive meaning-making process. Unfortunately, survivors with chronic spiritual problems could contend with challenging socioeconomic realities or live in difficult environments where there is an absence of relational supports and knowledge about healthy coping strategies or ways of persevering in resolving crises in meaning. For example, Ms. Lopez had long struggled with finances and had not cultivated close friendships with other women or participated in any type of community (church or otherwise) for many years. As such, appraisals of her traumatic episodes and unsafe coping were largely the products of her own isolated attempts to make sense of a pervasively stressful life.

One of the challenges in treating clients such as Ms. Lopez is to disentangle the possible interplay between psychiatric symptomatology and the individual's spiritual meaning system. In addition to a history of trauma, chronic spiritual problems may also overlap with psychiatric disorders (for a review, see Murray-Swank & Murray-Swank, 2013). That is, struggles with spirituality may serve as a risk factor for psychiatric disorders, and these types of problems may also shape one's spiritual life after trauma. For example, the depressive episode that precipitated Ms. Lopez's decision to seek help was antedated by maladaptive religious beliefs, and her spiritual struggles were simultaneously shaped by depressive symptomatology. In addition, unhealthy religious appraisals of her depression led Ms. Lopez to oppose adamantly several interventions that might have engendered efficient symptom relief, including consulting with a psychiatrist for medication and several attempts at self-care and behavioral activation (e.g., establishing an exercise routine).

Pretrauma themes of anxiety also seemed to contribute to Ms. Lopez's problems in spiritual and psychological domains. Partly due to a need to function with autonomy from an early age, Ms. Lopez had developed an overly strong sense of responsibility and inflexible expectations for her performance in life. Although this pseudo-maturity translated into much academic success, Ms. Lopez was vulnerable to self-recrimination and guilt about perceived shortcomings and failures in life. Foa and Rothbaum (1998) suggested that people with these types of rigid pretrauma beliefs might be more vulnerable to PTSD.

Specifically, whereas persons like Ms. Lopez may experience a confirmation of negative meanings, other maladaptive accommodators may struggle to reconcile darker dimensions of their traumas with an underdeveloped or naively positive faith system. Either way, clinicians should be mindful about how pretrauma beliefs may constrict survivors' ability to adaptively make meaning of their traumas and intersect with psychiatric problems in the therapeutic process.

Adaptive Accommodation: Spiritual Growth via Struggle

Although traumatic events can precipitate or perpetuate struggles in the spiritual domain, there is also consensus that these experiences hold the seeds for spiritual growth as well (Exline, 2012, 2013; Pargament, Murray-Swank, et al., 2005). When faced with a violation of sacred beliefs, goals, and values, many survivors will not surrender the possibility of faith, even in the context of chronic PTSD symptoms. Spiritual struggles may also promote greater awareness of specific weaknesses and help survivors discern ways in which they had somehow built their global meanings on the "sand," to use a biblical metaphor (Matthew 7:26). Negotiating spiritual struggles can also cause survivors to reevaluate their priorities, seek forgiveness, or cultivate new skills or sources of relational support in life. In such cases, finding footing on more solid ground in one's spiritual meaning system may entail discarding certain beliefs or values that had previously limited maturity in this domain.

For example, in processing struggles between her personal morality and God's perceived absence in her suffering, Ms. Lopez came to recognize that she had somehow come to view God as a "cosmic vending machine," who existed to fulfill her desires and reward her attempts at virtue and discipline in the domain of religion. As Ms. Lopez explored alternate theodicies in treatment sessions, she came to a deeper appreciation of her tradition's doctrine of grace and gradually relinquished a debilitating preoccupation with her performance in relationships with God and other authority figures.

In other instances, survivors may experience more extreme types of changes, which may lead to transferring to a new tradition or believing or practicing a set of spiritual teachings for the first time. As we noted in Chapter 3, periods of crisis are often reported in cases of religious conversion (for reviews, see Paloutzian, 2005; Paloutzian, Murken, Streib, & Rößler-Namini, 2013). These results do not, however, imply that all persons experiencing PTSD will have a religious conversion or that religious conversions reflect an adaptive accommodation of spiritual meaning for all survivors. Nonetheless, in the same way that trauma-related issues may lead some survivors to disengage from their faith, others may develop a newfound faith in the process of making meaning of their traumas. These possibilities suggest that traumas may serve as a "fork in the road" that can either lead to problems with despair and meaninglessness or provide an impetus for redirecting one's spiritual life in more constructive and satisfying directions (Exline, 2012, 2013; Pargament, Murray-Swank, et al., 2005).

Trauma survivors often report having grown spiritually from their experiences of suffering and recovery, despite evidence suggesting that most trauma survivors actually have decrements in their spirituality relative those who did not experience trauma. Still, perceptions of growth may be meaningful and part of an important path of recovery. Rather than cases of adaptive assimilation in which survivors draw on available resources in a manner that provides an affirmation of their faith system, perceived growth captures instances in which a survivor's spiritual development and functioning—and other resources—are perceived to surpass that which was present before the trauma occurred. Spiritual growth should therefore not simply be viewed as a return to baseline or recovery of pretrauma functioning (Bonanno, 2004). According to Tedeschi and Calhoun (2004), growth rather requires an encounter with a "seismic" stressor that challenges a person's most sacred beliefs and values, to the point where he or she can identify "fault lines" or structural deficiencies in global meaning that are in need of transformation.

Others have also argued that growth—whether in spiritual terms or not—should reflect an adaptive resolution of a potentially arduous process of accommodating one's situational meaning with one's global meaning system (Joseph & Linley, 2005). In addition, clinicians should anticipate that persons in this category may need support to identify ways to live out any constructive alterations in meaning via corresponding behavioral or lifestyle changes. For example, as Ms. Lopez successfully revisited her traumatic past in treatment (Phase 2), she found herself feeling more and more concerned about the many children in her new city who lacked stability in their home environments and were at risk of being abused. Hence, it seemed natural when she inquired with her therapist about the benefits of possibly volunteering with several advocacy organizations that served these vulnerable youth.

As we noted in Chapter 2, the world's major religions have long emphasized this potentially transformative potential of trauma. However, behavioral researchers have only just begun to study this phenomenon; findings have provided mixed support for the frequency of spiritual growth emerging out of spiritual struggle. In one study of churchgoing adults who were in close proximity to the Oklahoma City bombing, Pargament and colleagues (1998) found that engaging in a period of active spiritual struggle was in fact associated with greater self-reported perceptions of growth. Rather than cases of adaptive assimilation in which survivors draw on available resources in a manner that provides an affirmation of their faith system, perceived growth may capture instances in which a survivor's meaning system was challenged by a trauma and forced to change in positive ways. However, the few other studies on this topic with trauma-exposed samples have not found a link between spiritual struggles and growth (e.g., Harris et al., 2008; Ogden et al., 2011).

There are many possible explanations for these inconsistent findings, among which are a reliance on cross-sectional designs that could not test whether survivors' struggles in the spiritual domain were associated with the emergence of growth over time. Rather, these studies could only evaluate whether spiritual struggles overlapped with growth at the time of assessment, which for some survivors might have been in the midst of their struggles to adequately resolve meaning violations (Park, 2010). In addition, for studies that assessed both adaptive and maladaptive forms of spirituality, positive religious coping and related practices (e.g., prayer) were intertwined with perceptions of growth (e.g., Harris et al., 2008; Ogden et al., 2011). These latter findings converge with a general pattern for adaptive expressions of religiousness and spirituality (e.g., comforting appraisals, social support) to promote growth-inducing processes and activities that may eventuate in constructive life changes amid stressful situations (for a review, see Shaw, Joseph, & Linley, 2005). Looking ahead, behavioral researchers will have to implement longitudinal designs that may examine whether spiritual struggles lead to spiritual growth and how this adaptive transformation may occur.

From a clinical standpoint, it is important to recognize that survivors usually do not anticipate that their traumatic experiences will serve as catalysts for growth. Rather, most individuals in this category will experience growth as an epiphenomenon arising from simply persevering in the meaning-making process. Also, attributions of growth will typically not take place until safety needs have been addressed and the client has processed his or her trauma to an adequate degree in treatment. In addition, even for survivors who perceive growth, most would willingly exchange any constructive outcomes for undoing the consequences of the traumatic episode in their life story. Clinicians should, therefore, be prepared to affirm growth when it occurs but also to keep the treatment focused on alleviating distress and promoting reflection and other therapeutic activities that may lead to the restoration of global meaning.

Like Jacob's disabled leg after wrestling with God (Genesis 32:22–32), perceived growth also may occur alongside painful injuries that may persist to varying degrees over time. For example, in the process of struggling with the divine after repeated instances of lying and scheming to gain power and blessing from God, Jacob became less self-focused and grew in humility. Research has suggested that perceived growth is usually driven in part by distress and that survivors who struggle the most intensely with their traumas often lack the capacity to identify accurately positive changes during those times (e.g., P. Frazier et al., 2009). Clinicians should also be mindful that many spiritual traditions emphasize beliefs and values that are not comforting but could still become quite meaningful as clients experience a transformation in global meaning. As such, some clients may grow deeper in their faith while also experiencing certain painful emotions on a more frequent basis (i.e., growing "sadder but wiser" in light of the mysterious nature of God and divine providence).

Particularly for more devout persons, clinicians also should avoid viewing matters of faith simply in instrumental terms. Religion can certainly provide resources for healthy coping; however, most persons do not choose to engage in a relationship with God or adhere to specific doctrines or lifestyle practices to obtain these benefits in their time of need (for thoughtful discussion of these concerns, see Shuman & Meador, 2003). Instead, for clients like Ms. Lopez, faith may be far more complex and central to their identity, such that the possibility of using spirituality to cope and heal in the treatment setting could be offensive if not negotiated in a sensitive manner. We address these specific types of concerns in more depth in Chapter 12.

GENERAL SUMMARY OF MS. LOPEZ'S CASE

From a reciprocal meaning-making perspective, Ms. Lopez's case highlights what could be a common progression for clients with histories of complex trauma and related mental health concerns. Notwithstanding her fortitude as a child, unrelenting abuse eventually overwhelmed Ms. Lopez's faith system, and she lacked adequate resources for resolving her spiritual struggles and protecting herself from further exposure to trauma. In turn, she became entrenched in chronic spiritual struggles (primarily intrapersonal and divine domains) that were perpetuated by severe limitations in her home living environment and interpersonal relationships, unhealthy decisions about sexuality, and increasing contamination of her global meaning system.

When Ms. Lopez was raped in her first semester of college, her only option for restoring global meaning was to seek recourse to her damaged and insufficiently repaired spiritual beliefs and values. However, Ms. Lopez had many strengths and was able to achieve relative stability within the early months of treatment and experience relief from PTSD symptoms by processing traumatic memories via exposure interventions. At this point, Ms. Lopez no longer met criteria for a psychiatric disorder but was still asking the question that she raised in the first session: "What is my life about anyways?" In addition to maintaining therapeutic gains, the exploration and resolution of this question became the focus of her treatment. From this point forward, Ms. Lopez continued to consult with her therapist with decreasing frequency as she worked to reestablish a functional meaning system amidst intermittent declines in her mental health and as specific needs arose for support.

As Ms. Lopez progressed to focusing on Phase 3 aims, she likely found far more answers to her questions by immersing herself in her faith tradition than from consulting with her therapist. In this vein, a memorable moment occurred at the end of the first year of her treatment when Ms. Lopez completed the confirmation process and renewed her baptismal promises at the Easter vigil at a local Catholic church. The sacrament of baptism served as a tangible reflection of the healing that Ms. Lopez perceived in her life at that time. For example, she came to recognize that none of her traumas were her fault or a reflection of God's punishment or disdain for her. She also came to see that her compulsions for sexual risk taking did not mean that she was "unforgivable" or "dirty," but rather represented her best attempts at undoing the reality of the abuse and gaining a sense of mastery over her emptiness and anguish.

Rather than viewing God as another nonprotective and self-absorbed parental figure, she came to believe that God was compassionate and burned with anger about what she had to endure. Ms. Lopez also came to appreciate the mystery of Christ's crucifixion in her tradition and the love and suffering that this sacrificial act implied for her journey toward belonging and acceptance. These changes in meaning were aided by Ms. Lopez's regular involvement in her parish community along with her engagement in the Catholic student organization at her new university. In addition, Ms. Lopez grew increasingly impassioned by her tradition's teachings on social justice and opted to switch her major to a field of study that would allow her to work with at-risk youth. Through prayer and many conversations with her therapist and newfound friends in her spiritual community, Ms. Lopez also began to contemplate the possibility of going into the ministry herself. Although treatment ended at a point when Ms. Lopez was undecided about her professional goals, it was evident that she would "stand in the gap" for youth facing similar circumstances to those that she had had to overcome in her own life.

CONCLUSION

Ms. Lopez's case highlights the multifaceted role of spirituality in making meaning of traumas and recovering from PTSD and other trauma-related problems. In this chapter, we introduced a conceptual framework of possible trajectories of spiritual meaning making that clinicians might encounter in their work with traumatized clients such as Ms. Lopez. Upcoming chapters build on this theoretical foundation by providing practical suggestions for assessment (Chapter 6) as well as negotiating the treatment process (Chapter 7) from the standpoint of a reciprocal understanding of the possible interplay between spirituality and meaning making in the process of trauma recovery.

6

ASSESSMENT FROM THE RECIPROCAL MEANING-MAKING PERSPECTIVE

Previous chapters in this volume have addressed how spirituality can be a resource in responding to trauma but can also contribute to a variety of negative effects. Determining how spirituality can support treatment and recovery requires accurate assessment of both positive and negative aspects of spirituality for each client, with particular consideration of the roles that spirituality may play in manifold aspects of clients' lives and adjustment processes.

When assessing a client's spiritual beliefs, values, and behaviors, therapists have to go far beyond denominational labels, recognizing that although such labels may be informative (e.g., Table 2.1), there are considerable differences within these groups, such that not all Buddhists, Catholics, or Evangelical Christians are alike. For example, in the United States, 39% of Buddhists, 52% of Catholics, and 90% of Evangelical Christians reported being "absolutely certain" that there is a God (Pew Forum on Religion & Public Life,

http://dx.doi.org/10.1037/15961-006
Trauma, Meaning, and Spirituality: Translating Research Into Clinical Practice, by C. L. Park, J. M. Currier, J. I. Harris, and J. M. Slattery

2008). In other words, although one can make general predictions about religious beliefs and practices by knowing a person's religious affiliation, considerable variations exist within each group. Therapists are well advised to educate themselves and to consider a range of spiritual issues in assessment. This chapter describes several critical dimensions of spirituality that therapists may have to assess in their work with traumatized clients.

ASSESSMENT PROCESSES

We propose several tenets regarding assessment (Park & Slattery, 2009; Slattery & Park, 2011a). First, we propose that therapists should carefully assess trauma and the client's global meaning system, particularly how a client's trauma history has shaped his or her beliefs, values, and future goals. We encourage therapists to assess spirituality broadly and consider that it may—or may not—be a central aspect of an individual's global meaning system. Further, as emphasized in prior chapters, we assume that a person's spirituality and trauma history will reciprocally affect one another. Given that trauma is understood within the client's meaning system, we especially attend to discrepancies in spiritual meaning from the client's perspective. Consider, for example, that choosing to avoid worship services means something very different to a client who used to attend worship regularly compared with a client who historically rarely attended worship services or other group gatherings. The former may reflect maladaptive meanings whereas the latter would probably be nondiagnostic on this issue.

Second, as highlighted in Chapter 4, assessments should be broad and occur in a holistic context, also considering the client's functioning at work and school, in the family, and with peers; health concerns and medications; coping strategies; racial and ethnic identification; and personal and family histories of psychiatric problems and treatment (Park & Slattery, 2009; Slattery & Park, 2011a). We explicitly generate hypotheses about the meaning of discrepancies between global and situational meanings and form expectations for individuals based on their specific cultural, spiritual, and developmental groups. For example, we might consider what it means to lose a 3-year-old to cancer, which might be different for a 20-year-old parent than for a 45-year-old parent losing an only child to cancer at age 3. Finally, a 45-year-old Buddhist might perceive this situation differently from a 45-year-old Catholic. In addition to helping us better understand clients, such assessments prevent both over- and underfocusing on religion and spirituality, either of which could be problematic. Further, many changes in "secular" functioning may reflect changes in global meaning and spiritual functioning that may otherwise go unnoticed without careful assessment practices.

Finally, the client's relative strengths, weaknesses, and resources can be used to guide decision making throughout treatment. In addition to more commonly assessed secular strengths, weaknesses, and resources, these concerns can include specific spiritual resources as well as stages of psychospiritual development (see Chapter 2). Certain approaches to repairing and restoring global meaning could either be contraindicated or beneficial depending, for example, on where the client is in the recovery process (Herman, 1992). For instance, as the following case example illustrates, many clients might derive great comfort and a sense of stability from engaging in religious rituals and practices. However, with a possible violation of global meaning and maladaptive strategies for accommodating the trauma, they may abandon these spiritual resources as they attempt to make meaning (e.g., no longer praying or meditating, disengaging from spiritual activities). The following case example focuses especially on dimensions of the client's meaning system—global meaning, situational meaning, the meaning-making process, and meanings made—which will be considered throughout this discussion of assessment.

INTRODUCTION TO YASEMIN

Yasemin Yilmaz was 12 years old when her family fled to America. Her father had worked as a chemical engineer at a university in Turkey. However, when his research led to the development of new types of explosives, members of an organized crime group attempted to capture him. Initially, they broke into his lab and car, which he tolerated; however, when the family received threatening letters and a "stray bullet" went through the window of their flat, it became clear that he and his family were no longer safe in Turkey. They fled the country with only the clothes on their backs and the money they could carry.

Yasemin was overwhelmed by the changes she experienced in the United States. She had studied some English in school but was not prepared to do schoolwork in that language. She also lost a close companion in Turkey—she had to leave behind a much-loved cat. Without the necessary credentials, Yasemin's parents could not obtain the high-paying, professional positions they had held in Turkey. Further, her father was afraid to return to his previous career because he believed doing so would endanger his family. In addition, Yasemin's family had previously had servants who cared for the children, but given the family's change in socioeconomic status and the long hours her parents spent working in food service and janitorial jobs, Yasemin became the person primarily responsible for her younger brother's care. She could not tell her classmates much about her life in Turkey because she believed that would put her father and family at risk.

Yasemin felt very alone, experienced chronic and high levels of stress, and began having health problems. She missed a great deal of school due to disabling levels of back pain and asked to have her schoolwork sent home rather than attending school. Her doctors, however, found no medical explanation for her pain. They suggested—and her parents agreed—that stress and her discomfort with feeling different and isolated at school were likely a key source of her problems.

In their attempts to help, Yasemin's parents brought home a new kitten. However, Yasemin was not interested; her parents saw this as an indication that she was having serious problems. Her pediatrician helped them find a child psychologist, Dr. Khan, whom they carefully vetted. Yasemin initially found it difficult to talk to Dr. Khan because she was afraid that her disclosures would put her family in danger. Her parents repeatedly reassured her that she did not have to keep family secrets in that setting. Dr. Khan responded to her concerns by allowing her to take home a favorite stuffed elephant so she could practice sharing her secrets with it and then bring the elephant back to sessions to help her disclose what was going on.

Over time, a theme of loneliness and isolation emerged in sessions. Yasemin felt alone in her responsibility for her brother. Because of language, cultural, and religious differences, she had no friends at school. She believed her current concerns were small relative to the threats on their lives in Turkey; nonetheless, she was overwhelmed and worried, and because her parents worked long hours by necessity, she avoided talking to them so as not to cause them increased worry.

When Dr. Khan asked, "What do you miss most about your life in Turkey?" Yasemin replied, "I miss prayer time with the other girls in school." In the United States, she did not wear a hijab and did not pray with a Muslim community—in large measure to maintain the secrecy of their previous identities and keep the family safe. Yasemin went on to say,

> In Turkey, when I had a bad day at school, or I was mad at my brother or parents, I would pray, and Allah would give me wisdom to see what to do. But now I don't pray, so Allah does not help me anymore. I think that is why I get so much pain, and that is why my grades are so bad. I have left Allah, and Allah has left me.

Yasemin's child psychologist assumed that Yasemin may have been experiencing some difficulties in her spiritual and religious life and that these might reflect the possible traumas she had experienced. She had felt safe, respected, and connected to Allah, her family, and community in Turkey. She had global beliefs that if she maintained adherence to Muslim practices, she would be able to meet challenges. In her current situation, she was denied opportunities to maintain many of these practices and attributed her social isolation and physical and emotional stress to this change in spiritual practice. At her conventional level of psychospiritual development, she perceived spiritual practice rules as mandates. One could either follow the rules and be good, or fail to do so and be bad; this perspective categorically disrupted her identification as a committed Muslim and her relationship with Allah. She did not want to put additional demands on her parents, so she withdrew from them while spending much time in unproductive rumination and attempting to make meaning of her experiences in a manner that was almost impossible given her current level of development and access to resources.

Focusing on these different points in the meaning-making process— this example being just a small aspect of this process—helps therapists contextualize their client's behavior and symptoms, normalize parts that otherwise fail to make sense, and generate hypotheses about the meaning of events, symptoms, and behavior from the client's meaning system. In doing so, therapists may find themselves able to make more effective case conceptualizations and set more useful treatment goals. For example, Yasemin's therapist might choose to focus on ways to help her feel safe, disclose appropriately, and reconnect with Allah and her culture, family, and peers.

7 × 7 MODEL OF SPIRITUAL ASSESSMENT

Uncovering the meaning of an individual's spirituality requires a systematic look at the whole of the person's spiritual functioning in the context of medical, psychological, family systems, psychosocial, cultural, and social domains (Fitchett, 2002). In particular, Fitchett (2002) suggested that clinicians should examine seven aspects of spirituality to develop a comprehensive approach to spiritually sensitive assessment practices: (a) beliefs and meanings, (b) vocation and obligations, (c) experiences and emotions, (d) courage and growth, (e) rituals and practice, (f) community, and (g) authority and guidance in spiritual functioning (see Table 6.1). This information can be gathered using the clinical assessments described later in this chapter, in the course of the initial interview, and throughout treatment. Clinicians should use this information to develop hypotheses about adaptive and maladaptive meanings that clients may have drawn following the trauma. We now further describe these aspects of spirituality for Yasemin.

Beliefs and Meanings

Like many 12-year-old Muslims, Yasemin believed that if she followed the laws of her faith, prayed at the appropriate times, fasted during Ramadan, wore her hijab, and maintained spiritually responsible relationships with

TABLE 6.1

Domains of Spirituality to Include in an Assessment of the
Spiritual Domain, as Described in Fitchett's (2002) 7 × 7 Model

Belief and meaning	What beliefs have provided the client with a sense of meaning and purpose?
	What symbols reflect or express meaning for this person?
	What is the person's story? Do any current problems have a specific meaning or alter this meaning?
	Is the client affiliated with a formal system of belief (e.g., church or temple) either currently or in the past?
Vocation and obligations	Do the client's beliefs and sense of meaning in life create a sense of duty, vocation, calling or moral obligation? Will current problems compromise or conflict with a perceived ability to fulfill these duties?
	Are current problems seen as a sacrifice or atonement, or are they in any other way related to a perceived sense of duty?
Experience and emotion	What contacts with the sacred, divine, or demonic has the person had?
	What emotions have been experienced in these contacts and with the person's beliefs, meaning in life, and associated sense of vocation?
Courage and growth	Can views of the trauma be fit into existing beliefs and symbols? If not, can the person change or let these beliefs and symbols go to allow more helpful ones emerge?
Ritual and practice	What rituals and practices are associated with the survivor's beliefs and meaning in life? Has the trauma changed their perceived need for these, or in their ability to perform or participate in those that are important to them?
Community	Is the client part of one or more formal or informal communities of shared belief, meaning in life, ritual, or practice?
	What is the style of the client's participation in these communities?
	To what extent does the client experience these relationships— with the community, spiritual leader, God—as positive and supportive?
Authority and guidance	Where does the client find authority for beliefs, meaning in life, vocation, and rituals and practices?
	Where does the client look for guidance when faced with doubt, confusion, tragedy, or conflict?
	To what extent does the client look within or without for guidance?

others in her family and community, she would experience spiritual rewards for living a virtuous life (e.g., feelings of peace and confidence in her spiritual identity). When the circumstances of her forced immigration made it difficult and dangerous to observe the laws and customs of her Muslim faith, she believed she would lose her relationship with Allah and the inner strength that came from it.

Vocation and Obligations

Yasemin's spiritual understanding of her vocation was that she needed to fulfill certain obligations to help care for her family, especially her younger brother, and be responsive to adult authorities at home and school. She made every effort to do these things, but because she perceived a loss of spiritual strength (expressed alongside clinical depression and somatization), it became more difficult for her to find the energy to act on these perceived obligations.

Experiences and Emotions

Yasemin experienced a "catch-22" between her early religious training, which expected strict adherence to practices such as prayer and wearing the hijab, and parental instruction on leaving Turkey that she should not do these things because they would put her and her family in danger. As such, she experienced a discrepancy between her global value on adherence to Muslim practices and her ongoing love for her parents and concern for her family's safety (Phase 1 concern). This conflict was difficult to resolve, especially for a child at a conventional level of psychospiritual development. This conflict led to high levels of internal spiritual conflict characterized by guilt, anxiety, and depression.

Courage and Growth

In the course of treatment, Yasemin began to question whether she needed to alter her religious practices in the United States. These questions helped her and her family to examine more fully ways they could maintain their religious practices, even under threatening circumstances. Further, discussing these questions with her family helped her make more mature spiritual decisions. For example, as a preteen operating at a conventional level, Yasemin viewed it as wrong to go to school without a hijab. As she discussed her dilemma with her family and Dr. Khan, Yasemin began considering whether her religious values on modesty were more or less important than her ongoing commitment to care for and protect members of her family.

Rituals and Practice

In Turkey, Yasemin and her family strictly followed religious rituals related to prayer, dress, religious study, and diet. When she came to the United States, she had to drop many of these rituals to keep her family safe. Hence, she also lost the sense of peace and stability that came from her family's adherence to these practices both inside and outside their home.

Community

In Turkey, Yasemin's strict adherence to rituals such as prayer, dress, and studying the Koran was supported by her social and community context. In the United States, many of her teachers and peers viewed Islam as somehow threatening and did not understand her dietary restrictions; most important, her practice of rituals had the potential to put her family in danger. This disruption of her faith practices, as well as the loss of a supportive faith community, became central to addressing her mental health concerns.

Authority and Guidance in Spiritual Functioning

In Turkey, Yasemin's deference to religious and family authorities was both normal and adaptive. When instructed by her parents to change her spiritual practices, she experienced conflict between two separate sources of authority—those of Islam and those of her parents. When it became impossible to meet some of the values and expectations of her faith without violating others, she experienced significant spiritual struggles and had to evaluate critically how she should respond to these different sources of religious authority. This conflict forced Yasemin to struggle, at least temporarily, between an untenable conventional faith and a post-conventional faith that could critically evaluate these concerns. (Please refer to Table 2.2 for a review of these developmental considerations.)

USING THE RECIPROCAL MEANING-MAKING MODEL DURING ASSESSMENT

Fitchett's (2002) model helps describe Yasemin's functioning in these seven spiritual realms but does not include a strong focus on meaning-relevant domains (i.e., global meaning, situational meaning, meaning making, meaning made). We consider meaning to be the heart of clinical concerns, particularly for people struggling to move forward and live in satisfying and productive ways following a history of trauma. The Appendix provides a number of tools that may be useful in assessing these meaning-related domains.

Global Meaning

Assessments should address core elements of global meaning, including survivors' beliefs about how they should live out their beliefs, values, personal goals, and sense of purpose. In the course of an assessment, for example, clinicians might assess their clients' beliefs about a God, afterlife, and views about why suffering occurs and bad things happen (see Table 6.2). They might also

TABLE 6.2
Assessment of Global Spiritual Meaning

	Global meaning	Situational meaning
Beliefs	What story (or stories) have you told about who you are and why things happen? What are your beliefs in a higher power? If you believe in a higher power, what do you see as the nature of this higher power? What do you believe happens after people die? How do you believe that you should live out your beliefs?	What do you believe about why the trauma happened? How do you see and feel about yourself as a result of the trauma? In what ways, if any, have your stories about yourself and your world changed? What was your higher power's role, if any, in your trauma? Do you perceive your community of faith, higher power, and clergy as supportive of you? Have your beliefs about other people, your world, and your higher power changed? Do you feel any conflicts in your religious or spiritual beliefs? How do you resolve these conflicts?
Sense of purpose	How much does your life feel meaningful? When does your life feel more or less meaningful? What do you do to develop your sense of meaning and purpose? How much does your spiritual life contribute to your sense of meaning and purpose?	How did the trauma affect your sense of meaning and purpose? Have you experienced a change in your sense of meaning and purpose as a result of the trauma?
Goals and values	What provides meaning in your life? What is most important to you? How do you pursue and maintain those things most important to you? What are you doing to attempt to meet your spiritual and secular goals?	How did the trauma disrupt or take away the things that are important to you? Did it change your life direction? How have your goals or the values you hold changed? If you feel less able to meet your goals than before, what barriers do you perceive?

consider sources of meaning and purpose in life, as well as assessing their clients' spiritual and secular goals (which often have sacred overtones). Clinicians may also consider the means and strategies that clients use to actualize their beliefs, pursue goals, and develop a sense of meaning and purpose.

Religious Identity

Religious identity serves a number of important social and individual functions, including creating a sense of connection to a larger group, providing feelings of belongingness, and enhancing self-esteem. Religious identity is also positively associated with many indicators of mental health (Saroglou & Cohen, 2013). Research on religious identity has primarily studied the importance and salience of religion in a person's life, drawing on a single question: "Would you call yourself a strong Christian/Jew or a not very strong Christian/ Jew?" (Brenner, 2011). Brenner (2011) suggested that people who especially value their religious identity may overreport socially desirable behaviors associated with that identity (e.g., church attendance and tithing); knowing this might require therapists to cultivate a warm and respectful atmosphere that encourages honest reporting from religious clients. Religious identity can be assessed with a frequently used research survey assessing spiritual and social context (Spiritual and Demographic Survey, see Appendix), as well as the Religious Commitment Inventory–10 (see Appendix; Worthington et al., 2003).

It might also be useful to ask about the community in which a client lives. Answers to these questions may be complex. Individuals may be exposed to multiple religious groups and may synthesize unique religious identities that may not be readily apparent to therapists. In other cases, religious identity may interact with other identities (e.g., sexuality, ethnicity), which may lead to discrepancies in meaning. For example, Yasemin was disconnected from her former community of faith. She highly valued her identity as a Muslim, while also wanting to "fit in" in her new country. The resulting discrepancy between these values created intense distress for Yasemin.

Religious and Spiritual Beliefs

As discussed in previous chapters, religious and spiritual beliefs may buffer against posttraumatic stress disorder (PTSD) and other psychiatric problems by creating more benign situational appraisals, which in turn might minimize distress (Park, 2016). In this manner, benign religious beliefs can protect people against the daily wear and tear of stressors and help them face highly stressful or traumatic situations, whereas more malignant views can cause greater distress symptomatology (Park & Slattery, 2013a).

Many different religious beliefs may affect emotional well-being; some that may be particularly useful to assess include (a) that suffering can bring one closer to God, (b) that the devil causes temptation and suffering, (c) that one's behavior in this life determines one's afterlife, (d) that people deserve what happens to them (e.g., AIDS as God's punishment), (e) that scripture is the literal truth, and (f) that there is one true religion or way to God (e.g., Exline, 2008). Assessments of afterlife beliefs might include questions such as the following: What do you believe happens when people die? What do you expect will happen when you die? What do you believe you should do to have a positive afterlife (e.g., be good, believe, perform good acts, surrender to God, seek forgiveness for sin or acts of wrongdoing)?

Theodicy

Theodicies are theological explanations for the existence of suffering and evil in the universe or approaches to resolving discrepancies between global beliefs in a benevolent and omnipotent God with traumatic situations that such a God would theoretically never permit (Hale-Smith, Park, & Edmondson, 2012). Prior to the trauma, suffering and evil may simply be abstract ideas or, for people who hold naively positive or just world beliefs, the occurrence of trauma might be attributed to deservedness or personal reasons (e.g., the family that lost their house in a fire deserved it due to some earlier failing). Following trauma, however, people may ask how there can be a good and all-powerful God, given their experience of suffering and the clear demonstration that evil exists in the world.

One recent measure of theodicies, the Views of Suffering Scale (see Appendix; Hale-Smith et al., 2012), assesses a range of possible theodicies, including those of karma, randomness, and views of suffering as retribution and as soul building, along with beliefs that God has limited knowledge and that God suffers along with the sufferers. This measure, although incorporating viewpoints other than Christian ones, has been validated with a primarily Christian population. More research is needed to identify its utility with other faiths.

Spiritual Goals

Spiritual goals are one of the primary mechanisms for converting spiritual beliefs into a subjective sense of meaning and behavior (Schnitker & Emmons, 2013). Once individuals identify a goal as sacred, strivings and efforts consistent with that goal are associated with greater well-being (Pashak & Laughter, 2012; Schnitker & Emmons, 2013). In assessing spiritual goals, appropriate questions may include, "What are the most important things you want to accomplish in your life?" or "What activities help you feel that you have meaning or purpose?" Therapists should attend carefully to discrepancies between expressed spiritual goals and behavior because these discrepancies could be a source of distress. For example, as we highlight in the next chapter, a therapist may observe a therapeutically relevant discrepancy when a recently returned combat veteran identifies being a good father as a primary spiritual goal but reports spending most of his time at home alone and away from his children.

Religious beliefs and goals do not occur in a vacuum and can conflict with other global beliefs, values, and goals (e.g., religious beliefs about one's self-identification as being gay with values of self-expression and desires for a long-term, committed, loving relationship). As such, therapists should listen carefully for such discrepancies between two or more sets of goals, values, or beliefs, which can cause distress and interfere with adaptive coping. Yasemin, for example, valued her religious rituals and practices, which she perceived as conflicting with respect for her parents' authority and their request that she no longer wear the hijab or actively pray during school hours so as to keep the family safe.

Situational Meaning: Appraisals of the Trauma

Both global religious and spiritual beliefs and the specific context of the trauma influence trauma appraisals (Park, 2005, 2010; Park & Folkman, 1997; Slattery & Park, 2012a, 2012b). Post-trauma appraisals either can be comforting or a source of stress, and assessing their nature should be a regular part of treatment for PTSD and related concerns (Wortmann, Park, & Edmondson, 2011). It is these situational meanings rather than global meanings with which most trauma survivors consciously struggle. That is, most people do not worry about why God allows suffering in the world (i.e., a global existential problem), but instead wonder why God allowed this specific traumatic experience to happen at this particular time (i.e., a situational appraisal).

Traumatized clients are more likely to come to treatment holding threatening, rather than comforting, appraisals of their traumas. When these experiences are appraised as threatening to or having already damaged aspects of life that the person holds as sacred, these events can become imbued with spiritual meaning (Kusner & Pargament, 2012). Such a desecration might be especially relevant when people are physically abused by a religious or spiritual leader or in God's name, where the trauma may seem to have occurred with God's permission or endorsement. In other cases, the trauma may not appear to have clear spiritual overtones but acquires them over time. For people who believed that God was watching over them—or should have been—there is often now clear "evidence" that such is not the case or that God is not competent or sufficiently caring to remain active in the universe. Such overlays of spiritual meaning on secular events can intensify the trauma's hurtfulness and increase survivors' feelings of loss, distress, guilt, and shame (Worthington, Davis, et al., 2013).

Therapists should, therefore, be sensitive to the possibility that survivors perceive traumatic events as holding meaning and that even secular events can hold spiritual meaning. Discussions of feeling alone and unsupported may overtly refer to friends and family but can also reflect a deep sense of abandonment and of feeling unsupported by God. Feelings of being shameful or dirty may reflect survivors' beliefs that their God perceives them as having sinned. Expressing that they feel out of control may also reflect underlying spiritual doubts and feelings that they believe their God no longer listens to them (or never did).

Discrepancies Between Global and Situational Meanings

Throughout the assessment process, we look for discrepancies between a client's current status and ideal functioning (Slattery & Park, 2012a). Yasemin, for example, believed she would lose her relationship with Allah and the strength that came from it, and perceived herself as failing her obligations to Allah and her family. As such, she was torn between her values of loyalty in upholding religious rituals and practices on the one hand and her love and respect for her parents and family on the other. Over time, she also experienced a loss of community in the United States because her teachers and peers viewed her faith as a potential threat, and she recognized how her practice of that faith could endanger her family (Phase 1 concern). Each of these discrepancies was a source of distress for Yasemin.

As discussed in Chapter 3, when appraised meanings of events or situations are inconsistent with global meaning, people typically attempt to change or distort their appraisals to incorporate them into their global meaning (assimilation; Joseph & Linley, 2005). Presumably, trauma-related ruminations and intrusive thoughts are unsuccessful attempts to do so (Briñol, Petty, & Wheeler, 2006; Dalgleish & Power, 2004; Foa & Kozak, 1986; M. J. Gray, Maguen, & Litz, 2007). PTSD is, therefore, maintained, in part, because people assimilate negative beliefs about themselves and the world into their global meanings (e.g., bad things happen to bad people), perhaps even without being aware of doing so, and then avoid experiences that might challenge these rigidly held beliefs (M. J. Gray et al., 2007). This avoidance maintains their negative views of self and world (Foa, Huppert, & Cahill, 2006).

Discrepancies in meaning may be inferred in a number of ways. Survivors may directly describe what they had believed or hoped would happen. When asked about ways that they have changed since the trauma, they may be able to describe these changes (e.g., "I used to believe that the world was a safe place"). At other times, discrepancies can be inferred from the content of ruminative processes assessed in conversations with clients. Finally, as discussed in Chapter 5, therapists should be aware that some survivors may resolve discrepancies in maladaptive ways to gain a sense of cohesion and stability in life. At these points, as we discuss in later chapters, therapists may have to actively create discrepancies (e.g., "You say that no one has ever been there for you?"). The Global Meaning Violation Scale (see Appendix; Park et al., in press) can also be used to identify and explore discrepancies with clients.

Spiritual Meaning-Making Efforts

As discussed in the preceding chapter, efforts at assimilation or accommodation may be either adaptive or maladaptive in nature. Maladaptive assimilations might be incorporated into a fundamentally negative global meaning system, especially in cases of complex and repeated traumas (Type II). It is also possible for spiritual strugglers to over-accommodate their beliefs instead of grappling with the realities of their painful experiences, in which cases any trauma-related conclusions might then be generalized beyond the trauma (e.g., God is no longer powerful or no longer good).

In each of these cases, survivors may identify a discrepancy between global meaning (e.g., God is good) and situational meaning (e.g., God allowed this to happen). Therapists should assess both global and situational meanings, identify discrepancies, and then consider how the survivor is addressing possible distress related to these discrepancies. When the survivor responds to the trauma adaptively (either through assimilative or accommodative strategies), further clinical attention to the resolved discrepancy is not needed. If the survivor identifies the discrepancy and responds more negatively, such unsuccessful attempts at coping could require therapeutic attention. For example, Yasemin relied on a maladaptive accommodation in an attempt to resolve a discrepancy between her global religious values and her parents' situational instruction to stop wearing the hijab and praying in public places (e.g., "I have left Allah and Allah has left me"), which created self-blame and betrayal, thus adding to the stresses of leaving her homeland. Addressing safety needs was one part of helping Yasemin close this discrepancy.

Religious Coping

We discussed the relevance of religious coping in previous chapters. Just as prayer and ritual can serve different functions in one's life, people can use religion adaptively or maladaptively in the meaning-making process. Much of the research identifying positive and negative religious coping strategies has assessed them with the RCOPE and the Brief RCOPE (the latter is included in the Appendix; Pargament, Feuille, & Burdzy, 2011). Therapists can directly ask survivors about ways they use their religious beliefs, rituals, and communities to respond to the trauma as well as to other stressors. How has this use changed since the trauma? What happens when they use these coping strategies?

Spiritual Struggle

A person's spiritual life may be a source of strength, but it can also be characterized by struggle and become a source of clinical concerns. As discussed in Chapter 5, spiritual struggles can take a number of forms, including religious doubt, loss of faith, and anger toward God or members of the spiritual community. Spiritual struggle may involve either distancing or engagement, and can include both positive and negative emotions, both of which are assessed by the Religious and Spiritual Struggles Scales (see Appendix;

Exline, Pargament, Grubbs, & Yali, 2014). Because spiritual struggle and religious comfort are not significantly correlated with one another (e.g., Harris et al., 2008; Ogden et al., 2011), people can simultaneously experience severe struggle as well as high levels of religious comfort. This may set the stage for serious internal conflict and thus be an appropriate focus of therapy.

Assessments of spiritual struggle should, therefore, include questions about how clients cope with any spiritual struggles, rather than whether they are struggling, because some types of struggle may be more problematic than others (Exline & Rose, 2013). In so doing, therapists may reflect on questions such as these: "How do survivors see their relationship with their God?" "Can they maintain both positive and negative feelings toward their God?" "Can they be angry without walking away?" "Are they primarily using approach or avoidance strategies during their struggle?" Because agnostics and atheists report higher levels of anger toward God than other religious groups (Exline, Park, Smyth, & Carey, 2011), it can also be appropriate to consider spiritual struggle with these groups as well. The Religious and Spiritual Struggles Scale (see Appendix; Exline et al., 2014) can be a useful assessment tool for assessing this dimension of spirituality.

Despite her history of positive religious coping, Yasemin stopped using these resources after her family emigrated from Turkey. She experienced considerable spiritual struggle at the time of treatment, including perceptions of increased distance and mild anger, while retaining a desire for greater closeness to and support from Allah. She rarely overtly discussed these concerns as she avoided talking about anything she believed would put her family at risk.

Meanings Made

Discrepancies

When individuals reach a point of stable resolution of discrepancies between global and situational meaning, they achieve the "meaning made" point in the reciprocal meaning-making model. When meanings made of potential traumas are adaptive (e.g., regaining a sense that one's world and life have discernible meaning), survivors have better mental health, better treatment outcomes, fewer psychiatric symptoms, and higher levels of social support (Jim, Purnell, Richardson, Golden-Kreutz, & Andersen, 2006; Volkert, Schulz, Brutt, & Andreas, 2014). Furthermore, people who have a strong sense of purpose in life are more resilient when they later encounter physical and mental challenges (Boyle, Buchman, & Bennett, 2010). Of course, not all meanings made are adaptive. Addressing chronic, distressing meanings is a Phase 3 issue.

One potential approach to capturing the synchrony between global and situational meanings (i.e., meaning made) is the Integration of Stressful

Life Experiences Scale (ISLES; see Appendix), which identifies the degree to which trauma survivors have adaptively incorporated trauma into their global meaning and created harmony between their global and situational meanings (Holland, Currier, Coleman, & Neimeyer, 2010). Drawing on a sample of Iraq and Afghanistan veterans seeking health care in the Veterans Administration (VA) system, for example, Currier, Holland, Chisty, and Allen (2011) found that the ability to integrate trauma into global meaning, as assessed by the ISLES, was inversely linked with PTSD symptomatology and predicted fewer mental health referrals by VA clinicians over subsequent months. Another instrument that may be useful is the Meaning In Life Questionnaire (see Appendix; Steger, Frazier, Oishi, & Kaler, 2006). Serial assessments of meaning in life through a course of therapy can illuminate progress in the meaning-making process (or lack thereof).

When considering situational meanings with respect to her faith system, Yasemin expected that she should use her experience of adversity to facilitate her spiritual growth as a Muslim. On the night they left Turkey, she thought that she would have to spend extra time in prayer and study of the Koran to help herself and her family through this event. When she was subsequently denied opportunities to pursue spiritual development, the discrepancy between the expectations of her internalized spiritual meaning frameworks and her situation contributed to her distress; she felt paralyzed and unable to reengage her faith resources in her new cultural context.

Forgiveness

Most religions encourage and expect forgiveness, although views on forgiveness vary widely. Monotheistic religions often emphasize divine forgiveness, but also tend to encourage forgiveness of others (McCullough & Worthington, 1999). Forgiveness may be demanded or inspired by God (Rye et al., 2000), and may be perceived as a source for ending suffering for both oneself and others or as a way of creating happiness and approaching the divine.

Many religious clients perceive forgiveness as something they are required to give, regardless of their personal reactions or feelings about the offense or the offender (Wade, Johnson, & Meyer, 2008). As such, therapists may assess beliefs about forgiveness, including whether survivors perceive expectations to forgive, who they believe should be forgiven, and what that forgiveness process should look like. Yasemin, for example, felt unable to ask for forgiveness until she took steps to correct those behaviors, including failing to pray, which distanced her from Allah.

Assessments of meanings made regarding the issue of forgiveness should focus on attitudes and behaviors toward offender, self, and God, as well as the nature of the survivor's relationship with each and the degree to which these relationships have been imbued with the sacred. The Transgression-Related Interpersonal Motivations Scale–12 can be used to assess forgiveness (see Appendix; McCullough et al., 1998) in these respects. Worthington and Langberg (2012) suggested that responsible, rather than overly glib, self-forgiveness occurs within a context of (a) appealing to a higher power; (b) making amends for wrongs perpetrated; (c) readjusting unrealistic expectations when necessary and appropriate; (d) readjusting self-perceptions when necessary and appropriate to accept oneself as a "valuable, though fallen, human being" (p. 275); (e) practicing a life in which one habitually acts within one's morals and values; though (f) acknowledging that one is imperfect and will make mistakes despite attempts to live within one's moral beliefs.

SPIRITUAL RESOURCES

Studies of spirituality and adjustment among trauma survivors make it clear that spiritual resources are relevant to mental health (Harris et al., 2008; Ogden et al., 2011). Resources in the spiritual domain can take the form of supportive relationships with a higher power or community of faith and may include both instrumental support and coaching in effective coping.

Attachment to a Higher Power

Many people experience relationships with their higher power that are similar to the types of bonds they have with people; they might report feelings of closeness or distance, communicate with their higher power, often imagine their higher power with human features, and feel the same kinds of emotions toward that higher power that they might report feeling toward another human being (Wood et al., 2010). People's beliefs that God will protect them in times of danger or difficulty are also similar to those of a child's expectations of parents (Hill & Pargament, 2003). The Attachment to God Inventory (Beck & McDonald, 2004) assesses spiritual attachment. Sample items from the inventory include: "Without God I couldn't function at all," "I often feel angry with God for not responding to me when I want," and "I believe that people should not depend on God for things they should do for themselves."

Therapists should consider how their clients are viewing their higher power. How do they imagine their higher power is perceiving and responding to them? Do they perceive themselves as being judged? Abandoned? Supported? How are they, in turn, responding? Some of these attachment-related dynamics are quite evident in Yasemin's case. When she was required to give up practices that supported her attachment to Allah, she evidenced a parallel withdrawal from her parents. Furthermore, when denied social resources in her community, her desire for a closer relationship with Allah intensified, as did her grief about the loss of this attachment. Her functioning deteriorated during this period.

Spiritual Social Support

Support from one's higher power is not the only source of support that individuals experience in their religious lives; relationships in one's community of faith can also make an important contribution to meaning making and mental health in the face of adversity. Therapists should consider the ways that their clients' spiritual guides and spiritual communities are perceived as supportive or judgmental, critical, and rejecting. These perceptions might be different from their spiritual community's true reactions, and it may be helpful to refer clients to their spiritual leader to check out these perceptions (as discussed further in Chapter 12). Spiritual support can be measured using the Religious Comfort subscale of the Religious Comfort and Strains Scale (Exline, Yali, & Sanderson, 2000). Sample items from this subscale include: "Feeling like part of a religious or spiritual community," "Feeling that God is close to you," and "Good memories of past experiences with religion or religious people."

Stages of Spiritual Development

We outlined developmental considerations with respect to how spirituality might intersect with meaning making after trauma in Table 2.2. People's spiritual views are not stable and unchanging, but develop and change like other cognitive domains (e.g., as described by Piaget, Kohlberg, Erikson, and Gilligan). In general, across a lifespan, people gain greater amounts of knowledge, reality orientation, and complexity of thought, such that they can hold two or more apparently conflicting beliefs. The Fowler Religious Attitudes Scale–Revised (Harris & Leak, 2013) is designed to assess levels of psychospiritual development. Sample items from this scale include: "My religious orientation comes primarily from my church and the people who first taught me about my faith," and "It is not important that I keep the same religious views as my family of origin."

Therapists should listen to the ways in which clients talk about their spirituality, the trauma, themselves, and their God to discern their level of psychospiritual development. How do clients handle potential discrepancies in religious teachings? How do they prioritize apparently contradictory values? Yasemin was using early Stage 3 thinking when she was first referred for treatment, demonstrating some level of ambivalence in her relationship with Allah, while rarely being able to acknowledge both sides of her ambivalence. She focused on perceived religious imperatives (e.g., wearing a hijab) rather than other apparently competing values.

Therapists can facilitate survivors in making appraisals of themselves, the trauma, their world, and their higher power in a more sophisticated manner in many different ways (see Chapter 7). As we discuss in more depth in the next chapter, therapists can regularly offer empathic responses, discuss issues from other perspectives, reject dualities, encourage multiple perspectives, and provide opportunities for role taking (Day, 2013).

FOLLOW-UP WITH YASEMIN

Dr. Khan's work with Yasemin helped her make more sense of her changing sense of self, her world, and her relationship with Allah from multiple perspectives than did the more dualistic approach that she had previously adopted. As she came to trust him, she increasingly adopted some of his conclusions about her predicament, but also embraced his style of thinking about the world with significant complexity (e.g., he rarely accepted easy, simple answers). In fact, some parts of his comments and style reminded her of her imams in Turkey.

Dr. Khan and Yasemin's parents identified a number of ways they might be able to help her while remaining sensitive to the family's ongoing need for secrecy. They worked toward repairing her lost relationship with Allah by setting aside prayer space in their home and observing prayer time as a family when they were home together. Because other children in school were accustomed to seeing Yasemin go to the nurse's office, her parents asked the school nurse to take her out of the classroom at prayer time so she could pray during the school day. In addition, they began to set aside time to talk with both Yasemin and her brother every day, often after evening prayers, to help them manage the challenges they faced from their move and adjustment to a new country and culture. Dr. Khan helped them respond in a nonjudgmental manner as Yasemin talked about her concerns and feelings of abandonment by Allah. Although they did not directly address safety needs, these changes did help Yasemin feel safer.

In addition, they helped Yasemin develop social support from peers in ways that were not heavily language dependent, such as taking flute lessons at school—something she quickly excelled at—and that led to friendships with other musically interested peers. She and her parents talked about what she could and could not talk about with other girls to keep her family safe. With increased opportunities to talk with peers, both her English and her grades improved. As she and her family made these changes, Yasemin's back pain and depressive symptoms gradually subsided as well, and she began to feel increasingly at home in her new country.

CONCLUSION

Although religion and spirituality promote healing, there are other paths for achieving the sense of meaning, purpose, community, and connectedness that religion and spirituality provide. People may similarly derive these resources from family, achievement, overcoming oppression, creating change, or meeting other global goals (Park, 2005; Wong, 1998). A comprehensive, effective assessment will also identify the strengths and weaknesses in these other domains. Failures to attend to the client's meaning system as a whole will limit a therapist's ability to understand and engage clients, motivate change, and help them understand themselves (Park & Slattery, 2009).

As discussed in this chapter, spirituality can be part of every aspect of coming to terms with trauma, including the traumatic event itself; the meanings people draw about the event, themselves, other people, and their future; and their ability to cope with the trauma and other stressors (Kusner & Pargament, 2012). Spirituality can either increase or decrease clients' abilities to find meaning, purpose, and sense in the world; traumatic experiences can leave people feeling profoundly disconnected and misunderstood—or connected and supported.

Because spiritual issues can be experienced in different ways by clients, be a private part of their experience, and often be woven throughout their lives, they may also be difficult to disclose in treatment. Listening carefully, patiently, and respectfully can be essential. Incorporating spiritual language and meanings into reflective responses can address a client's deeper concerns and further facilitate discussion. Upcoming chapters address how to negotiate these types of treatment concerns in more depth (Chapter 7) and address possible issues with personal meaning that might emerge for therapists in the process of listening sensitively and deeply to trauma in this manner (Chapter 8).

7

OVERVIEW OF TREATMENT ISSUES FROM THE RECIPROCAL MEANING-MAKING MODEL

Spirituality can provide solace in the aftermath of trauma as well as resources for coping with posttraumatic stress disorder (PTSD) and other trauma-related sequelae. However, traumatic events can also undermine one's spiritual meaning system, and struggles in this domain might complicate the treatment process. In such cases, clients may experience painful discrepancies between their current experience and pretrauma global beliefs, values, and goals, often resulting in a profound void of purpose in life. As emphasized throughout this volume, difficulties in recovery may ensue from maladaptive efforts to resolve these discrepancies or an inability to reconcile the reality and sequelae of the trauma with spiritual meaning. Through negotiating these types of concerns in a sensitive manner over the course of treatment, therapists can support their clients' healing at deep emotional and spiritual levels.

http://dx.doi.org/10.1037/15961-007
Trauma, Meaning, and Spirituality: Translating Research Into Clinical Practice, by C. L. Park, J. M. Currier, J. I. Harris, and J. M. Slattery

Preceding chapters in this volume provided an overview of contemporary, evidence-based approaches to treating traumatized persons (Chapter 4), outlined general clinical concerns from the standpoint of a reciprocal meaning-making model (Chapter 5), and reviewed implications of this reciprocal perspective for assessment (Chapter 6). The reciprocal meaning-making model also identifies numerous places in the therapeutic process where clinicians can intervene with traumatized clients (e.g., reappraisal of the trauma, spiritual resources and coping strategies). This chapter describes three treatment objectives via the lens of a reciprocal meaning-making model: building the therapeutic alliance, resolving discrepancies in meaning, and creating new meaning in life. Drawing on insights gained from a veteran for whom religious faith factored prominently in his recovery from PTSD and related concerns, we again use a case-centered approach to illustrate applications to clinical practice.

INTRODUCTION TO MR. CUNNINGHAM

Jefferson Cunningham was a 42-year-old Caucasian male referred to a PTSD clinic at a Veterans Administration (VA) hospital following a neuropsychological evaluation for mild traumatic brain injury. He was born and raised in a mid-sized city as the older of two brothers. Mr. Cunningham's mother passed away abruptly from gastric cancer when he was 13, and he assumed primary responsibility for the care of a younger brother with Down syndrome because his father worked long hours outside the home. Mr. Cunningham indicated that although the loss of his mother was extremely difficult, he drew strength from his faith and church community. He also believed that God had ultimately used this experience to help him mature spiritually, eventually directing him to serve others with a career in professional ministry.

However, because of his vocational uncertainty in his late teens, along with a long-standing value on military service in his family, Mr. Cunningham enlisted in the army and served for 4 years after high school. The country was not at war during this period, and Mr. Cunningham was not deployed outside the continental United States. He completed a bachelor's degree in religious studies in the years following discharge and earned a master's of divinity at a major Christian Protestant seminary immediately thereafter. For the next decade, Mr. Cunningham served as a youth and associate pastor at a prominent evangelical church in the region where he grew up. He was married during this formative period, and the couple had four children. As a way of supplementing his modest income in ministry amid increasing financial pressures from his growing family, Mr. Cunningham joined the Army National Guard shortly before Operation Iraqi Freedom.

Mr. Cunningham's unit was attached to an active duty unit that experienced major casualties during the first deployment. As such, many of the members of Mr. Cunningham's Guard unit became integral for completing combat operational duties. Given his military background and sharpshooting skills, Mr. Cunningham was unexpectedly assigned the job of sniper and later reported that he believed he was responsible for the deaths of approximately a dozen combatants. In addition, he was at the front of a small reconnaissance group that discovered the scene of an ambush in which over 20 U.S. service members from another unit had been executed. Mr. Cunningham reported "going berserk" for an acute period after this event; however, in accordance with his overall propensity for resilience and adaptive coping, he performed well for the remainder of his war-zone deployment and was promoted to staff sergeant for his second deployment.

Mr. Cunningham was responsible for supervising security details in his new role in Iraq, which was much calmer than during his initial deployment. However, while securing a checkpoint late one night in an isolated area, he and three of his men were confronted with an ambiguous but highly threatening situation. Despite their best attempts to force an oncoming vehicle to change course, a driver approached the checkpoint at a high speed, and Mr. Cunningham had to give orders for his men to fire on the vehicle. On inspecting the vehicle, Mr. Cunningham discovered what appeared to be an Iraqi family that was grotesquely disfigured from the heavy artillery and crash, including a husband, wife, and what appeared to be four children. Mr. Cunningham was psychiatrically discharged shortly after this incident because of a "mental breakdown." He was hospitalized in a military facility for the next 6 months and, in the ensuing 4 years, had been referred three times for PTSD treatment by VA clinicians.

At the time of the most recent referral, Mr. Cunningham felt emotionally numb and distressed about his war-zone experiences. He had severed most social ties and had been increasingly misusing alcohol as a means of coping with severe re-experiencing symptoms related to the incident with the Iraqi family (e.g., nightmares, visions of one of the children with him most days, intrusive thoughts). He also reported a number of behavioral avoidance symptoms, including an inability to go to public places without "coming undone," emergence of alarming distress at disclosing details of his war-zone experiences, and limiting interactions and intimacy with his wife and children as much as possible (e.g., not eating dinner with the family). Mr. Cunningham was also "amped up" much of the time and struggled with a number of severe hyperarousal symptoms (e.g., inability to concentrate and complete tasks, insomnia, irritability and anger outbursts). As a result, his wife no longer felt safe with him and reported concerns about paranoid behaviors in the home as well (e.g., taking a gun into the shower). At the time of the referral, he fully met criteria for a DSM–5 (*Diagnostic and Statistical Manual of Mental Disorders*, fifth edition; American Psychiatric Association, 2013) diagnosis of PTSD.

BUILDING THE THERAPEUTIC ALLIANCE

Establishing safety and trust within the therapeutic relationship is a first-order priority in working with traumatized persons who might be struggling with their spirituality. However, whether treating traumatized clients or addressing other types of concerns, there is consensus across theoretical traditions that cultivating a strong therapeutic alliance is a prerequisite for promoting change in all forms of psychotherapy (for a comprehensive description of clinical strategies for negotiating the alliance over the course of treatment, see Safran & Muran, 2000). Notwithstanding diversity in definitions and measurement approaches, research has consistently found that the quality of the alliance between client and clinician in the initial sessions is a particularly robust predictor of successful outcomes later in treatment (e.g., Horvath & Greenberg, 1994; D. J. Martin, Garske, & Davis, 2000). Given the mistrust and sense of alienation that traumatized individuals can experience, these findings suggest that clinicians who attend closely to their relationships with these clients will be best equipped to build a foundation for possibly working through the trauma narrative and restoring global meaning over the treatment process. However, for clients such as Mr. Cunningham who might be experiencing layers of shame and grief over a profound violation of their spiritual beliefs, values, and goals, clinicians have to be intentional, from the outset of treatment, to convey a therapeutic posture of respect, empathy, and openness to exploring spiritual dimensions of the client's trauma-related difficulties.

Drawing on the ideas of Bordin (1979), the therapeutic alliance can be conceptualized as comprising three interrelated dimensions that clinicians must continually address: tasks, goals, and bond. The *tasks* of therapy entail the activities in which the client must engage to benefit from treatment. For example, as described in Chapter 4, cognitive behavior therapy–based therapies for PTSD, such as cognitive processing therapy (CPT; Resick & Schnicke, 1993) and prolonged exposure (PE; Foa, Hembree, & Rothbaum, 2007), rely on rational collaboration in structured exercises for challenging avoidance-based coping, processing the trauma memory, and revising maladaptive situational meanings related to the event. The *goals* of therapy refer to the endpoint or ultimate "telos" that the client hopes to attain by engaging in these procedures. For instance, the overarching goal of contemporary, evidence-based treatments for PTSD is typically to alleviate clients' posttraumatic symptomatology. Last, according to Bordin, the *bond* component captures the emotional or affective quality of the client–therapist relationship. Particularly when clients have to confront distressing thoughts and emotions or deconstruct aspects of their global meaning systems during the treatment, they first need to feel understood, valued, and respected by their therapist.

Building a strong alliance across these three components is a complex and dynamic endeavor for clinicians. For example, without developing a secure bond, clients might not feel comfortable voicing their disagreements about certain tasks and goals of the treatment. However, gaining a sense of efficacy in accomplishing tasks early on in treatment can deepen the client's confidence in the clinician and strengthen the bond. As such, clinicians have to cultivate a supportive relational atmosphere in this first phase and encourage dialogue about the client's emerging sense of confidence in the therapeutic relationship and inevitable ambivalence and obstacles to engaging in the tasks of therapy.

Clinicians should, therefore, explore clients' preconceptions about therapy as early as feasible in treatment, as well as discuss clients' assumptions about what will be required of them both within and outside of sessions. Depending on theoretical orientation and possible extratherapeutic parameters (e.g., managed care, clinic policies), therapists may not have to set rigid expectations about goals but rather allow individual clients' preferences to emerge gradually as they develop safety and trust in the relationship. Whatever the case, working to get on the same wavelength as clients across tasks, goals, and bond is critical for building the type of alliance that will provide the foundation for meaning making. When working with spiritually oriented clients, addressing spirituality can be an essential part of reducing fears about treatment and developing a warm and accepting relational environment for the implementation of treatment activities and procedures (for general discussions of the role of spirituality in building the therapeutic alliance, refer to Sperry, 2012; Verbeck et al., 2015; J. C. Young, Dowdle, & Flowers, 2009).

Although limited research has demonstrated the additive benefit of addressing spirituality with traumatized clients, findings from a sizeable group of veterans beginning a PTSD residential program has provided evidence for assuming a spiritually integrative perspective when clinically indicated (Currier, Holland, & Drescher, 2015). Results of this study indicated that adaptive and maladaptive dimensions of spirituality assessed at pretreatment were uniquely predictive of the severity of veterans' PTSD symptomatology at discharge from the program. In particular, participants who scored higher on adaptive spiritual factors (i.e., daily spiritual experiences, forgiveness, spiritual practices, positive religious coping, organizational religiousness) at baseline assessment fared better in treatment. In addition, negative religious coping at the start of treatment predicted poorer outcomes. In contrast, pretreatment levels of PTSD did not predict any of the spirituality variables following treatment. Overall, the results of this study suggest that clinicians who take steps to understand the spiritual context of trauma-related concerns will be better equipped to address PTSD among those clients who are struggling in their spirituality or who hope to draw on spiritual resources in meeting the tasks and goals of their treatment.

Exploring the spiritual context of trauma was an essential part of building an alliance with Mr. Cunningham. Despite the alarming consequences of his PTSD, he had precipitously dropped out of treatment on three prior occasions and had not adhered to an SSRI medication that might stabilize his anxiety and depressive symptoms. In discussing his mental health history and expectations for treatment, Mr. Cunningham blamed himself for a lack of follow through and spoke about disappointing other providers in a surprisingly self-deprecating manner. However, in probing deeper into his reasons for "bowing out" of treatment, Mr. Cunningham cautiously stated concerns about the secularized nature of recommended tasks and goals; he could not easily connect the rationale for these approaches with his conservative Christian, evangelical meaning system. Hence, although he had long desired to repair his family relationships and regain a sense of purpose in life, Mr. Cunningham was not willing to engage in any treatment procedures that might somehow betray these core convictions. As such, it was imperative to affirm the sustaining role of his faith and initiate an honest dialogue about his reluctance to engage in psychologically oriented approaches such as CPT or PE.

From the standpoint of the reciprocal meaning-making model, clients' behavior, problems, and attempted solutions make sense once their unique meanings can be understood. Insofar as clinicians can empathically enter clients' context and meaning systems, clients will begin to feel less out of control in their thoughts and emotions and more receptive to engaging in the many tasks that are required of them over the treatment process. In cases where spirituality factored prominently in identity formation and the development of global beliefs and values, clients should therefore not be expected to compartmentalize their most cherished sources of meaning outside of the therapeutic relationship or unavailable to the tasks and goals for their treatment. However, in light of the historical bias against spirituality in the mental health professions (Delaney, Miller, & Bisonó, 2007; P. Norris & Inglehart, 2004; Pew Research Center, 2002), combined with the stigma against mental health treatment in many churches and spiritual communities, spiritually oriented clients may feel conflicted about being disloyal to these values when pursuing treatment in secular contexts in which most therapists practice (Constantine, Myers, Kindaichi, & Moore, 2004; Jones, Cassidy, & Heflinger, 2002; Kane, 2003; Raue, Weinberger, Sirey, Meyers, & Bruce, 2011).

It might not be possible to build a therapeutic alliance in these cases without providing a rationale for how people recover from trauma in a manner that affirms the client's cultural background and possible faith system and language. Specifically, all the world's major religions have stories of epic figures who struggled with and successfully adapted to the reality and consequences of trauma. In building an alliance with spiritually oriented clients, therapists can, therefore, inquire about which doctrines or accounts from the client's sacred texts might illuminate his or her presenting concerns. For example, in discussing the consequences of Mr. Cunningham's reliance on avoidance-based coping and the persistence of painful emotions and meanings regarding his perceived role in the deaths of the Iraqi family, the clinician asked about relevant stories from the Old and New Testaments. In response, Mr. Cunningham quickly mentioned several biblical figures who experienced redemption after trauma (e.g., Job, Jesus Christ) and disclosed an abiding belief in a "God of truth" and a lifelong commitment to pursue intimacy with this deity regardless of the cost.

Taking steps to translate these early therapeutic conversations into Mr. Cunningham's faith language allowed an honest collaboration in determining the tasks and goals of his treatment. Considering Mr. Cunningham's core convictions, the therapist initiated a dialogue about different types of truth and suggested that PE's emphasis on "narrative truth" might serve as a catalyst for weaving his life narrative back into the ultimate story of God's redemption in the universe. Expanding on this line of reasoning, Mr. Cunningham then engaged in a psychoeducational discussion about PTSD and raised the possibility that re-experiencing symptoms could reflect a frustration of his God-given propensity to seek truth in his life. With this commitment to contextualize all aspects of the treatment to Mr. Cunningham's larger spiritual frame of reference, the therapeutic bond strengthened, which ultimately helped him to commit to beginning PE in future sessions.

Normalizing trauma-related distress and possible spiritual struggles can also be a critical part of building the therapeutic alliance with clients such as Mr. Cunningham (for a phase-based model of working with spiritual struggles, see Murray-Swank & Murray-Swank, 2012, 2013). When considering the meaning-making process, posttraumatic symptomatology can be adaptive insofar as the client is motivated to seek a deeper and more satisfying resolution of the problems. Most clients implicitly recognize that their current appraisals and global meanings are no longer adequate. However, they may also be struggling with self-criticism and view any maladaptive appraisals as absolute truisms rather than possibilities that could be revised in treatment. In these instances, offering gentle reframes that challenge and affirm the adaptive nature of problematic behavior or situations can reduce shame-inducing cognitions that limit motivation for meaning-based processing.

Instilling hope and developing a spirit of curiosity for new meanings can also enhance clients' willingness to engage in the tasks of treatment. In so doing, as clients gain emotional distance from appraisals about the trauma or negative changes in global meaning, they will be better equipped to discern how their attempts at coping conflict with previous sources of meaning in life.

Research has also suggested that people who attempt to make meaning of potential traumas can experience greater levels of distress in the short term than those who have already made meaning or who did not feel compelled to search for meaning in the first place (e.g., C. G. Davis, Wortman, Lehman, & Silver, 2000). These types of findings could be in part attributable to a pattern of maladaptive rumination about trauma (e.g., intrusive thoughts and imagery in PTSD) that often precedes deliberate attempts to introspect and make meaning of the experience. In cases in which clients have not yet begun to transition out of maladaptive rumination, clinicians might prioritize therapeutic tasks that promote safety in their thoughts, emotions, and behaviors. In addition, although both religious and nonreligious clients' functioning tends to improve as they begin to engage in adaptive meaning making, clients frequently have to be informed that they may experience a drop in functioning and greater distress during this early phase of treatment. Like the pain resulting from resetting a broken bone that healed improperly after many attempts to compensate for the injury, clients may experience a worsening of distress as they begin the process of addressing and healing violations of spiritual meaning.

When treating spiritually oriented clients, clinicians have to recognize that spirituality can similarly exacerbate distress in the short term in many cases. As discussed in Chapters 3 and 5, spirituality might promote adjustment through adaptive meaning making. However, when clients appraise a trauma as being a violation of deeply held spiritual beliefs and values (e.g., that there is a loving and benevolent God), they might have greater difficulties. For instance, although spirituality had a formative role in Mr. Cunningham's development of a coherent set of beliefs and values about himself, others, and God, the Iraqi family's deaths disrupted the foundations of his global meaning system. In keeping with the constellation of inappropriate guilt and shame that forms the heart of a moral injury (Litz, Gray, Bryant, & Adler, 2002), Mr. Cunningham was conflicted about his role in taking the lives of children who possibly had not yet heard the salvation account of Jesus Christ. In turn, he felt deserving of PTSD symptoms as his atonement for killing innocent persons and potentially sending children to hell. Hence, although spirituality played a powerful role in Mr. Cunningham's recovery over the later phases of treatment, his spiritual meaning system initially put Mr. Cunningham at risk of a range of posttraumatic symptomatology.

RESOLVING DISCREPANCIES IN MEANING

Once the foundations of a therapeutic alliance have been established, clinicians must begin to support traumatized clients in resolving discrepancies between aspects of situational and global meaning that contribute to PTSD and possible problems in the spiritual domain. Although clinicians have to transition into a more past-oriented approach to accomplish this aim, clients might benefit from an ongoing focus on current symptoms, situations, and events in conscious awareness rather than exclusively focusing on historical material from this point forward in the treatment. Traumatized clients can have serious difficulty regulating their emotions because of a lack of coping skills and the persistence of unsafe behaviors and relationships (Phase 1). Therefore, it is often imperative to regularly check in about self-care and affirm that they are regularly using the healthy coping strategies that had been discussed earlier in treatment. For example, as Mr. Cunningham began exposure exercises, the clinician still regularly inquired about his adherence to an SSRI medication and his success at practicing breathing retraining activities and other behavioral strategies for managing anxiety and depressive symptoms (e.g., maintaining regular exercise, sleeping, and eating routines). In this way, resolving his discrepancies between situational and global meaning entailed a variety of behavioral, cognitive, and emotional processes throughout the treatment process.

In shifting into a more past-oriented focus, helping clients develop a fuller and more cohesive account of the trauma can be a key part of the meaning-making process that precedes changes in global meaning. Traumatized clients can struggle to appreciate important contextual details as well as cognitive, emotional, and physical dimensions of their experience at the time of the trauma. Because global beliefs and values are more stable aspects of people's identities and lives that are not easily accessible via conscious awareness, they can be far more difficult to change. As such, before grappling with higher order issues related to global meaning that could be of a spiritual or existential nature, clinicians should initially identify situational meanings associated with discrepancies in meaning and incorporate tasks to flesh out the micronarrative of trauma in a careful and systematic manner. For example, rather than immediately processing Mr. Cunningham's self-appraisal about not being forgivable because of a perceived transgression of the seventh commandment, he was encouraged to repeatedly tell the story of the trauma using imaginal exposure exercises. In so doing, it became evident that he had gone to every length possible to spare the passengers' lives and ultimately gave the order to use heavy artillery out of his sense of duty and strong desire to protect his men rather than out of an intent to kill.

Whether spiritual or nonspiritual in nature, situational meanings can be complex and characterized by a variety of unstable dialectics. For example, clients might experience intense sadness and anxiety along with increasing moments of joy and gratitude, intimacy with others, and a sense of purpose over the course of treatment. As clients' posttraumatic symptomatology wanes, they can find themselves vacillating between a heightened awareness of a mismatch between their global meaning and how they have appraised the trauma to that point. In addition, clients frequently experience a strong pull to avoid thoughts and feelings related to such discrepancies, which may further complicate their ability to work through discrepancies in meaning.

Confronting these dialectics can be quite distressing, and clients may struggle not to oversimplify the trauma or exclusively focus on one pole at a time (e.g., God is cruel and cannot be trusted vs. God is all powerful and will always protect people). Rather than allowing clients to ruminate or engage in an unproductive cycle of repetition and avoidance, therapists have to encourage them to tolerate ambiguity and honor both poles of their dialectics. For example, as Mr. Cunningham grew increasingly dissatisfied with his trauma-related appraisals and how he had overaccommodated his spiritual meaning system since returning from the war, he was encouraged to commit to a period of pseudo-agnosticism in which he suspended attempts to resolve prematurely discrepancies in spiritual meaning without considering multiple perspectives on his experience.

Beyond attending to these more cognitive elements of situational and global meaning, attending to the emotional system is an indispensable part of re-storying the trauma as well. Following careful assessment and normalizing conflict and strain in the spiritual domain, Murray-Swank and Murray-Swank (2012, 2013) suggested that arousal and expression of trauma-related emotions are necessary for resolving discrepancies in spiritual meaning. Similarly, when considering the emotional processing theory that guides PE, Foa and Kozak (1986) suggested two essential conditions for revising a maladaptive fear structure: (a) internalized representations of feared stimuli (e.g., a possible insurgent for Mr. Cunningham), feared responses (e.g., increased heart rate), and meanings associated with these stimuli and responses must be activated in the context of therapeutic tasks and (b) new information in the trauma memory that challenges the content entrenched within the fear structure must become more accessible in conscious awareness and incorporated into the client's situational meaning.

From an emotional processing perspective, the conditioning of fear that underlies many cases of PTSD may then be characterized by a reinforcing interplay between distressing levels of physiological arousal and various strategies of behavioral avoidance. As Mr. Cunningham's case illustrates, Foa and colleagues' (2007) model of PTSD also highlights the potential importance of meanings related to clients' appraisals of how they behaved during the traumatic event, how they make sense of their posttraumatic symptoms, and interpersonal experiences related to the trauma. Hence, as discussed in Chapter 4, a deliberate and systematic revisiting of distressing emotions associated with the trauma memory is necessary for clients to modify trauma-related meanings and alleviate their posttraumatic symptomatology.

From an emotion-focused therapy (EFT) perspective (L. S. Greenberg, 2015; Paivio & Pascual-Leone, 2010), meaning making is similarly viewed as a dialectical process between affect and cognition in which clients must come into live contact with warded off emotions to accept and process them in treatment. In recognizing and expressing painful emotions, EFT suggests that clients will be able to reflect in more depth on their experience and develop fuller narratives about themselves and the trauma. From an EFT perspective, clients will, therefore, paradoxically not be able to "leave" their traumatic past until they have more fully "arrived" at the various emotions and cognitions related to different aspects of the trauma (L. S. Greenberg, 2015; Paivio & Pascual-Leone, 2010).

In keeping with general notions of exposure, clinicians using EFT have to maintain a patient and respectful posture as they challenge avoidance by implementing tasks that will support clients in approaching and tolerating uncomfortable emotions. In contrast with well-intentioned family and friends who may encourage clients to move on and get over the trauma, clinicians have to conversely follow a "pain compass," empathically supporting clients to move deeper "into" rather than "on from" emotions and cognitions associated with the traumatic narrative and possible violations in spiritual meaning. EFT also aims to change emotion with a process that alters clients' maladaptive emotional states by activating more adaptive ones in treatment sessions (e.g., transforming core shame with sadness; L. S. Greenberg, 2015).

Moving into painful meanings about his trauma was an indispensable part of resolving Mr. Cunningham's discrepancies. Mr. Cunningham participated in PE over a 4-month period in which he engaged in multiple lines of in vivo interventions that were negotiated with his spiritual values in mind. For example, many of the exercises focused on overcoming fear in Mr. Cunningham's family relationships (e.g., no longer carrying a gun around his home, participating in recreational activities with his wife and children) and gradually reengaging in his church community (e.g., reaching out to a former spiritual mentor, attending a weekly Bible study). In addition, Mr. Cunningham revisited the incident with the Iraqi family in depth via exposure exercises. In so doing, he recollected previously nonaccessible contextual details and identified a diversity of maladaptive emotions and cognitions for processing in session. For instance, Mr. Cunningham felt fearful about the uncertain intentions of the driver of the car at the start of the trauma narrative. However, after engaging in several imaginal exposures, it was evident that the most distressing part of the memory occurred after the threat was minimized. That is, the "hot spot" that factored most prominently in Mr. Cunningham's symptomatology at the time of treatment was when he inspected the vehicle and first discovered the family's remains.

Consistent with changes in the diagnostic criteria for PTSD (American Psychiatric Association, 2013), there is increasing consensus that trauma can entail a far more diverse array of stressors and emotions than has been appreciated historically (Litz et al., 2009). Consistent with fear conditioning models that have informed conceptualizations of PTSD, a recent mixed methods investigation by N. R. Stein et al. (2012) with 122 active duty personnel seeking treatment for PTSD found that many index traumas that were the focus of exposure interventions pertained to war-zone stressors that threatened injury or death for themselves (30%) or others (40%). However, in light of the other kinds of traumas that military personnel and other trauma-exposed groups might confront, N. R. Stein and colleagues also found that many of these individuals identified morally injurious experiences as being the most traumatic (defined as witnessing or being the victim of an act that violates one's moral beliefs and values [22%] or committing one of these acts themselves [12%]). When compared with life-threatening experiences, these latter types of traumas were also associated with distinct posttraumatic responses at the time of the study (e.g., humiliation, sadness, psychic numbness).

The reciprocal meaning-making model assumes that different therapeutic approaches will be more efficacious for resolving discrepancies in meaning associated with these varying types of posttraumatic emotions. Particularly in cases when core dimensions of spiritual meaning have been violated, clinicians may have to implement therapeutic tasks to address guilt and grave shame along with possible anxiety and fear-based symptomatology. In keeping with recent attempts to augment evidence-based practices for different types of military traumas (e.g., M. J. Gray et al., 2012; Steenkamp et al., 2011), Mr. Cunningham benefitted from incorporating EFT-based imaginal dialogues in the later stages of exposure exercises. That is, through several unfinished business dialogues with the oldest child, Mr. Cunningham was able to express a range of emotions about having to fire on the vehicle and asked the young girl for forgiveness.

At another point in one of these exercises, Mr. Cunningham also shared concerns about how the girl was faring in the afterlife. When instructed to speak from the child's position in the dialogue, Mr. Cunningham was forced to step outside his appraised meanings and surprisingly found himself acknowledging a sense of acceptance about the tragic and seemingly random nature of their encounter. Speaking from his imagined representation of the girl, arguably the climax in treatment occurred when Mr. Cunningham was able to move beyond maladaptive emotions to connect with deep sadness about his role in the deaths. In so doing, he also gained the capacity to draw on other teachings from his tradition about God's love and justice and came to perceive that the girl was likely in heaven and no longer suffering in any way—an image that transformed his persistent preoccupation with the bloody and mutilated body that had formed the heart of his re-experiencing symptomatology since returning home from the war.

CREATING NEW MEANINGS

Research has suggested that resolving discrepancies in meaning is associated with the amelioration of PTSD and other forms of symptomatology (e.g., Hembree & Foa, 2000). However, a reciprocal meaning-making model is not exclusively concerned with reducing distress. Rather, successful meaning making ultimately entails a process of developing a self-narrative that brings situational and global meaning together in a way that creates a fuller sense of purpose and more hopeful view of the future. Such a revised self-narrative may not only be linked with decreased symptomatology but also support clients' well-being and ability to identify areas of positive change that will bolster their resources for handling future stressors in an adaptive manner (see Chapter 11). Hence, as clients develop the capacity for resilience in their global meaning system, a reciprocal meaning-making model would predict that they will find themselves constructing more adaptive appraisals and positively coping with traumas that may occur in the future.

As the meaning-making process proceeds in treatment, therapists might, therefore, have to affirm perceptions of growth and be prepared to help clients to maintain a positive developmental trajectory over future chapters in their lives. Particularly with accommodative approaches to meaning making, clinicians have to find ways to help clients identify or develop growth-supporting beliefs and values that better align with changes in global meaning. However, as we highlighted in Chapter 5, some clients will not perceive growth in the meaning-making process, and others can be ambivalent about the notion that struggling with their trauma has paradoxically benefitted them. As such, even as clients take steps to restore global meaning and reconnect with others, it is best for clinicians not to shift into an explicit focus on promoting a subjective sense of purpose in life or other dimensions of perceived growth. Rather, as clients progress in the meaning-making process, therapists should reinforce therapeutic gains and implement tasks to facilitate a more authentic engagement in meaningful activities and relationships.

From a procedural standpoint, at this point in treatment clinicians may have to incorporate introspective tasks that resolve distress associated with discrepancies in meaning and possibly incorporate spirituality into global meaning. However, it may be necessary to support clients in responding to their distress through attempts at behavioral action. For example, Mr. Cunningham's severe posttraumatic symptomatology had impaired his ability to maintain consistent employment for several years, and his family was struggling financially. However, given his reputation and esteem in the region, Mr. Cunningham had an open invitation from the head pastor at his former church to return to work, and he had several other ministry-related job possibilities at other churches. As Mr. Cunningham recovered from PTSD and opened himself to the possibility of being forgiven, he grappled with his sense of vocation and what it would now mean for him to serve in a ministry-related position. Beyond in-session introspective tasks that supported Mr. Cunningham's work through his existential crisis, however, a crucial part of treatment entailed finding meaning through behavioral action outside of sessions.

With the encouragement of the therapist, Mr. Cunningham overcame his avoidance and reached out to his former employer for support in this process of vocational discernment. Mr. Cunningham viewed this man as a spiritual mentor who possessed wisdom and still cared about him greatly. Following coaching from the clinician, he was able to share the "newspaper version" of his trauma with the Iraqi family and disclosed his struggles with faith since returning from the war. In contrast to his fear of being chastised and rejected, Mr. Cunningham was met with compassion and admiration from his former employer. This acceptance helped him gradually repair other friendships and reintegrate into his spiritual community.

In all these ways, therapists working from the reciprocal meaning-making model can integrate aspects of cognitive, behavioral, and humanistic–existential approaches to support clients in gaining a fuller sense of purpose in life. For example, although cognitive–behavioral interventions emphasize the importance of beliefs and values, the reciprocal meaning-making model additionally considers the vital role of goals in structuring self-narratives and orienting clients to future chapters of their lives. As clients' stories become less contaminated and shaped by the micronarratives of their traumas, they may have to develop revised life goals and directions for valued living that better align with their revised global meaning system. In this vein, despite several supportive conversations with his former supervisor and mentor, Mr. Cunningham was still ambivalent about transitioning into a leadership position in the church. Hence, rather than simply reinserting Mr. Cunningham into his former job, the two men developed a more administratively oriented position that consisted of behind-the-scenes duties that had been neglected since Mr. Cunningham's war-zone service.

The reciprocal meaning-making model is also broader than existential perspectives that emphasize ultimate concerns or higher order meanings related to the human predicament (e.g., inevitability of death, freedom, meaninglessness; Yalom, 1980). As clients resolve discrepancies in meaning, it is not uncommon for a window of heightened existential awareness to emerge in which they grapple with ultimate concerns that assume a religious or spiritual form. In such cases, clients may feel conflicted about which tenets of their faith to accept and which appear to be wrong or misplaced on the basis of meanings they have made of their traumas over the course of treatment. This intrapersonal struggle with spirituality was exemplified in Mr. Cunningham's process of constructing alternate possibilities for the Iraqi girl's salvation that more closely aligned with his interpretation of scripture and beliefs about God's love and justice.

Murray-Swank and Murray-Swank (2012) also emphasized the helpfulness of creating spiritual meaning in these later stages of addressing spiritual struggles. In many cases, clients may opt to reject or revise religious beliefs that had once provided a sense of coherence and predictability. In other cases, clients might return to embrace certain tenets or doctrines that they had rejected amid their struggles to recover from posttraumatic symptoms. However, considering the need for cognitive flexibility and honoring both poles in resolving dialectics in meaning, clinicians should also appreciate the possibility that many clients represent a combination of these two options in creating new meaning.

Although Mr. Cunningham abandoned a notion of an unjust deity who would banish innocent children to eternal damnation, he also found himself embracing other teachings about God's character that he had rejected or not considered as fully since his war-zone service (e.g., merciful, loving, faithful). In keeping with the importance of working within the client's faith language, therapists may have to encourage clients to educate themselves about their tradition and seek the help of clergy or other religious professionals in this regard. We discuss considerations related to collaborating with pastoral professions in more detail in Chapter 12.

Compared with other models, the reciprocal meaning-making model emphasizes these higher order, existential concerns along with mundane, lower order aspects of global meaning that pertain to one's day-to-day life in concrete ways (e.g., work, parenting, health, leisure). Hence, as Mr. Cunningham gradually established a more satisfying spiritual life, he developed an intrinsic sense of motivation and was encouraged by his therapist to consider valued directions for living in his life roles at the time (e.g., husband, father, friend, pastor). For instance, beyond reaching out to his former employer and returning to work with a revised job description, Mr. Cunningham took a number of concrete steps to reestablish intimacy and connection with his wife (e.g., going for long walks each morning, scheduling a weekly date night). In addition, as in Mr. Denton's case in Chapter 4, Mr. Cunningham's wife participated in conversations at a later point in treatment for the purpose of improving the couple's communication, providing her with psychoeducation about trauma and discussing the impact of Mr. Cunningham's posttraumatic symptomatology on their relationship.

Although many of the same general therapeutic tasks were incorporated with Mr. Denton to promote a restoration of global meaning (e.g., PE), the success of Mr. Cunningham's treatment hinged on the clinician's willingness to incorporate his religious faith in the treatment. That is, as with many traumatized persons, Mr. Denton did not affiliate with a particular religious tradition, and his treatment culminated in reestablishing several traditional secular sources of meaning (e.g., focusing on generativity with children and grandchildren). In contrast, for a subjective sense of purpose to emerge, Mr. Cunningham had to resolve several types of spiritual struggles and internalize the resulting changes in spirituality back into global meaning. Hence, as he regained a sense of spiritual meaning and reconnected with God, he asked to devote the final treatment session to officiating a funeral service for the Iraqi girl. In so doing, Mr. Cunningham developed a brief liturgy and preached a eulogy for his therapist that affirmed the tragedy but also honored the girl's short life. In reflecting on being back in a pastoral role, Mr. Cunningham believed that this final therapeutic task was somehow necessary to "make things right" and to provide a sense of closure regarding this painful chapter of his life story.

CONCLUSION

This chapter has discussed several treatment issues from the perspective of the reciprocal meaning-making model. Although meaning making has captured the interest of researchers and scholars, there is little empirical evidence explicitly examining the role of incorporating spirituality into the therapeutic alliance or identifying how clinicians may support traumatized clients to resolve their discrepancies and create new meaning in life in psychotherapy. Rather, research has nearly exclusively focused on naturally occurring changes in meaning rather than developing or identifying interventions that might promote adaptive accommodations of spiritual meaning and changes that might lead to more satisfying global beliefs, values, and goals. When considering treatment issues from a reciprocal perspective, the association between meaning making and spirituality can also only be inferred at this point. Hence, the ideas presented in this chapter regarding how meaning making occurs and/or clinical strategies for resolving spiritual struggles are quite speculative. Moreover, although Chapter 10 outlines several promising intervention models for explicitly addressing spiritual concerns, there is also limited research on the value of addressing spirituality in an implicit manner (as partly exemplified in Mr. Cunningham's case). Given the salient role of spirituality in the inner life of many clients, we hope that researchers fill these important gaps in the empirical literature in coming years.

Drawing on the work of several scholars (e.g., Herman, 1992; van der Kolk, MacFarlane, & van der Hart, 1996), Chapter 4 outlined a phased-based model of restoring global meaning. Importantly, treatment issues that would be predicted by the reciprocal meaning-making model may align with these phases of recovery. For example, when clients are struggling to achieve emotional or physical safety, clinicians have to be responsive by focusing on stabilization and trust both within and outside the therapeutic relationship (Phase 1). As clinicians build the alliance in a manner that may begin to incorporate spirituality in this first phase, clients will stand on firmer ground for resolving discrepancies in meaning via the processing of the trauma memory (Phase 2). However, many clients will be too preoccupied with their traumatic past to address aims of Phase 3 until they have developed an adequate bond with the clinician and engaged in the necessary therapeutic tasks to alleviate their posttraumatic symptoms. Hence, although clinicians should maintain a respectful client-centered posture and be open to the emergence of a subjective sense of purpose throughout the course of treatment, many clients might not be prepared to pursue new meaning in life until they have satisfactorily healed the manner in which they are carrying their past in memory. In Chapter 9, we discuss how to address the past in more depth in treatment after considering, in Chapter 8, the role of the therapist in promoting meaning making from a reciprocal perspective.

8

THE THERAPIST'S PLACE IN THE RECIPROCAL MEANING-MAKING MODEL

Therapists are an inherent and essential part of a client's context and may, simply by being who they are, help clients frame themselves and their worlds. Their personal style of listening can help clients challenge maladaptive assumptions about their relationships with family, friends, and God. Further, they can actively help trauma survivors mobilize spiritual resources, draw on strengths, and think through spiritual issues in ways that reduce distress and help them move forward in positive ways. Therapists can, in turn, be affected by their work with clients. This chapter explores these transactional issues between therapist, client, and God; resulting changes in meaning experienced by both therapist and client; and how they can influence treatment.

http://dx.doi.org/10.1037/15961-008
Trauma, Meaning, and Spirituality: Translating Research Into Clinical Practice, by C. L. Park, J. M. Currier, J. I. Harris, and J. M. Slattery

CASE EXAMPLE: LYNDA JACCOBY AND SHEILA BROWNE

Dr. Lynda Jaccoby's personal journey of realizing her identity as a lesbian and learning how to manage being a member of an oppressed group was an important part of her decision to become a psychologist. She hoped to pursue research and clinical work to help others cope with similar oppression. Part of that journey included rejecting many of the Catholic beliefs with which she had been raised, especially the Catholic Church's beliefs about homosexuality. Replacing those beliefs with a Taoist approach that respects the life force in nature and the love that comes from that life force had helped her achieve a level of comfort with herself and her relationships, and ultimately helped her become healthy enough to become successful in her work as a psychologist. Because working with oppressed groups was important to her, she took a job as a psychologist working in a medical practice specializing in infectious diseases. Her caseload was largely made up of people learning to live with HIV.

When referred for counseling, Sheila Browne was distressed. Ms. Browne was a devout Catholic who did not use birth control, and she saw no reason to protect herself from sexually transmitted diseases in the context of what she thought was a good Catholic marriage. She contracted HIV, having assumed that her husband was monogamous. She struggled with her husband's betrayal, her anger and desire to dissolve her relationship with him, and the Catholic Church's beliefs about divorce. Dr. Jaccoby assured Ms. Browne that counseling could help her make the difficult decisions she faced and could provide her with support during a trying time.

Their first session seemed to go well. Ms. Browne received much-needed validation and support and discussed the goals she wanted to address in counseling. She scheduled a second session but did not show for her appointment. Dr. Jaccoby called several times without reaching her. Ms. Browne was unwilling to schedule another appointment when Dr. Jaccoby finally succeeded in connecting with her.

> *Dr. Jaccoby:*   Sheila, I'd like to learn more about why you decided to leave counseling. I'm wondering if there is something I could have done differently to be more helpful.
>
> *Ms. Browne:*   I just felt that you did not like me.
>
> *Dr. Jaccoby:*   Then I do need to learn more about this. Can you tell me what happened?
>
> *Ms. Browne:*   I was saying how I felt that this was not fair—I don't use IV drugs, I'm not gay, I don't have sex outside my marriage, I've done nothing to deserve to get HIV. And then you said how maybe I harshly judge people who have HIV if I think we deserve this illness.

Trauma survivors' relationships help create and inform their situational meaning following trauma, influencing whether they perceive themselves as damaged or resilient, supported or isolated, accepted or shameful. However, survivors are not just passive recipients of others' responses but also active contributors to their meaning-making process. As described next, survivors may misperceive even positive responses, assimilating their perceptions of others' actions into the meanings and explanations they have drawn for the trauma, human involvement, and God's role.

Support From Other People

Many clients experience a variety of interpersonal emotions following trauma, including feelings of guilt, shame, blame, and betrayal. These feelings do not derive solely from the nature of their relationships with the offender but also from those with their family, friends, and communities (see Figure 8.1). When trauma survivors experience support and positive responses from friends and family—and the offending party receives more negative responses—they are more able to challenge situational attributions

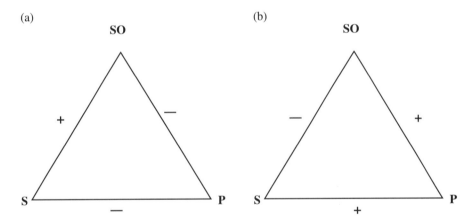

Figure 8.1. Relationship between survivor (S), perpetrator (P), and significant others (SO), which may include a higher power. A positive relationship with significant others and a negative one with the perpetrator is predictive of more positive outcomes (a). However, perceptions of negative appraisals and responses from significant others and a positive relationship with the perpetrator, as with abuse by a spiritual guide, is predictive of more negative outcomes (b). From *Just Before Dawn: Trauma Assessment And Treatment Of Sexual Victimization* (pp. 194–197), by J. Hindman, 1989, Alexandria, VA: Alexandria Associates. Copyright 1989 by Alexandria Associates. Adapted with permission.

that might otherwise lead to feelings of self-blame, shame, guilt, and betrayal and draw a positive situational meaning (see Figure 8.1a; Hindman, 1989; Worthington, Davis, et al., 2013).

However, many people lose support following trauma and, when they do, experience poorer outcomes (see Figure 8.1b; Brewin, Andrews, & Valentine, 2000; Hindman, 1989; Littleton, Axsom, & Grills-Taquechel, 2009). These losses can be clearly communicated (e.g., "What did you do to cause this?") or inferred (e.g., a man might conclude that he was "bad" when family and friends avoided him—even though he was the person who had initiated the relationship disruption). Losses of support can also be inferred from cultural messages. For example, in the United States, most people have been exposed to messages suggesting that bad things happen to bad people (Lerner & Miller, 1978). Losses may also be inferred from the difficulties that friends and family members have in discussing the trauma—and their outright avoidance of such discussions. As a result, trauma survivors may incorporate negative messages into their situational meaning and over-emphasize them (e.g., "I was hurt because I am bad and deserved it"), even though others had responded supportively. They may heavily weight negative cultural messages (the left side of Figure 8.1b) while concluding that the culture, their family and friends, or a higher power let offending parties off the hook (the right side of Figure 8.1b). Perceived support influences the meaning survivors make of trauma.

Perceptions of social support, however, depend on perceived safety. In a study of Chinese earthquake survivors, those with low levels of perceived safety reported more re-experiencing and hyperarousal symptoms than did survivors with greater perceived safety, regardless of the amount of social support they actually received (Cai, Ding, Tang, Wu, & Yang, 2014). Not feeling safe seemed to compromise survivors' ability to recognize and access social support. Cai and colleagues (2014) suggested that people who did not feel safe tended to perceive the support they received through their more negative global meaning: as pity or even as hostility.

As described in Chapter 5, therapists can help survivors reestablish a sense of safety. Creating such a sense of safety might include reducing risky behaviors, letting go of problematic relationships and developing more supportive ones, using adaptive coping strategies, and engaging in regular self-care. Reestablishing safety should also include focusing on the quality of the therapeutic relationship because, by extension from Cai et al. (2014), until safety is reestablished, trauma survivors may misperceive their therapists' actions through the lens provided by the global and situational meanings that they have drawn. Conversely, once survivors feel safe, they may be able to more accurately perceive their therapists' intentions and actions and collaborate more effectively with them.

Ms. Browne, for example, felt betrayed by her husband; blamed by her mother, who suggested that she had brought their marital problems on herself; and ashamed when out in public because she believed that her children's friends' parents perceived her as damaged and avoided her (although few, in fact, knew about either her husband's infidelity or her HIV status). She had previously perceived the world as a safe and accepting place, where people got what they deserved, but she now vacillated between believing that the world was just (and she bad) and that the world was unfair (and she good). With this frame of others' actions, she tended to reject even those acts with positive intents, including Dr. Jaccoby's reframe.

Relationship With Higher Power

Many people experience relationships with their higher power as similar to their relationships with other people. They report feelings of closeness or distance, communicate with their higher power, often imagine their higher power with human features, and feel the same kinds of emotions toward that higher power that they might have toward another human (Wood et al., 2010). People's beliefs that their higher power will protect them in times of danger or difficulty are also similar to those of a child's expectations of parents (Hill & Pargament, 2003). Thus, as discussed in Chapter 3, survivors may experience violations of global meaning (e.g., "God should protect me but didn't"), which can be experienced as a profound and devastating breach of trust (S. Smith, 2004; Wilson & Moran, 1998). They may attempt to resolve these discrepancies (e.g., "God is not all good," "I am not good nor worth protecting"), although maladaptive accommodations are problematic.

Not only are people's relationships with their higher power are similar to their feelings about other attachment figures in their lives but also, in their attempts to create consistency in their perceptions of the world, their relationships with that higher power may, in fact, be derived from those other relationships (e.g., people who perceived their parents as cruel were more likely to perceive God as cruel; Exline, Homolka, & Grubbs, 2013). People's relationships with their higher power might also be a reflection of their relationships with self and others (Exline, Park, Smyth, & Carey, 2011). That is, to the degree that survivors see themselves as unworthy, they might also expect rejection from their higher power. Further, the more securely attached they are to God, the more likely they will respond beneficently toward others (Worthington, Davis, et al., 2013).

Anger toward God is more common when people hold God responsible for negative events and when they have difficulty finding meaning following those events (Exline et al., 2011). Whereas anger toward God is common, anger often coexists with more positive emotions, although it is reported at lower levels. Ms. Browne, for example, expected rejection from God and, in later sessions, reported that she tended to distance herself from God, particularly when she wanted to share her fears and concerns, but easily turned to God with positive experiences. She believed God could only accept the good things she offered.

However, people with limited attachment resources or who have experienced major losses in their attachment networks may still maintain a relationship with their higher power and perceive it as an important resource (Keefer, Landau, & Sullivan, 2014). For example, a study of college students found that those with weak or anxious parental attachments still often reported close, secure attachments to their higher power (Kimball, Boyatzis, Cook, Leonard, & Flanagan, 2013). Such attachments might serve a corrective or reparative role, compensating for poor parental attachments. In one study, for example, people with little support from their community described closer relationships with their higher power (Granqvist & Hagekull, 1999). Similarly, people who have had a recent significant death or loss in their social network may experience compensation for their loss by drawing on their relationship with a higher power for support and intimacy (S. L. Brown, Nesse, House, & Utz, 2004).

Transference in Therapy

As noted earlier in this chapter, a number of authors have proposed triangular models to describe the relationships among the victim, offending parties, and others in their lives and how these affect the victim's perception of themselves and the event (D. E. Davis et al., 2014; Hindman, 1989; Worthington, Davis, et al., 2013; see Figure 8.1). Rejection by important others can cause survivors to create a global meaning in which they perceive themselves as unworthy and unacceptable (see Figure 8.1b). Acceptance and understanding from others, however, can lead to more positive meanings, including self-acceptance and self-empathy (see Figure 8.1a).

Therapists should be aware that people who have experienced trauma may believe that their higher power has rejected them, and they may experience damage to their global meaning—perhaps moving from a benign expectation of support to a more damaging belief that their higher power has turned away from them. When clients are experiencing spiritual struggle and believe that their higher power has abandoned them, they may create consistency in their global meaning by also expecting and believing that their therapist will reject them. Their therapists can work with this transference of feelings—from their higher power to their therapist—by recognizing and identifying it, then gently challenging it.

The Therapist as Proxy in the Healing Process

Although clients may experience negative transference toward their therapists, therapists can also be a healing part of a survivor's context post-trauma. Therapists can serve as proxies for families, friends, community, and God, challenging misperceptions about the client's place in these relationships. In that complex and sometimes difficult role, therapists can help clients generalize therapeutic feelings of safety, acceptance, and respect to the rest of their world (Exline et al., 2011). They can provide a corrective emotional experience and help survivors draw new meanings about the trauma, their higher power's involvement and response, and themselves.

Although Dr. Jaccoby's reframe may have been premature, it is likely that Ms. Browne's response to this reframe also reflected her self-perceptions and self-judgments. Ms. Browne appeared to have entered therapy believing that life is unfair, that God had abandoned her, and that others would also believe that she is worthless. As a result, her reaction toward Dr. Jaccoby's reframe appeared transferential: She expected that Dr. Jaccoby would react toward her as she believed the other important people in their life—her husband, family and friends, and God—had done. In calling Ms. Browne after she left therapy, Dr. Jaccoby began to challenge Ms. Browne's feelings of worthlessness.

THE THERAPIST'S ROLE IN THE THERAPEUTIC RELATIONSHIP

Therapists and Spirituality

As we discussed in Chapter 1 and will further discuss in Chapter 12, therapists, perhaps particularly psychologists, can have difficulties working with spiritual issues. They are less likely than the general public to report that they believe in God, attend religious services, or feel that religion is important in their lives (Delaney, Miller, & Bisonó, 2007; P. Norris & Inglehart, 2004; Pew Research Center, 2002). They may report bias against religion without feelings of embarrassment—although they would not express equally negative attitudes about race, culture, or gender (Brawer, Handal, Fabricatore, Roberts, & Wajda-Johnston, 2002).

In one meta-analysis, 82% of therapists surveyed reported that they had rarely or never discussed spiritual issues in the course of their graduate training (Walker, Gorsuch, & Tan, 2004). As a result, clinicians may have difficulty knowing how to approach religion and spirituality well (Brawer et al., 2002; Hage, 2006; McNeil, Pavkov, Hecker, & Killmer, 2012; Vieten et al., 2013; Vogel, McMinn, Peterson, & Gathercoal, 2013; Walker, Gorsuch,

& Tan, 2004, 2005). In fact, as we discuss in Chapter 10, therapists may perceive a requirement for "a separation between church and state," which may complicate their willingness to address the spiritual components of trauma or help clients access spiritual resources during their work in secular settings.

Although psychologists are frequently less religious than the population as a whole—and less religious than other therapists—they are also unlikely to be secular in orientation: Most perceive religion to be beneficial to mental health (Bilgrave & Deluty, 1998; Delaney et al., 2007; Russell & Yarhouse, 2006). Further, graduate students may be more interested in finding ways of incorporating religion and spirituality in treatment than are their professors (Brawer et al., 2002). About a quarter of graduate programs reported addressing religion and spirituality in supervision and, since 1996, psychiatry residency programs have been required to address religious and spiritual issues in their formal training (Brawer et al., 2002; Russell & Yarhouse, 2006). Further, in one somewhat dated study, 72% of psychologists reported that their religious values at least moderately contributed to their practice (Bilgrave & Deluty, 1998). Given the increasing focus on spirituality as a multicultural issue, this number is likely even higher now.

As we further discuss in Chapter 12, trauma therapists should spend time reflecting on their spiritual or religious background and recognize how their upbringing and beliefs influence their attitudes, perceptions, and assumptions about both psychological well-being and psychopathology, as well as their identification of problems and choices of interventions (Vieten et al., 2013). Both positive and negative attitudes about religion and spirituality may blind therapists to, respectively, the more negative or positive aspects of religion and spirituality (Cummings, Ivan, Carson, Stanley, & Pargament, 2014; Vieten et al., 2013).

Most issues can be approached from multiple directions; these directions are partially guided by the therapist's metaphysical assumptions and moral judgments (Delaney et al., 2007). For example, a Hindi therapist with strong beliefs about karma may let those beliefs guide her interpretation of and response to her client's stories, whereas a Catholic therapist may focus more on the importance of reconciliation and forgiveness. Carefully considering one's assumptions about the nature of a problem and the goals of treatment can both help therapists maintain their intentionality during treatment and maximize the potential for meeting ethical goals of beneficence and nonmaleficence (Tjeltveit, 2006).

Working With More Religious Clients or Clients From Other Faiths

Many people report preferring a therapist with similar religious and spiritual views (Gallup & Bezilla, 1994), and some clients question whether a therapist from a different spiritual background can actually listen and understand their concerns. In some cases, this may be an accurate concern—just as it can be a concern when therapists and clients differ on other dimensions. More religious therapists may especially attend to the ways that trauma affects the sacred and take such observations into account when setting treatment goals. However, less religious therapists may overlook interactions between trauma and the sacred or fail to recognize the ways in which the sacred plays an important role in clients' lives (Cummings et al., 2014). Such therapists may overlook the ways that spirituality offers support, coping strategies, and a sense of meaning or, conversely, how it can create strife and prevent forgiveness.

Nonetheless, although therapists may prefer clients with similar religious beliefs and values, their effectiveness with religious clients does not appear to be closely related to their own religiousness (Cummings et al., 2014; Propst, Ostrom, Watkins, Dean, & Mashburn, 1992). In fact, one study found that less religious therapists worked more effectively with religious clients when they incorporated religious beliefs and values into treatment than did more religious therapists (Propst et al., 1992). However, religious therapists in this study were not more effective when they incorporated religious content in treatment. In fact, moderate levels of differences in religiosity predicted the best treatment outcomes. Perhaps some similarities in global meaning systems sensitize therapists to their clients and allow them to engage empathically, whereas moderate differences free therapists to explore alternate situational meanings. However, therapists whose global meaning systems are too similar to that of their clients may not have the breadth to accompany explorations of alternate perspectives and meanings.

Sheila Browne and her therapist came from different faith traditions. Ms. Browne may not have considered the importance of religion in her choice of a therapist, or she perhaps did not have a choice because of the dictates of her health care system. Some clients may consciously choose an outsider, who they believe will consider their faith more "objectively" or allow them to more openly express their anger with God. Others may choose therapists of racial, ethnic, or spiritual groups that they perceive as having greater status or privilege. Finally, clients operating at a postconventional level of spiritual development (Fowler, 1981) may choose a therapist on the basis of perceived expertise rather than on religious similarity (see Table 2.2).

Most discussions of multicultural expertise have focused on race; however, a number of writers (e.g., Lam & Sue, 2001; Slattery & Park, 2011a) have argued that clients have multiple identities—including race, ethnicity, sexual orientation, socioeconomic status, ability status, gender, and age, as well as religion and spirituality—that influence their worldview and interactions with the world. Spirituality is only one dimension that should be examined in work with religious and spiritual clients, yet it may be as important to understand and engage as other parts of a client's identity (Vieten et al., 2013; Yakushko, Davidson, & Williams, 2009). Ms. Browne may have chosen her therapist because of Dr. Jaccoby's expertise in working with people with HIV—without recognizing the ways that her depression stemmed from her anger toward God.

Multiple identities are often seen as separate rather than as intersecting forces within each individual, and the salience of some aspects of identity may only appear at some points and in some contexts (Yakushko et al., 2009). For example, two clients may both present with symptoms of trauma following the death of their only child in a traffic accident, yet therapists may usefully conceptualize them differently by these multiple identities. The child's and parent's ages, for example, may help therapists understand the meaning of this death, including its cause, whether it was an off-time event, and whether the parent has other children. Still, the client's secular and spiritual views about the meaning of that event (e.g., perceived randomness, low perceptions of control, falling out of favor with God, or the possibility of an afterlife) may provide a greater richness in understanding that client's reactions.

Expressing Empathy for Spiritual Clients

Given the potential for mismatch between therapist and client, spiritual clients with a history of trauma may enter therapy with two strikes against them. Like many people with a history of trauma, they may feel different and believe that their experiences place them outside that of the balance of the population. As religion is often a great divide between people, clients may believe that their (probably) more secular therapist will be unable to empathize with and help them. Even people with the same religious affiliation may hold different perspectives on the world and have differing values, however (Joshanloo, 2014a). Further, Western views of well-being may be different from values and perspectives held by followers of Eastern religions (Joshanloo, 2014b).

One way that such a client–therapist mismatch may manifest is that therapists may leap to conclusions and intervene overly rapidly. In addition, therapists with a poor understanding of spirituality in general, and a client's religion in particular, may misperceive or misdiagnose symptoms and presentation (Vieten et al., 2013). Instead, it is helpful for the therapist to listen, build understanding, and share that understanding from the client's perspective before attempting to intervene (Slattery & Park, 2011a). As we discussed in Chapter 6, a strong assessment can build this sort of empathy. Therapists may ask what role religion serves in their clients' lives. What role would this client want it to serve? What situational meanings have their clients drawn

about the trauma, who they are now, and whether they can recover and reconcile with God and their community? Further, they might question whether
their clients' conclusions are helpful and consistent with religious teachings.

Therapists and Trauma

Given that estimates of trauma exposure involve a large proportion of
the population (Breslau, 2002), we should expect that many therapists have
been trauma exposed. In fact, in studies of therapists specializing in treating trauma, 50% to 75% reported also being trauma survivors (Creamer &
Liddle, 2005; Jenkins & Baird, 2002; Way, VanDeusen, Martin, Applegate,
& Jandle, 2004).

Many therapists may have chosen their profession as part of their personal meaning-making process, using their history of trauma to help survivors
come to peace with their trauma experiences. This decision can be appropriate and adaptive because there are many instances of therapists and psychiatrists making major contributions to the field by addressing practice issues
relevant to their personal experiences of psychopathology (e.g., Carey, 2011).

However, our profession may also include people who have confronted
emotional pain that they were unable to resolve with their existing spiritual
meaning-making resources. Such therapists may especially experience challenges while doing trauma work. They may over-identify with clients or take
on the role of savior in the course of trauma work. They might find such work
triggering and discover themselves responding primarily to their own issues
and concerns rather than their clients' needs. Therapists should actively and
consistently engage in self-care to maintain a healthy sense of meaning and
purpose, strengthen their spiritual health, and function effectively on the job
and throughout the rest of their lives (Schure, Christopher, & Christopher,
2008). Although true for therapists with a personal trauma history, self-care
and ongoing meaning making are important for all trauma therapists, including
those without a trauma history.

Therapists' global meaning can affect the course of therapy. For example, therapists' values predict whether they will believe a client's trauma
narrative. One study found that therapists who endorse more sexist attitudes
and more myths about childhood sexual abuse are less likely to believe clients'
narratives about childhood sexual abuse (DeMarni Cromer & Freyd, 2009).
However, when therapists are aware of the cultural dynamics of social power
and oppression, they can facilitate adaptive and contextualized meaning
making of trauma narratives (L. Brown, 2008).

Many types of trauma are more likely to affect people with more
limited social power and resources, such as children, people with lower
socioeconomic status, women, people with disabilities, and other cultural

minorities (Presidential Task Force on Posttraumatic Stress Disorder and Trauma in Children and Adolescents, 2008). Therapists often report that it is difficult to work with such problems without it affecting their values and sense of meaning. This may be why social justice has emerged as an important value in social work and counseling psychology—it may provide that sense of meaning and purpose that enables therapists to continue to do their work and do it well (Hayes, Pistorello, & Levin, 2012; National Association of Social Workers [NASW], 2013).

TRAUMA WORK'S IMPACT ON MEANING

Value changes associated with making meaning following trauma can take many forms and may be indications of growth, stress, or both (L. G. Calhoun, Cann, Tedeschi, & McMillan, 2000). As a culture, Americans responded to the collective trauma of the 9/11 terrorist attacks, for example, with an increased value on social order (Janoff-Bulman & Sheikh, 2006), whereas individual survivors and therapists from a range of disciplines appear to have moved in the opposite direction, by defining disciplinary ethics, research programs, and manualized interventions with clear values on social justice (e.g., Hayes et al., 2012; Kosutic & McDowell, 2008; National Association of Social Workers, 2013; Neacsiu, Ward-Ciesielski, & Linehan, 2012).

Therapists doing trauma work must remain aware of how their sense of meaning and their spiritual lives will inform and also be transformed, strengthened, or damaged by this work. In particular, therapists should be sensitive to issues of countertransference, vicarious traumatization, and burn-out, which may be especially raised by trauma work (Harrison & Westwood, 2009; Pearlman & Saakvitne, 1995; Saakvitne, 2002; Sabin-Farrell & Turpin, 2003). These factors may interfere with therapists' abilities to maintain the necessary sense of meaning and purpose that allow them to remain hopeful and effective during trauma work.

Countertransference

Therapists may experience a range of feelings in response to their work with trauma survivors, both those that have the ability to inform the thera-peutic work (countertransference) and those that interfere with the balance of the therapist's life (vicarious trauma). *Countertransference* includes the therapist's feelings, thoughts, and physical reactions to work in therapy, as well as conscious and unconscious defenses to distress and conflict among those feelings, thoughts, and physical reactions (Pearlman & Saakvitne, 1995). Therapists working with survivors of spiritual abuse, for example, report countertransferential feelings such as anger, outrage, and urges to justify one's higher power (Gubi & Jacobs, 2009).

Therapists' reactions to clients and their traumatic material are important sources of clinical data (Shubs, 2008). At the same time, many therapists may find it emotionally painful to stay empathically engaged with traumatic material; thus, many respond with defensive efforts to manage empathic pain, including avoidance and overidentification. Therapists may also have countertransferential responses to clients' religious identifications. When therapists are unable to recognize their own reactions and defenses, they can lose their effectiveness in therapy.

Dr. Jaccoby believed that she was providing Ms. Browne with a therapeutic reframe to help her think differently about her diagnosis. Under other circumstances, she may have been correct; however, with some reflection, she realized that she had expected to hear judgments about LGBT people from her devoutly Catholic client. Without realizing it, she had proactively defended herself—at a point in therapy when her client needed validation rather than challenge. Hers was probably a countertransferential reaction, reflecting her belief that a religious client such as Ms. Browne would reject her (as her family had done). It may have been helpful if Dr. Jaccoby had had a greater understanding of her own spiritual background and how this might influence her work with clients such as Ms. Browne (Vieten et al., 2013).

The bidirectionality of this interaction—including both clients' transferential and therapists' countertransferential responses—makes work with religious clients as difficult as work with nonreligious clients. Both nonreligious and religious clients may enter treatment with global meanings that lead them to expect rejection, criticism, and abandonment. When therapists are unable to manage their own feelings well, however, the therapeutic relationship can become judgmental, critical, unaccepting, and debate-filled, reinforcing maladaptive global beliefs and self-perceptions (Briere & Scott, 2006; see Figure 8.1). Given these considerations, therapy should be considered systemically, paying attention to the global meaning systems and interactional styles of client, therapist, offender(s), and other members of the client's world.

Vicarious Trauma

Vicarious trauma differs from countertransference in that it is a set of long-term, cumulative, and transformative changes in the therapist's global meaning system and behavior in relating to others that extend outside the therapy room. Vicarious trauma has also been called *secondary traumatic stress* and *compassion fatigue* (Way et al., 2004). Symptoms of vicarious trauma include altered cognitive schema, intrusive thoughts and imagery, avoidance, hypervigilance, decreased sense of personal safety, reduced self-esteem, cynicism, depression, and substance abuse (Way et al., 2004). Therapists with high levels of vicarious trauma are more likely to report poorer job satisfaction (Bride & Kintzle, 2011).

Early researchers of vicarious trauma hypothesized that therapists with a personal trauma history would be at greater risk of vicarious trauma because they were expected to be triggered by their work, to have more difficulty coping effectively, and to have more difficulty holding a positive sense of meaning. Findings in this area have been mixed (Creamer & Liddle, 2005; Jenkins & Baird, 2002; Pearlman & Mac Ian, 1995; Schauben & Frazier, 1995; Way et al., 2004). Across studies, however, it is clear that therapists who are at greatest risk are younger and less experienced, have more trauma survivors on their caseloads, and have had less education about trauma (Creamer & Liddle, 2005; Jenkins & Baird, 2002; Schauben & Frazier, 1995; Trippany, White Kress, & Wilcoxon, 2004; Way et al., 2004).

Studies of coping strategies used by successful trauma therapists are dominated by qualitative studies (Bober & Regehr, 2006; Harrison & Westwood, 2009; Killian, 2008; Trippany et al., 2004; Way et al., 2004). These therapists are more likely to use social support (especially peer support and peer supervision), self-awareness, cognitive complexity, deliberate optimism, and self-care across many domains of experience. They focus on maintaining appropriate boundaries with work, practicing empathy, finding ways to enhance professional satisfaction, engaging in ongoing meaning making, and accessing their spiritual resources and practices (Bober & Regehr, 2006; Harrison & Westwood, 2009; Killian, 2008; Trippany et al., 2004; Way et al., 2004). Risking Connection is a treatment protocol designed to help therapists recognize, manage, and treat vicarious trauma; to provide education about trauma and recovery for a wide range of mental health providers, including clergy; and to offer a structure to enhance professional support and address vicarious trauma (Saakvitne, Gamble, Pearlman, & Lev, 2000).

Although the early theoretical literature on vicarious trauma included a strong focus on therapist coping strategies as a potential buffer, empirical findings on the relationship between therapist coping strategies and rates of vicarious trauma have been mixed. Even when coping strategies have predicted outcomes, effect sizes have been relatively small (Bober & Regehr, 2006; Way et al., 2004). Nonetheless, personal coping strategies are often the only variables under a therapist's control, so proactive coping should not be ignored as a means of preventing or managing vicarious trauma. At the same time, however, when personal coping explains such a small proportion of the variance in outcomes, therapists should not be surprised or blame themselves when they recognize signs of vicarious trauma in their work or the balance of their lives (Bober & Regehr, 2006).

Burnout

Like vicarious trauma, *burnout* is a long-term, cumulative process. It differs from vicarious trauma, however, in being unrelated to the traumatic content of therapy; it has been documented in mental health professionals not specializing in trauma work (Jenkins & Baird, 2002; Maslach, 1982; Schauben & Frazier, 1995). Burnout has been described as a means of self-defense when the emotional and interpersonal demands of a job outweigh the supports available (Maslach, 1982). This process typically begins with overinvolvement in a work role, an overload of demands from work, and limited social support. These precipitating factors are typically followed by emotional exhaustion, feelings of being ineffective at work, decreased self-esteem, feelings of failure, and ultimately, defensive apathy and detachment from work concerns (Maslach, 1982). In sum, burnout seems to result from an inability to make or retain a sense of meaning in one's professional role.

Like vicarious trauma, burnout appears to be more common in younger, less experienced therapists and less common among therapists using evidence-based treatments (Craig & Sprang, 2010). Although much remains unknown about burnout, preliminary evidence has suggested that attempts to avoid thinking or feeling about a problem (avoidant coping) and burnout are linked. However, most of the available research is cross-sectional, making it difficult to make causal interpretations regarding the nature of the relationship between burnout and avoidant coping (Deighton, Gurris, & Traue, 2007).

Positive Changes

Although negative changes may occur in the course of work with trauma survivors, therapists may also perceive vicarious growth from such work, characterized by the same perceived increases in sense of meaning and personal strength, relationship functioning, and spiritual changes reported by some trauma survivors (Arnold, Calhoun, Tedeschi, & Cann, 2005; Brockhouse, Msetfi, Cohen, & Joseph, 2011). Studies of perceived vicarious growth among trauma therapists have indicated that those therapists with greater empathy report more vicarious growth, whereas those having a strong sense of coherence report lesser amounts (Brockhouse et al., 2011). This pattern is consistent with the reciprocal meaning-making model. More empathic therapists may have more flexible schemas and, thus, may be more able to assimilate in response to their work with survivors. However, therapists with a greater sense of coherence may be more likely to avoid the disruptions to global meaning that they might experience in work with survivors and, thus, have fewer opportunities for growth.

Harrison and Westwood's (2009) interviews of master trauma therapists offered some suggestions about why empathy may serve as a protective factor. They argued that when clinicians are able to maintain effective interpersonal boundaries (i.e., to get close without confusing the client's story and experiences with their own), their empathic attunement is helpful to the therapist as well as the client, in part because therapists recognize that their work is helpful to clients and are able to develop a deep sense of meaning and professional satisfaction.

Although the existing empirical findings about vicarious trauma are consistent with the reciprocal meaning-making model, it is important to recognize that this is a comparatively new area of research; no study has taken a longitudinal perspective, and most fail to control for factors such as trauma history, amount of personal therapy the therapist has undergone, supervisory support, and so forth (Chouliara, Hutchinson, & Karatzias, 2009). Further, symptoms consistent with vicarious trauma are not unique to therapists working with trauma survivors (Kadambi & Truscott, 2004). The bottom line is that being a therapist is stressful, regardless of specialization; providing therapy involves working with high levels of emotional pain.

CONCLUSION

Therapy with trauma survivors often involves meaning making at the relational level: Therapists' meaning systems can affect their clients' recovery process, and their clients can affect their therapists' ongoing ability to do this work. Therapists can create the sort of safe environment that can help clients build or rebuild a sense of meaning, a sense of purpose, and spiritual and secular beliefs and goals following trauma and take steps toward recovery. Conversely, therapists can feel overwhelmed, hopeless, and burned out as a result of their work with trauma survivors.

To remain effective in their work, trauma therapists must become aware of their global beliefs, attitudes, and biases about religion and spirituality (Vieten et al., 2013). They must also monitor their perceptions of their clients' beliefs and ways of living their spirituality. Therapists who pathologize—or idealize—the goals, beliefs, and strategies of religion and spirituality may have a more difficult time effectively helping clients mobilize those resources to resolve trauma. Those with a history of trauma must monitor the ways that their past affects their current work. Therapists who become skillful in their work with religious and spiritual meaning systems, however, might help clients steer clear of unhelpful theodicies, challenge maladaptive appraisals, and marshal spiritual resources and supports.

9

WORKING WITH BELIEFS, GOALS, AND VALUES

Trauma can disrupt a person's global meaning system. As a result, recovery often requires creating a new sense of one's place in the world and shifts in one's relationships with other people, and possibly with God. Therapists helping clients heal from trauma must help them explore how trauma-related changes affect and sometimes contaminate other parts of their lives; such maladaptive accommodations of global meaning can alter their sense of identity, goals, sense of purpose, and coping skills. Clients may also have to recognize how their relationships may have been damaged by their history of trauma so they can better relate to others and negotiate these life roles more effectively (e.g., parent, spouse, employee; McAdams, Reynolds, Lewis, Patten, & Bowman, 2001; Pals & McAdams, 2004).

Therapists can, therefore, help clients turn to, strengthen, and develop new spiritual coping strategies in the treatment process. Coping strategies such as mindfulness, meditation, prayer, and reliance on one's

http://dx.doi.org/10.1037/15961-009
Trauma, Meaning, and Spirituality: Translating Research Into Clinical Practice, by C. L. Park, J. M. Currier, J. I. Harris, and J. M. Slattery

spiritual community can help clients draw crucial distinctions between the past and present (or among parts of their current life), recognize ways they may revictimize themselves and stop doing so, turn to and feel supported by a higher power, and feel heard and accepted within their spiritual community.

Just as global meaning systems are often damaged by trauma, one fount of healing can come from accessing more adaptive global beliefs and goals, resolving trauma-induced discrepancies between situational and global meanings, and developing new and more helpful spiritual perspectives from which clients can understand the trauma, themselves, and their place in the world. Therapists may draw on a wide range of psychotherapeutic techniques and models in these endeavors to help clients search for and create new meaning. These ideas are explored in the following case, which we return to throughout the chapter.

INTRODUCTION TO MELODY

Melody was 14 years old when she was admitted to the pediatric ward of the state psychiatric hospital at 1:30 a.m. A 911 call had summoned police to her home after an apparent domestic incident: Furniture was overturned and many objects were broken, holes were made in walls, and a number of kitchen knives were plunged into furniture and other objects, including a violin. When the police arrived, only Melody and her mother were home. Melody's mother effusively thanked the police for coming, observing that she had been unable to control Melody and prevent her from damaging their home. Melody appeared timid and was small-framed and nonathletic; the police doubted she had the physical strength to create that much damage. As a result, they filed a report with Child Protective Services and took both mother and daughter for psychiatric observations and assessments.

During the morning report, night nurses described Melody as compliant, cooperative, and quiet. The only difficulty they had was that she responded to many questions with "I don't know" and volunteered no information that had not been specifically requested. Nurses reported that she did not appear to sleep, and although she went to the dining room for breakfast as instructed, barely ate anything. In addition, they reported that, on admission, she had a number of bruises and abrasions on her face, hands, and arms but did not complain about her injuries. Toxicology reports revealed no evidence of substance use.

Melody cooperated with standardized testing (e.g., Minnesota Multiphasic Personality Inventory—Adolescent [MMPI–A], Butcher et al., 1992; Wechsler Intelligence Scale for Children—IV, Wechsler, 2003). She was clearly of above average intelligence, and her MMPI–A profile described her as depressed, anxious, and overcontrolled. She provided only limited and concrete information (e.g., age, grade in school, address, her pediatrician's name). She reported she did not know where her father was and would not elaborate further. When asked about the events of the previous night, she only shook her head, blinked back tears, and said, "I can't tell you. I'll go to hell if I do."

THE PAST

People who experience changes in their sense of time immediately following trauma and who engage in trauma-related ruminations are more likely to develop posttraumatic symptoms (Kumpula, Orcutt, Bardeen, & Varkovitzky, 2011). These changes move a survivor's time focus from the present to the past, and especially to a view of the past as negative. Such a perspective is associated with a number of negative outcomes (Zimbardo & Boyd, 1999).

Trauma survivors are often avoidant pretrauma (Kumpula et al., 2011) and engage in more avoidance posttrauma, perhaps to avoid re-experiencing the trauma (e.g., through nightmares, flashbacks, and intrusive thoughts). Survivors are flooded by anxiety and struggle ineffectively to cope with it (Pyszczynski & Kesebir, 2011). Melody, for example, could not talk about her ordeal despite the fact that she was safe in the hospital.

Further, meaning violations associated with trauma often color and discolor the present: Melody was similarly frozen in her relationships with others, felt guilt regardless of what she did, and expected negative outcomes in spite of her best efforts. According to terror management theory (Pyszczynski & Kesebir, 2011), three things buffer against anxiety: cultural worldviews, self-esteem, and relationships. Each of these, as we have observed throughout this volume, is damaged by trauma (see, e.g., Bradley, Schwartz, & Kaslow, 2005; Janoff-Bulman, 1992; Janoff-Bulman & Frantz, 1997; Riggs, Monson, Glynn, & Canterino, 2009). In sum, trauma survivors often learn that nothing that they previously relied on—in Melody's case, God and her father—will keep them safe.

Thus, for some people, trauma can cause an existential crisis, shaking global meaning to the core. Some people attempt to cope with symptoms, without closing or resolving the meaning violation. Rather than resolving problems, these strategies can trap survivors in the past. Still others face the violation and attempt to work through it (a kind of rebirth), in the process creating a life narrative that acknowledges both terror and wisdom, good and evil, and connection and isolation.

TELLING MORE ADAPTIVE "STORIES"

Although global meaning systems are often damaged by trauma, meaning reparation can come from accessing more adaptive global beliefs and goals, resolving trauma-induced discrepancies between situational and global meanings, and developing new and more helpful spiritual perspectives from which clients can understand the trauma, themselves, and their place in the world. Meaning-based interventions can help trauma survivors develop a narrative that aligns appraised and global meanings of their past to rebuild a sense of meaning and purpose. Such interventions can help people recognize areas of positive change and growth that came about through their active coping. Interventions should not only reduce the tension or discrepancy between global and appraised meanings but also help survivors respond to that tension with action, growth, and greater meaning.

Friends and family members often encourage people to move on and get over their difficult perceptions and emotions rather than making sense of them (Neimeyer, Pennebaker, & van Dyke, 2009). Melody's mother, for example, dismissed Melody's feelings and concerns, warned her not to talk about the family to "outsiders," and often berated her when she cried. Rather than believing she could talk about her concerns, Melody avoided such discussions and even attempts to think about and make sense of her mother's actions.

Unfortunately, avoiding such thoughts and failing to marshal support can create a "crisis in meaning," depriving survivors "of a significant past, a comprehensible present and a purposeful future" (Neimeyer et al., 2009, p. 457). Instead, most researchers and clinicians contend that people who have been exposed to multiple traumas or who have developed symptoms of posttraumatic stress disorder (PTSD) should recount the trauma—sometimes on multiple occasions—and that, as a result, events will lose their power and associated negative affect (Adler, Bliese, McGurk, Hoge, & Castro, 2009; Rothbaum, Gerardi, Bradley, & Friedman, 2011). Telling their stories allows survivors to move "into" rather than "on from" distress symptomatology by meaningfully assimilating trauma into their life narrative.

According to McAdams and his colleagues (McAdams et al., 2001; Pals & McAdams, 2004), most survivors who do well acknowledge that the trauma shook up their life, yet tell a coherent and positive story that makes sense of themselves and their lives and identifies benefits from the trauma. They tell *redemption stories* in which negative events are transformed or redeemed by positive outcomes (e.g., "I felt God next to me, guiding me throughout"). Redemption stories allow survivors to continue perceiving meaning and purpose in life and bring coherence between situational and global meaning. However, people with negative outcomes are more likely to tell *contamination stories*. Life tends to start well in contamination stories, but then is ruined, contaminated, or undermined by events. In their stories, the world is bad and unfair; they recognize little control and do not expect things will improve in the future (e.g., "God has abandoned me"). Melody's was a contamination story when she first entered therapy: She saw herself as having failed to help her mother or keep her father safe. She sounded like Sisyphus—trying hard to push that rock up the hill but repeatedly failing. The treatment team helped Melody recognize the ways she had persevered even through great difficulties and the ways she could find meaning and purpose from this process.

Certainly, being able to tell a coherent and positive story is useful; however, survivors often tell stories that are extreme and dichotomous ways of appraising events. Any narrative that is narrow, rigid, and limiting is likely to become problematic at some point (Teasdale et al., 2001). Life is rarely all good or all bad; instead, most people experience both. Healthier survivors are able to recognize that their life histories are not wholly "contaminated" nor wholly damaged, identify both strengths and weaknesses, and see the strengths in their "weaknesses." In the Army's programs for returning soldiers, for example, service members are encouraged to acknowledge and normalize combat-related behaviors and reactions, reappraising postdeployment "symptoms" as combat-related strengths that are inappropriately used since their return (e.g., hypervigilance may be adaptive and necessary in the field but inappropriate at home; Adler et al., 2009). The army's programs help veterans develop more complex and adaptive narratives. Rather than blaming themselves for and ruminating on symptoms, they are encouraged to adapt combat-related behavioral and cognitive skills and strengths in home situations, thus developing a more coherent and positive explanation of postcombat behaviors.

Trauma may shatter global meaning and can cause survivors to make more negative reappraisals of their world and relationships. As described in Chapter 8, many people report parallel types of damage in their relationships with God and with others. Does God love me? Will I be safe and protected? Can I be accepted and belong? Telling new stories that integrate spiritual language and ideas into therapeutic language can strengthen restorying efforts by connecting survivors' secular and spiritual perspectives on the world, allowing them to tell stories that are meaningful and useful at multiple levels and that can be adaptively incorporated into their global meaning system (Van Eenwyk, 1996).

RESPONDING TO SPIRITUAL BARRIERS TO TREATMENT

Clients from many cultures, including African Americans, Latinos/as, Native Americans, older adults, and those from rural areas, may prefer clergy or spiritual healers over mental health providers—or have far better access to them. Preferences for clergy as a source of help for mental health issues can be predicted by minority status, a childhood history of religious education, a history of having attended religious services for at least 1 year, and perceptions of clergy as trustworthy and empathic (Constantine, Myers, Kindaichi, & Moore, 2004; Kane, 2010). In some cases, these preferences may stem from a degree of cultural distrust for conventional mental health services (Constantine et al., 2004; Jones, Cassidy, & Heflinger, 2002; Kane, 2003; Raue, Weinberger, Sirey, Meyers, & Bruce, 2011).

Cultural and spiritual meanings about participation in psychotherapy may serve as either barriers or opportunities to treatment (Beals et al., 2005; Blank, Mahmood, Fox, & Guterbock, 2002; El-Khoury et al., 2004; Kane, 2003; Neighbors, Musick, & Williams, 1998). These cultural barriers can occur when ethnic minority or immigrant cultures trust clergy more than medical providers or view mental health concerns as a symptom of spiritual problems (e.g., viewing depression as an indication that one is "not right with God"; Marwaha & Livingston, 2002; Mays, Caldwell, & Jackson, 1996; Molock, Matlin, Barksdale, Puri, & Lyles, 2008). In fact, in some cases, when survivors consult with clergy, they are less likely to engage with conventional mental health services (Blank et al., 2002; Neighbors et al., 1998).

Even when trauma survivors seek mental health treatment, specific religious beliefs and coping strategies may affect their willingness to engage in therapeutic tasks and activities. Preferences for seeking help from God often parallel preferences for seeking help from mental health providers. Both people who identify God as an important locus of control in negotiating mental health challenges and those who prefer collaborating with God to solve problems are more likely to seek mental health treatment, whereas those who prefer to solve problems without collaborating with God are less likely to seek help (Andrews, Stefurak, & Mehta, 2011; Kane, 2010).

Another spiritual consideration in trauma therapy involves survivors' spiritual meanings about disclosure. Survivors may have been told that they are somehow responsible for the abuse. In some cases, perpetrators may attempt to evoke guilt and shame to maintain survivors' silence (e.g., Ms. Lopez, Chapter 5; Schauer, Neuner, & Elbert, 2011). Family members and friends may respond to survivors using the frame of the just-world hypothesis (i.e., people deserve the things that happen to them; Lerner & Miller, 1978). Guilt and shame may be supported by explicitly spiritual references or their explanations of abuse as resulting from the survivor's sins or sinful nature. Melody's mother, for example, framed her own actions in this manner: She described Melody as the "Devil's child" and felt that she had to "rid the world of the evil that lives in [her]." Silence may also be induced by survivors' beliefs that forgiving perpetrators is a religious duty (Fortune, 1995; Imbens & Jonker, 1992). Other secular and religious beliefs and goals may also interfere with disclosures. Melody had a long history of protecting her mother especially, and saw disclosures as violating the precept "Honor thy mother and father." She believed she would go to hell if she described what had been occurring in the home.

Chaplains and other spiritual professionals can help survivors address such barriers to therapy and promote engagement in the therapeutic process. Although therapists often do not consider working with clergy when collaboration might be appropriate, most clergy are interested both in learning more about psychology and in reducing the divide between these two fields (Edwards, Lim, McMinn, & Dominguez, 1999; McRay, McMinn, Wrightsman, Burnett, & Ho, 2001). In addition, many clergy use individual and family counseling interventions in the context of their congregational ministry. To facilitate successful collaborations with clergy, clinicians should (a) recognize the many values that clinicians and clergy share (e.g., respect for individuals, confidentiality, and beneficence); (b) respect rather than dismiss clergy as a discipline with an important role in mental health services; (c) explore when such collaborations are appropriate, especially when the clergy's scope of practice is relevant to a survivor's concerns; and (d) communicate clearly with clergy to create an intervention or consultation plan (McMinn, Aikins, & Lish, 2003). We elaborate more on collaborating with ministry professionals in Chapter 12.

Because Melody was clearly identifying spiritual barriers to treatment, the treatment team asked the hospital chaplain to conduct a spiritual assessment. Perceived spiritual barriers may be veiled avoidance symptoms, however: Both Melody's spiritual beliefs and psychopathology could create significant barriers to treatment. In their discussion of the precept "honor thy mother and father," the hospital chaplain proposed a different interpretation from Melody's initial views. He indicated that this scripture advises that one should adopt a lifestyle that would make parents proud of their children, suggesting that lying or withholding the truth, even to protect parents, might be antithetical to such an honorable lifestyle. If Melody's mother had behaved violently the previous night, for example, she needed help, and the best way to get her that help would be to share truthfully what happened while her mother was in the hospital and could easily access that help. They also discussed the differences between sharing private information to be hurtful or embarrass someone and sharing information to help. This conversation allowed Melody to become actively involved in treatment. Because Melody continued to perceive a number of moral dilemmas to disclosing in therapy, however, she asked that the chaplain continue to join her in treatment.

SETTING THE STAGE FOR TREATMENT

As highlighted in Chapter 4, responding in empowering ways is especially important for people who have been victimized. Obtaining meaningful informed consent (or, in Melody's case, assent) is both empowering and necessary before beginning any therapy, particularly the exposure-based therapies that are often part of trauma work (Riggs, Cahill, & Foa, 2006; Walser & Westrup, 2007). Further, in Phase 1 of trauma therapies, establishing physical and psychological safety provides the basis for empowering meaningful participation in therapy (Herman, 1992). At the same time, these needs must be met quickly, so that efforts to address them do not reinforce avoidance behaviors (Resick, Monson, & Chard, 2008; Walser & Westrup, 2007). Melody had a number of pressing concerns that had to be addressed before she could commit to changing her internal narratives about the past: Would she be returning to her abusive mother, was her dog safe, and could she handle the responsibilities she felt at school and in her church? If Melody had continued to avoid treatment issues, her treatment team would have had to confront and challenge that avoidance.

The process of establishing physical and psychological safety requires careful assessment of the meanings the survivor makes of therapist behaviors. Particularly in inpatient care settings, it can be challenging to determine whether proposed interventions provide safety, foster dependence, or are empowering. As noted in Chapter 6, a client's goals and values play a critical role in therapy and should be assessed carefully. In this case, it was clear that Melody's goals and values focused on vocation and obligation (e.g., caring for her dog, continuing in her training as a violinist) and community (e.g., connecting with her school and church). She could only set aside acute anxieties to work in therapy when she was able to meet her expectations for herself in these areas.

ASSESSING MALADAPTIVE MEANINGS ABOUT THE PAST

Because trauma often damages a person's global meaning in profound ways, treatment can be difficult and slow. Many techniques, however, are available to facilitate recontextualizing, reframing, and reconstructing global meanings, providing for more adaptive assimilation and accommodation following trauma. Therapists can use strategies such as cognitive reframing, empty-chair techniques, and mindfulness skills to help clients search for and create new meanings. A variety of evidence-based treatments have been developed to create a coherent approach to this restorying process (e.g., acceptance and commitment therapy, cognitive processing therapy, building spiritual strength, and narrative exposure therapy), although they often are not always explicitly framed as attempts at restorying or creating new meanings.

Narrative exposure therapy (NET), with its comparatively simple, short-term structure, is particularly well suited to challenge meanings and allow some cognitive restructuring of traumatic experiences. NET was developed for use in refugee camps and other settings in which access to psychotherapy is limited and survivors are not yet in a safe environment (McPherson, 2012; Neuner, Schauer, Klaschik, Karunakara, & Elbert, 2004; Robjant & Fazel, 2010; Schauer et al., 2011). It has been successfully used with children (Neuner et al., 2008) and adults (Bichescu, Neuner, Schauer, & Elbert, 2007), and has demonstrated effectiveness as compared with no-treatment, waiting list, education about PTSD, and supportive counseling (Robjant & Fazel, 2010).

NET provides clients with an opportunity to create a narrative autobiography that contextualizes trauma with other aspects of the client's life, including developmental status, culture, and sociopolitical factors (Schauer et al., 2011). NET helps create new and more effective meanings about past traumatic events by relating the feelings clients had during the trauma to current feelings and contexts. NET "unfreezes" old cognitive constructs (narratives) about the trauma and creates healthier meanings and narratives for these events.

NET begins with psychoeducation regarding the sequelae of trauma and considers how distressing emotions and avoidance may combine to prevent trauma survivors from thinking clearly about traumatic experiences (Schauer et al., 2011). Therapists using NET then often create a "lifeline" to symbolize important life events, both positive and negative, placing the trauma in the context of the individual's social, cultural, historical, and political context (Schauer et al., 2011). In the process of creating such an autobiographical narrative, therapists facilitate survivors' reports of sensations, thoughts, feelings, actions, and decisions. According to NET, when survivors are able to describe their life in a sequential, logical narrative consistent with their educational and language capacity, the barriers to effective meaning making have been lifted and survivors will then be able to access more adaptive coping strategies for such events in the future (Schauer et al., 2011).

When Melody first arrived at the hospital, she had difficulty identifying positive experiences in her history. In developing her lifeline, Melody was able to tell stories both about negative experiences (e.g., her mother's hospitalizations, her father's disappearance under mysterious and perhaps traumatic conditions, and the events leading to her hospitalization) and also more positive ones (e.g., living with her aunt during her mother's early hospitalization, getting her puppy, joining her church's school, getting her violin;

see Figure 9.1). Identifying the negative experiences—which she labeled with rocks—helped her see these events as discrete rather than continuous. They also helped her therapist empathize with her experience. However, identifying positive events on her lifeline—which she labeled with flowers—helped Melody reframe her experience and begin to construct a redemption narrative. Further, her treatment team began to see the natural supports in her life that could be accessed and used in the course of treatment.

The NET lifeline identifies traumatic events that will require further processing and contextualizes them in the balance of the client's life (Schauer et al., 2011). For Melody, the lifeline also served as a window into matters of her values and identity. The positive caregivers in her life (i.e., her father, her aunt, and her Sunday school teacher) and social systems she viewed as important (e.g., church, school) provided a framework to help her treatment team understand the frames of reference through which she interpreted traumatic experiences. Her lifeline also created a road map of traumatic events for further narrative exposure (Schauer et al., 2011).

In NET, therapists not only identify critical life events but also solicit narratives about each, thus identifying failures in meaning making. These

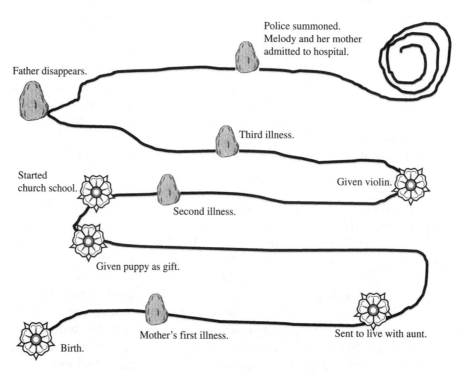

Figure 9.1. Melody's lifeline. Flowers = positive events; rocks = negative events.

narratives encourage clients to process relevant emotions and provide opportunities to reevaluate and reconstrue each event in context (Schauer et al., 2011). As seen in this narrative, Melody had particular difficulty identifying emotions and describing events associated with her father's disappearance in age-congruent ways. These difficulties are cues about areas in which survivors need further help recontextualizing an event and creating more functional situational meanings (Schauer et al., 2011).

Melody: At first, maybe, I thought he was in a hospital. He must have been hurt. I wanted to go to him so bad. But I didn't know where he was. I couldn't ask her; she was too sick.

Dr. Stein: What do you think would have happened if you had asked your Mom what happened?

Melody: I don't know. I think . . . she was so mad . . . I was afraid.

Dr. Stein: What were you afraid would happen?

Melody: Would she do to me what she did to him?

Dr. Stein: What do you think she did to him?

Melody: At first I thought he was just hurt. But he didn't come home and didn't come home and didn't come home. After a long time, no Dad, I started to think, she maybe did more than just hurt him.

Dr. Stein: Do you think he was killed?

Melody: [*Tearful.*] I don't know, I don't know, I don't know. Would he just leave me with her if he could get back home? I don't think he would leave me with her. He knows she's too sick for me to take care of her by myself. What if he couldn't get back home? What could keep him from coming home for me? If he was . . . what you said . . . I am so bad!

Dr. Stein: As I listen to you, I feel like I am hearing a terrible and confusing storm inside you. Can you tell me more about what you are feeling?

Melody: [*Now sobbing*] I want my Dad back so bad, and I don't deserve him because I did not take care of him or Mom enough to keep them OK.

Dr. Stein: You feel like it's your fault your Dad is gone and your Mom is sick?

Melody: Dad said we had to take care of Mom. I tried, I really tried. I work hard in school 'cause it makes her proud, and I take care of the house because she really can't when she's sick, and I take care of Brownie, and I don't ask her for anything 'cause it makes her madder, and I don't know what else to do. I prayed so hard for God to show me what I should do. But when Dad was gone, and still gone, and gone a long time, I should have done something. I should have told someone, but I didn't, because I was afraid she would kill me too. That's why, when she said she would kill Brownie, I broke the rules, and I put him out, and I called 911. I knew she would kill me if I told, but I deserve that because I didn't tell anyone about Dad because I was I was afraid she would kill me, and I would rather be dead than live knowing that I did not help Dad because I was too afraid.

Melody's narrative revealed a number of spiritual issues relevant to her ability to make meaning of this event. Her father's disappearance was an ambiguous loss (Boss, 2004): She did not know with any certainty what happened to him. Being with her father was a highly valued goal, and his sudden absence was a major violation of her global meaning; she struggled to find any meaningful reason for this disappearance. Further, she expressed a high level of perceived responsibility for others' behavior, consistent with her earlier accounts of the traumatic event that brought her to the hospital, yet she also believed that she had failed in meeting these responsibilities (maladaptive assimilation). Perhaps most important, her identity and self-worth appeared to be tied to her ability to respond to such highly ambiguous situations "correctly."

These types of inappropriate self-blame are so common among trauma survivors that the *Diagnostic and Statistical Manual of Mental Disorders* (fifth ed.; American Psychiatric Association, 2013) now includes them among the diagnostic criteria for PTSD. Trauma survivors often have guilt-evoking cognitions, including distorted perceptions of responsibility for the event, violated values, and an inability to predict or prevent the trauma (Kubany & Ralston, 2006). Unresolved guilt is associated with greater psychopathology. Once such appraisals are identified, however, they can be reframed or challenged.

WORKING WITH MORAL INJURY

When traumatic experiences challenge deeply held values, the result can be *moral injury*, a type of spiritual distress following traumas that overwhelm existing spiritual, moral, or existential meaning structures (Drescher et al., 2011; Litz et al., 2009; see also Chapter 6, this volume). Melody had internalized what were often abusive interactions with her mother and had had to make decisions about morally ambiguous dilemmas that she faced. Melody had attempted to be a good child and had maintained high grades in school, did most of the housework, attended Sunday school when she had a ride, and was a successful violinist with considerable promise as a musician; nonetheless, despite her best efforts, she could not please her mother or keep her safe. On the night the police intervened, her mother had accused her of coming home late and failing to complete her household chores before "gallivanting around." Her mother had punished her by destroying objects that were important to her, including her violin and books. Her mother had made other threats in the past, but this time threatened to kill Melody's dog, Brownie. Melody put Brownie outside to keep him safe, then called 911. As Melody talked about the incident, it was clear that she was in a catch-22 situation: She berated herself for being disobedient and letting Brownie outside, while certain that she could not live with herself if she allowed her mother to harm him. Whatever she did was likely to cause more guilt than she was capable of resolving successfully. Melody now felt guilty that she was not home to check on Brownie and see that he was safe and cared for.

This pattern of events in which Melody attempted to resolve an irresolvable dilemma was long-standing. When she was successful, she gained a sense of meaning; however, it often left her feeling alone and afraid and gave her a pervasive sense of helplessness—even as she attempted to take responsibility for events and situations beyond her control. Although this illusion of responsibility and control may have reduced her fears about her mother's apparently erratic behavior, she paid a high price for this control because she often felt inappropriate and damaging guilt, which she did not have the emotional or cognitive resources to resolve on her own.

When a survivor's initial spiritual meanings of the trauma include spiritually distressing cognitions (e.g., of divine punishment or self-blame), it may be useful to explore alternative global meanings (e.g., other theodicies explaining the presence of evil) and other situational meanings (e.g., alternatives to using self-blame, which seemed designed to perpetuate an illusion of control). It is clear, however, that when survivors' efforts to make meaning of a traumatic past cost them their moral or spiritual identity, their relationship with a previously valued higher power, or community of faith, engaging in a process of reconciling these meanings is essential.

Research on treating moral injury is relatively recent (Harris et al., 2011; Litz et al., 2009; Steenkamp et al., 2011), so clinical recommendations are tentative. However, current treatments frequently address damaged relationships, including the survivor's relationship with God, and foster both forgiveness and self-forgiveness. Such strategies include empty-chair techniques for facilitating dialogue with a higher power or another moral authority and focused work on forgiveness (Harris et al., 2011; Litz et al., 2009; Steenkamp et al., 2011).

CHALLENGING MALADAPTIVE APPRAISALS

Ultimately, creating new meaning requires expressing current appraisals and beliefs in relationship or dialogue so that meanings can be integrated back into social and cultural networks that provide the individual's context and identity (Alves et al., 2014). Virtually all therapeutic approaches designed to facilitate meaning making use some type of social expression (e.g., dialogue, group work, journaling) to help survivors make meaning of their experiences in social contexts (Allen & Wozniak, 2014; Alves et al., 2014; Demasure, 2012; Meston, Lorenz, & Stephenson, 2013; Tuval-Mashiach & Dekel, 2014). Melody often felt caught in her evaluations of her relationship with her mother: Were problems her fault (as her mother said)? Were they her mother's (as her father had intimated)? In some ways their hospitalizations reiterated this dilemma. However, it at least raised this question of responsibility—something her mother never did.

The therapy team, with Melody as an essential part of it, began to focus on the reciprocal meaning-making process. She was invited to reevaluate her perceived role in the family. Rather than accepting inappropriate responsibility for her parents' care, she began to recognize her parents' needs as clearly far more than an adolescent could meet. Nonetheless, she also became increasingly able to recognize how her belief that she could control the situation helped her function without being overcome by fear. When told that she would not be immediately returned to her mother's custody, she no longer had to maintain that belief, nor carry the paralyzing burden of guilt that came with it.

The therapy team also confronted Melody about her pattern of judging her responses to ambiguous situations. They worked with her on her tendency to attempt to categorize her actions as "right" or "wrong" and to judge herself harshly; they invited her to consider alternatives she might have chosen: She discovered she could find something "wrong" with every alternative. Working within her faith, the chaplain assured her that God did not want her to carry this unreasonable burden of guilt, pointing out that if she stopped blaming herself, she would have more energy to do things that would please God—like playing her violin in church.

Working with her concerns about her destroyed violin provided her with a helpful example of the ways that her thinking was distorted and unhelpful. Melody was concerned about paying the school back for the cost of the instrument and was fearful that her orchestra teacher would be angry with her. The team asked questions to assist her in viewing her role appropriately as an adolescent, rather than as parent to her mother: "Who actually broke the violin?" "Are you strong enough to physically stop your mother from breaking something she wants to break?"

Melody was able to articulate that she wanted to let go of the guilt and, at the same time, that she had been thinking this way so long that it was automatic for her: "like scales on my violin." Her psychologist helped her reframe guilt-evoking cognitions while the chaplain worked with her on skills such as praying for help to let go of guilt and practicing mantram meditation, reinforcing her worth in the eyes of God (i.e., adaptive accommodation; see Chapter 10).

SPIRITUALLY RELEVANT SOCIAL SUPPORT

In some cases, trauma—and the acting out behaviors that may accompany it—can be followed by a loss in social support from religious leaders and congregations. Such negative social interactions can include disapproval, criticism, and excessive demands and can cause people considerable distress (Exline, 2002). Such losses of support are related to poorer outcomes, including more depressive symptoms and lower well-being and self-esteem (Ellison, Zhang, Krause, & Marcum, 2009; Krause, 2003; see also Figure 8.1). Further, some people, like Melody, perceive criticism and a loss of social support following a trauma, even when no changes in social support have occurred.

Meaning making does not take place in a vacuum; people make meaning in the context of their community and culture (Demasure, 2012). Being a member of a community of shared faith can help survivors make new and sacred meanings of stressful events (Tuval-Mashiach & Dekel, 2014). The social support they receive from their community is a strong determinant of posttraumatic adjustment (Harris, Erbes, Winskowski, Engdahl, & Nguyen, 2014). Further, as seen with Melody, a community of faith can provide a spiritually and culturally relevant natural support system with a sphere of influence extending far beyond the support provided by mental health providers (Alves et al., 2014).

As discharge planning progressed, the treatment team involved Melody's community of faith. The police department had been unsuccessful in locating her father, so Child Protective Services followed up on Melody's request to ask her Sunday school teacher, Ms. Constantine, whether she would serve as her foster mother. Her teacher immediately agreed and visited Melody as soon as she learned what had happened and where Melody was. The staff was surprised and delighted to see the ordinarily over-controlled Melody greet Ms. Constantine with a warm hug and thank her for coming. The two sat and talked for a long time, each sharing how much they had missed the other during the period when Melody had been unable to go to church. Ms. Constantine asked Melody many questions—about school, her work with the violin, and her parents' well-being—demonstrating that the two had had a long and close relationship. Melody also shared her fears about Brownie. Ms. Constantine quickly assured her that Brownie was safe and would be living with them when Melody was released from the hospital.

Ms. Constantine was also able to help Melody reframe her management of the trauma:

> Melody, you are like Jesus: You love people even when they hurt you. A lot of kids would have tried to hurt your mom when she was hurting you, but you called the police and got her help. You were not only physically brave but spiritually brave. You did the right thing to help, even though she didn't want you to.

This reframe from a valued adult had far greater impact on Melody's maladaptive guilt than anything the therapy team could have done.

CONCLUSION

Survivors' global meaning is often tainted after a trauma, challenging their values and goals, sense of meaning and purpose, self-perceptions, and perceptions of others and other situations. Thought patterns may become ruminative and survivors may repeatedly question whether they should have handled the situation differently—and wonder why they did not. Their initial stories (contamination stories) may focus on the damage around them, causing them to respond adaptively by searching for ways to keep themselves safe in an unsafe world. It may also prevent them from seeing the resources and social support that they have. Nonetheless, the interventions described in this chapter help survivors challenge maladaptive situational meanings and enlarge and enrich their appraisals and life narrative.

10

INTERVENTIONS FOR HELPING CLIENTS RESOLVE SPIRITUAL STRUGGLE AND INCREASE SPIRITUAL WELL-BEING

As we reviewed in Chapter 9, trauma-exposed people often find that their old stories (e.g., about themselves as dirty or unworthy; about others hurting, failing, or judging them) get in the way of their engaging adaptively with partners, family, friends, and their community. Their stories trap them in the past and interfere with their ability to relate well with others. Not only do these stories prevent survivors from connecting with the people who were the main actors in their stories but they also often create distance between themselves and their significant others, leaving survivors feeling detached from their present and future. As seen in this next case, problems associated with trauma can cause a spiritual rift extending well beyond the immediate story.

Until recently, therapists had few strategies for helping clients with spiritual concerns following trauma and little guidance was available for thinking about how to approach these issues. In this chapter, we describe several

http://dx.doi.org/10.1037/15961-010
Trauma, Meaning, and Spirituality: Translating Research Into Clinical Practice, by C. L. Park, J. M. Currier, J. I. Harris, and J. M. Slattery

prevailing implicit and explicit approaches for incorporating spirituality into treatments for trauma survivors and consider some of the ethical issues raised by this work.

CASE EXAMPLE: MR. KENT

Allen Kent was 32 years old and in good recovery after a period of extensive therapy that helped him regain a sense of meaning and purpose following a history of child abuse in the family home, where his father had regularly sexually assaulted both children. Mr. Kent left the Roman Catholic faith early in his adolescence, well before starting therapy, because the Church's authority structure reminded him too much of his father's unquestioned authority in his family. At the time of treatment, Mr. Kent identified as agnostic, telling his therapist,

> If there is a God, I'm mad at Him. Anything that powerful could have stopped the abuse of little children. Night after night I prayed that my dad would stop doing this to me and, worse, stop hurting my little sister, but it never stopped—until I got big enough to defend myself, until my sister moved out of the house.

Although Mr. Kent experienced some internalized conflict and alienation from God, he did not experience that alienation as distressing, and outside of assessing the extent to which it was a concern for him, his spiritual identification was not discussed much in his therapy. However, when his first child, a daughter, was born, his wife wanted the child to be baptized. Although he had been out of therapy for several years, he reacted with strong feelings. For him, handing his child to a priest for baptism was like handing someone vulnerable, someone like his little sister, to a powerful authority who could not be trusted to have that child's best interests at heart. At the same time, he was aware of the benefits of his religious education (e.g., being kind, compassionate, and honest with others) and wanted his daughter to develop those values. However, he could not see introducing his daughter to the God, who, if real, allowed horrors to happen to little children, and he could not see this as helping her develop the kind of values he wanted for her.

Mr. Kent's internal conflict about this—coming at a time when his family was in transition, both parents were getting little sleep as they cared for their daughter, and their extended families were increasingly pressuring them to baptize their young daughter—led to an increase in symptoms. He began to have nightmares again, was increasingly irritable with his wife, and felt strong urges to act as a guard outside their daughter's room at night. He recognized that he was unable to make good decisions about the baptism with his symptoms at this level, and scheduled an appointment with his previous therapist.

Mr. Kent and his therapist discussed a number of possibilities, including family counseling to help the couple communicate well about decisions related to their child's spiritual upbringing, reviewing coping and relaxation skills so that Mr. Kent could get more sleep and be less reactive, and medications to help him sleep. After discussing these options, he decided to schedule a few sessions as a booster to improve his anxiety management, and he planned to ask his wife whether she could agree to put the subject of baptism on hold until he could identify what he wanted for their daughter's spiritual education. His therapist was certain that she could help Mr. Kent further develop his anxiety management skills but did not feel competent to help him with the spiritual parenting question. She suggested a referral to a spiritual director, who was trained to facilitate spiritual growth using both individual and group mentoring.

Mr. Kent was nervous about working with a spiritual director but quickly found that she did not pressure him into making any particular decision. She was genuinely concerned that his father may have so poisoned his concept of God that returning to a Judeo–Christian faith might not be an appropriate spiritual goal. She gave him room to discuss the extent to which he needed to have the same spirituality as his wife or child, and what spiritual principles he wanted his child to have. After listening carefully to his concerns and spiritual conflicts, she gave him a list of suggestions about other faiths and spiritual resources he could explore. She also suggested a way of resolving the family issue of baptism, by creating a sort of spiritual commitment ceremony for the child, whereby the parents could commit to spiritual principles on which they agreed, without identifying a specific faith.

For Mrs. Kent and her family, the traditional use of water was important, and they incorporated that into a ceremony, committing their daughter to "the spirit of love." At the ceremony, the spiritual director blessed the water as a symbol of ongoing life, and Mr. Kent held his daughter, sprinkled water on her forehead and, with his wife, committed to teaching her about love and compassion for others. Their families, although initially resistant to the ceremony, had a change of heart as they listened to the couple's sincere, rather than ritualized, vows to their child, believing this was the most spiritually genuine baptism they had witnessed.

Mr. Kent's symptoms remitted to baseline almost immediately after he and his wife found a satisfactory resolution to the baptism. In many ways, this "crisis" created an opportunity to set aside some of the old hurts he had experienced in childhood and to identify some ways that he could again experience some spiritual connections. In the course of his work with the spiritual director, Mr. Kent also discussed attaining some level of forgiveness for his father as a way of preventing future symptom exacerbations. Mr. Kent and the spiritual director were in agreement that he had no reason to reconcile his estranged relationship with his father, but he chose to explore ways of resolving some of his hurt and angry feelings about his father.

Survivors often enter therapy struggling with global spiritual meaning systems that are inadequate to accommodate their experience of trauma (Park, Edmondson, & Mills, 2010). Most Americans, for example, receive religious education only until about age 12, before many have developed the capacity for abstract cognitive operations (Pargament, 2007). Thus, their views of God, right and wrong, and themselves as spiritual beings tend to be dichotomous and simplistic (see Table 2.2). Their theodicies may be inadequate for explaining how a benevolent, omnipotent deity could allow bad things to happen to comparatively innocent and well-meaning people. In addition, people tend to be overly optimistic that God will protect them and that they can expect safety and security if they live a moral lifestyle. As a result, many people lack a spiritual meaning system adequate to the task of adaptively accommodating trauma. This lack might not be problematic—if they are not confronted with events exposing their naivety (Jost et al., 2014). Further, the acute distress associated with trauma exposure can make it difficult for clients to make constructive meanings of their experiences in the context of comparatively immature spiritual beliefs and goals (Pargament, 2007).

These difficulties trap survivors in the past, and they may attempt to resolve current problems using the rules and rubrics that made sense at that earlier time. Mr. Kent, for example, began obsessing about his daughter's safety in ways that made sense from the context of his childhood rather than through a reality-oriented consideration of his family's current situation: His reactions reflected the triggers and situational meanings associated with earlier developmental periods (e.g., Mr. Kent again had significant responsibility for a young and vulnerable child).

CONSIDERATIONS FOR INTEGRATING SPIRITUAL ISSUES INTO TREATMENT

Clients often use their spiritual beliefs, goals, and coping mechanisms as a basis for adaptive accommodation or assimilation. When that process fails, however, and spiritual meanings reflect maladaptive accommodation or assimilation (i.e., spiritual struggle), survivors often experience more psychopathology and may request help for spiritual concerns in mental health contexts (Exline, Yali, & Sanderson, 2000; Harris et al., 2008). As described in Chapter 5, spiritual struggles may be inferred when clients abandon their faith, leave a faith community, experience estrangement or conflict with a higher power or faith community, or have difficulty forgiving themselves. Spiritual struggles are associated with higher levels of psychopathology and more protracted courses of posttraumatic symptomatology (Harris et al., 2008; Ogden et al., 2011; Pargament, Smith, Koenig, & Perez, 1998); people who cannot resolve the struggle or who abandon their spiritual meaning system fare worse by clinical standards (Ben-Ezra et al., 2010; Fontana & Rosenheck, 2004).

Preliminary evidence has suggested that (a) spiritual struggle is associated with more severe symptoms of posttraumatic stress disorder (PTSD), (b) unresolved spiritual struggle predicts future posttraumatic symptoms (Harris et al., 2012; Koenig, Pargament, & Nielsen, 1998), and (c) interventions designed to address spiritual struggle also reduce symptoms of PTSD (Harris et al., 2011). These links reinforce our conclusion that we should direct clinical attention to meaning and spiritual concerns, although we should do so when it makes sense for that particular survivor. For example, Mr. Kent was comfortable with his decision to disengage from his spiritual roots early in his recovery, although this disengagement was no longer an effective solution with the birth of his daughter.

Many mental health professionals may find resolving spiritual distress challenging because many current therapists received little or no training in handling spirituality, and therapists in training are often either implicitly or explicitly taught to avoid spiritual material (Kahle & Robbins, 2004). Until recently, psychologists sensitive to clients' spiritual concerns had to make referrals to chaplains, clergy, or spiritual directors for supportive counseling or values clarification. Increasingly, however, attending to spiritual concerns in psychotherapy is seen as an essential aspect of ethical and culturally sensitive treatment (e.g., Saunders, Miller, & Bright, 2010; Sperry, 2012; Sperry & Shafranske, 2005; Vieten et al., 2013). Approaches mental health providers might use to develop competence in addressing spiritual distress include (a) personal study of research on spirituality in therapy, using resources such as this book and the ever-increasing base of journal articles available on the topic, (b) consultation or supervision with clergy who have a background in counseling (e.g., clinical pastoral education or equivalent programs) or other mental health providers who have a strong background in this area, or (c) participation in increasingly available graduate courses in psychology of spirituality and related topics.

Mental health treatment occurs on a continuum from spiritually avoidant to spiritually integrated care (Saunders et al., 2010), as illustrated in Figure 10.1. Spiritually avoidant care avoids addressing spiritual beliefs, goals, and behaviors, even when the client raises these issues in treatment. Even treatment that does not explicitly address spiritual issues may create spiritual changes, however. For example, Mr. Kent's wife respected his efforts to manage aggressively his symptoms, so became willing to defer spiritual decisions

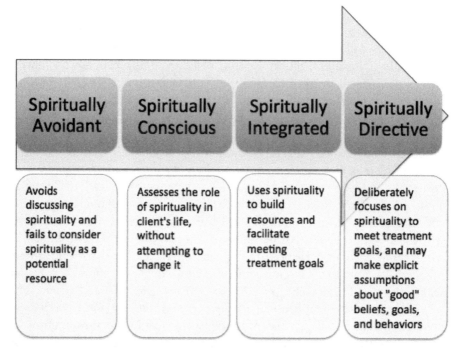

Spiritually Avoidant	Spiritually Conscious	Spiritually Integrated	Spiritually Directive
Avoids discussing spirituality and fails to consider spirituality as a potential resource	Assesses the role of spirituality in client's life, without attempting to change it	Uses spirituality to build resources and facilitate meeting treatment goals	Deliberately focuses on spirituality to meet treatment goals, and may make explicit assumptions about "good" beliefs, goals, and behaviors

Figure 10.1. Continuum of spiritual care in treatment.

about their daughter, even agreeing to set boundaries with extended family members who were pressuring them to baptize her. His wife's decision allowed him to connect with rather than avoid spiritual goals.

Spiritually conscious care involves respectfully and sensitively assessing and considering the client's spiritual background, without necessarily attempting to support, leverage, or transform spiritual beliefs, goals, and behaviors. This level of integration of spirituality with treatment seems to meet the American Psychological Association (APA; 2010) ethical principles on respect for human rights and dignity, at least at a minimal level. Spiritually directive care focuses treatment directly on spiritual beliefs and can be associated with a variety of ethical problems, including failure to respect the client's spiritual belief system, imposition of spiritual beliefs on clients, problems with competency, and difficulties with confused roles and boundaries.

Finally, spiritually integrated therapy considers a client's own spiritual meaning systems as a tool for meeting treatment goals; it tailors treatment to the client's belief system rather than imposing another belief system. Such treatment can help survivors continue their spiritual growth and focus on a spiritual present, rather than stalling at a stage of spiritual development where they were frozen in time by pathological meanings of trauma. The available evidence supports spiritually integrated care, particularly with trauma survivors (e.g., Shafranske & Cummings, 2013; Walker, Courtois, & Aten, 2015).

In general, therapists should monitor where they are on this continuum of spiritual care. Although clients may choose to dodge spiritual issues in treatment, ethical therapists should not sidestep relevant spiritual issues—and the cases when they might adopt more spiritually directive approaches should be carefully considered given the client's clinical goals and spiritual values. Mr. Kent's first round of treatment was spiritually conscious: His therapist assessed spiritual issues but respected that he did not identify resolving spiritual struggle as a goal. When Mr. Kent returned to treatment, his therapist took a spiritually integrative approach, particularly in their work on self-forgiveness. His therapist, who did not feel competent to help him explore strategies for fostering his daughter's spiritual growth, referred him to a spiritual director, which allowed the therapist to feel comfortable in her ability to maintain effective roles and boundaries in treatment.

Most mental health professionals have little training in addressing spiritual concerns (Shafranske & Cummings, 2013; Shafranske & Malony, 1990). Personal experience or familiarity with a religious tradition or faith group does not make one competent to deal with clients' spiritual issues. Therapists must both restrict their practice to their area of competence and, at the same time, seek out training or make referrals when spirituality appears relevant to the clinical issue presented (APA, 2010; see Standards 2.01–2.06). As such, it is important to evaluate one's competence on an ongoing basis and seek further education, consultations, supervision, or referrals as needed when working with clients who have clinically relevant spiritual concerns (Rosenfeld, 2011). As with any other domain of practice, knowledge of the research literature on spirituality and mental health is critical when addressing spiritual struggle or accessing spiritual beliefs and practice during treatment (Gonsiorek, Richards, Pargament, & McMinn, 2009; Plante, 2007; Saunders et al., 2010). We address these ethical concerns in greater depth in Chapter 12. Along with scope of practice and competency, therapists should also carefully consider aspects of billing regarding spiritually integrated care, noting the difference between psychotherapeutic techniques that have empirical support versus spiritual care more appropriately provided by chaplains or clergy (Gonsiorek et al., 2009).

SPIRITUALLY INTEGRATED CARE IN TRADITIONAL PSYCHOTHERAPIES

Spirituality can be addressed in three ways in traditional, psychologically oriented approaches for PTSD and related concerns. First, as discussed in Chapter 4, clinicians can draw on psychological interventions to achieve psychological outcomes. Although they might assume a spiritually avoidant approach, simply alleviating posttraumatic symptomatology might indirectly support a client's spirituality, existential-mindedness, and ability to meet valued goals. A second approach is to assume a spiritually conscious or spiritually integrative approach and adapt psychological interventions to address spiritual concerns when doing so will be helpful for a specific client. For example, clinicians might explore maladaptive cognitions about God in restructuring exercises, develop in vivo exposure interventions that promote reconnection with one's spiritual tradition or community, or inquire about possible spiritual meanings of traumatic experiences after imaginal exposure exercises (e.g., "Where do you believe God might have been when this event occurred?"). A final option for integrating spirituality with traumatized clients is to refer to or collaborate with ministry professionals or incorporate spiritual interventions that explicitly attempt to achieve both psychological and spiritual outcomes (see Figure 10.1).

Such attempts at spiritually integrated care often occur in the context of psychotherapies that were not designed with spiritual goals in mind. For example, in cognitive behavior therapy, therapists may encounter clients with a "punishing God" distortion of their faith following trauma, and cognitive interventions can be effective in addressing this as a negative, global cognition (Daniels & Fitzpatrick, 2013). In acceptance and commitment therapy, spiritual values are likely to be nominated by the client during goal development, in which case treatment explicitly focuses on spiritual values (Hayes, Pistorello, & Levin, 2012). In psychodynamic and interpersonal therapies, the client's early experiences learning about God, as well as transference related to parents, clergy, God, and even the therapist, may be material to be processed in sessions (Daniels & Fitzpatrick, 2013). In client-centered therapies, therapists may focus on spiritual concerns and spiritual growth consistent with the client's meaning system, express confidence in the client's ability to reach spiritual goals, and be present with the client while resolving spiritual concerns (Daniels & Fitzpatrick, 2013). In each case, however, treatment relies on developing and using spiritually competent attitudes, knowledge, and skills (Daniels & Fitzpatrick, 2013; Vieten et al., 2013).

Recently, several spiritually informed approaches for trauma survivors were developed and empirically tested. These approaches can be divided into two classes: *implicit* approaches, which use spiritual practices such as meditation or yoga to address psychological symptoms; and *explicit* approaches, which use spiritually integrated interventions to directly address spiritual struggle. In the balance of this chapter, we consider implicit and explicit approaches to spiritual issues in trauma therapy and explore further the sometimes complex ethical issues relevant to providing spiritually integrated therapies.

IMPLICIT SPIRITUAL APPROACHES

Meditation

Meditation comprises myriad Eastern spiritual practices, all of which help clients calm the mind, experience peace, increase their sense of integration with the universe, become enlightened, and attain higher levels of spiritual maturity (K. W. Chen et al., 2012). A number of meditative approaches to trauma recovery have been developed to date; these vary substantially in the degree to which they retain the spiritual content of Eastern meditation practices (Cuellar, 2008).

Mindfulness-based stress reduction (MBSR) is a standardized program of instruction in mindfulness meditation, which was originally based on Buddhist Vipassana traditions, although the overt spiritual content has been removed. The focal elements of MBSR include body scanning and awareness, accepting one's experience, and adopting an attitude of curiosity (Kearney, McDermott, Malte, Martinez, & Simpson, 2012). A strong body of research on mindfulness meditation and MBSR supports its efficacy in treating anxiety (K. W. Chen et al., 2012), although only a few studies have focused specifically on PTSD (Kearney et al., 2012; Kimbrough, Magyari, Langenberg, Chesney, & Berman, 2010; Nakamura, Lipschitz, Landward, Kuhn, & West, 2011).

Although most research on mindfulness meditation involves MBSR, there are studies of mindfulness skills training in other therapeutic contexts (e.g., as part of dialectical behavior therapy; Linehan, 1993a). Uncontrolled studies of mindfulness skills training for people with PTSD symptoms (child abuse survivors and veterans) have indicated that, relative to baseline, participants reported increased mindfulness skills and fewer symptoms of depression (Kearney et al., 2012; Kimbrough et al., 2010). In a more methodologically rigorous study, veterans in a mindfulness-based sleep intervention had better sleep and fewer PTSD symptoms than did veterans in a standardized sleep education protocol (Nakamura et al., 2011). These findings suggest that mindfulness has strong potential as an intervention for PTSD, although further, better-controlled studies examining a broader range of outcomes are necessary. There are no studies examining changes in spiritual distress associated with MBSR or mindfulness training, however. Such studies would be essential for determining the extent to which the action of mindfulness training occurs through addressing spiritual distress.

Like the MBSR program, the Mantram Repetition Program (MRP) is a standardized intervention for teaching mantram meditation, which develops a meditative focus on a spiritual word or phrase (Bormann, Liu, Thorp, & Lang, 2012). Because of the necessary language content in the mantram, this type of meditation is less removed from its spiritual content in Western contexts than is MBSR, and may thus provide easier therapeutic entry to addressing spiritual distress. As such, it provides a point of focus that may be especially appropriate for clients with high levels of re-experiencing symptoms (e.g., intrusive memories or flashbacks).

A randomized controlled trial comparing treatment as usual with treatment augmented with MRP indicated that MRP was associated with reduced PTSD and depressive symptoms (Bormann et al., 2012). This reduction in PTSD symptoms was largely related to changes in hyperarousal, and the effects of the intervention were mediated by increases in spiritual well-being (Bormann et al., 2012). Further research on MRP may demonstrate that it can enhance mental health providers' ability to effectively address spiritual distress associated with trauma.

Therapists considering integrating meditation into treatment should consider their skills and training in teaching these skills as well as the meaning of meditation in the client's spiritual meaning system. Clients from some Christian denominations may object to the use of a spiritual practice they view as being outside their religious tradition; however, meditative processes are natural parts of many religious traditions (e.g., praying the rosary) and may be able to be adapted to fit those traditions.

Yoga

Yoga is a mind–body practice derived from East Indian spirituality that integrates physical postures, breath control, and meditation (Sakuma et al., 2012). Yoga may promote change via many of the same pathways as meditation and thus help practitioners reach the same goals. In addition, in the West, yoga is an embodied practice, with the physical postures typically being a central part of the practice. This component may be particularly relevant for trauma survivors like Mr. Kent who may have difficulty being quiet and still and who experience greater stress and distress at these points (Streeter, Gerbarg, Saper, Ciraulo, & Brown, 2012; van der Kolk et al., 2014).

Like research on meditation, research on yoga's role in facilitating trauma recovery is comparatively new. In a quasi-experimental study of flood survivors, for example, a daily intervention including loosening exercises, physical postures, breathing techniques, and guided relaxation decreased their sadness and anxiety relative to survivors on the wait list (Telles, Singh, Joshi, & Balkrishna, 2010). Another important yoga study compared three conditions—yoga breathing, yoga breathing with exposure therapy, and a wait-list control group—among tsunami survivors. Those in both intervention groups reported fewer symptoms of PTSD and depression than did those in the control group, and gains were maintained over 24 weeks (Descilo et al., 2010). A feasibility study of a yoga intervention for veterans with combat-related PTSD found that veterans who participated in 12 sessions of yoga training over 6 weeks reported less hyperarousal and better sleep (Staples, Hamilton, & Uddo, 2013). Another trial of a yoga intervention for veterans with chronic PTSD that used intensive yoga training scheduled with monthly follow-up sessions found that over 6 months, those randomized to the intervention group had reduced symptoms compared with those in the control group (Carter et al., 2013).

Like research on meditation, these studies did not measure spiritual variables, nor do they effectively describe the extent to which spiritual content may have been relevant to the interventions used. At the same time, these results are promising, suggesting that further research may illuminate mechanisms that affect spiritual meaning systems.

Evaluation of Implicit Approaches

Meditation and yoga have several advantages in treating trauma. They do not have the side effects and interaction risks associated with pharmaceutical interventions. In addition, they cost less, are less stigmatizing, and are more accessible than traditional psychotherapy or psychiatric services (K. W. Chen et al., 2012). Further, at face value, it is reasonable to speculate that spiritual practices designed to help people effectively manage affective arousal will be useful in managing PTSD and other conditions characterized by hyperarousal. It is unclear, however, whether spirituality or meaning making, per se, is the mechanism of action of these interventions, although at least one meditation study demonstrated that increases in spiritual well-being were associated with reductions in PTSD symptoms, as noted earlier (Bormann et al., 2012). Finally, when used well, these practices encourage participants to "let go" and come into the present rather than ruminating over either the past or future.

Nonetheless, some survivors may use these techniques to facilitate avoidance, and therapists should monitor whether they are using meditation with appropriate moderation. Because others may experience periods of unanticipated distress during meditation, therapists should inform survivors that happiness per se is not the goal of meditation and that they may experience distress as they begin to look within. They should also be guided to develop strategies for responding to and handling any distress they do experience.

Meta-analyses of research on meditation have demonstrated that the effect sizes for these interventions are greater in Eastern cultures, where the spiritual meaning systems on which the interventions are based are also the spiritual bedrock of the culture (K. W. Chen et al., 2012). If Eastern approaches are more effective in Eastern cultures, it may be that spiritually integrated approaches consistent with monotheist spiritualities that dominate Western culture—Christianity, Judaism, and Islam—may be more accessible and more effective in Western cultures; however, this hypothesis has yet to be empirically tested. Nonetheless, a number of explicitly spiritually integrated interventions have been developed, all drawn from Western cultures. These interventions show promise in reducing survivors' spiritual distress.

EXPLICIT APPROACHES AND SPIRITUALLY INTEGRATED INTERVENTIONS

Although research on interventions designed to create spiritual meaning making has lagged behind that on meditative approaches, several intervention models have received preliminary empirical support (Cole & Pargament, 1999; Harris et al., 2011; Murray-Swank & Pargament, 2005, 2008; Pargament, 2007). These interventions provide clinicians with tools for helping clients resolve spiritual distress and effectively use healthy spiritual foundations to facilitate growth and resilience in the face of future traumatic experiences. These approaches include opportunities to discuss spiritual meanings associated with trauma, teach spiritual coping strategies that can help clients develop a new narrative of their experience, and facilitate spiritual meanings that contribute to more tenable global meanings. Many of the explicit approaches overlap with implicit approaches in that they include work with meditative practices or spiritual practices such as prayer. Three specific approaches that have garnered empirical support are Re-Creating Your Life (Cole, 2005; Cole & Pargament, 1999), Solace for the Soul (Murray-Swank & Pargament, 2005, 2008), and Building Spiritual Strength (Harris et al., 2011).

Re-Creating Your Life is a manualized group intervention for individuals actively dealing with cancer (Cole, 2005; Cole & Pargament, 1999). Although cancer is not necessarily trauma, as defined in the *Diagnostic and Statistical Manual of Mental Disorders* (fifth ed.; American Psychiatric Association, 2013), the range of existential concerns patients with cancer report is often similar to those experienced by other kinds of trauma survivors. Therapeutic goals include facilitating highly effective spiritual coping and reducing spiritual distress. Treatment offers opportunities to discuss stories, narratives, and experiences of cancer survivors; access peer support from within the group; build problem-solving and meditation skills; and use guided imagery and empty-chair exercises for facilitating communication with a higher power (Cole, 2005; Cole & Pargament, 1999). In preliminary studies, those participating in the therapeutic intervention reported stable levels of depression and pain, whereas those in a no-treatment control group reported increasing levels of each (Cole, 2005). However, in this small trial of 16 patients, randomization was not used; instead, participants self-selected to their group, rendering results tentative.

Solace for the Soul is a manualized individual intervention for women who have survived sexual abuse (Murray-Swank & Pargament, 2005, 2008). This intervention includes techniques for helping clients develop a positive image of God, reconcile anger and abandonment issues, create a base of spiritual support, and facilitate healthy spiritual values related to their bodies and sexuality. The program includes therapeutic prayer, breathing exercises, spiritual imagery, poetry, a two-way journal for communication with God, and spiritual rituals. Studies of this intervention to date have used each participant's baseline scores as controls and have had few participants, but participants have reported reductions in psychological symptoms (as measured by the Trauma Symptoms Checklist and the Brief Symptom Inventory) and less negative religious coping compared with their baselines (Murray-Swank & Pargament, 2005, 2008).

Building Spiritual Strength (BSS) is a manualized group program facilitating resolution of spiritual distress, originally developed for survivors of combat trauma (Harris et al., 2011). The protocol includes opportunities for mutual support among group members and empty-chair and journaling exercises to facilitate relationships with a higher power. Group sessions focus on considering theodicies; learning active prayer and meditative coping techniques; exploring forgiveness of self, other, or higher power; and planning for ongoing spiritual support after the end of the group. In a randomized controlled trial of veterans who were struggling with PTSD, BSS participants reported a greater reduction of posttraumatic symptoms relative to the wait-list controls; symptom reduction was stable over the study period (Harris et al., 2011). Further studies are necessary to determine the extent to which resolving spiritual distress, rather than nonspecific factors such as group and therapist support, is responsible for the intervention's success.

Psychologists can implement these spiritually integrated interventions in a number of ways. Those with training, experience, or ongoing supervision can implement them independently or in consultation with a therapist who has sufficient background in spiritual concerns to provide needed support. Others may work collaboratively with clergy, including chaplains or spiritual directors. Another model is to have the intervention provided by clergy with a strong background in mental health interventions or to have clergy provide the intervention as a coleader or in consultation with a therapist with an appropriate clinical background. Many people, especially those from some ethnic minority groups, may find chaplains, clergy, or spiritual directors less stigmatizing, more accessible, and culturally preferred sources of support. Therefore, as we discussed in Chapter 9, spiritually integrated interventions provided by or in conjunction with clergy may be available to many people who would otherwise not access treatment.

FORGIVENESS INTERVENTIONS

Forgiveness is a nearly universal value across spiritual approaches and religions, and forgiveness of self and other is often at the core of recovery from trauma, a critical meaning made. Forgiveness can also be a powerful technique for moving away from the past and creating a new and preferred present (e.g., less rumination, greater peace). Studies on relationships between forgiveness and posttraumatic adjustment support the clinical attention to this area, especially because trauma survivors who are having difficulties forgiving themselves and others have reported higher levels of PTSD symptoms, depression, and anxiety (Hamama-Raz, Solomon, Cohen, & Laufer, 2008; Witvliet, Phipps, Feldman, & Beckham, 2004).

Everett Worthington and his colleagues have published a wealth of both foundational and applied research on forgiveness, including several intervention manuals based on their REACH model (Wade, Hoyt, Kidwell, & Worthington, 2014). The six-step model involves recalling the painful event, making an effort to empathize with the offender, offering forgiveness, making a commitment to forgive, and maintaining forgiveness (Wade et al., 2014). This model of forgiveness intervention has been developed in several individual, group, and self-help workbook formats and has been shown to facilitate positive mental health outcomes (Van Tongeren, Burnette, O'Boyle, Worthington, & Forsyth, 2014).

Denton and Martin (1998) defined *forgiveness* as internally resolving negative feelings without seeking revenge. However, forgiveness may have other, perhaps maladaptive, spiritual and religious meanings for survivors. Therapists should assess these meanings and clear up misconceptions before recommending implementing forgiveness interventions. Some survivors may prematurely pursue forgiveness out of a sense of religious duty or in an effort to foreclose feelings of anger (Linn, Linn, & Linn, 1997). Others, like Mr. Kent, may refuse to consider forgiveness because they mistakenly believe forgiving indicates that the perpetrator did no wrong, that they are not experiencing problems as a result of the trauma, or that forgiveness requires reconciliation with the perpetrator (Denton & Martin, 1998; Enright & Fitzgibbons, 2014). Regardless of their perspective on forgiveness, therapists should allow clients to decide whether they will pursue forgiveness at any given point in time.

The BSS manual described earlier includes two sessions addressing forgiveness (Harris et al., 2011). It invites clients to consider entering into forgiveness processes with themselves, with others who have hurt them, and with God or their higher power as well. In these sessions, forgiveness is considered a means of freeing oneself from distressing feelings rather than as a religious obligation. These sessions distinguish between forgiveness (an internal process of working through the pain and letting go of the grudge) and reconciliation (an interpersonal process where trust and safety are reestablished) because reconciliation is not always wise or appropriate. Sessions reframe the difficulties survivors may experience in reconciling: When others still actively seek to harm, preventing them from doing so is a kindness. Finally, these sessions describe forgiveness as a process rather than an event. In the BSS intervention, clients are given permission to experience rather than deny feelings of anger and to perceive anger positively, as evidence that the forgiveness process is still under way (Harris et al., 2011). As Mr. Kent worked in therapy and found ways to forgive his father (not reconcile with him because he continued to experience his father as dangerous), his symptoms decreased.

Another well-researched intervention is forgiveness therapy (Enright & Fitzgibbons, 2014; Reed & Enright, 2006), a manualized individual intervention comprising weekly individual sessions for 7 to 12 months to facilitate forgiveness (Reed & Enright, 2006). The intervention is complex and includes (a) defining forgiveness and discriminating between forgiveness and reconciliation; (b) exploring survivors' anger, defenses, and grief; (c) identifying areas in which a perpetrator may have taught the survivor shame or self-blame; (d) using empathy and compassion to reframe the offender's behavior; (e) practicing forgiveness and goodwill by refusing revenge; and (f) making new meaning of the offense by finding purpose and meaning in unjust suffering and finding new ways to help others (Reed & Enright, 2006). Meta-analyses of forgiveness therapy have indicated that it is helpful to survivors of several types of interpersonal trauma, including spousal abuse and incest (Baskin & Enright, 2004; Enright & Fitzgibbons, 2014; Reed & Enright, 2006).

ETHICAL CONSIDERATIONS IN SPIRITUALLY INTEGRATED INTERVENTIONS

Ethical issues often arise in the process of attending to trauma survivors' spiritual concerns; importantly, ethical recommendations in this domain have been changing rapidly (Rosenfeld, 2011). For example, some have argued that spiritually integrated interventions should not be used for clients with psychotic spectrum disorders (Hathaway, 2011; Hathaway & Ripley, 2009), whereas others have specifically stated that this diagnosis does not contraindicate these interventions (e.g., Sperry, 2005). Others have suggested that spiritual coping may play an important role for those with serious mental illness and have noted that this population may have elevated needs for spiritually integrated therapies (Rosenfeld, 2011). Because there is no broad agreement on some issues, practitioners should review the literature, obtain training in these approaches, and seek consultation from professionals with this expertise before using them.

Specific ethical considerations for implementing spiritually integrated therapies include (a) scope of practice, (b) considering "church and state" issues when working in public health settings, and (c) maintaining group environments that are respectful of spiritual diversity. Chapter 12 provides a fuller discussion of ethics via the lens of the reciprocal meaning-making model; however, given their relevance for conducting spiritually integrative interventions, these concerns are each briefly described next.

Scope of Practice

Clinicians should be clear about the nature and limits of their roles when offering spiritually integrated interventions so that clients do not rely on them for theological or religious guidance outside their scope of practice (Plante, 2007; Richards & Bergin, 2014). Although clinicians can appropriately explore possible distortions of theology or other religious doctrines, they should not set themselves up as authorities on the nature of any higher power, community of faith, or religious belief system. Collaborating with the client's clergy or other sources of religious authority can help therapists maintain appropriate relationship boundaries, so they do not unwittingly serve as both clergy and therapist (Plante, 2007; Richards & Bergin, 2014). Mr. Kent's therapist made a referral to a spiritual advisor to support clear boundaries and roles in treatment.

Separation of Church and State

When they are practicing in a public health or government-funded setting, some therapists believe they should avoid discussion of spiritual issues to maintain a clear separation of church and state (e.g., avoiding the appearance of promoting religion using state funds). This approach is misguided. Therapists must attend to spirituality as an important individual difference and respect their clients' rights and dignity by respecting their faith and relevant concerns (APA, 2010; Richards & Bergin, 2014). Further, hospitals are typically required to respond to Joint Commission (2015) requirements to provide spiritually sensitive care.

This dilemma can be addressed by considering how rather than whether spirituality should be addressed in treatment. Spiritually integrated interventions that explore and resolve spiritual distress based on the client's own religious meaning system are appropriate in public health settings; interventions that are specific to particular faith groups and perspectives are inappropriate. Spiritually conscious care would minimally meet ethical standards whereas spiritually integrated care would be appropriate with informed consent.

Spiritually Respectful Environments

Most therapists are steeped in respect for multicultural differences from early in their training, but this respect becomes more difficult when facilitating spiritually integrative interventions in group formats. In these settings, there is no guarantee that other clients will share that respect. During the informed consent process, therapists should educate group members about respecting diverse spiritual ideas; this step is critical to implement ethically a spiritually integrated group intervention. When Mr. Kent began attending a group in the spiritual director's practice, the respect and safety he experienced in that environment helped him feel more open to both his spiritual director's recommendations and feedback from the group.

Clients who belong to faiths that require evangelism may be interested in spiritual coping and concerned about addressing spiritual distress and, therefore, may be more likely to be drawn to such groups. Nonetheless, it will be important to clearly place proselytizing and practicing evangelism off limits. With such clients, it may be important to validate that they should indeed proselytize if it is a tenet of their faith but to also emphasize that group is an inappropriate context for that practice. Many clients respond well to the reframe that by working hard at using their faith to recover, they will represent their faith positively to others and that such quiet evangelism is more appropriate, more respectful, and potentially more effective in this setting than overt evangelism.

CONCLUSION

With clients like Mr. Kent, who present with spiritual distress related to past trauma, therapists can consider many resources and directions to facilitate a more effective and present-centered spirituality. It can be especially helpful to complete a careful assessment of the client's religious culture and background that includes the meaning of that background to that particular client, as discussed in Chapter 6. Mr. Kent's religion had become a symbol of abusive authority, and conventional ways of conceptualizing spirituality were likely to exacerbate rather than ameliorate his symptoms. Nonetheless, as the source of his current distress was clearly spiritual in nature, it was impossible to address fully his symptoms without also addressing spiritual concerns. His therapist's decision to work with Mr. Kent using symptom management and family interventions, while a spiritual director addressed issues of spiritual parenting, was especially useful because it helped him find ways to make meaning of his spiritual values while avoiding ethical concerns that might have been raised if his therapist had attempted to address both.

Implicit and explicit spiritual approaches can be used either as a primary therapeutic intervention or, more commonly, as a complementary intervention supplementing a more standard evidence-based therapy such as cognitive processing therapy or prolonged exposure. According to the phase-based model of trauma recovery discussed in Chapter 4, implicit spiritual approaches such as yoga and meditative interventions may be most appropriate for helping clients learn how to maintain safety and manage symptoms well enough to prepare for more difficult therapeutic work. Explicit spiritual approaches are likely to be more useful in Phases 2 and 3, as clients first work toward creating new, more adaptive meanings about spiritual aspects of trauma exposure and then learn ways to implement these new meanings in their social context. Mr. Kent's first therapy had emphasized more Phase 1 work, and he had begun practicing yoga at that point. His more recent work emphasized Phase 3 and used more implicit spiritually integrative interventions.

Therapists differ in their fluency with spiritually integrative interventions, as well as the implicit and explicit spiritual approaches described in this chapter. Some can comfortably teach yoga or meditation skills whereas others might be more comfortable working with prayer language. Clinical choices about interventions should be based on the client's needs, the therapist's skill set, supervision and training resources, and available community spiritual resources such as spiritual direction and chaplaincy.

11

DEVELOPING RESILIENCE

So far, we have focused on identifying and treating distress symptoms that often present following exposure to trauma. Nonetheless, as Bonanno (2004) and others have pointed out, people do not inevitably develop post-traumatic stress disorder (PTSD) or other mental health problems following a potentially traumatic event. In fact, the number of people diagnosed with PTSD following possible traumas is surprisingly low (depending on the trauma, between 6.6% and 17.8%; Bonanno, 2004). Further, in studies conducted around the world, even in places where risk of trauma exposure is quite high, most people report fairly high levels of subjective well-being (Dunkel Schetter & Dolbier, 2011; Myers, 2000).

People can experience a variety of outcomes following exposure to trauma (Bonanno, 2004; Carver, 1998; Mancini & Bonanno, 2012; Steinhardt & Dolbier, 2008; Wortmann, Park, & Edmondson, 2011). Some people function poorly after trauma and do not improve for years or decades (chronic

http://dx.doi.org/10.1037/15961-011
Trauma, Meaning, and Spirituality: Translating Research Into Clinical Practice, by C. L. Park, J. M. Currier, J. I. Harris, and J. M. Slattery

distress). Others struggle for a certain period and, although their level of functioning improves, continue to function more poorly than before the trauma occurred (diminished functioning). Still others return to baseline fairly quickly (recovery), and others thrive and report doing even better than they were doing pre-trauma (thriving). Finally, recent research findings suggest that some people may initially do well but nonetheless experience a trauma-related decline in functioning months or years later (delayed distress response; e.g., Pietrzak et al., 2014; Pietrzak, Van Ness, Fried, Galea, & Norris, 2013; Solomon, Horesh, Ein-Dor, & Ohry, 2012).

That some people develop posttraumatic symptoms following traumatic experiences while others do not suggests that there may be something that a person does that leads to these differing responses (e.g., mental health symptoms, a relatively benign response, or growth). This chapter focuses on the roles that spirituality and meaning making may play in preventing problems and maximizing trauma-related recovery and possible growth. In addition, we identify interventions that could be helpful in facilitating resilient trajectories in the aftermath of stress and trauma.

DEFINING RESILIENCE

Elsewhere, we defined *resilience* as a longitudinal trajectory of continued favorable functioning, even after an event increased one's risk of poor outcomes (Park & Slattery, 2013b). We propose that resilience is the outcome of an active process that can be learned, rather than simply an innate and static characteristic; that is, resilience results when people use a set of skills or behaviors that help them understand or manage a stressful event of some kind (Park & Slattery, 2013b; White, Driver, & Warren, 2010). Resilience is a multidimensional phenomenon (e.g., affecting physical, emotional, spiritual, social, and family life domains); people may experience declines in functioning on some dimensions, yet evidence resilience on others (Costanzo, Ryff, & Singer, 2009).

Even when people possess skills that make them more resilient, their resilience can vary across different types of stressors (Newman, 2005; Sturgeon & Zautra, 2010). For example, some people who are resilient when experiencing chronic pain have difficulty with environmental or emotional stressors—and vice versa (Sturgeon & Zautra, 2010). In addition, most people's level of functioning fluctuates to some degree across time; thus, a person's resilience is best identified after several assessments, rather than after a single observation (Berntsen et al., 2012). Although it can be quite challenging for researchers to obtain repeated follow-up assessments, the information derived from these types of studies highlights the inevitable fluctuations in functioning that even the most resilient persons may experience on difficult days or weeks relative to their overall adaptive adjustment.

This process view of resilience has several implications for identifying strategies for working with people exposed to trauma. First, whereas many people see mental health problems as a fixed and unchanging characteristic of themselves (e.g., "I have been ruined by my rape," "God has abandoned me"), we can approach treatment with a growth mind-set, on the basis of the assumption that survivors can develop more helpful ways of appraising themselves, the event, God, and the world (e.g., "Right now I am having a hard time handling being raped," "I have difficulty feeling God's presence at this time"; Dweck, 2006). Rather than accepting maladaptive initial appraisals of the trauma, we can help survivors make more adaptive reappraisals, working toward developing adaptive assimilations and accommodations of the trauma.

Second, therapists should keep in mind that trauma survivors always have strengths, even when those strengths are only healthy intentions that cause additional problems. For example, Yasemin Yilmaz Chant, the client discussed in Chapter 6 and again later in this chapter, withdrew socially so she would not overburden her already stressed parents. Accessing and affirming these strengths can help survivors make more positive self-appraisals relative to the trauma, marshal their resources, and respond more effectively. Third, conceptualizing resilience in this manner can influence our intervention strategies, such that we can intentionally help clients transfer skills to situations not immediately related to the event. Finally, we should consider the skills, processes, and contexts that can lead to resilience when designing interventions to not only help survivors recover but also enhance their resilience to future stressful experiences (see Table 11.1).

We discuss two kinds of resilience-promoting strategies in this chapter: primary and secondary prevention. Mental health professionals and clergy may help people who have never experienced a trauma develop a global meaning system and meaning-making strategies that will facilitate more resilient responses if they encounter subsequent traumas at some future time (*primary prevention*). Mental health professionals and clergy can also intervene shortly after the occurrence of a possible trauma to help people cope effectively and reduce the probability of distress symptomatology enduring over time (*secondary prevention*; Park & Slattery, 2013b). In addition, because people with a history of trauma exposure are at greater risk of being retraumatized, interventions should include a future-oriented focus to prevent PTSD and other mental health problems in the event that survivors encounter additional traumas.

TABLE 11.1
Resources Associated With Greater Resilience

Resources	Examples
Positive individual and cultural global beliefs	Loving God, benevolence, comprehensibility, mattering, significance, collectivism, familism
Positive global goals	Having a happy, productive life; being of service to God or humankind; having a successful career; living a morally righteous life and going to Heaven
Tendencies to make positive situational meanings	Hopefulness, optimism, positive emotion, empathy, hardiness, sense of coherence
Self-appraisals	Self-esteem, self-confidence, mastery, control, agency, self-efficacy, autonomy, independence
Meaning-making skills	Reappraisal, acceptance, emotional regulation, positive religious and spiritual coping
Other positive coping skills	Relaxation skills, mindfulness, spiritual rituals, active and proactive coping, cognitive flexibility
Interpersonal and social connections	Spiritual community, social connectedness, perceived support, high quality relationships
Other resources	Socioeconomic status, intelligence, predisposition for good health, temperament, healthy behavioral practices, physical fitness, previous success with adversity

PRIMARY PREVENTION: MR. O'MALLEY

James O'Malley (age 55) was relatively resilient after hitting with his car and killing a child while traveling home from an out-of-town trip (recovery trajectory). The child, who had been diagnosed with autism, had darted onto a major highway near his home and into oncoming traffic. Mr. O'Malley observed,

> The only way that I survived was to believe that there wasn't anything else that I could have done differently. I responded as well as I could, given my driving skills. Maybe someone else could have handled it better, but it was a judgment call. That's life.

Mr. O'Malley noted that his way of thinking about the accident stemmed from his Jesuit education, which emphasized that "you can't understand everything intellectually." He found it helpful to trust in God's plan, even though he sometimes had difficulty understanding it. He also noted that he coped "in the usual male way by trying not to think about it." In addition, the child's teacher left a message on the O'Malleys' answering machine, encouraging him not to blame himself because this had been "an accident waiting to happen." Although they never talked to this teacher, Mr. O'Malley and his wife saw this reframe as being helpful in changing their initial maladaptive appraised meanings about the accident.

PRIMARY PREVENTION OF PROBLEMS FOLLOWING TRAUMA

Primary prevention interventions are conducted with the general population outside the context of trauma and target people regardless of their history of trauma exposure. Their goal is to boost resilience to possible exposures to traumas in the future. Such interventions have been administered to both low-risk populations (e.g., school-age children; Huppert & Johnson, 2010) and those at greater risk (e.g., firefighters and army recruits; Pargament & Sweeney, 2011; B. W. Smith et al., 2011). In designing and implementing primary prevention interventions, we attempt to mitigate any loss in functioning in the event of trauma exposure—so that people exposed to trauma experience less distress for shorter durations than they would otherwise (i.e., recovery trajectory; Carver, 1998; Layne et al., 2009).

Primary prevention interventions attempt to bolster adaptive aspects of global meaning (i.e., beliefs, goals, and sense of meaning and purpose in life), enabling people to withstand and manage stress and engage in adaptive assimilation processes in the event of a possible trauma. Mr. O'Malley described a number of aspects of his Jesuit education 40 years earlier that helped him accept this incomprehensible predicament following the child's death and continue trusting in God. For example, he believed that he could not expect to understand God's plan from his more limited viewpoint. Because he was still able to perceive his world as making sense after the child's death, he was able to respond to the accident with fairly low distress and remain hopeful that he could go on without lasting impairment.

Spirituality and Primary Prevention

As noted in Chapter 3, some types of spiritual meaning making have been consistently related to both mental and physical well-being (Park & Slattery, 2012, 2013a). Parents and other caregivers can help children become more resilient to trauma by helping them develop more realistic global beliefs about mistakes, problems, and trauma, as well as more flexible rather than dichotomous situational attributions about trauma. More helpful types of spirituality are flexible and offer strategies for making sense of difficult experiences. They can be linked with a theodicy that explains suffering in a way that individuals find acceptable, while helping them maintain adaptive views of themselves, their world, and God. They help people accept the reality of the situation, draw on spiritual resources, engage in positive problem-solving strategies, make meaning, and cultivate or reaffirm a sense of purpose (Pargament & Sweeney, 2011). They can provide alternative appraisals of trauma to help survivors better cope with and make sense of traumatic situations. For example, Mr. O'Malley's global belief that God has a plan—even if he could not know it—transformed an apparently senseless event into something that remained consistent with his global meaning system, thus minimizing discrepancies and resultant distress.

Second, religious communities, spiritual leaders, and beliefs about God can promote resilience by providing people with positive messages and forms of support that can help them manage traumatic experiences (see Saroglou & Cohen, 2013; Worthington, Davis, et al., 2013). This support can take many forms, but at the very least, religious communities and spiritual leaders should create a setting in which people feel listened to, believed, and accepted even when they judge themselves harshly. They can be given resources that will help them perceive themselves in positive ways rather than as being punished for perceived sins, maintain a positive sense of the sacred, and develop adaptive strategies for reconciling with God (Bowland, Biswas, Kyriakakis, & Edmond, 2011; Fortune, 1995). Rather than being protected from problems, children can be encouraged to learn and grow from them (cf. Dweck, 2006).

Third, survivors can develop a practice of prayer and ritual that will help them maintain an adaptive global meaning system and remain resilient following a trauma. For example, they may ask for help from God, thus retaining a belief in their ability to maintain a relative sense of control in their lives. Such practices may return a sense of normalcy by providing continuity with social norms. Instead of feeling groundless following trauma, people engaging in these processes can retain the coherence of their beliefs, goals, and values, allowing them to feel calm and safe. Nonetheless, spirituality in general, and spiritual rituals and prayer in particular, are not always helpful or benign, an issue to which clergy and therapists should remain sensitive.

Using prayer to ask for help, facilitate acceptance, and access calm and focus when attempting to manage anxiety or PTSD symptoms is associated with positive outcomes (e.g., Harris et al., 2008; Harris, Schoneman, & Carrera, 2005). These uses of prayer can promote perceiving trauma in less aversive ways by making connections with the highest levels of meaning, longest time frames, and broadest perspectives (Zell & Baumeister, 2013). However, one study of college students found that using prayer to defer or avoid stressors was related to more anxiety than were other approaches to prayer (Harris et al., 2005). From a meaning-making perspective, using prayer to defer or avoid stressors may reflect immature beliefs about God and the support expected to be received from God (see discussion of spiritual development in Chapter 2). Treatment can help clients use these distinctions to identify more helpful ways of approaching prayer.

In addition, most religions include health-promoting practices and clear standards, both of which promote self-control (Zell & Baumeister, 2013). These standards can remove triggers to health-interfering behaviors by encouraging people to spend time at their place of worship with people sharing similar moral standards and values. Such actions can help people avoid triggering behaviors and situations or distract them in the midst of such behaviors and situations. Religion's health-promoting practices and standards can remind people of their highest goals and thus of what not to do (e.g., "Don't do this or you will go to hell"), while often emphasizing moral accountability to self, others in the religious community, and God. Such practices facilitate the ability to self-monitor, identify when one is off-track, and automatize virtuous behavior. In sum, beliefs that "God wants me to do this" can provide the ultimate reason to behave in health-promoting ways as well as help people persist on dull or aversive tasks (Zell & Baumeister, 2013). Such practices and standards may be particularly important in helping people maintain a sense of meaning following trauma and engage in behaviors that will keep them safe.

Mr. O'Malley, for example, wanted to stay home in the days following the accident, but he never considered as an option missing Mass and some of the positive, health-promoting aspects of his spirituality. Further, he perceived common maladaptive coping mechanisms (e.g., drinking to excess) as inconsistent with his spiritual beliefs, despite temptations to distance himself from his distress in maladaptive ways (e.g., consuming alcohol to the point of intoxication).

Spiritual and Meaning-Focused Interventions Designed to Build Primary Resilience

As discussed in Chapter 10, resilience-promoting strategies that directly address spirituality and meaning (explicit interventions) and those that incorporate spirituality but that may not directly address it (implicit interventions such as yoga and meditation) can foster primary resilience. For example, mindfulness is active and open attention to the present moment; thoughts and feelings are observed objectively and nonjudgmentally rather than from the midst of emotional responsiveness. In a meta-analysis of school-based interventions, teaching mindfulness to children and youth in school settings showed small to moderate effects on resilience and various resilience-related realms, including well-being, positive and constructive emotions or affect, social skills and positive relationships, and self-concept and self-esteem (Zenner, Herrnleben-Kurz, & Walach, 2014). In a study with firefighters, mindfulness was more strongly related to positive outcomes than were other resilience resources, including social support, optimism, and personal mastery (B. W. Smith et al., 2011). Mindfulness interventions and other implicit interventions may promote resilience by fostering more mature spirituality and flexible global meaning systems, thereby building intrapersonal resources, a focus on the present rather than worrying about the future, and acceptance of "what is" rather than remaining fixed on obtaining a specific outcome (B. W. Smith et al., 2011). A review of the literature on mindfulness in military populations demonstrated evidence of a significant and positive relationship with resources related to resilience (Rees, 2011).

The U.S. Army has introduced interventions to increase spiritual fitness and resilience as part of a comprehensive intervention plan that also addresses physical, material, and mental well-being (Pargament & Sweeney, 2011). This plan is designed to build primary resilience (at least relative to deployment) and decrease the probability of psychological problems, including PTSD and substance abuse. The spiritual fitness program uses a three-tiered approach that (a) identifies what gives soldiers their life meaning and purpose, assesses current life directions relative to building a meaningful and fulfilling life, and creates a spiritual development plan; (b) builds skills to help them access spiritual resources (e.g., normalize spiritual struggle, make meaning, learn to meditate); and (c) creates deeper connections with other people and the world. At this point, however, this program has not received strong empirical support (Eidelson & Soldz, 2012).

Just as developing such programs is likely to be difficult, so will assessing them. Follow-ups will have to be long term rather than only, for example, a part of a soldier's homecoming assessment. Because survivors often follow resilience trajectories, resilience interventions will need to be evaluated with regard to both immediate and long-term benefits on a range of outcomes. Further, one must consider who will most profit from the interventions. This may depend on factors such as spiritual interest, spiritual development, and spiritual resources.

SECONDARY PREVENTION: HELPING PEOPLE RECOVER OR THRIVE IMMEDIATELY POSTTRAUMA

Secondary prevention strategies target persons who were exposed to trauma and attempt to facilitate a relatively rapid return to baseline functioning or even an improvement in functioning (e.g., recovery and thriving trajectories). Most trauma-exposed people, even those initially presenting with psychiatric symptoms, report few symptoms of PTSD several months later (Bonanno, 2004). For example, in telephone interviews, about 7.5% of respondents met criteria for a diagnosis of PTSD 1 month following the 9/11 terrorist attacks, whereas only 0.6% met criteria at 6 months (Galea et al., 2003).

Spirituality in Secondary Prevention

Trauma survivors often report feeling support from God, religious communities, and religious leaders that help them create adaptive meanings of their traumatic experiences (Bowland et al., 2011; Fortune, 1995; Nason-Clark, 1997). Participating in faith communities may provide opportunities to make more adaptive global meanings through action in a socially supportive environment, making support from a higher power more concrete in the context of a community of faith.

Others may have a global meaning that includes theological beliefs or views of God that could impede recovery, especially beliefs that lead a person to feel powerless or shameful or that promote unhealthy selflessness (Bowland et al., 2011). Such beliefs may include negative messages about women from Bible stories, expectations of self-sacrifice to meet others' needs, passive acceptance of suffering, and equation of submissiveness with spiritual maturity (Imbens & Jonker, 1992). Further, survivors may believe they should forgive and seek reparation with offenders quickly, even when the offender denies the offense, continues to abuse the survivor, or shows no feelings of sorrow or regret (Fortune, 1995; Imbens & Jonker, 1992). Such beliefs may be activated when a person is exposed to trauma.

As described in Chapters 2 and 3, survivors may also perceive themselves as abandoned or punished by God for past sins or lack of devotion (Exline, 2002; Exline & Rose, 2013). In so doing, they may experience a series of apparent paradoxes between global and situational meanings that they must somehow reconcile: the sinfulness of humanity with the desire to be worthy of God's love, feeling punished by God despite their innocence, feeling abandoned by God during the traumatic experience despite global beliefs in a loving God, and discrepancies between how they experience their faith community and what it could or should be (Bowland et al., 2011).

Trauma survivors may also experience distress when they perceive little support from their faith community and religious leaders (Bowland et al., 2011). They may perceive these people as minimizing or denying their personal experiences of trauma and may even believe that violence within the home is accepted or condoned (Nason-Clark, 1997). Further, some religious communities can promote simplistic theological responses to interpersonal traumas, including equating forgiveness with forgetting offenses and reconciliation, encouraging unconditional (and premature) forgiveness of the offender, attributing trauma to punishments for sin, or encouraging survivors to suffer silently to achieve rewards in the afterlife (Fortune, 1995; Imbens & Jonker, 1992; Nason-Clark, 1997). Nason-Clark (1997) concluded that these problems occur in part due to clergy holding overly optimistic attitudes about violence that might occur in families—that men want to stop their abusive actions, that they can change with help, and that violent families can easily be transformed into more healthy ones. These types of responses may induce maladaptive accommodations that lead to blame- and shame-promoting appraisals (e.g., "My husband cannot stop beating me because I deserve beatings," "Even God believes that I should forgive and forget what my husband did"). As described in Chapter 6, therapists should be especially careful to assess such beliefs and determine whether a survivor's beliefs and support system are, in fact, supportive.

Secondary Prevention Strategies Immediately Posttrauma

Recovery appears to be the most common trajectory following exposure to potential traumas (Bonanno, 2004; Leaman & Gee, 2012). As a result, we should be cautious about pathologizing restorative processes and unintentionally undermining natural recovery processes and resilience. Some mental health professionals have argued that what is appropriate in helping survivors with the most significant symptoms to recover from trauma may not be appropriate for people who are more resilient (e.g., Adler, Bliese, McGurk, Hoge, & Castro, 2009; Bonanno, 2004). In fact, following the 9/11 attacks on the World Trade Center, Goldstein and her colleagues (2001) urged therapists to avoid encouraging survivors to recount their experiences. They argued that such practices were "not only likely to be ineffective, but can be iatrogenic" (p. 4). From the stance of the reciprocal meaning-making model, forcing all people who have been exposed to a trauma to receive treatment could remove their sense of choice, feelings of control, and preferences for privacy, thus increasing rather than decreasing feelings of anger and frustration (Litz, Gray, Bryant, & Adler, 2002). Requiring people to recount their experience with the trauma—when they may not feel the need to do so—might suggest that they should be more distressed, causing them to appraise themselves as damaged and, thus increase their feelings of distress.

This idea—that not all trauma survivors should receive therapy or other interventions following trauma exposure—is somewhat counterintuitive, perhaps because most people with histories of trauma who are seen by therapists are already struggling with PTSD or other symptoms. Therapists may then overgeneralize from their experiences with survivors in treatment and conclude that all people exposed to traumatic events will be traumatized. Through the lens of the reciprocal meaning-making model, however, triage makes perfect sense: intervene with people whose situational appraisals may cause them to need help in returning to baseline, but support those who are presenting with more normative distress to draw on their available resources to recover in an efficient and natural manner.

Rather than intervening with everyone immediately following a trauma, current best practices suggest focusing on those at greatest risk of developing trauma-related symptoms (e.g., those with histories of prior trauma; low social support; greater neuroticism; and symptoms of hyperarousal, depression, or emotional problems), as well as those who still have symptoms

3 months after the trauma (Berntsen et al., 2012; Bonanno, 2004; Dougall, Herberman, Delahanty, Inslicht, & Baum, 2000; Litz et al., 2002). Instead of offering blanket interventions immediately following a trauma, survivors might be offered psychological first aid (e.g., comfort, support, information, and resources to meet immediate material and emotional needs), characterized by an initial screening to identify those who may need additional help, an assessment 1 week following the potentially traumatic event, and psychotherapy only when indicated (Litz et al., 2002). All survivors should be encouraged to access and use positive social support whenever possible. Such interventions normalize early responses, dampen hyperarousal, and encourage survivors to appraise themselves as temporarily distressed rather than permanently damaged.

Instead of recounting the trauma in therapeutic conversations, early interventions should help survivors access material, social, spiritual, and psychological resources they need to restore or maintain meaning (Hobfoll, Dunahoo, & Monnier, 1995; Hobfoll, Tracy, & Galea, 2006; Hobfoll et al., 2009; Litz et al., 2002). For example, in phone interviews of New Yorkers following the 9/11 attacks, losing resources (e.g., hope, material resources) predicted development of both PTSD and depression to a greater degree than did other risk factors (Hobfoll et al., 2006). However, resource gain (e.g., increase in a sense of purpose, time with loved ones) neither predicted nor prevented psychiatric problems. Resource gains may rapidly become the "new normal," whereas survivors may continue to appraise losses as such and mourn them. As a result, many people exposed to trauma may need more help in preventing or stopping cycles of loss and restoring a sense of normalcy than in pursuing more traditional therapeutic goals (Hobfoll et al., 2006).

The reciprocal meaning-making model can guide and inform early prevention efforts among trauma-exposed individuals. Clinical staff can consider how to help trauma survivors retain a sense of meaning and draw helpful situational attributions. Hobfoll and his colleagues (2009) described five goals of such work: fostering a sense of safety, calm, self- and community efficacy, connectedness, and hope. Promoting a sense of safety takes a number of forms, including providing material safety; reconnecting survivors with friends and families both emotionally and physically; removing and avoiding negative rumors, gossip, and media; and addressing negative and extreme beliefs (e.g., "the world is an extremely dangerous place") to help survivors distinguish between situations that accurately predict danger and those harmless stimuli that were accidentally linked to the dangerous situation. Calmness can be promoted by normalizing responses to a situation, teaching anxiety management strategies and problem-focused coping, reminding survivors of their pre-trauma strengths and efficacy, rebuilding their sense that they can effectively cope with trauma-related events, and empowering their family and community to respond competently to the trauma and its possible sequelae. Survivors may need help accessing the support they require and ensuring that such support is positive rather than undermining their self-image and self-efficacy (Ahrens, 2006; Hobfoll et al., 2009).

Trauma can threaten and change global meaning, lead to foreshortened views of the future, and cause feelings of depression and despair (Janoff-Bulman, 1992). Interventions such as those described by Hobfoll and his colleagues (2009) might create a needed sense of hope by accessing or rebuilding positive and adaptive global beliefs and goals, retrieving or regaining spiritual and other helpful resources, building a positive sense of coherence, and identifying and rediscovering personal strengths.

BUILDING AND EXTENDING RESILIENCE: YASEMIN YILMAZ CHANT

In Chapter 6, we examined Yasemin Yilmaz Chant's response after being displaced from Turkey following death threats to her family. She responded well to a series of therapeutic interventions that revitalized her faith and reconnected her to her family, peers, and spiritual community. For the purpose of considering the role of the reciprocal meaning-making model in conceptualizing resilience over the life course, we now discuss her response to stressors she encountered some years later, as an adult.

Ms. Chant's childhood was difficult, and so was her adult life. She attended college and became a pharmacy assistant, building a romantic relationship with an American man in her class. When they told their families about their intentions to marry, his family reacted negatively, accusing him of marrying a "heathen." The two finally eloped. His family essentially disowned the couple and subsequently maintained minimal contact with them.

The couple had been married for 3 years when Ms. Chant's husband was paralyzed in a motorcycle accident. At this point, she had to provide financial support for the household while supporting and caring for him through a long regimen of physical therapies. Although these changes were initially difficult, Ms. Chant rapidly rose to the challenges and handled them well. When her brother visited her husband in the hospital, he asked her,

> How do you do this? His family has abandoned him and you, and you are all alone to take care of him. You struggled so much when we moved from Turkey, but your husband almost died, and you seem OK. How are you really? What is going on in your heart?

Ms. Chant replied simply, "When we moved from Turkey, I tried to do it without Allah. Now I know, no matter what happens, I don't have to do it alone. As long as I reach out to Allah, Allah will be with me and help me."

What allowed Ms. Chant to be relatively resilient now, when she had struggled earlier? In her earlier treatment, she learned important coping skills and was supported in cultivating a well-functioning personal meaning system. She discovered that she was indeed strong enough to continue functioning under stress, and she developed effective strategies for responding to stressful situations in her later years. She had also learned how to access spiritual resources when other supports and resources were less available, and she developed a theodicy that allowed her to see Allah as present, even when things were not as she preferred. She confidently applied these skills to subsequent challenges in her life.

DEVELOPING RESILIENCE SUBSEQUENT TO INITIAL TRAUMAS

As highlighted in the opening chapter of this book, nearly everyone encounters highly stressful events over their life stories. People with significant trauma histories, however, are more likely to be retraumatized and are at greater risk of developing PTSD when they encounter additional traumas (e.g., Cloitre, 2009; Cloitre, Stovall-McClough, Zorbas, & Charuvastra, 2008; Herman, 1992). They are also more likely to engage in behaviors that put them at greater risk of trauma (see Chapter 4). Further, they may have made maladaptive assimilations and accommodations that compromise their appraisals of subsequent traumas; that is, these maladaptive changes in global meaning can be reinforced through additional trauma exposures.

Unfortunately, some people may need to deal repeatedly with potentially traumatizing situations in their occupational roles (e.g., soldiers, police officers, firefighters, emergency personnel). They need to be able to maintain emotional safety on the job; decompress, debrief, and retain a sense of meaning and purpose when off the job; and apply and cope effectively with subsequent exposures. Given these needs, an essential aspect of treatment includes helping already traumatized people become more resilient to future traumas (as with Yasemin Yilmaz Chant).

As described in Chapter 4, contemporary therapies for trauma survivors address safety issues (Phase 1), including decreasing risk taking and increasing social supports. In addition, there are several research-supported approaches that address problematic situational meanings that might prevent recovery from PTSD (Phase 2). Both Phase 1 and Phase 2 interventions should decrease the probability of retraumatization as well. In so doing, therapists will be better positioned to promote Phase 3 aims related to restoration of global meaning and promoting spiritual and relational connections that can help trauma survivors develop ways of thinking and behaving that promote resilience in response to subsequent trauma.

The Roles of Spirituality and Meaning in Creating Long-Term Resilience

It appears likely that the spiritual and meaning-making strategies that help survivors reframe and respond to their past effectively can also help them develop greater capacities for resilience in the face of future stressors. As we described in Chapter 3, helping survivors develop new, more realistic ways of thinking about and seeing their world, as well as a tougher, more complex, and more mature spiritual meaning system, can render people less prone to PTSD and distress when they encounter subsequent stressors. Interventions that foster these spiritual coping strategies include helping survivors identify personal, family, and community strengths; develop more supportive spiritual beliefs and a supportive community; expand their coping skills and access these skills as needed; and cultivate global beliefs that acknowledge evil, pain, and hardship, but also recognize ongoing opportunities for joy, connection, and ease.

As a young child, for example, Yasemin Yilmaz Chant withdrew from social and spiritual supports and developed a number of negative meanings about herself and her world. Therapy allowed her to begin to perceive and access both social and spiritual resources. Perhaps her increased resilience as an adult stemmed from her prior success in using these resources and her expectations for future success in doing so. Similarly, a decade after his car accident, Mr. O'Malley began going blind. Although his work and preferred recreational activities depended heavily on his eyesight, when talking about his pending blindness, he was able to adopt a philosophical stance: "Nothing hurts and I don't have any choice." He then laughed and said, "The worst thing is not driving. Really, people have dramatically worse situations than me." Rather than adopting a punitive or overly demanding global meaning system—"If God loves me, He won't let me go blind"—his earlier Jesuit education and experiences led him to believe and accept that God's plan may sometimes be difficult to understand. Mr. O'Malley maintained a strong sense of life meaning and purpose and strong positive connections to his faith, despite losing his vision and other losses that occurred as a result.

CONCLUSION

Chronic symptomatology is not inevitable following trauma, and many people, in fact, continue to do well (Bonanno, 2004; Leaman & Gee, 2012). Therapists, clergy, and educators can be forward thinking and help people develop a strong and flexible global meaning system that integrates spirituality and a sense of meaning and purpose, which will help them be resilient when encountering future tragedies (as was the case for both Mr. O'Malley and Ms. Chant). Other people exposed to trauma may need assistance in creating helpful narratives and redeveloping an adaptive sense of meaning (through either adaptive assimilative or accommodative processes).

Although there is significant research on resilience, most is cross-sectional rather than longitudinal or prospective in nature. It would be helpful to follow both trauma survivors and the general population across time, monitoring their global beliefs about themselves, their world, and God. What interventions best help people make and retain meaning following trauma? What best helps them respond resiliently to additional trauma? What factors best predict future resilience or the severity of mental and physical sequelae of trauma? Although answers to these questions await additional research, it is clear that therapists have many opportunities to facilitate their clients' development of resources to promote their resilience.

12

ETHICAL CONSIDERATIONS FOR ADDRESSING SPIRITUALITY WITH TRAUMA SURVIVORS FROM A RECIPROCAL PERSPECTIVE

In preceding chapters, we considered the reciprocal meaning-making model with respect to theory, research, and clinical practice with trauma survivors. We described this model in depth and outlined implications of a reciprocal understanding of trauma and spirituality for assessment, treatment, and self-care for professionals working with this population. We share the conviction that this information holds promise for informing future research and enhancing the effectiveness of clinical strategies for posttraumatic stress disorder (PTSD) and other trauma-related concerns. However, we are also well aware that if researchers and clinicians are truly to honor the universal ethical mandate across mental health professions to address respectfully spirituality in their work, an array of thorny ideological and practical considerations may emerge. Hence, if progress is to be made in this worthwhile venture, mental health professionals will have to both anticipate and embrace the messiness of becoming conscious and sensitive to the spirituality of their clients.

http://dx.doi.org/10.1037/15961-012
Trauma, Meaning, and Spirituality: Translating Research Into Clinical Practice, by C. L. Park, J. M. Currier, J. I. Harris, and J. M. Slattery

In Chapter 10, we considered several ethical concerns related to implementing spiritually integrative interventions. Given the importance of this topic, we provide, in this chapter, a more general discussion of professional ethics related to addressing spirituality in mental health professions through a meaning-making lens. We begin with a supervision dyad in which spiritual concerns were largely avoided, and we refer to the case in applying the reciprocal model throughout this chapter.

A SUPERVISION SCENARIO: DR. MARSHA ROBYN AND MS. JILL FORSTER

Dr. Marsha Robyn was concerned when Ms. Jill Forster, her supervisee and a practicum student in her third year of psychology graduate training, called her about an hour and a half after the training clinic had closed for the day. "I'm sorry to bother you," Ms. Forster said, "but I suspect that my last client may be stalking me." Dr. Robyn was aware that Ms. Forster had concerns about this particular client, who had a history of becoming abusive in relationships with women. Dr. Robyn had supported Ms. Forster as she worked hard to maintain a therapeutic stance and set appropriate boundaries with a client who repeatedly asked why she could not date her clients and who would often wait until the session was over and the two were in the hallways, away from the cameras in the training clinic session rooms, to tell Ms. Forster that he had romantic feelings for her. Tonight, in session, Ms. Forster planned to discuss transferring his care to a different therapist because his strong feelings for Ms. Forster were stifling progress in the treatment. Ms. Forster had been sufficiently concerned about the session that she had asked another student in her practicum group to observe the session over the video relay, in the event that her client's behavior began to escalate into aggression.

Ms. Forster explained to her supervisor that she had finished the session, met with the other student who had observed the session for debriefing, and completed her session note before leaving the clinic. However, when Ms. Forster got into her car, she saw that the client was still sitting in his vehicle, parked next to hers, in the clinic parking lot. He then tailed her in his car as she left. Ms. Forster first drove around the block to see whether the client would follow a route that made no sense. He did. She then drove to the campus security building and parked right next to the door; the client finally drove on out of sight. Ms. Forster waited some time, not asking for help from security for fear that she would violate her client's confidentiality, and drove home in the hopes that her client was not waiting for her. She then called her supervisor from the safety of her home. Once Dr. Robyn was reasonably certain that Ms. Forster was not in immediate danger, she scheduled a supervisory appointment for the next morning.

In processing Ms. Forster's experience and considering next steps with this case, she told Dr. Robyn, "I'd rather not tell you this, but I believe that I ethically must. I think there are some elements of my background that may affect my objectivity with this client." Ms. Forster then informed Dr. Robyn that she had been physically and sexually abused by her father throughout her childhood. She was a successful therapist in the graduate training program, excelling in academics, being sought out by her peers for consultation in practicum, and developing insightful lines of clinical research. Other clinical faculty had similarly not observed any difficulties with stress, anxiety, or inappropriate reactivity in Ms. Forster at any point in her various training activities.

Dr. Robyn observed that Ms. Forster's hands were shaking as she went on to explain,

> This client often justifies his abuse of his domestic partners by quoting Bible passages about how the man is the head of the household. My father used to quote those same passages to tell my mother why she should not interfere with abuse of me. I have been trying to manage my countertransference to this client, but at this point I am frightened by his efforts to push my boundaries, and I really recoil from the faith perspective he espouses in sessions. I don't think I've been providing effective therapy with him recently, and as afraid as I am of him now, I don't feel that I am at all objective. I don't think I can ethically continue to work with him. I've never been in this place with a client before, and I'm not sure what to do next.

SELF-AWARENESS AND MANAGING RELIGIOUS BIAS

Dating back to the writings of Freud (1961) and other prominent figures, psychology and other mental health disciplines historically have maintained ambivalent or even negative views of religion. As we highlighted in earlier chapters, available findings have suggested that psychologists in particular seldom endorse forms of spirituality tied to conventional forms of religiousness (e.g., Bilgrave & Deluty, 1998; Delaney, Miller, & Bisonó, 2007; Shafranske & Cummings, 2013; Shafranske & Malony, 1990). Hence, when compared with the majority of the U.S. population, who embrace religious or theistically oriented forms of spirituality, mental health professionals are less likely to endorse a belief in God or higher power and may lack synchrony with other aspects of global meaning with many of the people who might seek their expertise.

Such a mismatch may engender a variety of negative biases among non-religious clinicians (e.g., religious faith equated with low intelligence or poor coping). Although likely not as common, religious clinicians might similarly be at risk of forming negative evaluations of nonreligious clients who are espousing beliefs or values or engaging in reckless behaviors that are not sanctioned by their faith tradition (e.g., substance misuse, unsafe sex). In fact, attitudes on both sides of the spectrum might limit the ability of clinicians to appraise accurately adaptive and maladaptive dimensions of spirituality (Cummings, Ivan, Carson, Stanley, & Pargament, 2014). Hence, regardless of one's religious or spiritual background, the ethical principle of respect for people's rights and dignity requires that clinicians respect clients' religious and spiritual identifications. Deepening self-awareness of religious bias and gaining appreciation for how prejudices may affect research and practice in one's discipline are, therefore, important ethical considerations for any mental health professional.

When considering the macrolevel beliefs and values of psychology and mental health disciplines that equip clinicians for working with trauma survivors, there is a shared commitment to secularism and contextualizing one's professional expertise to processes, relationships, and events that can be observed in the natural world (i.e., naturalism). Beginning with a historical push during the Enlightenment to separate medieval science from religion, professionals trained in the behavioral sciences can feel constrained from discussing supernatural or metaphysical phenomena in their work. Whether focusing on PTSD or other topics, scientific questions and hypotheses, study designs, and interpretation of results are inherently appraised via a naturalist worldview. For example, even as research on the intersection of trauma and spirituality grows, researchers might be reluctant to interpret their findings with respect to central dimensions of global meaning that capture the beliefs and values of participants being studied (e.g., role of divine intervention in recovery from PTSD). In extreme cases, behavioral scientists might be explicitly prejudiced against spiritual beliefs and values that cannot be easily assimilated into this agreed-on meaning system in the larger academic or professional community. Hence, although research has made it apparent that posttraumatic adjustment commonly entails salient spiritual dimensions, professionals could feel that they are somehow being unscientific by incorporating this knowledge into their work.

In fact, in a concerted effort to avoid negative bias against spirituality or religious faith, mental health professionals frequently strive for a posture of acceptance and neutrality in their work. Although done with the best intentions, some have argued that this stance of respectful neutrality to theism and other nonnaturalistic worldviews has engendered a pervasive implicit bias in psychology that might apply to other mental health fields as well (e.g., Slife

& Reber, 2009). For example, because naturalism has been equated with traditional science and is somehow viewed as being impartial to nonnaturalistic beliefs and values that undergird spiritual traditions throughout the world, Slife and Reber (2009) suggested that unintentional or implicit prejudices against nonnaturalistic systems for meaning making typically shape the interpretive frameworks and professional behavior of researchers and clinicians. Paradoxically, whether a mental health professional is conventionally religious or not, maintaining a doggedly neutral stance toward religious faith or spirituality in one's work might be seen as the most effective way to avoid discriminating against religious clients. However, because implicit prejudices and practices against nonnaturalistic paradigms have become so covert and institutionalized, Slife and Reber argued that this strategy can increase the likelihood of transgressing against one's professional code of ethics through discriminatory practices against individuals who do not make meaning via a purely secular or naturalistic lens.

This unintended religious bias can assume many forms in clinical practice with trauma survivors. Like Ms. Forster's reluctance to discuss her client's unhealthy religious beliefs about women, clinicians might feel they are being unethical by accommodating their therapeutic approaches to account for phenomena that cannot be easily fitted into a naturalistic or secular paradigm. For example, even if Ms. Forster had acquired skills for assessing and conceptualizing the role of maladaptive religious beliefs in her client's interpersonal problems with women, she might have intentionally refrained from addressing these concerns during sessions or bringing them up with Dr. Robyn at earlier points in treatment.

Out of a genuine desire to convey respect, Ms. Forster also did not question aspects of her client's meaning system that he identified as being religious. With greater knowledge about her client's faith tradition, Ms. Forster might have gained an appreciation for within-group variance and recognized that he was an outlier in his toxic beliefs and values, behaviors, and relationships with women when compared with others who share his religious identification. As discussed in Chapter 5, clients managing high levels of stress and psychopathology may present with concrete and rigid reasoning that spans into the spiritual domain. In such cases, failing to explore how aspects of a client's global meaning system align with accepted teachings and practices in the faith group might convey a lack of knowledge on the part of the clinician and complicity with pathological distortions of the particular tradition.

Such a spiritually avoidant approach could, of course, also apply to supervisors. Despite available evidence for how distorted interpretations about male leadership in certain biblical passages can be used to justify oppression and violence toward women (e.g., Levitt, Swanger, & Butler, 2008), Dr. Robyn did not inquire about religious determinants of the client's attitudes toward women and provocative manner of relating with Ms. Forster in the sessions. In addition, prior to the client's verbal threat and dangerous behavior, Dr. Robyn did not encourage Ms. Forster to consider how her spiritual background and experiences might affect her ability to establish a therapeutic bond with this particular client and address his problems in a competent and concerned manner. By omitting spirituality from the supervisory relationship, Dr. Robyn possibly further confirmed Ms. Forster's assumption that spirituality was not clinically relevant and off limits for discussion in their supervision sessions as well.

As a result, Ms. Forster lacked an opportunity to receive consensual validation from Dr. Robyn and went on to privately blame herself for her negative evaluation of the client's toxic attitudes and behaviors toward women. Over the course of treatment, Ms. Forster internalized her client's problems as being her burden, and her sense of frustration and guilt worsened to the point where she could no longer maintain a therapeutic posture. Although there are differences between relationships with clients and those with supervisees, supervisors cannot expect their supervisees to avoid religious bias if they have not been able first to cultivate self-awareness and skills in addressing spirituality themselves. In other words, supervisors cannot truly expect to support supervisees in gaining self-awareness of their meaning systems if they are unwilling to engage in their spiritual journeys as mental health professionals.

Implicit ethical transgressions might also occur with negotiating tasks and goals of treatment. As such, clinicians have to be aware of value conflicts between the naturalistic worldview of their disciplines and supernatural or metaphysical beliefs and values that may define the global meaning systems of their clients (Yarhouse & Johnson, 2013). Given the possibility that survivors may reorganize or revise their spiritual meanings in the course of treatment, respect for their faith identifications can become especially complicated. For example, disengaging or exiting from faith is a possible resolution for trauma survivors who are struggling with their spirituality and feeling angry with God or a higher power (Exline, Kaplan, & Grubbs, 2012; Exline, Park, Smyth, & Carey, 2011). However, findings suggest that clients who abandon their faith system might experience poorer rates of recovery from PTSD and other problems (Ben-Ezra et al., 2010; Falsetti, Resick, & Davis, 2003; Fontana & Rosenheck, 2004). Hence, clinicians frequently have to encourage clients to suspend a possible compulsion to overaccommodate their faith system prior to establishing safety and working through their posttraumatic symptomatology (see Chapter 7).

When solely considering such a case from a naturalistic paradigm, clinicians may thereby lack the ability to appraise the functionality of the client's pretrauma nonnaturalistic meaning system. Out of a humane desire to alleviate the client's suffering as fully and efficiently as possible, a clinician may inadvertently encourage the client to move away from his or her faith system. However, as with Ms. Forster's trajectory of adaptive accommodation, many trauma survivors may opt to distance themselves from their faith or certain spiritual beliefs and practices. So as to avoid bias in either direction, clinicians have to respect clients' spiritual identification of origin as well as their decision to transition or remain in that faith tradition. For those who de-convert or leave a faith tradition in the context of adaptively accommodating their traumatic experiences, clinicians have to respect the right to do so while also providing a safe place to explore possible ways of resolving clients' crises in spiritual meaning.

Because no psychotherapy is truly value free, the only means of maintaining ethical practice in an age of increasing pluralism in religion and spirituality is to develop a high level of awareness of personal and professional values, beliefs, and biases (Vieten et al., 2013; Yarhouse & Johnson, 2013). As discussed in Chapter 10, clinicians should have the skills to provide spiritually conscious care for all clients, and some professionals may specialize further in gaining advanced skills for spiritually integrative or spiritually directive care. Regardless of where one falls on such a continuum of spiritual care in psychotherapy (Saunders, Miller, & Bright, 2010), clinicians do not have to abandon naturalism in avoiding religious bias in their work with trauma survivors. In fact, this approach is not possible and will unintentionally lead to a variety of other types of ethical transgressions. Rather, from a meaning-making perspective, clinicians have to develop awareness of (a) their personal beliefs and values with respect to spirituality, (b) the naturalistic worldview prevalent in psychology and other mental health disciplines and how it is not neutral to most spiritual meaning systems, and (c) how these personal and institutionalized levels of bias will inevitably shape one's research and practice with trauma survivors. In gaining self-awareness along these lines, clinicians can then assume a position of humility that can truly respect the many possible meaning frameworks of their clients.

OBTAINING COMPETENCE IN ADDRESSING SPIRITUALITY

The culture of mental health professions may differ significantly from the spiritual meaning systems of aspiring clinicians. As we discussed in Chapter 8, available findings have suggested that graduate programs seldom address spiritual concerns in coursework, supervision, and other training opportunities (Brawer, Handal, Fabricatore, Roberts, & Wajda-Johnston, 2002; Schafer, Handal, Brawer, & Ubinger, 2011; Vogel, McMinn, Peterson, & Gathercoal, 2013). Culturally speaking, a lack of standardized training opportunities might be one of the "mechanisms" by which religious bias pervades research and clinical practice in mental health professions such as psychology. Because most professors and other training faculty have not received formal education and systematic training in this area, they may feel inadequate or have blind spots about addressing spirituality with their students. As a result, even though many emerging professionals may value spirituality in their personal lives, they may complete their education and training without acquiring fundamental skills for addressing this domain in their professional endeavors.

For example, a national survey of 1,000 American Psychological Association (APA) members found that most were open to religion and spirituality being important to clients (Hathaway, Scott, & Garver, 2004). However, more than half of this sample of psychologists reported that they rarely or never assessed how psychological conditions affect their clients spiritually or developed treatment plans with their clients' spiritual meaning systems in mind (Hathaway et al., 2004). Notwithstanding possible attempts at neutral acceptance of religion and spirituality in such cases, these findings align with other evidence that clinicians frequently lack even the most rudimentary skills for providing spiritually sensitive care (e.g., Vieten et al., 2013).

From a meaning-making standpoint, educational and training experiences may serve to acculturate and socialize mental health professionals to the values, traditions, and rituals into the larger cultural milieu of their respective fields. In providing a model of ethical acculturation for psychologists, Handelsman, Gottlieb, and Knapp (2005) identified the following values as core components of acculturating into this particular mental health profession: scientific thinking, the appreciation of the complexity of behavior, scientifically informed practice, the search for truth, lifelong learning, the sharing of knowledge, the desire to improve society, tolerance for diversity, and social justice. Of course, spiritual traditions frequently uphold many of these same values. However, just as critical life events can precipitate assimilative and accommodative processes of meaning making, Handelsman and colleagues argued that aspiring clinicians also have to reconcile their personal ethics of origin in the process of identifying with the ethics of their profession. As highlighted in Figure 12.1, many aspiring clinicians may have to redefine their cultural identity in their training and professional development.

Regardless of one's faith identification, Handelsman and colleagues' (2005) model suggests that students will ideally engage in an integrative strategy of ethical acculturation in which they adopt the values of their profession while also maintaining adaptive dimensions of their personal meaning systems (i.e., integration). In honoring the values of each of these systems of meaning, students might then develop a richer appreciation of both. However, given that many clinicians do not identify with organized religions or place importance on religious or spiritual concerns, a substantial subset might have been drawn into mental health professions by a sense of harmony with secular or

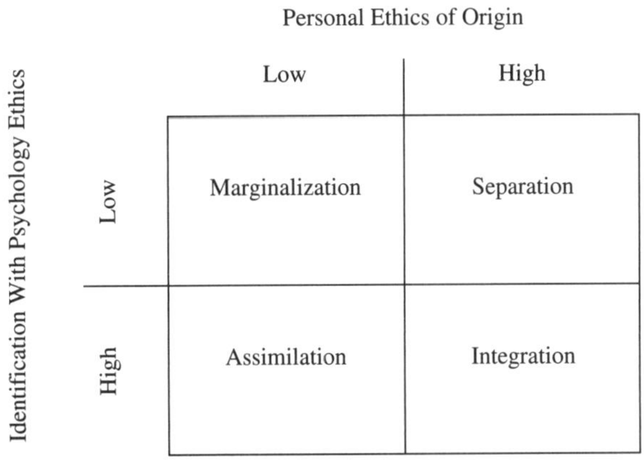

Personal Ethics of Origin

Figure 12.1. Model of ethical acculturation. From "Training Ethical Psychologists: An Acculturation Model," by M. M. Handelsman, M. C. Gottlieb, and S. Knapp, 2005, *Professional Psychology: Research and Practice*, *36*, p. 60. Copyright 2005 by the American Psychological Association.

naturalistic meaning systems from the start. Many of these students may lack awareness of their assumptions about the spiritual domain, such that they underemphasize their personal ethics of origin in acculturating into their profession over their careers (i.e., assimilation).

When considering ethical implications for this assimilative strategy for acculturating into mental health professions, clinicians might not consider their lack of competence for addressing spirituality problematic or may even feel resistant to gaining skills in this domain. In another survey, this one of 300 APA members, psychologists who ascribed less personal importance to religion and spirituality were less open to obtaining competence in this area or using clinical strategies to incorporate their clients' spiritual beliefs and values into the treatment (R. E. Frazier & Hansen, 2009). Hence, despite increasing evidence of the relevance of spirituality for recovery from trauma along with an emphasis on enhancing multicultural competence across mental health disciplines, some clinicians working on the frontlines with trauma survivors might not be readily amenable to spiritually sensitive approaches to treatment.

In such cases, if clinicians are to accommodate their practice in a manner that addresses spirituality at the most basic level (i.e., assessing and conceptualizing the possible role of spirituality in the client's life; see Chapter 6), they may need heightened awareness of a discrepancy between a spiritually sensitive approach and predominant clinical models that inform approaches to treating trauma survivors. In turn, they will have the opportunity to revise their professional identity in such a manner that they can draw on evidence-based approaches to trauma care along with an appreciation for the role of spirituality among many trauma survivors who might seek their expertise.

Other clinicians may not require this consciousness-raising step in the process of obtaining competence. In fact, available findings have suggested that a substantial minority of psychologists indeed ascribe some degree of importance to spirituality in their lives, and many maintain an affiliation with conventional religious groups (Shafranske & Cummings, 2013; Shafranske & Malony, 1990). In these cases, clinicians might be quite aware of a discrepancy between their personal meaning system and their professional code of ethics. Although detailed prospective findings are limited, some students may struggle to adapt to a secular framework while not overaccommodating their spiritual meaning systems in the process of acculturation (Handelsman et al., 2005). As shown in Figure 12.1, clinicians might feel marginalized or alienated in their personal and professional lives in such cases. According to Handelsman et al. (2005), low identification with personal ethics of origin and professional ethics represents the most problematic situation. That is, unlike integration or assimilation, clinicians would only address spirituality with clients when personally convenient and would not intervene from a strong sense of moral obligation. In addition, they would not do so with concern for adhering to the ethics and values that undergird the cultural frameworks of their profession or possible faith tradition.

This type of marginalization strategy might apply to cases in which clinicians change their religious identification over the course of their training and/or careers. As in Ms. Forster's history of spiritual abuse, mental health professionals may distance or de-convert from faith systems and practices as part of normative psychospiritual developmental processes and/or in response to trauma or stressful experiences (Paloutzian, 2005). In other cases, students might desire to develop a professional identity so strongly that they disengage or separate from the traditions that endowed life with purpose and previously guided their life stories. In fact, when compared with their religious affiliations during childhood, a survey found that psychologists reported a 44% drop in Christian Protestant affiliations, 36% decrease in affiliations to Roman Catholicism, and 20% drop in Jewish affiliation as adults (Shafranske & Malony, 1990). In contrast, when compared with affiliations with Judeo-Christian traditions as children, rates of psychologists who endorsed no religious affiliation at the time of the survey had increased tenfold from 3% to 30%.

In contrast, in the absence of formalized training, other religious clinicians might rely on a separation strategy of ethical acculturation in which they mistakenly equate their faith experiences and backgrounds with being competent clinically (see Figure 12.1). For example, clinicians may assume that because of their devoutness or personal knowledge, they are uniquely positioned to incorporate spirituality into their professional work and minimize the relevance of professional ethics. As such, clinicians in these cases might feel as though their way of expressing their spiritual values is sufficient to help their clients and that they do not need additional ethical standards. Such a naive assumption threatens to trivialize spirituality as being a valid area of clinical expertise with trauma survivors, particularly among clinicians who will likely feel the most passionate about addressing spirituality in the first place. Without developing expertise via the same types of standardized training experiences that are an unquestionable requisite for other areas of professional practice, clinicians relying on this strategy are at risk of failing to socializing into their profession and inadvertently discriminating against their clients' meaning frameworks in the process—even in cases in which clients affiliate with the same religious tradition (Handelsman et al., 2005).

When considering possible diversity concerns that may emerge between different types of therapeutic dyads, clinicians may believe that synchrony in spiritual identifications might be sufficient for obtaining competence in this area. Further, clinicians might assume that differences in spirituality will unavoidably interfere with building a therapeutic alliance with certain clients. In either case, such misperceptions about obtaining competence in spirituality grossly oversimplify concepts of multiculturalism and threaten the efficacy of clinicians' work with clients from diverse spiritual backgrounds. Differences in spirituality might, in fact, aid clinicians in recognizing the importance of managing their biases via careful assessment of the client's spiritual beliefs and values (as outlined in Chapter 6).

Even if a client shares a similar spiritual identification, inevitable within-group variability across religious traditions might lead clinicians to underestimate discordant beliefs and values in therapeutic dyads in these cases. From a meaning-making view, clinician–client dyads with too much perceived concordance in spirituality might fall into a false consensus bias. For example, clinicians in these cases might refrain from exploring alternate ways of appraising traumas or neglect to support clients in adopting new practices that might be helpful for alleviating their distress (e.g., mindfulness). However, dyads with too little similarity may engender a false difference bias that prevents clinicians from being flexible in accommodating their approach in a manner that honors a client's faith system.

Vieten and her colleagues (2013) proposed a set of empirically derived spiritual and religious competencies for psychologists, which may also apply to other mental health professions, that equip clinicians to work with trauma survivors. By offering this list, Vieten et al. noted, "Our goal is not to require that [clinicians] employ religious or spiritual interventions, nor to encourage them to adopt personally any form of spiritual or religious beliefs and practices" (p. 138). According to Saunders et al.'s (2010) continuum of spiritual care described in Chapter 10, clinicians may not take steps to gain proficiency in actively drawing on spiritually integrative or spiritually directive interventions in treating trauma survivors. Instead, these competencies might help clinicians avoid bias when spiritual concerns emerge in treatment and enable them to identify and address spiritual struggles as well as incorporate spiritual resources in their therapeutic tasks and goals. Vieten et al.'s list might also provide a set of baseline standards for content that might be incorporated into graduate training programs across mental health professions.

In brief, Vieten et al.'s (2013) list of competencies spans three inter-related domains—attitudes, knowledge, and skills—that clinicians should possess for effective and ethical practice. When considering implicit and explicit views that people frequently hold about religion and spirituality, Vieten et al. recommended that clinicians have to demonstrate empathy, respect, and appreciation for clients' religious and spiritual backgrounds and affiliations. Also, they must view spirituality and religion as important aspects of human diversity and develop awareness of how their beliefs may influence their clinical practice. Regarding the second domain, Vieten et al. offered several competencies for obtaining information, facts, concepts, and awareness of empirical sources (e.g., diversity of forms of religion and spirituality, intersection between spirituality and psychopathology, developmental considerations of religious beliefs and practices, legal and ethical considerations of addressing religion and spirituality). Finally, Vieten et al. offered six competencies for applying this knowledge of religion and spirituality in clinical work with clients. For example, clinicians must develop necessary skills for conducting empathic and effective psychotherapy with clients from diverse religious backgrounds as well as assessing for and conceptualizing clients' backgrounds. Vieten et al.'s work should stimulate dialogue and discussion that can lead to systematic changes in improving coverage of spiritual concerns for mental health professions in the years to come.

PRACTICAL ISSUES FOR INCORPORATING SPIRITUALITY INTO WORK WITH TRAUMA SURVIVORS

Aspirational values such as respect and competence serve a crucial identity-forming function across the many mental health professions that equip clinicians to help individuals and communities affected by trauma. However, in attempting to provide spiritually conscious care, clinicians can encounter a variety of practical ethical issues in their day-to-day decisions and behaviors. We now shift to considering several practical issues that have particular relevance for applying a reciprocal meaning-making model: informed consent, collaboration with ministry professionals, and personal problems. Useful resources for more general and comprehensive discussion of these concerns include APA's *Ethical Principles of Psychologists and Code of Conduct* (2010; hereinafter Ethics Code) and Resolution on Religious,

Religion-Based, and/or Religion Derived Prejudice (APA, 2008), preliminary guidelines on the use of spiritually oriented interventions (Hathaway, 2011; Hathaway & Ripley, 2009), checklists for managing ethical concerns in spiritually integrated interventions (Richards & Bergin, 2014), and articles outlining relevant ethical concerns with addressing spirituality (e.g., Gonsiorek, Richards, Pargament, & McMinn, 2009; Rosenfeld, 2011; Sperry, 2005).

Informed Consent

Whether directly targeting spiritual concerns or not, clinicians have to receive informed consent from the client before implementing any therapeutic procedures (APA, 2010). In so doing, the client needs an adequate understanding of the rationale, provisional timeline of the treatment, and possible consequences for engaging in specific tasks and goals. As discussed in Chapter 7, efficacy can be enhanced when clinicians provide a spiritually safe environment in which they take steps to understand a client's beliefs and values and contextualize their interventions in his or her global meaning system. However, even when spirituality clearly intersects with the presenting problems and goals, trauma survivors might not wish to discuss this domain or conceptualize their problems from a spiritual perspective.

Particularly in cases of a spiritual struggle when appraisals of a trauma or dimensions of spiritual meaning are playing a destructive role, clients may have experienced a pervasive violation of their faith system. As a result, they may be angry with God or a higher power and feel abandoned by their church or spiritual community. Other survivors might be grappling with intrapersonal struggles such as religious doubting, self-forgiveness, and shame (see Chapter 5). In such cases, survivors who are struggling with their faith or spirituality might have first sought help from a pastoral professional or religious leader. If these initial attempts at help seeking went poorly, clients might feel even more ambivalent about addressing spiritual concerns with a psychologist or other type of mental health provider. As such, they may fear being treated in the same way by a psychotherapist if he or she explicitly addressed spiritual concerns in the treatment.

Obtaining informed consent in these situations might precipitate tension for clinicians between the competing ethical obligations to respect a client's autonomy while also intervening with integrity and concern. From a reciprocal viewpoint, spirituality might influence every aspect of the meaning-making process (see Chapter 3). We have provided case examples throughout this volume to illustrate ways in which resources and struggles in the spiritual domain factored prominently in restoring global meaning. Although research is making it increasingly clear that effective treatments with survivors of trauma might have to encompass the spiritual domain, clinicians ultimately have to respect clients' autonomy in establishing the tasks and goals of their treatments. Hence, clinicians may encounter situations in which clients are not open to addressing spirituality, but clinicians' empirical and theoretical knowledge of the reciprocal meaning-making model leads them to recognize the potentially dire consequences of not doing so. These situations might engender unique ethical concerns for clinicians who are practicing in a spiritually conscious manner.

One practical solution in such cases is for clinicians to disclose in a respectful and thoughtful manner their sense of concern over leaving spiritual struggles unaddressed during treatment. In addition, clinicians can offer empathic exploration of the resistance as well as psychoeducation about the possible reciprocal interplay between spirituality and meaning making in the consenting process. Depending on the client's preferences, clinicians might then agree to not explicitly incorporate spirituality in the treatment or request the client's permission to discuss this concern at a later point in treatment. That is, as discussed in Chapter 4, clinicians might agree to promote emotional safety and processing of the trauma in the initial phases of treatment. As the therapeutic alliance becomes stronger and the client's PTSD is alleviated, the clinician might then reassess possible spiritual struggles and revisit the need for addressing this domain if it appears to be clinically relevant.

Other practical issues can emerge when trauma survivors desire to incorporate spirituality in their treatment. Because spiritually integrative and spiritually directive approaches explicitly attempt to change aspects of a client's spiritual meaning system, survivors have to grasp fully the consequences of successfully achieving their goals. In many cases, clients' spiritual changes might be entirely consistent with their existing faith identification and require little accommodation in beliefs and behaviors. For example, if survivors foreclosed on appraising their trauma as being "God's will" and had not considered other theodicies that their religious tradition might also endorse, they may be apt to self-blame and struggle to stay connected in their relationships with God and their spiritual community. Spiritual change might then entail adaptive assimilation in which clients grow to practice their faith more effectively and experience a strengthening of core aspects of their identity. In such cases, clients might cultivate deeper relationships and reaffirm their beliefs in the context of their preexisting tradition (Pargament, 2007).

However, depending on the functionality of a client's spiritual meaning system, the risks of spiritual change might be far greater in other cases. For instance, if adaptive accommodation culminates in changing a religious affiliation, a reverberating series of transitions might follow in one's family relationships, employment, and other life domains. For example, as Ms. Forster discussed the process of dealing with her history of spiritual abuse, Dr. Robyn learned that she ultimately de-converted from her childhood faith. In addition, as Ms. Forster discussed her progress in her education and developed a more secular meaning system, Dr. Robyn came to understand how difficult it had become for Ms. Forster to maintain healthy connections with her family. As such, part of the informed consent process should acknowledge that even without explicitly addressing spirituality in treatment, survivors might experience spiritual change as part of their recovery. However, by consensually incorporating spirituality into the treatment, clients have to understand how these therapeutic tasks might facilitate or accelerate this process.

Collaborating With Ministry Professionals

In cases when one cannot ensure competence in addressing spiritual concerns, a viable solution is to refer to or collaborate with ministry professionals on the case (e.g., chaplains, clergy, spiritual directors). According to the APA (2010) Ethical Principles of Psychologists and Code of Conduct, "When indicated and professionally appropriate, psychologists [are to] cooperate with other professionals in order to serve their clients effectively and appropriately" (p. 7). For example, depending on one's scope of expertise, clinicians might also have to consult with a psychiatrist for medication needs. Given the possible physical health consequences of PTSD (Qureshi, Pyne, Magruder, Schulz, & Kunik, 2009), clinicians might also have to refer to physicians with other specialties and consult about their clients' medical needs and treatments. In cases of domestic violence, child abuse, or other types of ongoing traumatic exposures, clinicians might have to collaborate with an attorney, caseworker, or other community professional to facilitate physical safety as a first order objective. Ministry professionals might similarly play an adjunctive role in treatment or be positioned to meet the needs of trauma survivors in certain cases. However, possibly because of differences in meaning systems that organize clinicians' personal and professional lives, research has suggested that a lack of trust and confidence persists between many mental health and ministry professionals (Nieuwsma et al., 2013).

Although collaboration may enhance mental health care and correct the possibility of disjointed services, special competencies apply to working well with ministry professionals. Focusing on samples of 94 clergy and 145 psychologists, McMinn, Aikins, and Lish (2003) examined the importance of several such principles of effective collaboration between these professions. In general, clergy endorsed favorable experiences working with psychologists who offered unique expertise compared with their training backgrounds, possessed awareness of spiritual and religious dimensions of life, and were perceived as being trustworthy and respectful in their interactions. In addition, clergy appreciated working with psychologists who shared common values and goals with individuals they were conjointly attempting to help. With the exception of complementary expertise, psychologists similarly appreciated each of these principles. In addition, although clergy were less concerned about quality of personal relationships, psychologists in McMinn et al.'s study had the most favorable experiences working with clergy who took the time to get to know them on a more personal level.

These latter results speak to the importance among many clinicians for developing interpersonal familiarity and trust with professionals with whom they are collaborating. At the most basic level, McMinn et al.'s (2003) findings also underscore that clinicians should be sufficiently familiar with ministry professionals with whom they can seek consultation and/or offer referrals when spiritual concerns emerge that go beyond their expertise. Given the underrepresentation of conventionally religious persons in mental health professions, many clinicians might, therefore, have to learn about religious and/or spiritual traditions and organizations in their communities as part of their professional work and development.

As we highlighted in Chapter 6, clinicians should also assess their clients' possible relationships with ministry professionals at the start of treatment and be open to communicating with them over the course of treatment. Although clinicians do not have to possess synchrony in spiritual meaning with ministry professionals, they have to respect them as coprofessionals and take care not to undermine efforts at spiritual care with clients who desire an integrative approach. Hence, for religious and nonreligious clinicians alike, the first step is to become knowledgeable about ministry professionals' background and skills and to understand how they might help clients. In the same way that gaining knowledge of clients' spiritual lives might enhance treatment efficacy, conflicts in values and goals will less likely emerge with ministry professionals when respect and understanding have been established at the front end.

Notwithstanding the possible helpfulness of collaborating with ministry professionals, a variety of ethical issues might emerge. As emphasized throughout this chapter, in working with clients, clinicians similarly have to develop awareness of synchrony and/or differences in their meaning systems with ministry professionals if they are to minimize religious bias. In the same manner that concordance in spiritual meaning might detract from treatment efficacy, clinicians who collaborate with ministry professionals from the same tradition might have to negotiate dual relationships and remain cognizant about maintaining their professional role in the case. In contrast, in cases of worldview differences, clinicians might also assume a spiritually avoidant approach by not considering the need for collaborating with ministry professionals. In addition, as with obtaining informed consent for incorporating spirituality into treatment, clinicians should similarly not disclose information about clients to other professionals without first obtaining the client's consent in written form. However, before releasing any information, clinicians have to ascertain first whether ministry professionals possess the requisite skills and take steps to define their respective roles, establish parameters for communication, and possibly discuss how differences in values and goals might detract from the care of the client.

In taking these steps, clinicians should also consider their ethical obligation to uphold confidentiality. According to the APA (2010) Ethics Code, "Psychologists have a primary obligation and take reasonable precautions to protect confidential information" (p. 7). Although there might be strong concordance in global values (e.g., integrity, justice, respect), ministry professionals often do not approach confidentiality in the same manner as do psychologists and other mental health professionals. In some cases, ministry professionals are more protected from breaching confidentiality (e.g., chaplains working in military contexts, priests practicing the sacrament of confession). However, particularly when collaborating with a leader or member of a client's spiritual community, dual relationships can emerge in which ministry professionals might struggle to hold information about the client's life in confidence.

As such, clinicians should disclose information only to the degree that it might be beneficial and work with clients to similarly disclose details about their lives that will be helpful for them. For example, when working with trauma survivors, it is essential to limit certain details about their lives and to share only the "newspaper version" of their traumas with ministry professionals when clinically indicated. However, as highlighted in Chapter 5 by Ms. Lopez's decision to discuss her sexual abuse with a priest before engaging in exposure exercises with her therapist, some clients might find it easier to discuss painful aspects of their lives with ministry professionals. In these cases, clinicians may opt not to dissuade the client from sharing painful aspects of their life stories with ministry professionals, but they should also be prepared to process these interactions and provide consultation at the front end about how to decrease the likelihood that they will be retraumatizing in any way.

Personal Problems

A final practical ethical concern is the need for clinicians to responsibly manage their own problems in life. Whether working with trauma survivors or other clinical populations, clinicians have to grapple with their own emotional and spiritual struggles during their professional journeys. Given the possibility that clinicians will have histories of victimization themselves, these types of personal problems may arise from their direct exposure to trauma. Treating trauma can also entail indirect exposure to trauma in a manner that engenders a variety of emotional and/or spiritual concerns that can limit one's efficacy as a clinician (e.g., vicarious traumatization, compassion fatigue, burnout; see Chapter 8). Given the ubiquitous realities of suffering and change in human life, clinicians might also have to negotiate chronic stressors and transitions in life (e.g., divorce, caregiving to aging parent, birth of child). In the same way that we have argued throughout the pages of this volume that spirituality and meaning are best viewed from a reciprocal perspective, challenges in professional and personal domains often cannot be compartmentalized and may affect one another in manifold ways.

From a meaning-making view, these types of personal problems can emerge for a variety of reasons. The motivations of many clinicians for working with trauma survivors may involve altruistic reasons or spiritual values and goals (e.g., alleviating suffering and injustice, making the world a better place). In confronting tragic events and intense suffering with traumatized clients, clinicians might increasingly struggle to situate their lives in a broader system of meaning and lose a subjective sense of purpose in their work. In addition, if treatment is to support survivors in restoring global meaning and connection with others, treatment can progress slowly and clinicians may have to revisit the most painful parts of these narratives (see Chapter 4). Even if one has not been exposed to a significant trauma or has not struggled with their own spirituality, helping clients to reestablish functional meaning systems can violate the meaning systems of clinicians and lead to a painful discrepancy that might be difficult to resolve adaptively through assimilative processes. Hence, these therapeutic encounters might jeopardize the functionality of clinicians' meaning systems and necessitate accommodative meaning-making strategies.

Depending on the severity of threat to one's meaning system, clinicians may falter in their clinical decision making and ability to perform work-related duties in such cases. Beyond not initiating activities in which there is a substantial probability that problems in one's life will engender difficulties in following through with clinical responsibilities in a competent manner, the APA (2010) Ethics Code states, "When psychologists become aware of personal problems that may interfere with their performing work-related duties adequately, they take appropriate measures" (p. 5). As with Ms. Forster's decision to set up a transfer for her client, clinicians might have to limit, suspend, or terminate their work-related duties as a way of ensuring the quality of the client's care. From an ethical standpoint, clinicians' chief obligation in renegotiating their professional role in the client's life is to ensure that his or her needs will be adequately addressed in the future. However, in so doing, clinicians have to maintain a therapeutic posture with clients who may cause distress for them or threaten the foundations of their meaning system.

Effectively negotiating personal problems can be especially difficult when countertransference concerns emerge because of a convergence in life histories with respect to traumatic experiences. Ms. Forster found herself in the challenging predicament of promoting change and meaning making with a religious man who embodied many of the same disturbing qualities that existed in her father and led to her history of sexual and spiritual abuse. Ms. Forster did not meet criteria for PTSD or any other psychiatric condition that might limit her efficacy as a clinician with this client. In addition, she lacked foreknowledge about the man's toxic faith system and attitudes toward women. Hence, Ms. Forster had no forewarning about the ethical dilemma that would evolve for her in attempting to provide treatment in this case. However, she nonetheless felt limited in her clinical decision making and skill because of the reactivation of distressing thoughts and emotions from her trauma history.

Ethically speaking, there are no definitive rules for clinicians about working with clients who might remind them of traumatic experiences in their lives. Considering rates of exposure to trauma (P. Frazier, 2012; F. H. Norris & Slone, 2007), a proportion of clinicians in mental health professions will undoubtedly have histories of abuse or victimization. As such, many clinicians might pursue this type of work as a "meaning project" and promote healing and growth with survivors of similar traumas. However, as with Ms. Forster, other clinicians will not pursue a specialization in trauma but nonetheless encounter clients who stir up painful aspects of their life stories. Regardless of intentionality or motivation, clinicians have an ethical obligation to seek consultation and relational support when personal problems emerge.

The case example highlights several ethical concerns for clinicians and supervisors. Although Dr. Robyn had appropriately guided Ms. Forster to transfer the client, the supervisor did not create an atmosphere for Ms. Forster to get to the heart of the matter until the situation escalated to a dangerous point. The same clinical decision might have been reached if Ms. Forster had been supported to explore the intersection between her history of spiritual abuse and ambivalence about confronting the client. However, her meaning system would possibly not have been so threatened, and the client would have been afforded an earlier opportunity to change and grow in the context of mental health treatment.

Regardless of one's trauma history, a helpful ethical principle is that clinicians who desire to provide spiritually integrative care to trauma survivors will often have to engage in the same procedures and processes of meaning making that they implement with clients. Although all clinicians confront personal problems that may precipitate discrepancies in meaning, we should not attempt to guide our clients toward psychological, relational, and (possible) spiritual outcomes in ways in which we have been unwilling to engage in our own journeys. Chapter 11 provided a conceptualization of resilience as resulting from an adaptive resolution of a crisis in meaning in treatment. In other words, we argued that one of the most important goals of effective treatment for PTSD and other trauma-related problems is to promote a restoration of a functional meaning system that will increase the likelihood of adaptive coping in face of future traumas or critical life events. We now similarly encourage clinicians to intentionally cultivate their own resilience in their professional journeys. As we highlighted in Chapter 8, clinicians might struggle to find an adaptive balance between meeting the multifaceted needs of their clients and paying attention to their own well-being.

Many clinicians may cope with personal problems by drawing on their natural strengths. However, given the nature and intensity of working with trauma survivors, Buckwalter (2011) suggested that clinicians also have to pursue intentionally four sets of global values and goals to offset the potential effects of chronic stress: health, pleasure, love, and purpose. That is, when considering how to address the personal hazards of working with this population, clinicians have to engage first in a lifelong commitment to nurturing one's physical body (e.g., maintaining a regular sleep routine, eat healthfully, and developing a consistent exercise routine according to ever-changing abilities and limitations). Second, clinicians should continually invest in enhancing the quality of their relationships with family, friends, and other significant characters in their life story. Third, beyond attempts to change the world via one's professional work, we encourage clinicians to seize opportunities to enjoy deeply those situations or activities that truly enrich and satisfy them (e.g., poetry, novels, travel, nature).

Finally, in keeping with the distal outcome of a functional meaning system, we encourage clinicians also to find purpose in life. In keeping with a reciprocal meaning-making model, this final factor is more elusive than the other domains. Beyond the fulfillment that might come from supporting survivors in restoring global meaning following trauma, clinicians may cultivate an abiding sense of purpose in life by way of many different pathways (e.g., pursuing one's own psychotherapy, becoming an advocate or social activist, serving in one's community, engaging more deeply in one's faith tradition or spiritual life). In the same way that trauma survivors might have to revise and expand their meaning systems in a manner that can account for the reality of their traumatic past along with the possibility of purpose and hope, we contend that clinicians might also take steps to refine their philosophies of trauma and suffering. In pursuing these values and goals, clinicians will still encounter traumatized clients whom they are unable to help, and they might find themselves in ethical predicaments similar to the one that Ms. Forster encountered. However, we contend that addressing the concerns of traumatized clients will more likely be a rewarding experience if clinicians are taking deliberate steps to attend to their own spiritual journeys.

CONCLUSION

In the way that the reciprocal meaning-making model can enhance assessment and treatment practices, a reciprocal understanding might also illumine ethical concerns for incorporating spirituality in working with trauma survivors. Drawing on a supervision dyad of Dr. Robyn and Ms. Forster, this chapter discussed macrolevel issues related to managing religious bias and obtaining competence. Next, we discussed three practical concerns that clinicians have to negotiate in applying the reciprocal model to their work with clients. We were not able to fully resolve the many ethical concerns that will emerge if mental health professions are to implement systematic changes to more adequately equip clinicians and researchers to conduct spiritually conscious work with trauma survivors. Beyond the need for coherent conceptual models and evidence-based assessment and intervention practices, we contend that mental health professions will have to address squarely a variety of complex ethical concerns in more fully attending to the possible psychological, social, physical, and spiritual needs of clients struggling to come to terms with traumatic experiences. We hope that this chapter will support this dialogue in the years to come.

13

APPLICATIONS AND FUTURE DEVELOPMENT OF THE RECIPROCAL MEANING-MAKING MODEL

The increasing recognition of the need for more effective treatments for individuals seeking treatment for trauma as well as for clients who may be in treatment for other concerns but who also have a history of trauma is leading to increases in clinical research efforts (U.S. Department of Veterans Affairs, 2015). As we have emphasized throughout this book, this increased attention to effective treatments for trauma and recovery must include a focus on spiritual dimensions: Trauma often threatens the core of one's meaning system, and spiritual issues are, for many, an inherent and essential aspect of their recovery. Yet, in spite of the increased attention given to treating survivors of trauma, we see little effort being made in the broader trauma field to integrate spirituality into treatment. One exception is the increased attention to moral injury, which does address spirituality, albeit often only tangentially.

Our hope is that this volume will advance efforts to integrate spirituality into trauma research and treatment, using the reciprocal meaning-making

http://dx.doi.org/10.1037/15961-013

Trauma, Meaning, and Spirituality: Translating Research Into Clinical Practice, by C. L. Park, J. M. Currier, J. I. Harris, and J. M. Slattery

model as a framework for these efforts. Drawing on this model throughout this volume, we have illustrated how aspects of spirituality often infuse individuals' global beliefs and goals as well as their sense of meaning and purpose in life. Their global meaning systems are critical determinants of the situational meanings that survivors assign to traumatic events. For example, for many people, their specific beliefs about God and God's role in causing events or protecting them from harm will shape their understanding of why an event happened and why it happened to them. When events are perceived as massively violating one's global meaning, the resulting distress can be resolved only through intensive meaning making. Survivors of trauma frequently draw on their spiritual resources as they reappraise situational meanings so that they can assimilate the event into their global beliefs and goals or accommodate the event by changing their global meaning. These meaning-making processes, in turn, will influence clients' levels of recovery and the meanings they make from their trauma, often including a reenvisioned or transformed spirituality.

This reciprocal meaning-making model is supported by a fair amount of empirical literature and provides the basis for the therapeutic approaches advocated here. Yet much remains to be learned about this reciprocal meaning-making model and its centrality to therapies addressing spirituality and meaning following trauma. More research is needed to further develop the theoretical model and to create and test interventions that more holistically help traumatized individuals who are struggling in the spiritual domain as well as in their emotions and relationships.

FUTURE RESEARCH ON THE RECIPROCAL MEANING-MAKING MODEL

Interest in research to better understand global meaning and meaning-making processes has increased in recent years, and researchers have been developing new approaches to assess meaning and track changes over time. In addition to introducing new survey instruments to tap aspects of meaning (for a review, see Park & George, 2013), researchers have adopted creative methods such as using priming, neuroimaging, diaries, and social media analysis (Buhle et al., 2014; Doré, Ort, Braverman, & Ochsner, 2015; LoSavio et al., 2011; Yuan, Ding, Liu, & Yang, 2015). Successfully capturing the dynamic, fluid processes of meaning making requires longitudinal research and, ideally, some elements of prospective assessment to truly examine changes in meaning pre- to posttrauma. That is, without assessing global meaning prior to the exposure to trauma, researchers cannot ascertain trajectories in meaning making. Unlike research on other topics, behavioral scientists should not manipulate the occurrence of traumatic events in the lives of their participants. Hence, if substantive progress is to be made in studying the reciprocal model, researchers will have to implement innovative strategies in the years ahead for gauging factors associated with pre- to posttrauma changes in meaning.

Important, too, from our perspective, is that this research should explicitly incorporate attention to spiritual components of global and situational meaning. Many of the best current studies of trauma impact and recovery do not, unfortunately, include even a mention of spirituality, let alone a focus on it (Bonanno, Brewin, Kaniasty, & La Greca, 2010). Conducting such complex research is highly challenging and time and resource intensive, yet our ability to accurately conceptualize meaning and meaning making in the aftermath of trauma greatly depends on it. We encourage researchers to adopt methodologically sophisticated approaches to investigate spirituality and meaning in the context of trauma. Some of the specific topic areas in which there is the greatest need for deeper knowledge include issues about how global meaning develops over time and is affected by trauma; the relative impacts of secular and spiritual meanings; the roles of spiritual struggle, distress, and moral injury posttrauma; the process of meaning making and drawing meanings; and strategies for more effectively building resilience.

Trauma and Global Meaning Development

As we noted in Chapter 2, surprisingly little is known about how global meaning systems develop. Although it is safe to assume that global beliefs are to some extent formed by one's personal experiences, these beliefs are substantially influenced by one's already-existing meaning systems as well as by one's social environment and broader culture (Koltko-Rivera, 2004; Ozorak, 2005). Few theories have been offered as to how global goal systems or meanings in life develop. For example, important questions for empirical inquiry may include the following: How do some individuals develop complex and integrated goal hierarchies while others' goal systems remain relatively simple and fragmented? Why do some individuals have spirituality as their superordinate goal, infusing their entire goal hierarchy and providing a strong sense of meaning in life, whereas others keep spirituality as a separate goal that competes for attention with more secular goals?

Our reciprocal meaning-making model adds another layer of complexity to these questions in that it proposes not only that these global meanings influence how survivors appraise stressful and traumatic events but also that stressful and traumatic events shape their global meaning systems. This reciprocal influence is not limited to childhood but rather occurs throughout the life course. The development of global meaning systems and the interplay between development and stressful or traumatic encounters are clearly areas ripe for empirical inquiry. Again, looking ahead, it is hoped that researchers will implement the types of longitudinal and prospective designs that may illumine the role of trauma exposure in the overall process of developing global meaning systems.

Secular Versus Spiritual Meanings

As we noted earlier, for many people, religion and spirituality are core components of their lives, and research has demonstrated that religion and spirituality are often brought to bear in times of high stress and trauma (e.g., Pargament, 1997). However, we do not have a clear sense of when and for whom secular situational meanings will dominate and when spiritual meanings will prevail. There is some suggestion that traumas without a clear human agent (e.g., natural disasters) will draw forth more spiritual meanings than will those perpetrated by another human (e.g., terrorist attacks; Park, 2016). However, although human agency accounts for proximal causality, the question of "Why me?" often remains. Further, regardless of its cause, the damage sustained and the recovery required may still lead individuals to rely on their spirituality to understand and make sense of their trauma as well as move beyond it. Future research should identify the characteristics of an individual, his or her meaning system, and past experiences, as well as characteristics of the event and context, that influence the specific kinds of situational meanings that are made. Particularly for clinicians working with survivors of various types, this fine-grain information may promote an increased understanding of the diverse ways that their clients might make meaning of their traumas.

Spiritual Struggles and Distress

We have discussed how trauma survivors often experience spiritual distress and struggle following trauma: possibly questioning God's love for them, doubting their worth in the eyes of God, and feeling angry and abandoned by God or their fellow believers. Often such struggles coexist with many positive aspects of spirituality in the course of trauma recovery (Exline, Pargament, Grubbs, & Yali, 2014). However, only a few studies have examined spiritual struggle in the context of trauma (see Currier, Drescher, & Harris, 2014; Harris et al., 2008, 2011, 2012; Ogden et al., 2011). We need to know much more about how spiritual struggle operates in concert with other aspects of spirituality in the meaning-making process following trauma. There is also preliminary research indicating that psychospiritual development may be related to spiritual struggles, but there are far more questions than answers about the nature and dynamics of this relationship (Harris & Leak, 2013).

One intriguing notion is that spiritual struggle may lead to spiritual growth (Pargament, Desai, & McConnell, 2006). A core assumption of most religious and philosophic traditions across the world is that adaptive resolution of spiritual struggles can lead to maturation or positive changes in spirituality. Some have, therefore, argued that such struggle can be an important pathway to more mature spirituality (e.g., Exline, 2012; Harris & Leak, 2013; Klaassen & McDonald, 2002). Although this theoretical notion is appealing, there is little evidence that spiritual struggles lead to positive outcomes (see Pargament et al., 2006); in fact, where spiritual struggle is chronic rather than transitory, outcomes are consistently poorer (Harris et al., 2012; Pargament, Koenig, Tarakeshwar, & Hahn, 2001). However, research has yet to examine how spiritual struggles are resolved over time and the factors that might be associated with spiritual growth. That is, we have to learn how spiritual struggles track with positive aspects of meaning making and the forms that resolution of struggles after trauma take.

Moral Injury

Throughout this book, we have discussed the increased attention that trauma researchers and therapists are giving to moral injury. Because this is a nascent area of research, little is known about how moral injuries may occur and how we might conceptualize the possible points of intersection with spirituality. That is, excluding longer standing discussion in theological and philosophical literature, moral injury is not considered an inherently spiritual construct. In the same way that not all survivors endow their trauma with spiritual meaning or draw on resources in the spiritual domain in their coping process, not every morally injured individual experiences spiritual distress or struggle. However, given the inextricable connections between morality and religion/spirituality, clinical evidence and emerging empirical findings have also suggested that spiritual concerns are often at the heart of survivors' experiences of being morally injured (Harris, Park, Currier, Usset, & Voecks, 2015). As such, future research should identify how pretrauma global meaning systems can shape the manifestation of spiritual and nonspiritual forms of moral injury. This line of research may support clinicians in refraining from spiritualizing moral injury when clients are not struggling along these lines but also prepare them to address spirituality when these concerns factor prominently in the development and disruption of global meaning.

Research on psychospiritual and adult cognitive development may be especially valuable in discerning the ways in which young adult combatants make meaning while balancing civilian and military moral contexts (e.g., Harris et al., 2015). The extent to which meaning making, psychospiritual development, and resolution of spiritual struggle may be mechanisms of action in current treatments for moral injury is an important topic for future research in this area. Although military service carries the risk of a unique set of moral and ethical challenges, this construct might apply to other trauma-exposed groups as well. For example, a study of teachers in El Salvador who were working in violent communities throughout the country found that exposure to potentially morally injurious events that may occur in this professional context was uniquely associated with greater posttraumatic stress disorder (PTSD) symptoms and burnout in the presence of direct victimization (Currier, Holland, Rojas-Flores, Herrera, & Foy, 2015). Although research on moral injury in military populations has to continue, these types of findings suggest the need to examine the interplay between meaning and moral injury among other professionals who might confront people who are experiencing suffering and injustice in the world (e.g., humanitarian aid workers, clergy and other ministry professionals).

Meaning Making

One of the core elements of the reciprocal meaning-making model is the actual processing of the traumatic event: the reappraising and other strategies that survivors use to restory and reframe the trauma to render it less toxic and more consistent with their global meaning or the reconsidering of their global beliefs and goals. In their restorying process, survivors must ask themselves a series of uncomfortable questions, including whether the world is controllable and safe or whether their current life priorities are the ones they want to pursue. Researchers have documented this process using both qualitative (Brinn & Auerbach, 2015; Grossman, Sorsoli, & Kia-Keating, 2006) and quantitative (Currier, Holland, & Malott, 2015; Currier et al., 2013) methods. To date, this body of research is consistent with the basic tenets of the reciprocal meaning-making model (Park, 2010), but the findings are quite preliminary. That is, virtually all this research on meaning making has been cross-sectional. Further, in spite of their rich conceptualizations, most researchers assess meaning making simplistically. Thus, we have to learn much more about how the various aspects of meaning making—secular and spiritual—operate, interact, and change across time.

Meanings Made

An important assertion of the reciprocal meaning-making model is that through the processes of meaning making and reconciling what happened to them and how they understand it in regard to their global meaning, trauma survivors will create new understandings of themselves and God, how things happen, and the nature of other people and the world. Often, they revise their goals, values, and strivings as well as their understanding of the trauma. However, few studies have demonstrated pre- to posttrauma changes in global beliefs and goals, and most of the research on this topic is anecdotal. For example, the phenomenon of "posttraumatic growth" has received a great deal of research attention in recent years, yet these self-reports of improvements following trauma have not been shown to reflect accurately any true changes (P. Frazier et al., 2009) and are typically highly positively associated with PTSD symptoms (Park, 2016). There is also little research that has carefully documented changing appraisals of an event over time and how those changes are a function of various types of meaning making; such studies could greatly inform us about the specific ways that individuals' appraised meanings of their traumas change and, ideally, link those changes to the processes that bring these changes about.

Resilience

In addition to learning more about how people recover from highly stressful situations, we are also interested in more fully illumining the factors— both secular and spiritual—that help people to be less adversely affected by traumatic exposures or to recover more quickly from them. These are typically considered *resilience factors* (King et al., 2012). As we have discussed throughout this book, aspects of one's meaning system constitute major resilience factors, determining the extent to which global meaning may be violated by traumatic events and, thus, the distress people experience. Research has suggested that some types of global beliefs may be protective, such as those that are realistic about the likelihood of even good, morally upstanding, or beneficent people encountering adversity and trauma (C. G. Davis & Asliturk, 2011). Yet, we have much to learn about the specifics of meaning systems that render individuals more or less vulnerable to highly stressful or traumatic events. Future research is needed, particularly prospective research that will allow us to see how different pretrauma aspects of meaning (e.g., attachments, views of God, beliefs in fairness and justice, sacred goals) influence the course of trauma and recovery following trauma exposure.

FUTURE DIRECTIONS IN CLINICAL APPLICATIONS OF THE RECIPROCAL MEANING-MAKING MODEL

As the research findings accumulate on the reciprocal meaning-making model, they should be incorporated into our clinical approaches to working with trauma survivors. Some of the important issues regarding clinical applications include further development and empirical testing of interventions, training and competence for clinicians, and the potential for developing interventions that promote resilience.

Developing Interventions

Currently, there is little empirical evidence explicitly examining the role of incorporating spirituality into the therapeutic alliance or identifying how clinicians may support traumatized clients in resolving their discrepancies and creating new meaning in life in the context of psychotherapy. Rather, as detailed earlier, research has nearly exclusively focused on naturally occurring changes in meaning rather than on developing or identifying interventions that might promote adaptive accommodations of spiritual meaning and changes that might lead to more satisfying global beliefs, values, and goals.

In Chapter 10, we reviewed some of the different ways that spirituality may be included in treatment. Some approaches are implicit (e.g., mindfulness therapies, yoga), whereas, in others, spirituality is directly addressed as a central part of the therapy. These explicit approaches may be interwoven into already-established secular therapy modalities (e.g., cognitive behavior therapy) or may take the form of manual-based interventions such as Building Spiritual Strength (Harris et al., 2011). All of these approaches have some preliminary evidence demonstrating efficacy but require much more testing to determine their efficacy and effectiveness.

Given our nation's concerns about PTSD in veterans as well as in survivors of child abuse, domestic violence, sexual assault, and others traumas, federal and private support for research on trauma is widely available; nonetheless, funding for research on meaning and spiritual issues with this population is comparatively scarce. Some federal funding has been offered to study implicit spiritual approaches such as meditation and yoga; however, research on explicit spiritual approaches has been almost exclusively accomplished with private funding. Although concerns about separation of church and state may understandably make federal funding sources skittish, there are reasons to reconsider the dearth of federal funding in this area.

Spiritual approaches appear more effective when they are based on the most common religious views in the culture (K. W. Chen et al., 2012); the fact that federal research funding is rarely available for interfaith interventions that are consistent with relevant ethics codes likely limits the development of and access to the types of meaning making and spiritually integrative interventions that may be most effective for trauma survivors in our society. Given increasing emerging evidence that spiritual distress is a cause of more prolonged and severe symptoms of PTSD (e.g., Currier, Holland, & Drescher, 2015; Harris et al., 2012), ignoring spiritual meaning-making in funding for research is likely to slow progress in developing effective treatments in the years to come.

Assessing the Benefits of the Integrative Approaches

Although early research on spiritually integrated interventions indicated the utility of this approach, at least for some clients, little research comparing spiritually integrated approaches with conventional approaches in randomized controlled designs has been published. Such research is necessary to determine the extent to which common factors, such as therapeutic alliance and support from group members, may or may not explain variance in clinical outcomes associated with spiritually integrated therapies. Such studies may also include a broader range of outcomes, such as spiritual distress, community integration, and quality of life, to determine whether there are rehabilitative effects of spiritually integrated interventions that may not be identified using standard symptom measures.

Identifying Optimal Interventions for Clients

Although spiritually integrated interventions for traumatic stress are increasing, the available research does not yet provide guidance about "what works best for whom." Certainly, it would be inappropriate to compel clients to pursue spiritually integrated care if that is not their choice, but there are further considerations. Culture, values, religious affiliation, level of spiritual development, diagnostic considerations, and many other individual variables may be relevant to decisions about the appropriateness of spiritually integrated interventions; such questions await future inquiry. Some preliminary findings have suggested that African American and Latino/Latina clientele may derive greater benefit from spiritually integrated interventions (Harris et al., 2011), although there is little research regarding this important issue of who benefits most.

Training for Clinicians

Because spirituality is central to the lives of so many people and is particularly relevant in the context of trauma, our model suggests that competent therapy requires at minimum spiritually conscious approaches (Saunders, Miller, & Bright, 2010), meaning that therapists are at least aware of the ways that spirituality may play a role in clinical presentations and clinical work. As emphasized in Chapter 10, the bare minimum requirement for spiritually conscious care is to provide a spiritually supportive atmosphere and implement assessment strategies to gather the necessary information to conceptualize the role of spirituality in clients' lives. However, some therapists may opt to go beyond this basic awareness and acquire competence in addressing the interplay of spirituality, meaning, and trauma in their interventions.

This leads us to three recommendations regarding therapist training and competence. First, therapists who regularly work with trauma survivors in their clinical practices should integrate spirituality into their current approaches to assessment and possibly treatment (e.g., cognitive behavioral therapy, prolonged exposure, cognitive processing therapy). Second, we encourage therapists who regularly focus on issues of spirituality and meaning to learn more about trauma and the ways that such experiences may shape individuals' beliefs and behaviors in the spiritual domains as well as the issues they present in therapy. Third, we suggest that all therapists should consider the ways that global meaning has changed or is changing as a result of the issues bringing clients to seek therapy, as well as how spiritual and meaning-based interventions may facilitate recovery and greater resilience in the years after treatment has ended.

Clinicians should also be competent to seek appropriate consultation and collaborative relationships with clergy. As previously discussed, clinicians have to understand clients' religious culture well enough to consult appropriate clergy; for example, consultation with a Wisconsin Synod Lutheran minister may not be appropriate for a client who is a member of the Evangelical Lutheran Church of America. The scope and boundaries of practice, particularly when the client is consulting both a mental health provider and clergy, are also essential areas of training.

Prevention and Resilience

Finally, we would like to raise the hope that the research and clinical focus on meaning and spirituality will ultimately promote prevention and resilience. Knowing what helps individuals minimize distress following trauma exposure may inform the development of more effective secondary resilience programs (C. G. Davis & Asliturk, 2011). We should continue to consider when such interventions are helpful, for whom, and with what sort of traumas. Further, future research on resources that may enhance meaning-making skills, such as cognitive complexity or postconventional religious reasoning, may yield findings that could be applied in the schools and military to prevent anticipated problems.

CONCLUSION

The reciprocal model of meaning making provides a solid framework for building a much deeper and richer understanding of how spirituality influences the meaning systems of individuals, particularly in the context of trauma. The increased sophistication of research endeavoring to explicate and illuminate these processes is encouraging, and even more so are the numbers of researchers attending to the influence of spirituality in these processes. The empirical attention to interventions drawing on this expanding body of knowledge is, however, lagging, and many challenges remain. We have high hopes that in coming years, the clinical applications developed will prove to be effective and will increasingly be seen as important in a respectful approach to meeting the needs of clients in their recovery from traumatic experiences.

APPENDIX: ASSESSMENT TOOLS FOR THE RECIPROCAL MEANING-MAKING APPROACH

The following are assessment tools that the authors have found useful in clinical and research settings. A caveat is that these instruments are largely designed for research rather than clinical use and in many cases do not have established norms or cutoffs that diagnose or designate specific clinical concerns. This appendix is designed to be a resource for researchers. Clinicians may find these instruments useful on a more qualitative basis—for example, as an entry point for discussion of the specific types of spiritual distress that may be relevant for specific clients.

Spiritual and Demographic Survey

1. Please choose which of the following statements best describes your beliefs (circle one):
   - I believe in a God or higher power.
   - I believe that there might be a God or higher power, but I'm not certain.
   - I believe in some spiritual aspects of life, but not in any God or higher power.
   - I do not believe in anything like a God or higher power.
2. What is your current religious affiliation? (circle all that apply)

   Buddhist   Catholic   Hindu   Jewish   Muslim   Atheist
   Agnostic   Protestant   Other (please specify): _____

   Denomination or subgroup of your religious affiliation: _____

   (If these categories are inadequate to describe your religious beliefs, please feel free to write in this space to clarify.)
3. Is your current religious affiliation the same affiliation with which you were raised? (circle one)

   Yes   No   Other (please explain): _____

4. How often do you attend worship services in public or in your home? (circle the one that best describes you)
   - Never or almost never
   - Once or twice a year
   - 4–11 times a year
   - Once or twice a month
   - Once a week
   - 2–6 times per week
   - Every day
   - More than once a day
5. How often do you pray? (circle the one that best describes you)
   - Never or almost never
   - Once or twice a year
   - 4–11 times a year
   - Once or twice a month
   - Once a week
   - 2–6 times per week
   - Every day
   - More than once a day
6. How often do you engage in scripture study or other studies of your religion? (circle one)
   - Never or almost never
   - Once or twice a year
   - 4–11 times a year
   - Once or twice a month
   - Once a week
   - 2–6 times per week
   - Every day
   - More than once a day
7. List any other community groups (besides your faith community) in which you hold membership:
8. How would you describe your sexual orientation? (circle the best descriptor for you)

   Straight   Bisexual   Gay   Lesbian   Transgender   Asexual

Note. This is an unpublished survey that has been used in research studies to characterize participant religious and social contexts, but which could also be used in interview format. There are no subscales or scoring guides.

Religious Commitment Survey

For each item below, rate the item for how well it describes you. Use the following scale:

1. Not at all true of me
2. Mostly not true of me
3. Neither completely true or untrue of me
4. Mostly true of me
5. Totally true of me

_____ 1. I often read books and magazines about my faith.
_____ 2. I make financial contributions to my religious organization.
_____ 3. I spend time trying to grow in understanding of my faith.
_____ 4. Religion is especially important to me because it answers many questions about the meaning of life.
_____ 5. My religious beliefs lie behind my whole approach to life.
_____ 6. I enjoy spending time with others of my religious affiliation.
_____ 7. Religious beliefs influence all my dealings in life.
_____ 8. It is important to me to spend periods of time in private religious thought and reflection.
_____ 9. I enjoy working in the activities of my religious organization.
_____10. I keep well informed about my local religious group and have some influence in its decisions.

Note. No items are reverse scored. Higher scores are indicative of higher religious commitment. From "The Religious Commitment Inventory–10: Development, Refinement and Validation of a Brief Scale for Research and Counseling," by E. L. Worthington, N. E. Wade, T. L. Hight, J. S. Ripley, M. E. McCullough, J. W. Berry, . . . L. O'Connor, 2003, *Journal of Counseling Psychology, 50,* p. 87. Copyright 2003 by the American Psychological Association.

Views of Suffering Scale

For each of the following statements, indicate the choice that best indicates the extent of your belief or disbelief. Please use "God" however your faith defines God or a higher power. Response choices are as follows:

strongly disagree	moderately disagree	mildly disagree
mildly agree	moderately agree	strongly agree

1. God could prevent evil and/or suffering from happening, but God chooses not to because God isn't entirely good.
2. God is all-good and all-powerful, but God is not obligated to relieve suffering.
3. No one knows why bad things happen to good people; it's all pretty random.
4. The most important thing when we experience hard things is to keep asking God questions, even if we don't understand the answers.
5. The main obstacle to God preventing suffering is that God doesn't know when it will happen.
6. Individuals suffer because of their deeds in the past.
7. By praying and having faith we can take control over suffering.
8. When we suffer, God is suffering along with us.
9. Suffering is intended by God to be a source of personal growth.
10. Everything that we experience—including suffering—is planned in detail by God.
11. God allows suffering because God is not all-loving.
12. Suffering happens randomly, not because of anything people have done wrong.
13. We shouldn't resist suffering because God has planned every detail of our experiences—even the bad ones.
14. God is all-powerful and can change situations to alleviate suffering.
15. We know God is good in the midst of pain because God suffers with us.
16. Karma is the best explanation for individuals' suffering.
17. God will stop our suffering if we pray and have faith.
18. The most important thing to remember about human suffering is that God is above and beyond it all; we might never get answers to our questions.
19. We suffer because God wants us to become a better people through experiencing hard things.
20. There's no need to strive against suffering because God will ultimately control everything we experience.
21. When we suffer, God does God's best within chosen boundaries.
22. God's primary role when we encounter suffering is to experience it with us.
23. Suffering just happens without purpose or underlying reason.
24. We know that God is not all-good because there is suffering in the world.
25. Suffering is a way to encounter a God who is above and beyond human experience and comprehension.
26. God cares about people who are suffering, but can't protect them because God doesn't know in advance what will happen.
27. People can stop or get out of their experiences of suffering by praying.
28. God intends suffering to be a catalyst for growth.
29. The main impediment to God protecting people from suffering is that God doesn't know when or how it will happen.
30. Individuals experience suffering as a result of their past wrongdoing.

Note. Subscales include Unorthodox (Items 1, 11, 24), Random (Items 3, 12, 23), Retribution (Items 6, 16, 30), Limited Knowledge (Items 5, 26, 29), Suffering God (Items 8, 15, 22), Overcoming (Items 7, 17, 27), Soul Building (Items 9, 19, 28), Encounter/Divine Responsibility (Items 2, 4, 14, 18, 21, 25). From "Measuring Beliefs About Suffering: Development of the Views of Suffering Scale," by A. Hale-Smith, C. L. Park, and D. Edmondson, 2012, *Psychological Assessment, 24,* p. 863. Copyright 2012 by the American Psychological Association.

Global Meaning Violation Scale

Please rate the stressful event you identified using the following scale: 1 (*not at all*), 2 (*slightly*), 3 (*moderately*), 4 (*quite a bit*), 5 (*very much*).

When you think about how you felt before and after your most stressful experience

1. How much does the occurrence of this stressful experience violate your sense of the world being fair or just?
2. How much does this stressful experience violate your sense that other forces have control in the world?
3. How much does this stressful experience violate your sense that God is in control?
4. How much does this stressful experience violate your sense of being in control of your life?
5. How much does this stressful experience violate your sense that the world is a good and safe place?

How much does your stressful experience interfere with your ability to accomplish each of these?

6. Social support and community
7. Self-acceptance
8. Physical health
9. Inner peace
10. Educational achievement
11. Achievement in my career
12. Creative or artistic accomplishment
13. Intimacy (emotional closeness)

Note. Subscales include Belief Violations (Items 1, 2, 3, 4, 5), Intrinsic Goal Violations (Items 16, 7, 8, 9, 13), Extrinsic Goal Violations (Items 10, 11, 12). From *Assessing Disruptions in Meaning: Development of the Global Meaning Violation Scale,* by C. L. Park, K. E. Riley, L. George, I. Gutierrez, A. Hale, D. Cho, and T. Braun, 2015, in press. Copyright held by authors.

Brief RCOPE

The following items deal with ways you coped with the most distressing event you identified earlier in this survey. There are many ways to try to deal with problems. These items ask what you did to cope with this negative event. Obviously, different people deal with things in different ways, but we are interested in how you tried to deal with it. Each item says something different about a particular way of coping. We want to know to what extent you did what the item says. *How much or how frequently.* Don't answer on the basis of what worked or not, just whether or not you did it. Try to rate each item separately in your mind from the others. Make your answers as true FOR YOU as you can.

	Not at all			A great deal
1. Looked for a stronger connection with God.	0	1	2	3
2. Sought God's love and care.	0	1	2	3
3. Sought help from God in letting go of my anger.	0	1	2	3
4. Tried to put my plans into action with God.	0	1	2	3
5. Tried to see how God might be trying to strengthen me in this situation.	0	1	2	3
6. Asked forgiveness for my sins.	0	1	2	3
7. Focused on religion to stop worrying about my problems.	0	1	2	3
8. Wondered whether God had abandoned me.	0	1	2	3
9. Felt punished by God for my lack of devotion.	0	1	2	3
10. Wondered what I did for God to punish me.	0	1	2	3
11. Questioned God's love for me.	0	1	2	3
12. Wondered whether my church had abandoned me.	0	1	2	3
13. Decided the devil made this happen.	0	1	2	3
14. Questioned the power of God.	0	1	2	3

Note. Subscales include Positive Religious Coping (Items 1–7) and Negative Religious Coping (Items 8–14). From "The Brief RCOPE: Current Psychometric Status of a Short Measure of Religious Coping," by K. L. Pargament, M. Feuille, and D. Burdzy, 2011, *Religion*, *2*, p. 57. Creative Commons. In the public domain.

Religious and Spiritual Struggles Scale

At times in life many people experience struggles, concerns or doubts regarding spiritual or religious issues. Over the last month, to what extent have you had each of these experiences listed below? There are no right or wrong answers; the best answer is the one that most accurately reflects your experience.

1.	Felt as though God had let me down.	1	2	3	4	5
2.	Felt angry at God.	1	2	3	4	5
3.	Felt as though God had abandoned me.	1	2	3	4	5
4.	Felt as though God was punishing me.	1	2	3	4	5
5.	Questioned God's love for me.	1	2	3	4	5
6.	Felt tormented by the devil or evil spirits.	1	2	3	4	5
7.	Worried that problems I was facing were the work of the devil or evil spirits.	1	2	3	4	5
8.	Felt attacked by the devil or by evil spirits.	1	2	3	4	5
9.	Felt as though the devil (or an evil spirit) was trying to turn me away from what was good.	1	2	3	4	5
10.	Felt hurt, mistreated, or offended by religious/ spiritual people.	1	2	3	4	5
11.	Felt rejected or misunderstood by religious/spiritual people.	1	2	3	4	5
12.	Felt as though others were looking down on me because of my spiritual beliefs.	1	2	3	4	5
13.	Had conflicts with other people about religious/ spiritual matters.	1	2	3	4	5
14.	Felt angry at organized religion.	1	2	3	4	5
15.	Wrestled with attempts to follow my moral principles.	1	2	3	4	5
16.	Worried that my actions were morally or spiritually wrong.	1	2	3	4	5
17.	Felt torn between what I wanted and what I knew was morally right.	1	2	3	4	5
18.	Felt guilty for not living up to my moral standards.	1	2	3	4	5
19.	Questioned whether life really matters.	1	2	3	4	5
20.	Felt as though my life had no deeper meaning.	1	2	3	4	5
21.	Questioned whether my life will really make any difference in the world.	1	2	3	4	5
22.	Had concerns about whether there is any ultimate purpose to life or existence.	1	2	3	4	5
23.	Struggled to figure out what I really believe about religion/spirituality.	1	2	3	4	5
24.	Felt confused about my religious/spiritual beliefs.	1	2	3	4	5
25.	Felt troubled by doubts or questions about religion/ spirituality.	1	2	3	4	5
26.	Worried about whether my beliefs about religion/ spirituality were correct.	1	2	3	4	5

Note. Subscales include Divine (Items 1–4), Demonic (Items 6–9), Interpersonal (Items 6–9), Moral (Items 10–14), Ultimate Meaning (Items 15–19), Doubt (Items 23–26). From "The Religious and Spiritual Struggles Scale: Development and Initial Validation," by J. J. Exline, K. I. Pargament, J. B. Grubbs, and A. M. Yali, 2014, *Psychology of Religion and Spirituality, 6*, p. 213. Copyright 2014 by the American Psychological Association.

The Integration of Stressful Life Experiences Scale (ISLES)

Please indicate the extent to which you agree or disagree with the following statements with regard to your recent loss. Read each statement carefully and be aware that a response of agreement or disagreement may not have the same meaning across all items.

	Strongly agree	Agree	Neither agree nor disagree	Disagree	Strongly disagree
1. Since this loss, the world seems like a confusing and scary place.	1	2	3	4	5
2. I have made sense of this loss.	1	2	3	4	5
3. If or when I talk about this loss, I believe people see me differently.	1	2	3	4	5
4. I have difficulty integrating this loss into my understanding about the world.	1	2	3	4	5
5. Since this loss, I feel like I'm in a crisis of faith.	1	2	3	4	5
6. This loss is incomprehensible to me.	1	2	3	4	5
7. My previous goals and hopes for the future don't make sense anymore since this loss.	1	2	3	4	5
8. I am perplexed by what happened.	1	2	3	4	5
9. Since this loss happened, I don't know where to go next in my life.	1	2	3	4	5
10. I would have an easier time talking about my life if I left this loss out.	1	2	3	4	5
11. My beliefs and values are less clear since this loss.	1	2	3	4	5
12. I don't understand myself anymore since this loss.	1	2	3	4	5
13. Since this loss, I have a harder time feeling like I'm part of something larger than myself.	1	2	3	4	5

The Integration of Stressful Life Experiences Scale (ISLES) *(Continued)*

Please indicate the extent to which you agree or disagree with the following statements with regard to your recent loss. Read each statement carefully and be aware that a response of agreement or disagreement may not have the same meaning across all items.

	Strongly agree	Agree	Neither agree nor disagree	Disagree	Strongly disagree
14. This loss has made me feel less purposeful.	1	2	3	4	5
15. I haven't been able to put the pieces of my life back together since this loss.	1	2	3	4	5
16. After this loss, life seems more random.	1	2	3	4	5

Note. This scale has been slightly modified from its original form to make it more relevant for bereaved individuals (i.e., the word *loss* is substituted for the word *event*). With the exception of Item 2 (which should be reverse scored), all items should be scored using the 1 (*strongly agree*) to 5 (*strongly disagree*) format presented above. A sum of all items can be taken to compute a total ISLES score. Likewise, Items 1, 3, 5, 7, 9, 11, 12, 13, 14, 15, and 16 can be summed to compute the Footing in the World subscale, and Items 2, 4, 6, 8, and 10 can be summed to compute the Comprehensibility subscale. From "The Integration of Stressful Life Experiences Scale (ISLES): Development and Initial Validation of a New Measure," by J. M. Holland, J. M. Currier, R. A. Coleman, and R. A. Neimeyer, 2010, *International Journal of Stress Management, 17,* p. 337. Copyright 2010 by the American Psychological Association.

Meaning in Life Questionnaire

Please take a moment to think about what makes your life feel important to you. Please respond to the following statements as truthfully and accurately as you can, and also please remember that these are very subjective questions and that there are no right or wrong answers. Please answer according to the scale below:

1. Absolutely untrue
2. Mostly untrue
3. Somewhat untrue
4. Can't say true or false
5. Somewhat true
6. Mostly true
7. Absolutely true

1. _____ I understand my life's meaning.
2. _____ I am looking for something that makes my life feel meaningful.
3. _____ I am always looking to find life's purpose.
4. _____ My life has a clear sense of purpose.
5. _____ I have a good sense of what makes my life meaningful.
6. _____ I have discovered a satisfying life purpose.
7. _____ I am always searching for something that makes my life feel significant.
8. _____ I am seeking a purpose of mission for my life.
9. _____ My life has no clear purpose.
10. _____ I am searching for meaning in my life.

Note. Subscales include Presence of Meaning (Items 1, 4, 5, 6, 9—reverse coded) and Searching for Meaning (Items 2, 3, 7, 8, 10). From "The Meaning in Life Questionnaire: Assessing the Presence of and Search for Meaning in Life," by M. F. Steger, P. Frazier, S. Oishi, and M. Kaler, 2006, *Journal of Counseling Psychology, 53,* p. 93. Copyright 2006 by the American Psychological Association.

Transgression-Related Interpersonal
Motivations Scale—12-Item Form (TRIM–12)

For the following questions, please indicate your current thoughts and feelings about the person who hurt you. Use the following scale to indicate your agreement with each of the questions.

1 = Strongly disagree, 2 = Disagree, 3 = Neutral, 4 = Agree, 5 = Strongly agree

1. I'll make him/her pay.
2. I keep as much distance between us as possible.
3. I wish that something bad would happen to him/her.
4. I live as if he/she doesn't exist, isn't around.
5. I don't trust him/her.
6. I want him/her to get what he/she deserves.
7. I find it difficult to act warmly toward him/her.
8. I avoid him/her.
9. I'm going to get even.
10. I cut off the relationship with him/her.
11. I want to see him/her hurt and miserable.
12. I withdraw from him/her.

Note. Subscales include Avoidance Motivations (Items 2, 4, 5, 7, 8, 10, 12) and Revenge Motivations (Items 1, 3, 6, 9, 11). From "Interpersonal Forgiving in Close Relationships: II. Theoretical Elaboration and Measurement," by M. E. McCullough, K. C. Rachal, S. J. Sandage, E. L. Worthington Jr., S. W. Brown, and T. L. Hight, 1998, *Journal of Personality and Social Psychology, 75*, p. 1603. Copyright 1998 by the American Psychological Association.

REFERENCES

Adler, A. B., Bliese, P. D., McGurk, D., Hoge, C. W., & Castro, C. A. (2009). Battlemind debriefing and battlemind training as early interventions with soldiers returning from Iraq: Randomization by platoon. *Journal of Consulting and Clinical Psychology, 77*, 928–940. http://dx.doi.org/10.1037/a0016877

Ahrens, C. E. (2006). Being silenced: The impact of negative social reactions on the disclosure of rape. *American Journal of Community Psychology, 38*, 31–34. http://dx.doi.org/10.1007/s10464-006-9069-9

Aldwin, C. M. (2007). *Stress, coping, and development: An integrative perspective* (2nd ed.). New York, NY: Guilford Press.

Aldwin, C. M., Park, C. L., Jeong, Y.-J., & Nath, R. (2014). Differing pathways between religiousness, spirituality, and health: A self-regulation perspective. *Psychology of Religion and Spirituality, 6*, 9–21. http://dx.doi.org/10.1037/a0034416

Allen, K. N., & Wozniak, D. F. (2014). The integration of healing rituals in group therapy for women survivors of domestic violence. *Social Work in Mental Health, 12*, 52–68. http://dx.doi.org/10.1080/15332985.2013.817369

Alves, D., Fernández-Navarro, P., Baptista, J., Ribeiro, E., Sousa, I., & Gonçalves, M. M. (2014). Innovative moments in grief therapy: The meaning reconstruction approach and the processes of self-narrative transformation. *Psychotherapy Research, 24*, 25–41. http://dx.doi.org/10.1080/10503307.2013.814927

American Psychiatric Association. (1980). *Diagnostic and statistical manual of mental disorders* (3rd ed.). Washington, DC: Author.

American Psychiatric Association. (2000). *Diagnostic and statistical manual of mental disorders* (4th ed., text rev.). Washington, DC: Author.

American Psychiatric Association. (2013). *Diagnostic and statistical manual of mental disorders* (5th ed.). Washington, DC: Author.

American Psychological Association. (2008). Resolution on religious, religion-based, and/or religion-derived prejudice. *American Psychologist, 63*, 431–434.

American Psychological Association. (2010). *Ethical principles of psychologists and code of conduct (2002, Amended June 1, 2010)*. Retrieved from http://www.apa.org/ethics/code/index.aspx

Andrews, S. L., Stefurak, J. T., & Mehta, S. (2011). Between a rock and a hard place? Locus of control, religious problem-solving, and psychological help-seeking. *Mental Health, Religion & Culture, 14*, 855–876. http://dx.doi.org/10.1080/13674676.2010.533369

Arnold, D., Calhoun, L. G., Tedeschi, R., & Cann, A. (2005). Vicarious posttraumatic growth in psychotherapy. *Journal of Humanistic Psychology, 45*, 239–263. http://dx.doi.org/10.1177/0022167805274729

Austin, J. T., & Vancouver, J. B. (1996). Goal constructs in psychology: Structure, process, and content. *Psychological Bulletin, 120*, 338–375. http://dx.doi.org/10.1037/0033-2909.120.3.338

Baskin, T. W., & Enright, R. D. (2004). Intervention studies on forgiveness: A meta-analysis. *Journal of Counseling & Development, 82*, 79–90. http://dx.doi.org/10.1002/j.1556-6678.2004.tb00288.x

Baumeister, R. F. (1991). *Meanings of life*. New York, NY: Guilford Press.

Beals, J., Novins, D. K., Whitesell, N. R., Spicer, P., Mitchell, C. M., & Manson, S. M. (2005). Prevalence of mental disorders and utilization of mental health services in two American Indian reservation populations: Mental health disparities in a national context. *The American Journal of Psychiatry, 162*, 1723–1732. http://dx.doi.org/10.1176/appi.ajp.162.9.1723

Beck, R., & McDonald, A. (2004). Attachment to God: The Attachment to God Inventory, tests of working model correspondence, and in exploration of faith group differences. *Journal of Psychology and Theology, 32*, 92–103.

Ben-Ezra, M., Palgi, Y., Sternberg, D., Berkley, D., Eldar, H., Glidai, Y., . . . Shrira, A. (2010). Losing my religion: A preliminary study of changes in belief pattern after sexual assault. *Traumatology, 16*, 7–13. http://dx.doi.org/10.1177/1534765609358465

Benore, E. R., & Park, C. L. (2004). Death-specific religious beliefs and bereavement: Belief in an afterlife and continued attachment. *International Journal for the Psychology of Religion, 14*, 1–22. http://dx.doi.org/10.1207/s15327582ijpr1401_1

Berntsen, D., Johannessen, K. B., Thomsen, Y. D., Bertelsen, M., Hoyle, R. H., & Rubin, D. C. (2012). Peace and war: Trajectories of posttraumatic stress disorder symptoms before, during, and after military deployment in Afghanistan. *Psychological Science, 23*, 1557–1565. http://dx.doi.org/10.1177/0956797612457389

Bichescu, D., Neuner, F., Schauer, M., & Elbert, T. (2007). Narrative exposure therapy for political imprisonment-related chronic posttraumatic stress disorder and depression. *Behaviour Research and Therapy, 45*, 2212–2220. http://dx.doi.org/10.1016/j.brat.2006.12.006

Bilgrave, D., & Deluty, R. (1998). Religious beliefs and therapeutic orientations of clinical and counseling psychologists. *Journal for the Scientific Study of Religion, 37*, 329–349. http://dx.doi.org/10.2307/1387532

Bisson, J., & Andrew, M. (2005). Psychological treatment of post-traumatic stress disorder (PTSD). *Cochrane Database of Systematic Reviews, 190*, CD003388.

Bisson, J. I., Ehlers, A., Matthews, R., Pilling, S., Richards, D., & Turner, S. (2007). Psychological treatments for chronic post-traumatic stress disorder. Systematic review and meta-analysis. *The British Journal of Psychiatry, 190*, 97–104. http://dx.doi.org/10.1192/bjp.bp.106.021402

Bjorck, J. P., & Thurman, J. W. (2007). Negative life events, patterns of positive and negative religious coping, and psychological functioning. *Journal for the Scientific Study of Religion, 46*, 159–167. http://dx.doi.org/10.1111/j.1468-5906.2007.00348.x

Blank, M. B., Mahmood, M., Fox, J. C., & Guterbock, T. (2002). Alternative mental health services: The role of the black church in the South. *American Journal of Public Health, 92*, 1668–1672. http://dx.doi.org/10.2105/AJPH.92.10.1668

Bober, T., & Regehr, C. (2006). Strategies for reducing secondary or vicarious trauma: Do they work? *Brief Treatment and Crisis Intervention, 6*, 1–9. http://dx.doi.org/10.1093/brief-treatment/mhj001

Boehnlein, J. K. (2007). Religion and spirituality after trauma. In L. J. Kirmayer, R. Lemelson, & M. Barad (Eds.), *Understanding trauma. Integrating biological, clinical and cultural perspectives* (pp. 259–274). New York, NY: Cambridge University Press. http://dx.doi.org/10.1017/CBO9780511500008.018

Bonanno, G. A. (2004). Loss, trauma, and human resilience: Have we underestimated the human capacity to thrive after extremely aversive events? *American Psychologist, 59*, 20–28. http://dx.doi.org/10.1037/0003-066X.59.1.20

Bonanno, G. A., Brewin, C. R., Kaniasty, K., & La Greca, A. M. (2010). Weighing the costs of disaster: Consequences, risks, and resilience in individuals, families, and communities. *Psychological Science in the Public Interest, 11*, 1–49. http://dx.doi.org/10.1177/1529100610387086

Bordin, E. (1979). The generalizability of the psychoanalytic concept of the working alliance. *Psychotherapy: Theory, Research & Practice, 16*, 252–260. http://dx.doi.org/10.1037/h0085885

Bormann, J. E., Liu, L., Thorp, S. R., & Lang, A. J. (2012). Spiritual wellbeing mediates PTSD change in veterans with military-related PTSD. *International Journal of Behavioral Medicine, 19*, 496–502. http://dx.doi.org/10.1007/s12529-011-9186-1

Boss, P. (2004). Ambiguous loss, research, theory and practice: Reflections after 9/11. *Journal of Marriage and Family, 66*, 551–566. http://dx.doi.org/10.1111/j.0022-2445.2004.00037.x

Bovin, M. J., & Marx, B. P. (2011). The importance of the peritraumatic experience in defining traumatic stress. *Psychological Bulletin, 137*, 47–67. http://dx.doi.org/10.1037/a0021353

Bowland, S., Biswas, B., Kyriakakis, S., & Edmond, T. (2011). Transcending the negative: Spiritual struggles and resilience in older female trauma survivors. *Journal of Religion, Spirituality & Aging, 23*, 318–337. http://dx.doi.org/10.1080/15528030.2011.592121

Boyle, P. A., Buchman, A. S., & Bennett, D. A. (2010). Purpose in life is associated with a reduced risk of incident disability among community-dwelling older persons. *The American Journal of Geriatric Psychiatry, 18*, 1093–1102. http://dx.doi.org/10.1097/JGP.0b013e3181d6c259

Bradley, R., Greene, J., Russ, E., Dutra, L., & Westen, D. (2005). A multidimensional meta-analysis of psychotherapy for PTSD. *The American Journal of Psychiatry, 162*, 214–227. http://dx.doi.org/10.1176/appi.ajp.162.2.214

Bradley, R., Schwartz, A. C., & Kaslow, N. J. (2005). Posttraumatic stress disorder symptoms among low-income, African American women with a history of intimate partner violence and suicidal behaviors: Self-esteem, social support, and religious coping. *Journal of Traumatic Stress, 18,* 685–696. http://dx.doi.org/10.1002/jts.20077

Braswell, G. S., Rosengren, K. S., & Berenbaum, H. (2012). Gravity, God and ghosts? Parents' beliefs in science, religion, and the paranormal and the encouragement of beliefs in their children. *International Journal of Behavioral Development, 36,* 99–106. http://dx.doi.org/10.1177/0165025411424088

Brawer, P. A., Handal, P. J., Fabricatore, A. N., Roberts, R., & Wajda-Johnston, V. A. (2002). Training and education in religion/spirituality within APA-accredited clinical psychology programs. *Professional Psychology: Research and Practice, 33,* 203–206. http://dx.doi.org/10.1037/0735-7028.33.2.203

Brenner, P. S. (2011). Identity importance and the overreporting of religious service attendance: Multiple imputation of religious attendance using the American Time Use Study and the General Social Survey. *Journal for the Scientific Study of Religion, 50,* 103–115. http://dx.doi.org/10.1111/j.1468-5906.2010.01554.x

Breslau, N. (2002). Epidemiologic studies of trauma, posttraumatic stress disorder, and other psychiatric disorders. *Canadian Journal of Psychiatry/La Revue canadienne de psychiatrie, 47,* 923–929.

Breslau, N., Kessler, R. C., Chilcoat, H. D., Schultz, L. R., Davis, G. C., & Andreski, P. (1998). Trauma and posttraumatic stress disorder in the community: The 1996 Detroit Area Survey of Trauma. *Archives of General Psychiatry, 55,* 626–632. http://dx.doi.org/10.1001/archpsyc.55.7.626

Breuer, J., & Freud, S. (2000). *Studies on hysteria: The definitive edition* (J. Strachey, Trans.). New York, NY: Basic Books.

Brewin, C. R., Andrews, B., & Valentine, J. D. (2000). Meta-analysis of risk factors for posttraumatic stress disorder in trauma-exposed adults. *Journal of Consulting and Clinical Psychology, 68,* 748–766. http://dx.doi.org/10.1037/0022-006X.68.5.748

Brewin, C. R., Lanius, R. A., Novac, A., Schnyder, U., & Galea, S. (2009). Reformulating PTSD for *DSM–V*: Life after Criterion A. *Journal of Traumatic Stress, 22,* 366–373. http://dx.doi.org/10.1002/jts.20443

Bride, B. E., & Kintzle, S. (2011). Secondary traumatic stress, job satisfaction and occupational commitment in substance abuse counselors. *Traumatology, 17,* 22–28. http://dx.doi.org/10.1177/1534765610395617

Briere, J. (2013). Mindfulness, insight, and trauma therapy. In C. K. Germer, R. D. Siegel, & P. R. Fulton (Eds.), *Mindfulness and psychotherapy* (2nd ed., pp. 208–224). New York, NY: Guilford Press.

Briere, J., & Scott, C. (2006). *Principles of trauma therapy: A guide to symptoms, evaluation, and treatment.* Thousand Oaks, CA: Sage.

Brinn, A. J., & Auerbach, C. F. (2015). The warrior's journey: Sociocontextual meaning-making in military transition. *Traumatology, 21,* 82–89. http://dx.doi.org/10.1037/trm0000030

Briñol, P., Petty, R. E., & Wheeler, S. C. (2006). Discrepancies between explicit and implicit self-concepts: Consequences for information processing. *Journal* of *Personality and Social Psychology, 91,* 154–170. http://dx.doi.org/10.1037/0022-3514.91.1.154

Brockhouse, R., Msetfi, R. M., Cohen, K., & Joseph, S. (2011). Vicarious exposure to trauma and growth in therapists: The moderating effects of sense of coherence, organizational support, and empathy. *Journal of Traumatic Stress, 24,* 735–742. http://dx.doi.org/10.1002/jts.20704

Brown, L. (2008). *Cultural competence in trauma therapy: Beyond the flashback.* Washington, DC: American Psychological Association. http://dx.doi.org/10.1037/11752-000

Brown, S. L., Nesse, R. M., House, J. S., & Utz, R. L. (2004). Religion and emotional compensation: Results from a prospective study of widowhood. *Personality and Social Psychology Bulletin, 30,* 1165–1174. http://dx.doi.org/10.1177/0146167204263752

Buckwalter, G. (2011). *My definition of resilience.* Retrieved from http://www.headington-institute.org/files/resiliencedefinition_edited-copy_74370.pdf

Buhle, J. T., Silvers, J. A., Wager, T. D., Lopez, R., Onyemekwu, C., Kober, H., . . . Ochsner, K. N. (2014). Cognitive reappraisal of emotion: A meta-analysis of human neuroimaging studies. *Cerebral Cortex, 24,* 2981–2990. http://dx.doi.org/10.1093/cercor/bht154

Burke, L. A., & Neimeyer, R. A. (2014). Complicated spiritual grief I: Relation to complicated grief symptomatology following violent death bereavement. *Death Studies, 38,* 259–267. http://dx.doi.org/10.1080/07481187.2013.829372

Butcher, J. N., Williams, C. L., Graham, J. R., Archer, R. P., Tellegen, A., Ben-Porath, Y. S., & Kaemmer, B. (1992). *Minnesota Multiphasic Inventory—Adolescent (MMPI–A).* Minneapolis: University of Minnesota Press.

Butler, L. D., Blasey, C. M., Garlan, R. W., McCaslin, S. E., Azarow, J., Chen, X.-H., . . . Spiegel, D. (2005). Posttraumatic growth following the terrorist attacks of September 11, 2001: Cognitive coping, and trauma symptom predictors in an Internet convenience sample. *Traumatology, 11,* 247–267. http://dx.doi.org/10.1177/153476560501100405

Cahill, S. P., Rothbaum, B. O., Resick, P. A., & Follette, V. M. (2009). Cognitive–behavioral therapy for adults. In E. B. Foa, T. M. Keane, M. J. Friedman, & J. A. Cohen (Eds.), *Effective treatments for PTSD: Practice guidelines from the International Society for Traumatic Stress Studies* (2nd ed., pp. 139–222). New York, NY: Guilford Press.

Cai, W., Ding, C., Tang, Y.-L., Wu, S., & Yang, D. (2014). Effects of social supports on posttraumatic stress disorder symptoms: Moderating role of perceived safety. *Psychological Trauma: Theory, Research, Practice, and Policy, 6,* 724–730. http://dx.doi.org/10.1037/a0036342

Calhoun, L. G., Cann, A., Tedeschi, R. G., & McMillan, J. (2000). A correlational test of the relationship between posttraumatic growth, religion, and cognitive processing. *Journal of Traumatic Stress, 13,* 521–527. http://dx.doi.org/10.1023/A:1007745627077

Calhoun, L., & Tedeschi, R. G. (2006). *Handbook of post-traumatic growth.* Mahwah, NJ: Erlbaum.

Calhoun, P. S., Hertzberg, J. S., Kirby, A. C., Dennis, M. F., Hair, L. P., Dedert, E. A., & Beckham, J. C. (2012). The effect of draft DSM–V criteria on posttraumatic stress disorder prevalence. *Depression and Anxiety, 29,* 1032–1042. http://dx.doi.org/10.1002/da.22012

Carey, B. (2011, June 23). Expert on mental illness reveals her own fight. *The New York Times,* p. A1. Retrieved from http://www.nytimes.com/2011/06/23/health/23lives.html?pagewanted=all

Carone, D. A., Jr., & Barone, D. F. (2001). A social cognitive perspective on religious beliefs: Their functions and impact on coping and psychotherapy. *Clinical Psychology Review, 21,* 989–1003. http://dx.doi.org/10.1016/S0272-7358(00)00078-7

Carter, J. J., Gerbarg, P. L., Brown, R. P., Ware, R. S., D'Ambrosio, C., Anand, L., . . . Katzman, M. A. (2013). Multi-component yoga breath program for Vietnam veteran post-traumatic stress disorder: Randomized controlled trial. *Journal of Traumatic Stress Disorders & Treatment, 2,* 3. http://dx.doi.org/10.4172/2324-8947.1000108

Carver, C. S. (1998). Resilience and thriving: Issues, models, and linkages. *Journal of Social Issues, 54,* 245–266. http://dx.doi.org/10.1111/j.1540-4560.1998.tb01217.x

Chen, K. W., Berger, C. C., Manheimer, E., Forde, D., Magidson, J., Dachman, L., & Lejuez, C. W. (2012). Meditative therapies for reducing anxiety: A systematic review and meta-analysis of randomized controlled trials. *Depression and Anxiety, 29,* 545–562. http://dx.doi.org/10.1002/da.21964

Chen, Y. Y., & Koenig, H. G. (2006a). Do people turn to religion in times of stress? An examination of change in religiousness among elderly, medically ill patients. *Journal of Nervous and Mental Disease, 194,* 114–120. http://dx.doi.org/10.1097/01.nmd.0000198143.63662.fb

Chen, Y. Y., & Koenig, H. G. (2006b). Traumatic stress and religion: Is there a relationship? A review of empirical findings. *Journal of Religion and Health, 45,* 371–381. http://dx.doi.org/10.1007/s10943-006-9040-y

Chouliara, Z., Hutchinson, C., & Karatzias, T. (2009). Vicarious traumatisation in practitioners who work with adult survivors of sexual violence and child sexual abuse: Literature review and directions for future research. *Counselling and Psychotherapy Research, 9,* 47–56. http://dx.doi.org/10.1080/14733140802656479

Christiansen, C. (2000). Identity, personal projects and happiness: Self construction in everyday action. *Journal of Occupational Science, 7,* 98–107. http://dx.doi.org/10.1080/14427591.2000.9686472

Cloitre, M. (2009). Effective psychotherapies for posttraumatic stress disorder: A review and critique. *CNS Spectrums, 14*(Suppl. 1), 32–43.

Cloitre, M., Stolbach, B. C., Herman, J. L., van der Kolk, B., Pynoos, R., Wang, J., & Petkova, E. (2009). A developmental approach to complex PTSD: Childhood and adult cumulative trauma as predictors of symptom complexity. *Journal of Traumatic Stress, 22,* 399–408. http://dx.doi.org/10.1002/jts.20444

Cloitre, M., Stovall-McClough, C., Zorbas, P., & Charuvastra, A. (2008). Attachment organization, emotion regulation, and expectations of support in a clinical sample of women with childhood abuse histories. *Journal of Traumatic Stress, 21*, 282–289. http://dx.doi.org/10.1002/jts.20339

Cole, B. S. (2005). Spiritually focused psychotherapy for people diagnosed with cancer: A pilot outcome study. *Mental Health, Religion & Culture, 8*, 217–226. http://dx.doi.org/10.1080/13694670500138916

Cole, B. S., Hopkins, C. M., Tisak, J., Steel, J. L., & Carr, B. I. (2008). Assessing spiritual growth and spiritual decline following a diagnosis of cancer: Reliability and validity of the spiritual transformation scale. *Psycho-Oncology, 17*, 112–121. http://dx.doi.org/10.1002/pon.1207

Cole, B., & Pargament, K. (1999). Re-creating your life: A spiritual/psychotherapeutic intervention for people diagnosed with cancer. *Psycho-Oncology, 8*, 395–407. http://dx.doi.org/10.1002/(SICI)1099-1611(199909/10)8:5<395::AID-PON408>3.0.CO;2-B

Constantine, M. G., Myers, L. J., Kindaichi, M., & Moore, J. L., III. (2004). Exploring indigenous mental health practices: The roles of healers and helpers in promoting well-being in people of color. *Counseling and Values, 48*, 110–125. http://dx.doi.org/10.1002/j.2161-007X.2004.tb00238.x

Costanzo, E. S., Ryff, C. D., & Singer, B. H. (2009). Psychosocial adjustment among cancer survivors: Findings from a national survey of health and well-being. *Health Psychology, 28*, 147–156. http://dx.doi.org/10.1037/a0013221

Courtois, C. A. (2004). Complex trauma, complex reactions: Assessment and treatment. *Psychotherapy: Theory, Research, Practice, Training, 41*, 412–425. http://dx.doi.org/10.1037/0033-3204.41.4.412

Craig, C. D., & Sprang, G. (2010). Compassion satisfaction, compassion fatigue, and burnout in a national sample of trauma treatment therapists. *Anxiety, Stress, & Coping, 23*, 319–339. http://dx.doi.org/10.1080/10615800903085818

Creamer, T. L., & Liddle, B. J. (2005). Secondary traumatic stress among disaster mental health workers responding to the September 11 attacks. *Journal of Traumatic Stress, 18*, 89–96. http://dx.doi.org/10.1002/jts.20008

Cuellar, N. G. (2008). Mindfulness meditation for veterans—Implications for occupational health providers. *Workplace Health & Safety, 56*, 357–363. http://dx.doi.org/10.3928/08910162-20080801-02

Cummings, J. P., Ivan, M. C., Carson, C. S., Stanley, M. A., & Pargament, K. I. (2014). A systematic review of relations between psychotherapist religiousness/spirituality and therapy-related variables. *Spirituality in Clinical Practice, 1*, 116–132. http://dx.doi.org/10.1037/scp0000014

Currier, J. M., Drescher, K., & Harris, J. I. (2014). Spiritual functioning among veterans seeking residential treatment for PTSD: A matched control group study. *Spirituality in Clinical Practice, 1*, 3–15. http://dx.doi.org/10.1037/scp0000004

Currier, J. M., Holland, J. M., Chisty, K., & Allen, D. (2011). Meaning made following deployment in Iraq or Afghanistan: Examining unique associations with posttraumatic stress and clinical outcomes. *Journal of Traumatic Stress, 24*, 691–698. http://dx.doi.org/10.1002/jts.20691

Currier, J. M., Holland, J. M., & Drescher, K. D. (2015). Spirituality factors in the prediction of outcomes of PTSD treatment for U.S. military veterans. *Journal of Traumatic Stress, 28*, 57–64. http://dx.doi.org/10.1002/jts.21978

Currier, J. M., Holland, J. M., & Malott, J. (2015). Moral injury, meaning making, and mental health in returning veterans. *Journal of Clinical Psychology, 71*, 229–240. http://dx.doi.org/10.1002/jclp.22134

Currier, J. M., Holland, J. M., & Neimeyer, R. A. (2006). Sense-making, grief, and the experience of violent loss: Toward a mediational model. *Death Studies, 30*, 403–428. http://dx.doi.org/10.1080/07481180600614351

Currier, J. M., Holland, J. M., Rojas-Flores, L., Herrera, S., & Foy, D. (2015). Morally injurious experiences and meaning in Salvadorian teachers exposed to violence. *Psychological Trauma: Theory, Research, Practice, and Policy, 7*, 24–33. http://dx.doi.org/10.1037/a0034092

Currier, J. M., Holland, J. M., Rozalski, V., Thompson, K., Rojas-Flores, L., & Herrera, S. (2013). Teaching in violent communities: The contributions of meaning made of stress on psychiatric distress and burnout. *International Journal of Stress Management, 20*, 254–277. http://dx.doi.org/10.1037/a0033985

Dalgleish, T., & Power, M. J. (2004). Emotion-specific and emotion-non-specific components of posttraumatic stress disorder (PTSD): Implications for a taxonomy of related psychopathology. *Behaviour Research and Therapy, 42*, 1069–1088. http://dx.doi.org/10.1016/j.brat.2004.05.001

Daniels, C., & Fitzpatrick, M. (2013). Integrating spirituality in counselling and psychotherapy: Theoretical and clinical perspectives. *Canadian Journal of Counselling and Psychotherapy, 47*, 315–341.

Davis, C. G., & Asliturk, E. (2011). Toward a positive psychology of coping with anticipated events. *Canadian Psychology/Psychologie canadienne, 52*, 101–110. http://dx.doi.org/10.1037/a0020177

Davis, C. G., Nolen-Hoeksema, S., & Larson, J. (1998). Making sense of loss and benefiting from the experience: Two construals of meaning. *Journal of Personality and Social Psychology, 75*, 561–574. http://dx.doi.org/10.1037/0022-3514.75.2.561

Davis, C. G., Wortman, C. B., Lehman, D. R., & Silver, R. C. (2000). Searching for meaning in loss: Are clinical assumptions correct. *Death Studies, 24*, 497–540. http://dx.doi.org/10.1080/07481180050121471

Davis, D. E., Van Tongeren, D. R., Hook, J. N., Davis, E. B., Worthington, E. L., Jr., & Foxman, S. (2014). Relational spirituality and forgiveness: Appraisals that may hinder forgiveness. *Psychology of Religion and Spirituality, 6*, 102–112. http://dx.doi.org/10.1037/a0033638

Day, J. M. (2013). Constructs of meaning and religious transformation: Cognitive complexity, postformal stages, and religious thought. In H. Westerink (Ed.),

Constructs of meaning and religious transformation: Current Issues in the psychology of religion (pp. 59–79). Vienna, Austria: Vienna University Press.

Decker, L. R. (1993). The role of trauma in spiritual development. *Journal of Humanistic Psychology, 33*(4), 33–46. http://dx.doi.org/10.1177/00221678930334004

Deighton, R. M., Gurris, N., & Traue, H. (2007). Factors affecting burnout and compassion fatigue in psychotherapists treating torture survivors: Is the therapist's attitude to working through trauma relevant? *Journal of Traumatic Stress, 20,* 63–75. http://dx.doi.org/10.1002/jts.20180

Delaney, H. D., Miller, W. R., & Bisonó, A. M. (2007). Religiosity and spirituality among psychologists: A survey of clinician members of the American Psychological Association. *Professional Psychology: Research and Practice, 38,* 538–546. http://dx.doi.org/10.1037/0735-7028.38.5.538

Del Gaizo, A. L., Elhai, J. D., & Weaver, T. L. (2011). Posttraumatic stress disorder, poor physical health and substance use behaviors in a national trauma-exposed sample. *Psychiatry Research, 188,* 390–395. http://dx.doi.org/10.1016/j.psychres.2011.03.016

DeMarni Cromer, L., & Freyd, J. J. (2009). Hear no evil, see no evil? Associations of gender, trauma history, and values with believing trauma vignettes. *Analyses of Social Issues and Public Policy, 9,* 85–96. http://dx.doi.org/10.1111/j.1530-2415.2009.01185.x

Demasure, K. (2012). The passion of the possible: Life story as a pastoral means of accompanying others. *Counselling and Spirituality/Counseling et spiritualité, 31,* 49–73.

Denton, R. T., & Martin, M. W. (1998). Defining forgiveness: An empirical exploration of process and role. *American Journal of Family Therapy, 26,* 281–292. http://dx.doi.org/10.1080/01926189808251107

Descilo, T., Vedamurtachar, A., Gerbarg, P. L., Nagaraja, D., Gangadhar, B. N., Damodaran, B., . . . Brown, R. P. (2010). Effects of a yoga breath intervention alone and in combination with an exposure therapy for post-traumatic stress disorder and depression in survivors of the 2004 South-East Asia tsunami. *Acta Psychiatrica Scandinavica, 121,* 289–300. http://dx.doi.org/10.1111/j.1600-0447.2009.01466.x

Devlin, H., Roberts, M., Okaya, A., & Xiong, Y. M. (2006). Our lives were healthier before: Focus groups with African American, American Indian, Hispanic/Latino, and Hmong people with diabetes. *Health Promotion Practice, 7,* 47–55. http://dx.doi.org/10.1177/1524839905275395

Dew, R. E., Daniel, S. S., Goldston, D. B., McCall, W. V., Kuchibhatla, M., Schleifer, C., . . . Koenig, H. G. (2010). A prospective study of religion/spirituality and depressive symptoms among adolescent psychiatric patients. *Journal of Affective Disorders, 120,* 149–157. http://dx.doi.org/10.1016/j.jad.2009.04.029

Doré, B., Ort, L., Braverman, O., & Ochsner, K. N. (2015). Sadness shifts to anxiety over time and distance from the national tragedy in Newtown, Connecticut. *Psychological Science, 26,* 363–373. http://dx.doi.org/10.1177/0956797614562218

Dougall, A. L., Herberman, H. B., Delahanty, D. L., Inslicht, S. S., & Baum, A. (2000). Similarity of prior trauma exposure as a determinant of chronic stress responding to an airline disaster. *Journal of Consulting and Clinical Psychology, 68,* 290–295. http://dx.doi.org/10.1037/0022-006X.68.2.290

Drescher, K. D., & Foy, D. W. (2008). When they come home: Posttraumatic stress, moral injury, and spiritual consequences for veterans. *Reflective Practice: Formation and Supervision in Ministry, 28,* 85–102.

Drescher, K. D., Foy, D. W., Kelly, C., Leshner, A., Schutz, K., & Litz, B. (2011). An exploration of the viability and usefulness of the construct of moral injury in war veterans. *Traumatology, 17,* 8–13. http://dx.doi.org/10.1177/1534765610395615

Drescher, K. D., Rosen, C. S., Burling, T. A., & Foy, D. W. (2003). Causes of death among male veterans who received residential treatment for PTSD. *Journal of Traumatic Stress, 16,* 535–543. http://dx.doi.org/10.1023/B:JOTS.0000004076.62793.79

Dunkel Schetter, C. D., & Dolbier, C. (2011). Resilience in the context of chronic stress and health in adults. *Social and Personality Psychology Compass, 5,* 634–652. http://dx.doi.org/10.1111/j.1751-9004.2011.00379.x

Dunn, K. S., & Horgas, A. L. (2004). Religious and nonreligious coping in older adults experiencing chronic pain. *Pain Management Nursing, 5,* 19–28. http://dx.doi.org/10.1016/S1524-9042(03)00070-5

Dweck, C. S. (2006). *Mindset: The new psychology of success.* New York, NY: Ballantine.

Edwards, L. C., Lim, B. R., McMinn, M. R., & Dominguez, A. W. (1999). Examples of collaboration between psychologists and clergy. *Professional Psychology: Research and Practice, 30,* 547–551. http://dx.doi.org/10.1037/0735-7028.30.6.547

Eidelson, R., & Soldz, S. (2012). Does Comprehensive Soldier Fitness work? CSF research fails the test. *Coalition for an Ethical Psychology.* Retrieved from http://www.ethicalpsychology.org/Eidelson-&-Soldz-CSF_Research_Fails_the_Test.pdf

Einolf, C. J. (2011). The link between religion and helping others: The role of values, ideas, and language. *Sociology of Religion, 72,* 435–455. http://dx.doi.org/10.1093/socrel/srr017

El-Khoury, M. Y., Dutton, M. A., Goodman, L. A., Engel, L., Belamaric, R. J., & Murphy, M. (2004). Ethnic differences in battered women's formal help-seeking strategies: A focus on health, mental health, and spirituality. *Cultural Diversity and Ethnic Minority Psychology, 10,* 383–393. http://dx.doi.org/10.1037/1099-9809.10.4.383

El Leithy, S., Brown, G. P., & Robbins, I. (2006). Counterfactual thinking and posttraumatic stress reactions. *Journal of Abnormal Psychology, 115,* 629–635. http://dx.doi.org/10.1037/0021-843X.115.3.629

Ellison, C. G., & Lee, J. (2010). Spiritual struggles and psychological distress: Is there a dark side of religion? *Social Indicators Research, 98,* 501–517. http://dx.doi.org/10.1007/s11205-009-9553-3

Ellison, C., Zhang, W., Krause, N., & Marcum, J. (2009). Does negative interaction in the church increase psychological distress? Longitudinal findings from the

Presbyterian Panel Survey. *Sociology of Religion, 70*, 409–431. http://dx.doi.org/10.1093/socrel/srp062

Emmons, R. A. (1999). *The psychology of ultimate concerns.* New York, NY: Oxford University Press.

Emmons, R. A. (2003). Personal goals, life meaning, and virtue: Wellsprings of a positive life. In C. L. M. Keyes & J. Haidt (Eds.), *Flourishing: Positive psychology and the life well-lived* (pp. 105–128). Washington, DC: American Psychological Association. http://dx.doi.org/10.1037/10594-005

Emmons, R. A. (2005). Emotion and religion. In R. F. Paloutzian & C. L. Park (Eds.), *Handbook of the psychology of religion and spirituality* (pp. 235–252). New York, NY: Guilford Press.

Emmons, R. A., Colby, P. M., & Kaiser, H. A. (1998). When losses lead to gains: Personal goals and the recovery of meaning. In P. T. P. Wong & P. S. Fry (Eds.), *The human quest for meaning* (pp. 163–178). Mahwah, NJ: Erlbaum.

Enright, R. D., & Fitzgibbons, R. P. (2014). *Forgiveness therapy: An empirical guide for resolving anger and restoring hope.* Washington, DC: American Psychological Association.

Erbes, C. R., Polusny, M. A., MacDermid, S., & Compton, J. S. (2008). Couple therapy with combat veterans and their partners. *Journal of Clinical Psychology, 64*, 972–983. http://dx.doi.org/10.1002/jclp.20521

Eriksson, C. B., Holland, J. M., Currier, J. M., Snider, L., Ager, A., Kaiser, R., & Simon, W. (2015). Trajectories of spiritual change among expatriate humanitarian aid workers: A prospective longitudinal study. *Psychology of Religion and Spirituality, 7*, 13–23. http://dx.doi.org/10.1037/a0037703

Esser-Stuart, J. E., & Lyons, M. A. (2002). Barriers and influences in seeking health care among lower income minority women. *Social Work in Health Care, 35*, 85–99. http://dx.doi.org/10.1300/J010v35n03_06

Exline, J. J. (2002). Stumbling blocks on the religious road: Fractured relationships, nagging vices, and the inner struggle to believe. *Psychological Inquiry, 13*, 182–189. http://dx.doi.org/10.1207/S15327965PLI1303_03

Exline, J. J. (2008). Beliefs about God and forgiveness in a Baptist Church sample. *Journal of Psychology and Christianity, 27*, 131–139.

Exline, J. J. (2012). The flame of love as a refining fire: Gifts of spiritual struggle. In M. T. Lee & A. Yong (Eds.), *Godly love: Impediments and possibilities* (pp. 57–74). Lanham, MD: Lexington Books.

Exline, J. J. (2013). Religious and spiritual struggles. In K. I. Pargament (Ed.), *APA handbook of psychology, religion, and spirituality: Vol. 1. Context, theory, and research* (pp. 459–475). Washington, DC: American Psychological Association.

Exline, J. J., Homolka, S. J., & Grubbs, J. B. (2013). Negative views of parents and struggles with God: An exploration of two mediators. *Journal of Psychology and Theology, 41*, 200–212.

Exline, J. J., Kaplan, K. J., & Grubbs, J. B. (2012). Anger, exit, and assertion: Do people see protest toward God as morally acceptable? *Psychology of Religion and Spirituality, 4*, 264–277. http://dx.doi.org/10.1037/a0027667

Exline, J. J., Pargament, K. I., Grubbs, J. B., & Yali, A. M. (2014). The Religious and Spiritual Struggles Scale: Development and initial validation. *Psychology of Religion and Spirituality, 6*, 208–222. http://dx.doi.org/10.1037/a0036465

Exline, J. J., Park, C. L., Smyth, J. M., & Carey, M. P. (2011). Anger toward God: Social–cognitive predictors, prevalence, and links with adjustment to bereavement and cancer. *Journal of Personality and Social Psychology, 100*, 129–148. http://dx.doi.org/10.1037/a0021716

Exline, J. J., & Rose, E. D. (2013). Religious and spiritual struggles. In R. F. Paloutzian & C. L. Park (Eds.), *Handbook of the psychology of religion and spirituality* (2nd ed., pp. 380–398). New York, NY: Guilford Press.

Exline, J. J., Yali, A. M., & Sanderson, W. C. (2000). Guilt, discord, and alienation: The role of religious strain in depression and suicidality. *Journal of Clinical Psychology, 56*, 1481–1496. http://dx.doi.org/10.1002/1097-4679(200012)56:12<1481::AID-1>3.0.CO;2-A

Fallot, R. D., & Heckman, J. P. (2005). Religious/spiritual coping among women trauma survivors with mental health and substance use disorders. *The Journal of Behavioral Health Services & Research, 32*, 215–226. http://dx.doi.org/10.1007/BF02287268

Falsetti, S. A., Resick, P. A., & Davis, J. L. (2003). Changes in religious beliefs following trauma. *Journal of Traumatic Stress, 16*, 391–398. http://dx.doi.org/10.1023/A:1024422220163

Fitchett, G. (2002). *Assessing spiritual needs: A guide for caregivers*. Lima, OH: Academic Renewal Press.

Flannelly, K. J., Ellison, C. G., Galek, K., & Koenig, H. G. (2008). Beliefs about life-after-death, psychiatric symptomatology and cognitive theories of psychopathology. *Journal of Psychology and Theology, 36*, 94–103.

Foa, E. B., Hembree, E. A., & Rothbaum, B. O. (2007). *Prolonged exposure therapy for PTSD: Emotional processing of traumatic experiences*. New York, NY: Oxford University Press.

Foa, E. B., Huppert, J. D., & Cahill, S. P. (2006). Emotional processing theory: An update. In B. O. Rothbaum (Ed.), *Pathological anxiety: Emotional processing in etiology and treatment* (pp. 3–24). New York, NY: Guilford Press.

Foa, E. B., Keane, T. M., Friedman, M. J., & Cohen, J. A. (2009). *Effective treatments for PTSD: Practice guidelines from the International Society for Traumatic Stress Studies* (2nd ed.). New York, NY: Guilford Press.

Foa, E. B., & Kozak, M. J. (1986). Emotional processing of fear: Exposure to corrective information. *Psychological Bulletin, 99*, 20–35. http://dx.doi.org/10.1037/0033-2909.99.1.20

Foa, E. B., & Rothbaum, B. O. (1998). *Treating the trauma of rape: Cognitive–behavioral therapy for PTSD*. New York, NY: Guilford Press.

Fontana, A., & Rosenheck, R. (2004). Trauma, change in strength of religious faith, and mental health service use among veterans treated for PTSD. *Journal of Nervous and Mental Disease, 192*, 579–584. http://dx.doi.org/10.1097/01.nmd.0000138224.17375.55

Fortune, M. M. (1995). Forgiveness: The last step. In C. J. Adams & M. M. Fortune (Eds.), *Violence against women: A Christian theological sourcebook* (pp. 201–206). New York, NY: Continuum.

Fowler, J. W. (1981). *Stages of faith*. New York, NY: Harper & Row.

Foy, D. W., & Drescher, K. D. (2015). Faith and honor in trauma treatment for military personnel and their families. In D. F. Walker, C. A. Courtois, & J. D. Aten (Eds.), *Spiritually oriented trauma psychotherapy* (pp. 233–252). Washington, DC: American Psychological Association. http://dx.doi.org/10.1037/14500-012

Franklin, M. D., Schlundt, D. G., & Wallston, K. A. (2008). Development and validation of a religious health fatalism measure for the African-American faith community. *Journal of Health Psychology, 13*, 323–335. http://dx.doi.org/10.1177/1359105307088137

Frazier, P. (2012). Trauma psychology. In E. M. Altmaier & J. C. Hansen (Eds.), *The Oxford handbook of counseling psychology* (pp. 807–836). New York, NY: Oxford University Press.

Frazier, P., Tennen, H., Gavian, M., Park, C., Tomich, P., & Tashiro, T. (2009). Does self-reported posttraumatic growth reflect genuine positive change? *Psychological Science, 20*, 912–919. http://dx.doi.org/10.1111/j.1467-9280.2009.02381.x

Frazier, R. E., & Hansen, N. D. (2009). Religious/spiritual psychotherapy behaviors: Do we do what we believe to be important? *Professional Psychology: Research and Practice, 40*, 81–87. http://dx.doi.org/10.1037/a0011671

Freud, S. (1961). *Civilization and its discontents*. London, England: Norton.

Friedman, M. J., Davidson, J. R. T., & Stein, D. J. (2009). Psychopharmacotherapy for adults. In E. B. Foa, T. M. Keane, M. J. Friedman, & J. A. Cohen (Eds.), *Effective treatments for PTSD: Practice guidelines from the International Society for Traumatic Stress Studies* (2nd ed., pp. 245–268). New York, NY: Guilford Press.

Friedman, M. J., Keane, T. M., & Resick, P. A. (Eds.). (2007). *Handbook of PTSD: Science and practice*. New York, NY: Guilford Press.

Friedman, M. J., Resick, P. A., Bryant, R. A., & Brewin, C. R. (2011). Considering PTSD for *DSM–5*. *Depression and Anxiety, 28*, 750–769. http://dx.doi.org/10.1002/da.20767

Furnham, A., & Brown, L. B. (1992). Theodicy: A neglected aspect of the psychology of religion. *International Journal for the Psychology of Religion, 2*, 37–45. http://dx.doi.org/10.1207/s15327582ijpr0201_4

Galea, S., Vlahov, D., Resnick, H., Ahern, J., Susser, E., Gold, J., . . . Kilpatrick, D. (2003). Trends of probable post-traumatic stress disorder in New York City after the September 11 terrorist attacks. *American Journal of Epidemiology, 158*, 514–524. http://dx.doi.org/10.1093/aje/kwg187

Gall, T. L. (2006). Spirituality and coping with life stress among adult survivors of childhood sexual abuse. *Child Abuse & Neglect, 30*, 829–844. http://dx.doi.org/ 10.1016/j.chiabu.2006.01.003

Gall, T. L., & Guirguis-Younger, M. (2013). Religious and spiritual coping: Current theory and research. In K. I. Pargament (Ed.), *APA handbook of psychology, religion, and spirituality: Vol. 1. Context, theory, and research* (pp. 349–364). Washington, DC: American Psychological Association. http://dx.doi.org/ 10.1037/14045-019

Gallup, G. H., Jr., & Bezilla, R. (1994, January 22). More find religion important. *Washington Post*, p. G10.

Garbarino, J., & Bedard, C. (1996). Spiritual challenges to children facing violent trauma. *Childhood, 3*, 467–478. http://dx.doi.org/10.1177/0907568296003004004

George, L., & Park, C. L. (2014). Existential mattering: Bringing attention to a neglected but central aspect of meaning? In P. Russo-Netzer & A. Batthyany (Eds.), *Meaning in positive and existential psychology* (pp. 39–51). New York, NY: Springer. http://dx.doi.org/10.1007/978-1-4939-0308-5_3

Gillies, J., & Neimeyer, R. A. (2006). Loss, grief, and the search for significance: Toward a model of meaning reconstruction in bereavement. *Journal of Constructivist Psychology, 19*, 31–65. http://dx.doi.org/10.1080/10720530500311182

Gold, S. D., Marx, B. P., Soler-Baillo, J. M., & Sloan, D. M. (2005). Is life stress more traumatic than traumatic stress? *Journal of Anxiety Disorders, 19*, 687–698. http://dx.doi.org/10.1016/j.janxdis.2004.06.002

Goldstein, N., Gist, R., McNally, R. J., Acierno, R., Harris, M., Devilly, G. J., . . . Foa, E. (2001, November). Psychology's response. *Monitor on Psychology, 32*(10). Retrieved from http://www.apa.org/monitor/nov01/letters.aspx

Gonsiorek, J. C., Richards, P. S., Pargament, K. I., & McMinn, M. R. (2009). Ethical challenges and opportunities at the edge: Incorporating spirituality and religion into psychotherapy. *Professional Psychology: Research and Practice, 40*, 385–395. http://dx.doi.org/10.1037/a0016488

Granqvist, P., & Hagekull, B. (1999). Religiousness and perceived childhood attachment: Profiling socialized correspondence and emotional compensation. *Journal for the Scientific Study of Religion, 38*, 254–273. http://dx.doi.org/10.2307/1387793

Granqvist, P., & Kirkpatrick, L. A. (2013). Religion, spirituality, and attachment. In K. I. Pargament (Ed.), *APA handbook of psychology, religion, and spirituality: Vol. 1. Context, theory, and research* (pp. 139–155). Washington, DC: American Psychological Association.

Gray, K., & Wegner, D. M. (2010). Blaming God for our pain: Human suffering and the divine mind. *Personality and Social Psychology Review, 14*, 7–16. http://dx.doi.org/ 10.1177/1088868309350299

Gray, M. J., Maguen, S., & Litz, B. T. (2007). Schema constructs and cognitive models of Posttraumatic Stress Disorder. In L. P. Riso, P. L. du Toit, D. J. Stein, & J. E. Young (Eds.), *Cognitive schemas and core beliefs in psychological problems:*

A scientist–practitioner guide (pp. 59–92). Washington, DC: American Psychological Association. http://dx.doi.org/10.1037/11561-004

Gray, M. J., Schorr, Y., Nash, W., Lebowitz, L., Amidon, A., Lansing, A., . . . Litz, B. T. (2012). Adaptive disclosure: An open trial of a novel exposure-based intervention for service members with combat-related psychological stress injuries. *Behavior Therapy, 43,* 407–415. http://dx.doi.org/10.1016/j.beth.2011.09.001

Greenberg, L. S. (2015). *Emotion-focused therapy: Coaching clients to work through their feelings* (2nd ed.). Washington, DC: American Psychological Association. http://dx.doi.org/10.1037/14692-000

Greenberg, L. S., & Malcolm, W. (2002). Resolving unfinished business: Relating process to outcome. *Journal of Consulting and Clinical Psychology, 70,* 406–416. http://dx.doi.org/10.1037/0022-006X.70.2.406

Greenberg, M. A. (1995). Cognitive processing of traumas: The role of intrusive thoughts and reappraisals. *Journal of Applied Social Psychology, 25,* 1262–1296. http://dx.doi.org/10.1111/j.1559-1816.1995.tb02618.x

Grossman, F. K., Sorsoli, L., & Kia-Keating, M. (2006). A gale force wind: Meaning making by male survivors of childhood sexual abuse. *American Journal of Orthopsychiatry, 76,* 434–443. http://dx.doi.org/10.1037/0002-9432.76.4.434

Gubi, P. M., & Jacobs, R. (2009). Exploring the impact on counsellors of working with spiritually abused clients. *Mental Health, Religion & Culture, 12,* 191–204. http://dx.doi.org/10.1080/13674670802441509

Hage, S. M. (2006). A closer look at the role of spirituality in psychology training programs. *Professional Psychology: Research and Practice, 37,* 303–310. http://dx.doi.org/10.1037/0735-7028.37.3.303

Hale-Smith, A., Park, C. L., & Edmondson, D. (2012). Measuring beliefs about suffering: Development of the Views of Suffering Scale. *Psychological Assessment, 24,* 855–866. http://dx.doi.org/10.1037/a0027399

Hall, M., & Johnson, E. (2001). Theodicy and therapy: Philosophical/theological contributions to the problem of suffering. *Journal of Psychology and Christianity, 20,* 5–17.

Hamama-Raz, Y., Solomon, Z., Cohen, A., & Laufer, A. (2008). PTSD symptoms, forgiveness, and revenge among Israeli Palestinian and Jewish adolescents. *Journal of Traumatic Stress, 21,* 521–529. http://dx.doi.org/10.1002/jts.20376

Handelsman, M. M., Gottlieb, M. C., & Knapp, S. (2005). Training ethical psychologists: An acculturation model. *Professional Psychology: Research and Practice, 36,* 59–65.

Harper, A. R., & Pargament, K. I. (2015). Trauma, religion, and spirituality: Pathways to healing. In K. E. Cherry (Ed.), *Traumatic stress and long-term recovery* (pp. 349–367). New York, NY: Springer. http://dx.doi.org/10.1007/978-3-319-18866-9_19

Harris, J. I., Erbes, C. R., Engdahl, B. E., Ogden, H., Olson, R. H. A., Winskowski, A. M., . . . Mataas, S. (2012). Religious distress and coping with stressful life events: A longitudinal study. *Journal of Clinical Psychology, 68,* 1276–1286. http://dx.doi.org/10.1002/jclp.21900

Harris, J. I., Erbes, C. R., Engdahl, B. E., Olson, R. H., Winskowski, A. M., & McMahill, J. (2008). Christian religious functioning and trauma outcomes. *Journal of Clinical Psychology, 64,* 17–29. http://dx.doi.org/10.1002/jclp.20427

Harris, J. I., Erbes, C. R., Engdahl, B. E., Thuras, P., Murray-Swank, N., Grace, D., . . . Le, T. (2011). The effectiveness of a trauma focused spiritually integrated intervention for veterans exposed to trauma. *Journal of Clinical Psychology, 67,* 425–438. http://dx.doi.org/10.1002/jclp.20777

Harris, J. I., Erbes, C. R., Winskowski, A. M., Engdahl, B. E., & Nguyen, X. (2014). Social support as a mediator in the relationship between religious comforts and strains and trauma symptoms. *Psychology of Religion and Spirituality, 6,* 223–229. http://dx.doi.org/10.1037/a0036421

Harris, J. I., & Leak, G. K. (2013). The Revised Faith Development Scale: An option for a more reliable self-report measurement of postconventional religious reasoning. In R. L. Piedmont & A. Village (Eds.), *Research in the social scientific study of religion* (Vol. 24, pp. 1–13). Boston, MA: Brill. http://dx.doi.org/10.1163/9789004252073_002

Harris, J. I., Park, C. L., Currier, J. M., Usset, T. J., & Voecks, C. D. (2015). Moral injury and psycho-spiritual development: Considering the developmental context. *Spirituality in Clinical Practice, 2,* 256–266. http://dx.doi.org/10.1037/scp0000045

Harris, J. I., Schoneman, S. W., & Carrera, S. R. (2005). Preferred prayer styles and anxiety control. *Journal of Religion and Health, 44,* 403–412. http://dx.doi.org/10.1007/s10943-005-7179-6

Harrison, R. L., & Westwood, M. J. (2009). Preventing vicarious traumatization of mental health therapists: Identifying protective practices. *Psychotherapy: Theory, Research, Practice, Training, 46,* 203–219. http://dx.doi.org/10.1037/a0016081

Hathaway, W. L. (2011). Ethical guidelines for using spiritually oriented interventions. In J. D. Aten, M. R. McMinn, & E. L. Worthington (Eds.), *Spiritually oriented interventions for counseling and psychotherapy* (pp. 65–81). Washington, DC: American Psychological Association. http://dx.doi.org/10.1037/12313-003

Hathaway, W. L., & Ripley, J. W. (2009). Ethical concerns around spirituality and religion in clinical practice. In J. D. Aten & M. M. Leach (Eds.), *Spirituality and the therapeutic process: A comprehensive resource from intake to termination* (pp. 25–52). Washington, DC: American Psychological Association. http://dx.doi.org/10.1037/11853-002

Hathaway, W. L., Scott, S. Y., & Garver, S. A. (2004). Assessing religious/spiritual functioning: A neglected domain in clinical practice? *Professional Psychology: Research and Practice, 35,* 97–104. http://dx.doi.org/10.1037/0735-7028.35.1.97

Hayes, S. C., Pistorello, J., & Levin, M. E. (2012). Acceptance and Commitment Therapy as a unified mode of behavior change. *The Counseling Psychologist, 40,* 976–1002. http://dx.doi.org/10.1177/0011000012460836

Hembree, E. A., & Foa, E. B. (2000). Posttraumatic stress disorder: Psychological factors and psychosocial interventions [Special issue]. *Journal of Clinical Psychiatry*, *61*(Suppl. 7), 33–39.

Henry, J. D., Phillips, L. H., Ruffman, T., & Bailey, P. E. (2013). A meta-analytic review of age differences in theory of mind. *Psychology and Aging*, *28*, 826–839. http://dx.doi.org/10.1037/a0030677

Herman, J. (1992). *Trauma and recovery: The aftermath of violence—From domestic abuse to political terror*. New York, NY: Basic Books.

Hill, P. C., & Pargament, K. I. (2003). Advances in the conceptualization and measurement of religion and spirituality: Implications for physical and mental health research. *American Psychologist*, *58*, 64–74. http://dx.doi.org/10.1037/0003-066X.58.1.64

Hindman, J. (1989). *Just before dawn: Trauma assessment and treatment of sexual victimization*. Ontario, OR: Alexandria Associates.

Hobfoll, S. E., Dunahoo, C. A., & Monnier, J. (1995). Conservation of resources and traumatic stress. In J. R. Freedy & S. E. Hobfoll (Eds.), *Traumatic stress: From theory to practice* (pp. 29–47). New York, NY: Plenum Press. http://dx.doi.org/10.1007/978-1-4899-1076-9_2

Hobfoll, S. E., Tracy, M., & Galea, S. (2006). The impact of resource loss and traumatic growth on probable PTSD and depression following terrorist attacks. *Journal of Traumatic Stress*, *19*, 867–878. http://dx.doi.org/10.1002/jts.20166

Hobfoll, S. E., Watson, P., Bell, C. C., Bryant, R. A., Brymer, M. J., Friedman, M., . . . Ursano, R. J. (2009). Five essential elements of immediate and mid-term mass trauma intervention: Empirical evidence. *Focus*, *7*, 221–242. http://dx.doi.org/10.1176/foc.7.2.foc221

Holland, J. M., Currier, J. M., Coleman, R. A., & Neimeyer, R. A. (2010). The Integration of Stressful Life Experiences Scale (ISLES): Development and initial validation of a new measure. *International Journal of Stress Management*, *17*, 325–352. http://dx.doi.org/10.1037/a0020892

Hood, R. W., Hill, P. C., & Spilka, B. (2009). *The psychology of religion: An empirical approach* (4th ed.). New York, NY: Guilford Press.

Horvath, A. O., & Greenberg, L. S. (Eds.). (1994). *The working alliance: Theory, research, and practice*. New York, NY: Wiley.

Huppert, F. A., & Johnson, D. M. (2010). A controlled trial of mindfulness training in schools: The importance of practice for an impact on well-being. *The Journal of Positive Psychology*, *5*, 264–274. http://dx.doi.org/10.1080/17439761003794148

Imbens, A., & Jonker, I. (1992). *Christianity and incest*. Minneapolis, MN: Fortress Press.

Institute of Medicine. (2008). *Treatment of posttraumatic stress disorder: An assessment of the evidence*. Washington, DC: National Academies Press.

Inzlicht, M., McGregor, I., Hirsh, J. B., & Nash, K. (2009). Neural markers of religious conviction. *Psychological Science*, *20*, 385–392. http://dx.doi.org/10.1111/j.1467-9280.2009.02305.x

Janoff-Bulman, R. (1992). *Shattered assumptions: Towards a new psychology of trauma.* New York, NY: Free Press.

Janoff-Bulman, R., & Frantz, C. M. (1997). The impact of trauma on meaning: From meaningless world to meaningful life. In M. J. Power & C. R. Brewin (Eds.), *The transformation of meaning in psychological therapies: Integrating theory and practice* (pp. 91–106). Hoboken, NJ: Wiley.

Janoff-Bulman, R., & Sheikh, S. (2006). From national trauma to moralizing nation. *Basic and Applied Social Psychology, 28,* 325–332. http://dx.doi.org/10.1207/s15324834basp2804_5

Jenkins, S. R., & Baird, S. (2002). Secondary traumatic stress and vicarious trauma: A validational study. *Journal of Traumatic Stress, 15,* 423–432. http://dx.doi.org/10.1023/A:1020193526843

Jim, H. S., Purnell, J. Q., Richardson, S. A., Golden-Kreutz, D., & Andersen, B. L. (2006). Measuring meaning in life following cancer. *Quality of Life Research, 15,* 1355–1371. http://dx.doi.org/10.1007/s11136-006-0028-6

Johnson, S. M. (2002). *Emotionally focused couple therapy with trauma survivors: Strengthening attachment bonds.* New York, NY: Guilford Press.

Joint Commission. (2015). *Comprehensive accreditation manual for hospitals.* Oakbrook Terrace, IL: Author.

Jones, D. L., Cassidy, L., & Heflinger, C. A. (2002). "You can talk to them. You can pray": Rural clergy responses to adolescents with mental health concerns. *Journal of Rural Mental Health, 36,* 24–33. http://dx.doi.org/10.1037/h0094777

Joseph, S., & Linley, P. A. (2005). Positive adjustment to threatening events: An organismic valuing theory of growth through adversity. *Review of General Psychology, 9,* 262–280. http://dx.doi.org/10.1037/1089-2680.9.3.262

Joshanloo, M. (2014a). Differences in the endorsement of various conceptions of well-being between two Iranian groups. *Psychology of Religion and Spirituality, 6,* 138–149. http://dx.doi.org/10.1037/a0035510

Joshanloo, M. (2014b). Eastern conceptualizations of happiness: Fundamental differences with western views. *Journal of Happiness Studies, 15,* 475–493. http://dx.doi.org/10.1007/s10902-013-9431-1

Jost, J. T., Hawkins, C. B., Nosek, B. A., Hennes, E. P., Stern, C., Gosling, S. C., & Graham, J. (2014). Belief in a just God (and a just society): A system justification perspective on religious ideology. *Journal of Theoretical and Philosophical Psychology, 34,* 56–81. http://dx.doi.org/10.1037/a0033220

Kadambi, M. A., & Truscott, D. (2004). Vicarious trauma among therapists working with sexual violence, cancer, and general practice. *Canadian Journal of Counselling, 38,* 260–276.

Kahle, P. A., & Robbins, J. M. (2004). *The power of spirituality in therapy: Integrating spiritual and religious beliefs in mental health practice.* New York, NY: Haworth Pastoral Press.

Kane, M. N. (2003). Skilled help for mental health concerns: Comparing the perceptions of Catholic priests and Catholic parishioners. *Mental Health, Religion & Culture, 6*, 261–275. http://dx.doi.org/10.1080/1367467031000100993

Kane, M. N. (2010). Predictors of university students' willingness in the USA to use clergy as sources of skilled help. *Mental Health, Religion & Culture, 13*, 309–325. http://dx.doi.org/10.1080/10371390903381106

Kangas, M. (2013). *DSM–5* trauma and stress-related disorders: Implications for screening for cancer-related stress. *Frontiers in Psychiatry, 4*. http://dx.doi.org/10.3389/fpsyt.2013.00122

Karoly, P. (1999). A goal systems-self-regulatory perspective on personality, psychopathology, and change. *Review of General Psychology, 3*, 264–291. http://dx.doi.org/10.1037/1089-2680.3.4.264

Kearney, D. J., McDermott, K., Malte, C., Martinez, M., & Simpson, T. L. (2012). Association of participation in a mindfulness program with measures of PTSD, depression and quality of life in a veteran sample. *Journal of Clinical Psychology, 68*, 101–116. http://dx.doi.org/10.1002/jclp.20853

Keefer, L. A., Landau, M. J., & Sullivan, D. (2014). Non-human support: Broadening the scope of attachment theory. *Social and Personality Psychology Compass, 8*, 524–535. http://dx.doi.org/10.1111/spc3.12129

Keesee, N. J., Currier, J. M., & Neimeyer, R. A. (2008). Predictors of grief following the death of one's child: The contribution of finding meaning. *Journal of Clinical Psychology, 64*, 1145–1163. http://dx.doi.org/10.1002/jclp.20502

Kelly, G. A. (1969). Personal construct theory and the psychotherapeutic interview. In B. Maher (Ed.), *Clinical psychology and personality: The selected papers of George Kelly* (pp. 224–264). New York, NY: Wiley.

Kennedy, J. E., Davis, R. C., & Taylor, B. G. (1998). Changes in spirituality and well-being among victims of sexual assault. *Journal for the Scientific Study of Religion, 37*, 322–328. http://dx.doi.org/10.2307/1387531

Kennedy, P., & Drebing, C. E. (2002). Abuse and religious experience: A study of religiously committed evangelical adults. *Mental Health, Religion & Culture, 5*, 225–237. http://dx.doi.org/10.1080/13674670110112695

Kessler, R. C., Sonnega, A., Bromet, E., Hughes, M., & Nelson, C. B. (1995). Posttraumatic stress disorder in the National Comorbidity Survey. *Archives of General Psychiatry, 52*, 1048–1060. http://dx.doi.org/10.1001/archpsyc.1995.03950240066012

Killian, D. (2008). Helping till it hurts? A multimethod study of compassion fatigue, burnout, and self-care in clinicians working with trauma survivors. *Traumatology, 14*, 32–44. http://dx.doi.org/10.1177/1534765608319083

Kimball, C. N., Boyatzis, C., Cook, K. V., Leonard, K. C., & Flanagan, K. S. (2013). Attachment to God: A qualitative exploration of emerging adults' spiritual relationship with God. *Journal of Psychology and Theology, 41*, 175–188.

Kimbrough, E., Magyari, T., Langenberg, P., Chesney, M., & Berman, B. (2010). Mindfulness intervention for child abuse survivors. *Journal of Clinical Psychology, 66*, 17–33.

King, L. A., Pless, A. P., Schuster, J. L., Potter, C. M., Park, C. L., Spiro, A., III, & King, D. W. (2012). Risk and protective factors for traumatic stress disorders. In G. Beck & D. Sloan (Eds.), *Oxford handbook of traumatic stress disorders* (pp. 333–346). New York, NY: Oxford University Press. http://dx.doi.org/10.1093/oxfordhb/9780195399066.013.0022

Klaassen, D. W., & McDonald, M. J. (2002). Quest and identity development: Re-examining pathways for existential search. *International Journal for the Psychology of Religion, 12*, 189–200. http://dx.doi.org/10.1207/S15327582IJPR1203_05

Kleim, B., & Ehlers, A. (2009). Evidence for a curvilinear relationship between posttraumatic growth and posttrauma depression and PTSD in assault survivors. *Journal of Traumatic Stress, 22*, 45–52. http://dx.doi.org/10.1002/jts.20378

Klinger, E. (1998). The search for meaning in evolutionary perspective and its clinical implications. In P. P. Wong & P. S. Fry (Eds.), *The human quest for meaning: A handbook of psychological research and clinical applications* (pp. 27–50). Mahwah, NJ: Erlbaum.

Klinger, E. (2012). The search for meaning in evolutionary goal-theory perspective and its clinical implications. In P. P. Wong (Ed.), *The human quest for meaning: Theories, research, and applications* (2nd ed., pp. 23–56). New York, NY: Routledge/Taylor & Francis.

Koenig, H. G., Pargament, K. I., & Nielsen, J. (1998). Religious coping and health status in medically ill hospitalized older adults. *Journal of Nervous & Mental Disease, 186*, 513–521. http://dx.doi.org/10.1097/00005053-199809000-00001

Koltko-Rivera, M. E. (2004). The psychology of worldviews. *Review of General Psychology, 8*, 3–58. http://dx.doi.org/10.1037/1089-2680.8.1.3

Koltko-Rivera, M. E. (2006–2007). Religions influence worldviews; worldviews influence behavior: A model with research agenda. *Psychology of Religion Newsletter: Division 36—American Psychological Association, 32*, 1–10.

Kosutic, I., & McDowell, T. (2008). Diversity and social justice issues in the family therapy literature: A decade review. *Journal of Feminist Family Therapy, 20*, 142–165. http://dx.doi.org/10.1080/08952830802023292

Krause, N. (2003). Exploring race differences in the relationship between social interaction with clergy and feelings of self-worth in late life. *Sociology of Religion, 64*, 183–205. http://dx.doi.org/10.2307/3712370

Krause, N., Ellison, C. G., & Wulff, K. M. (1998). Church-based emotional support, negative interaction, and psychological well-being: Findings from a national sample of Presbyterians. *Journal for the Scientific Study of Religion, 37*, 725–741. http://dx.doi.org/10.2307/1388153

Kubany, E. S., & Ralston, T. (2006). Cognitive therapy for trauma-related guilt and shame. In V. M. Follette & J. I. Ruzek (Eds.), *Cognitive–behavioral therapies for trauma* (pp. 258–289). New York, NY: Guilford Press.

Kumpula, M. J., Orcutt, H. K., Bardeen, J. R., & Varkovitzky, R. L. (2011). Peri-traumatic dissociation and experiential avoidance as prospective predictors of posttraumatic stress symptoms. *Journal of Abnormal Psychology, 120,* 617–627. http://dx.doi.org/10.1037/a0023927

Kushner, H. S. (1981). *When bad things happen to good people.* New York, NY: Avon Books.

Kusner, K., & Pargament, K. I. (2012). Shaken to the core: Understanding and addressing the spiritual dimension of trauma. In R. A. McMackin, E. Newman, J. M. Fogler, & T. M. Keane (Eds.), *Trauma therapy in context: The science and craft of evidence-based practice* (pp. 211–230). Washington, DC: American Psychological Association. http://dx.doi.org/10.1037/13746-010

Lam, A. G., & Sue, S. (2001). Client diversity. *Psychotherapy: Theory, Research, Practice, Training, 38,* 479–486. http://dx.doi.org/10.1037/0033-3204.38.4.479

Lawler-Row, K. A. (2010). Forgiveness as a mediator of the religiosity–health relationship. *Psychology of Religion and Spirituality, 2,* 1–16. http://dx.doi.org/10.1037/a0017584

Lawson, R., Drebing, C., Berg, G., Vincellette, A., & Penk, W. (1998). The long term impact of child abuse on religious behavior and spirituality in men. *Child Abuse & Neglect, 22,* 369–380. http://dx.doi.org/10.1016/S0145-2134(98)00003-9

Layne, C. M., Beck, C. J., Rimmasch, H., Southwick, J. S., Moreno, M. A., & Hobfoll, S. E. (2009). Promoting "resilient" posttraumatic adjustment in childhood and beyond: "Unpacking" life events, adjustment trajectories, resources, and inter-ventions. In D. Brom, R. Pat-Horenczyk, & J. D. Ford (Eds.), *Treating trauma-tized children: Risk, resilience and recovery* (pp. 13–47). New York, NY: Routledge/ Taylor.

Lazarus, L. F., & Folkman, S. (1984). *Stress, appraisal, and coping.* New York, NY: Springer.

Leaman, S. C., & Gee, C. B. (2012). Religious coping and risk factors for psycho-logical distress among African torture survivors. *Psychological Trauma: Theory, Research, Practice, and Policy, 4,* 457–465. http://dx.doi.org/10.1037/a0026622

Leary, M. R., & Tangney, J. P. (2003). The self as an organizing construct in the behavioral sciences. In M. R. Leary & J. P. Tangney (Eds.), *Handbook of self and identity* (pp. 3–14). New York, NY: Guilford Press.

Leblanc, A. J., Driscoll, A. K., & Pearlin, L. I. (2004). Religiosity and the expan-sion of caregiver stress. *Aging & Mental Health, 8,* 410–421. http://dx.doi.org/10.1080/13607860410001724992

Lerner, M. J., & Miller, D. T. (1978). Just world research and the attribution process: Looking back and ahead. *Psychological Bulletin, 85,* 1030–1051. http://dx.doi.org/10.1037/0033-2909.85.5.1030

Levitt, H. M., Swanger, R. T., & Butler, J. B. (2008). Male perpetrators' perspectives on intimate partner violence, religion, and masculinity. *Sex Roles, 58,* 435–448. http://dx.doi.org/10.1007/s11199-007-9349-3

Linehan, M. M. (1993a). *Cognitive behavioral treatment of borderline personality disorder.* New York, NY: Guilford Press.

Linehan, M. M. (1993b). *Skills training manual for treating borderline personality disorder.* New York, NY: Guilford Press.

Linn, D., Linn, S. F., & Linn, M. (1997). *Don't forgive too soon: Extending the two hands that heal.* New York, NY: Paulist Press.

Littleton, H. L., Axsom, D., & Grills-Taquechel, A. E. (2009). Adjustment following the mass shooting at Virginia Tech: The roles of resource loss and gain. *Psychological Trauma: Theory, Research, Practice, and Policy, 1,* 206–219. http://dx.doi.org/10.1037/a0017468

Litz, B. T., Gray, M. J., Bryant, R. A., & Adler, A. B. (2002). Early intervention for trauma: Current status and future directions. *Clinical Psychology: Science and Practice, 9,* 112–134. http://dx.doi.org/10.1093/clipsy.9.2.112

Litz, B. T., Stein, N., Delaney, E., Lebowitz, L., Nash, W. P., Silva, C., & Maguen, S. (2009). Moral injury and moral repair in war veterans: A preliminary model and intervention strategy. *Clinical Psychology Review, 29,* 695–706. http://dx.doi.org/10.1016/j.cpr.2009.07.003

LoSavio, S. T., Cohen, L. H., Laurenceau, J., Dasch, K. B., Parrish, B., & Park, C. L. (2011). Reports of stress-related growth from daily negative events. *Journal of Social and Clinical Psychology, 30,* 760–785. http://dx.doi.org/10.1521/jscp.2011.30.7.760

Mahoney, A., Pargament, K. I., Cole, B., Jewell, T., Magyar, G. M., Tarakeshwar, N., . . . Phillips, R. (2005). A higher purpose: The sanctification of strivings in a community sample. *International Journal for the Psychology of Religion, 15,* 239–262. http://dx.doi.org/10.1207/s15327582ijpr1503_4

Mahoney, A., Pargament, K. I., Jewell, T., Swank, A. B., Scott, E., Emery, E., & Rye, M. (1999). Marriage and the spiritual realm: The role of proximal and distal religious constructs in marital functioning. *Journal of Family Psychology, 13,* 321–338. http://dx.doi.org/10.1037/0893-3200.13.3.321

Mancini, A. D., & Bonanno, G. A. (2012). Differential pathways to resilience after loss and trauma. In R. A. McMackin, E. Newman, J. M. Fogler, & T. M. Keane (Eds.), *Trauma therapy in context: The science and craft of evidence-based practice* (pp. 79–98). Washington, DC: American Psychological Association. http://dx.doi.org/10.1037/13746-004

Manne, S., Ostroff, J., Fox, K., Grana, G., & Winkel, G. (2009). Cognitive and social processes predicting partner psychological adaptation to early stage breast cancer. *British Journal of Health Psychology, 14,* 49–68. http://dx.doi.org/10.1348/135910708X298458

Martin, D. J., Garske, J. P., & Davis, M. K. (2000). Relation of the therapeutic alliance with outcome and other variables: A meta-analytic review. *Journal of Consulting and Clinical Psychology, 68,* 438–450. http://dx.doi.org/10.1037/0022-006X.68.3.438

Martin, L. H. (2015). The continuing enigma of "religion." *Religion, Brain and Behavior, 5,* 125–131.

Marwaha, S., & Livingston, G. (2002). Stigma, racism or choice. Why do depressed ethnic elders avoid psychiatrists? *Journal of Affective Disorders, 72,* 257–265. http://dx.doi.org/10.1016/S0165-0327(01)00470-0

Maslach, C. (1982). *Burnout: The cost of caring.* Englewood Cliffs, NJ: Prentice-Hall.

Mays, V. M., Caldwell, C. H., & Jackson, J. S. (1996). Mental health symptoms and service utilization patterns of help-seeking among African American women. In H. W. Neighbors & J. S. Jackson (Eds.), *Mental Health in Black America* (pp. 161–176). Thousand Oaks, CA: Sage.

McAdams, D. P., Reynolds, J., Lewis, M., Patten, A. H., & Bowman, P. J. (2001). When bad things turn good and good things turn bad: Sequences of redemption and contamination in life narrative and their relation to psychosocial adaptation in midlife adults and students. *Personality and Social Psychology Bulletin, 27,* 474–485. http://dx.doi.org/10.1177/0146167201274008

McCaslin, S. E., de Zoysa, P., Butler, L. D., Hart, S., Marmar, C. R., Metzler, T. J., & Koopman, C. (2009). The relationship of posttraumatic growth to peritraumatic reactions and posttraumatic stress symptoms among Sri Lankan university students. *Journal of Traumatic Stress, 22,* 334–339. http://dx.doi.org/10.1002/jts.20426

McCullough, M. E., Bono, G., & Root, L. M. (2005). Religion and forgiveness. In R. F. Paloutzian & C. L. Park (Eds.), *Handbook of the psychology of religion and spirituality* (pp. 394–411). New York, NY: Guilford Press.

McCullough, M. E., Rachal, K. C., Sandage, S. J., Worthington, E. L., Jr., Brown, S. W., & Hight, T. L. (1998). Interpersonal forgiving in close relationships: II. Theoretical elaboration and measurement. *Journal of Personality and Social Psychology, 75,* 1586–1603. http://dx.doi.org/10.1037/0022-3514.75.6.1586

McCullough, M. E., & Worthington, E. L., Jr. (1999). Religion and the forgiving personality. *Journal of Personality, 67,* 1141–1164. http://dx.doi.org/10.1111/1467-6494.00085

McGregor, I., & Little, B. R. (1998). Personal projects, happiness, and meaning: On doing well and being yourself. *Journal of Personality and Social Psychology, 74,* 494–512. http://dx.doi.org/10.1037/0022-3514.74.2.494

McIntosh, D. N. (1995). Religion-as-schema, with implications for the relation between religion and coping. *International Journal for the Psychology of Religion, 5,* 1–16. http://dx.doi.org/10.1207/s15327582ijpr0501_1

McIntosh, D. N., Silver, R. C., & Wortman, C. B. (1993). Religion's role in adjustment to a negative life event: Coping with the loss of a child. *Journal of Personality and Social Psychology, 65,* 812–821. http://dx.doi.org/10.1037/0022-3514.65.4.812

McMinn, M. R., Aikins, D. C., & Lish, R. A. (2003). Basic and advanced competence in collaborating with clergy. *Professional Psychology: Research and Practice, 34,* 197–202. http://dx.doi.org/10.1037/0735-7028.34.2.197

McMinn, M. R., & Campbell, C. D. (2007). *Integrative psychotherapy: Toward a comprehensive Christian approach.* Downers Grove, IL: Intervarsity Press.

McNeil, S. N., Pavkov, T. W., Hecker, L. L., & Killmer, J. M. (2012). Marriage and family therapy graduate students' satisfaction with training regarding religion and spirituality. *Contemporary Family Therapy: An International Journal, 34,* 468–480. http://dx.doi.org/10.1007/s10591-012-9205-7

McPherson, J. (2012). Does narrative exposure therapy reduce PTSD in survivors of mass violence? *Research on Social Work Practice, 22,* 29–42. http://dx.doi.org/10.1177/1049731511414147

McRay, B. W., McMinn, M. R., Wrightsman, K., Burnett, T. D., & Ho, S. T. D. (2001). What Evangelical pastors want to know about psychology. *Journal of Psychology and Theology, 29,* 99–105.

Meston, C. M., Lorenz, T. A., & Stephenson, K. R. (2013). Effects of expressive writing on sexual dysfunction, depression, and PTSD in women with a history of childhood sexual abuse: Results from a randomized clinical trial. *Journal of Sexual Medicine, 10,* 2177–2189. http://dx.doi.org/10.1111/jsm.12247

Michael, T., Ehlers, A., Halligan, S. L., & Clark, D. M. (2005). Unwanted memories of assault: What intrusion characteristics are associated with PTSD? *Behaviour Research and Therapy, 43,* 613–628. http://dx.doi.org/10.1016/j.brat.2004.04.006

Moghaddam, F. M., Warren, Z., & Love, K. (2013). Religion-as-schema, with implications for the relation between and the staircase to terrorism. In R. F. Paloutzian & C. L. Park (Eds.), *Handbook of the psychology of religion and coping* (2nd ed., pp. 632–648). New York, NY: Guilford Press.

Molock, S. D., Matlin, S., Barksdale, C., Puri, R., & Lyles, J. (2008). Developing suicide prevention programs for African American youth in African American churches. *Suicide and Life-Threatening Behavior, 38,* 323–333. http://dx.doi.org/10.1521/suli.2008.38.3.323

Monson, C. M., Fredman, S. J., & Adair, K. C. (2008). Cognitive—behavioral conjoint therapy for posttraumatic stress disorder: Application to operation enduring and Iraqi Freedom veterans. *Journal of Clinical Psychology, 64,* 958–971. http://dx.doi.org/10.1002/jclp.20511

Morris, B. A., Shakespeare-Finch, J., & Scott, J. L. (2012). Posttraumatic growth after cancer: The importance of health-related benefits and newfound compassion for others. *Supportive Care in Cancer, 20,* 749–756. http://dx.doi.org/10.1007/s00520-011-1143-7

Murray-Swank, A., & Murray-Swank, N. A. (2013). Spiritual and religious problems: Integrating theory and clinical practice. In K. I. Pargament (Ed.), *APA handbook of psychology, religion, and spirituality: Vol. 2. An applied psychology of religion and spirituality* (pp. 421–437). Washington, DC: American Psychological Association. http://dx.doi.org/10.1037/14046-022

Murray-Swank, N. A., & Murray-Swank, A. B. (2012). Navigating the storm: Helping clients in the midst of spiritual struggles. In J. D. Aten, K. A. O'Grady, & E. L. Worthington, Jr. (Eds.), *The psychology of religions and spirituality for clinicians: Using research in your practice* (pp. 217–244). New York, NY: Routledge.

Murray-Swank, N. A., & Pargament, K. I. (2005). God, where are you? Evaluating a spiritually-integrated intervention for sexual abuse. *Mental Health, Religion & Culture, 8*, 191–203. http://dx.doi.org/10.1080/13694670500138866

Murray-Swank, N. A., & Pargament, K. I. (2008). Solace for the soul: Evaluating a spiritually-integrated counselling intervention for sexual abuse. *Counselling and Spirituality/Counseling et spiritualité, 27*, 157–174.

Myers, D. G. (2000). The funds, friends, and faith of happy people. *American Psychologist, 55*, 56–67. http://dx.doi.org/10.1037/0003-066X.55.1.56

Najavits, L. M. (2002). *Seeking Safety: A treatment manual for PTSD and substance abuse.* New York, NY: Guilford Press.

Najavits, L. M., & Hien, D. (2013). Helping vulnerable populations: A comprehensive review of the treatment outcome literature on substance use disorder and PTSD. *Journal of Clinical Psychology, 69*, 433–479. http://dx.doi.org/10.1002/jclp.21980

Nakamura, Y., Lipschitz, D. L., Landward, R., Kuhn, R., & West, G. (2011). Two sessions of sleep-focused mind-body bridging improve self-reported symptoms of sleep and PTSD in veterans: A pilot randomized controlled trial. *Journal of Psychosomatic Research, 70*, 335–345. http://dx.doi.org/10.1016/j.jpsychores.2010.09.007

Nason-Clark, N. (1997). *The battered wife: How Christians confront family violence.* Louisville, KY: Westminster John Knox.

National Association of Social Workers. (2013). *Social justice.* Retrieved from http://www.socialworkers.org/pressroom/features/issue/peace.asp

Neacsiu, A. D., Ward-Ciesielski, E. F., & Linehan, M. M. (2012). Emerging approaches to counseling intervention: Dialectical behavior therapy. *Counseling Psychologist, 40*, 1033–1060. http://dx.doi.org/10.1177/0011000011421023

Neighbors, H. W., Musick, M. A., & Williams, D. R. (1998). The African American minister as a source of help for serious personal crises: Bridge or barrier to mental health care? *Health Education & Behavior, 25*, 759–777. http://dx.doi.org/10.1177/109019819802500606

Neimeyer, R. A., Pennebaker, J. W., & van Dyke, J. G. (2009). Narrative medicine: Writing through bereavement. In H. M. Chochinov & W. Breitbart (Eds.), *Handbook of psychiatry in palliative medicine* (2nd ed., pp. 454–469). New York, NY: Oxford University Press.

Neuner, F., Onyut, P. L., Ertl, V., Odenwald, M., Schauer, E., & Elbert, T. (2008). Treatment of posttraumatic stress disorder by trained lay counselors in an African refugee settlement: A randomized controlled trial. *Journal of Consulting and Clinical Psychology, 76*, 686–694. http://dx.doi.org/10.1037/0022-006X.76.4.686

Neuner, F., Schauer, M., Klaschik, C., Karunakara, U., & Elbert, T. (2004). A comparison of narrative exposure therapy, supportive counseling, and psychoeducation for treating posttraumatic stress disorder in an African refugee settlement. *Journal of Consulting and Clinical Psychology, 72*, 579–587.

Newman, R. (2005). APA's Resilience Initiative. *Professional Psychology: Research and Practice, 36*, 227–229. http://dx.doi.org/10.1037/0735-7028.36.3.227

Newton, A. T., & McIntosh, D. N. (2009). Associations of general religiousness and specific religious beliefs with coping appraisals in response to Hurricanes Katrina and Rita. *Mental Health, Religion & Culture, 12*, 129–146. http://dx.doi.org/10.1080/13674670802380400

Newton, A., & McIntosh, D. N. (2013). Unique contributions of religion to meaning. In J. A. Hicks & C. Routledge (Eds.), *The experience of meaning in life* (pp. 257–269). New York, NY: Springer. http://dx.doi.org/10.1007/978-94-007-6527-6_20

Nieuwsma, J. A., Rhodes, J. E., Jackson, G. L., Cantrell, W. C., Lane, M. E., Bates, M. J., . . . Meador, K. G. (2013). Chaplaincy and mental health in the Department of Veterans Affairs and Department of Defense. *Journal of Health Care Chaplaincy, 19*, 3–21.

Norenzayan, A., & Lee, A. (2010). It was meant to happen: Explaining cultural variations in fate attributions. *Journal of Personality and Social Psychology, 98*, 702–720. http://dx.doi.org/10.1037/a0019141

Norris, F. H., & Slone, L. B. (2007). The epidemiology of trauma and PTSD. In M. J. Friedman, T. M. Keane, & P. A. Resick (Eds.), *Handbook of PTSD: Science and practice* (pp. 78–98). New York, NY: Guilford Press.

Norris, P., & Inglehart, R. (2004). *Sacred and secular: Religion and politics worldwide*. New York, NY: Cambridge University Press. http://dx.doi.org/10.1017/CBO9780511791017

Ogden, H., Harris, J. I., Erbes, C., Engdahl, B., Olson, R., Winskowski, A. M., & McMahill, J. (2011). Religious functioning and trauma outcomes among combat veterans. *Counselling and Spirituality/Counseling et spiritualité, 30*, 71–89.

Oman, D. (2013). Defining religion and spirituality. In R. F. Paloutzian & C. L. Park (Eds.), *Handbook of the psychology of religion and spirituality* (pp. 23–47). New York, NY: Guilford Press.

Ozorak, E. W. (2005). Cognitive approaches to religion. In R. F. Paloutzian & C. L. Park (Eds.), *Handbook of the psychology of religion and spirituality* (pp. 216–234). New York, NY: Guilford Press.

Paivio, S. C., & Pascual-Leone (2010). *Emotion-focused therapy for complex trauma*. Washington, DC: American Psychological Association.

Paloutzian, R. F. (2005). Religious conversion and spiritual transformation: A meaning-system analysis. In R. F. Paloutzian & C. L. Park (Eds.), *Handbook of the psychology of religion and spirituality* (pp. 331–347). New York, NY: Guilford Press.

Paloutzian, R. F., Murken, S., Streib, H., & Rößler-Namini, S. (2013). Conversation, deconversion, and spiritual transformation: a multilevel interdisciplinary view. In R. F. Paloutzian & C. L. Park (Eds.), *Handbook of the psychology of religion and spirituality* (2nd ed., pp. 399–421). New York, NY: Guilford Press.

Paloutzian, R. F., & Park, C. L. (2015). Religiousness and spirituality: The psychology of multilevel meaning making behavior. *Religion, Brain, and Behavior, 5*, 166–178. http://dx.doi.org/10.1080/2153599X.2014.891254

Pals, J. L., & McAdams, D. P. (2004). The transformed self: A narrative understanding of posttraumatic growth. *Psychological Inquiry, 15*, 65–69.

Pargament, K. I. (1996). Religious methods of coping: Resources for the conservation and transformation of significance. In E. Shafranske (Ed.), *Religion and the clinical practice of psychology* (pp. 215–239). Washington, DC: American Psychological Association.

Pargament, K. I. (1997). *Psychology of religion and coping: Theory, research, practice*. New York, NY: Guilford Press.

Pargament, K. I. (2007). *Spiritually integrated psychotherapy: Understanding and addressing the sacred*. New York, NY: Guilford Press.

Pargament, K. I. (Ed.). (2013). *APA handbook of psychology, religion and spirituality: Vol. 1. Context, theory, and research*. Washington, DC: American Psychological Association.

Pargament, K. I., Desai, K. M., & McConnell, K. M. (2006). Spirituality: A pathway to posttraumatic growth or decline? In L. G. Calhoun & R. G. Tedeschi (Eds.), *Handbook of posttraumatic growth: Research and practice* (pp. 121–137). Mahwah, NJ: Erlbaum.

Pargament, K. I., Falb, M. D., Ano, G. G., & Wachholtz, A. B. (2013). The religious dimension of coping: Theory, advances in theory, research, and practice. In R. F. Paloutzian & C. L. Park (Eds.), *Handbook of the psychology of religion and spirituality* (2nd ed., pp. 560–579). New York, NY: Guilford Press.

Pargament, K. I., Feuille, M., & Burdzy, D. (2011). The Brief RCOPE: Current psychometric status of a short measure of religious coping. *Religions, 2*, 51–76. http://dx.doi.org/10.3390/rel2010051

Pargament, K. I., & Hahn, J. (1986). God and the just world: Causal and coping attributions to God in health situations. *Journal for the Scientific Study of Religion, 25*, 193–207. http://dx.doi.org/10.2307/1385476

Pargament, K. I., Koenig, H. G., Tarakeshwar, N., & Hahn, J. (2001). Religious struggle as a predictor of mortality among medically ill elderly patients: A 2-year longitudinal study. *Archives of Internal Medicine, 161*, 1881–1885. http://dx.doi.org/10.1001/archinte.161.15.1881

Pargament, K. I., Koenig, H. G., Tarakeshwar, N., & Hahn, J. (2004). Religious coping methods as predictors of psychological, physical and spiritual outcomes among medically ill elderly patients: A two-year longitudinal study. *Journal of Health Psychology, 9*, 713–730. http://dx.doi.org/10.1177/1359105304045366

Pargament, K. I., Magyar-Russell, G. M., & Murray-Swank, N. A. (2005). The sacred and the search for significance: Religion as a unique process. *Journal of Social Issues, 61*, 665–687. http://dx.doi.org/10.1111/j.1540-4560.2005.00426.x

Pargament, K. I., Mahoney, A., Exline, J. J., Jones, J. W., & Shafranske, E. P. (2013). Envisioning an integrative paradigm for the psychology of religion and spirituality. In K. I. Pargament (Ed.), *APA handbook of psychology, religion and spirituality: Vol. 1. Context, theory, and research* (pp. 3–19). Washington, DC: American Psychological Association. http://dx.doi.org/10.1037/14045-001

Pargament, K. I., Murray-Swank, N. A., Magyar, G. M., & Ano, G. G. (2005). Spiritual struggle: A phenomenon of interest to psychology of religion. In W. R. Miller

& H. D. Delaney (Eds.), *Judeo Christian perspectives on psychology: Human nature, motivation, and change* (pp. 245–268). Washington, DC: American Psychological Association. http://dx.doi.org/10.1037/10859-013

Pargament, K. I., Smith, B. W., Koenig, H. G., & Perez, L. (1998). Patterns of positive and negative religious coping with major life stressors. *Journal for the Scientific Study of Religion, 37*, 710. http://dx.doi.org/10.2307/1388152

Pargament, K. I., & Sweeney, P. J. (2011). Building spiritual fitness in the Army: An innovative approach to a vital aspect of human development. *American Psychologist, 66*, 58–64. http://dx.doi.org/10.1037/a0021657

Park, C. L. (2005). Religion as a meaning-making framework in coping with life stress. *Journal of Social Issues, 61*, 707–729. http://dx.doi.org/10.1111/j.1540-4560.2005.00428.x

Park, C. L. (2009). Overview of theoretical perspectives. In C. L. Park, S. Lechner, M. H. Antoni, & A. Stanton (Eds.), *Positive life change in the context of medical illness: Can the experience of serious illness lead to transformation?* (pp. 11–30). Washington, DC: American Psychological Association. http://dx.doi.org/10.1037/11854-001

Park, C. L. (2010). Making sense of the meaning literature: An integrative review of meaning making and its effects on adjustment to stressful life events. *Psychological Bulletin, 136*, 257–301. http://dx.doi.org/10.1037/a0018301

Park, C. L. (2016). Meaning making in the context of disasters. *Journal of Clinical Psychology.* Advance online publication. http://dx.doi.org/10.1002/jclp.22270

Park, C. L., & Cohen, L. H. (1993). Religious and nonreligious coping with the death of a friend. *Cognitive Therapy and Research, 17*, 561–577. http://dx.doi.org/10.1007/BF01176079

Park, C. L., Edmondson, D., Fenster, J. R., & Blank, T. O. (2008). Meaning making and psychological adjustment following cancer: The mediating roles of growth, life meaning, and restored just-world beliefs. *Journal of Consulting and Clinical Psychology, 76*, 863–875. http://dx.doi.org/10.1037/a0013348

Park, C. L., Edmondson, D., & Hale-Smith, A. (2013). Why religion? Meaning as motivation. In K. I. Pargament (Ed.), *APA handbook of psychology, religion, and spirituality: Vol. 1. Context, theory, and research* (pp. 157–171). Washington, DC: American Psychological Association.

Park, C. L., Edmondson, D., & Mills, M. A. (2010). Religious worldviews and stressful encounters: Reciprocal influence from a meaning-making perspective. In T. Miller (Ed.), *Handbook of stressful transitions across the lifespan* (pp. 485–501). New York, NY: Springer. http://dx.doi.org/10.1007/978-1-4419-0748-6_25

Park, C. L., & Fenster, J. R. (2004). Stress-related growth: Predictors of occurrence and correlates with psychological adjustment. *Journal of Social and Clinical Psychology, 23*, 195–215. http://dx.doi.org/10.1521/jscp.23.2.195.31019

Park, C. L., & Folkman, S. (1997). Meaning in the context of stress and coping. *Review of General Psychology, 1*, 115–144. http://dx.doi.org/10.1037/1089-2680.1.2.115

Park, C. L., & George, L. S. (2013). Assessing meaning and meaning making in the context of stressful life events: Measurement tools and approaches. *The Journal of Positive Psychology, 8*, 483–504. http://dx.doi.org/10.1080/17439760.2013.830762

Park, C. L., Riley, K. E., George, L., Gutierrez, I., Hale, A., Cho, D., & Braun, T. (in press). *Assessing disruptions in meaning: Development of the Global Meaning Violation Scale*.

Park, C. L., & Slattery, J. M. (2009). Including spirituality in case conceptualizations: A meaning system approach. In J. Aten & M. Leach (Eds.), *Spirituality and the therapeutic practice: A comprehensive resource from intake to termination* (pp. 121–142). Washington, DC: American Psychological Association. http://dx.doi.org/10.1037/11853-006

Park, C. L., & Slattery, J. M. (2012). Spirituality, emotions, and physical health. In L. J. Miller (Ed.), *The Oxford handbook of the psychology of spirituality and consciousness* (pp. 379–387). Oxford, England: Oxford University Press.

Park, C. L., & Slattery, J. M. (2013a). Religion and emotional health and well-being. In R. F. Paloutzian & C. L. Park (Eds.), *Handbook of the psychology of religion and spirituality* (2nd ed., pp. 540–559). New York, NY: Guilford Press.

Park, C. L., & Slattery, J. M. (2013b). Resilience interventions with a focus on meaning and values. In M. Kent, M. C. Davis, & J. W. Reich (Eds.), *The resilience handbook: Approaches to stress and trauma* (pp. 270–282). New York, NY: Routledge.

Pashak, T. J., & Laughter, T. C. (2012). Measuring service-mindedness and its relationships with spirituality and life satisfaction. *College Student Journal, 46*, 183–192.

Pearlman, L. A., & Mac Ian, P. S. (1995). Vicarious traumatization: An empirical study of the effects of trauma work on trauma therapists. *Professional Psychology: Research and Practice, 26*, 558–565. http://dx.doi.org/10.1037/0735-7028.26.6.558

Pearlman, L. A., & Saakvitne, K. W. (1995). *Trauma and the therapist: Countertransference and vicarious traumatization in psychotherapy with incest survivors*. New York, NY: Norton.

Perera, S., & Frazier, P. A. (2013). Changes in religiosity and spirituality following potentially traumatic events. *Counselling Psychology Quarterly, 26*, 26–38. http://dx.doi.org/10.1080/09515070.2012.728883

Peres, J. F., Moreira-Almeida, A., Nasello, A. G., & Koenig, H. G. (2007). Spirituality and resilience in trauma victims. *Journal of Religion and Health, 46*, 343–350. http://dx.doi.org/10.1007/s10943-006-9103-0

Peterson, C., Park, N., & Seligman, M. E. P. (2005). Orientations to happiness and life satisfaction: The full life versus the empty life. *Journal of Happiness Studies, 6*, 25–41. http://dx.doi.org/10.1007/s10902-004-1278-z

Pew Forum on Religion & Public Life. (2008). *U.S. religious landscape survey*. Retrieved from http://religions.pewforum.org/pdf/report2-religious-landscape-study-full.pdf

Pew Research Center. (2002). *Americans struggle with religion's role at home and abroad.* Retrieved from http://www.people-press.org/2002/03/20/part-1-religion-in-america/

Pew Research Center. (2015). *U.S. public becoming less religious.* Retrieved from http://www.pewforum.org/2015/11/03/u-s-public-becoming-less-religious/

Pietrzak, R. H., Feder, A., Singh, R., Schechter, C. B., Bromet, E. J., Katz, C. L., . . . Southwick, S. M. (2014). Trajectories of PTSD risk and resilience in World Trade Center responders: An 8-year prospective cohort study. *Psychological Medicine, 44,* 205–219. http://dx.doi.org/10.1017/S0033291713000597

Pietrzak, R. H., Goldstein, R. B., Southwick, S. M., & Grant, B. F. (2011). Medical comorbidity of full and partial posttraumatic stress disorder in US adults: Results from Wave 2 of the National Epidemiologic Survey on Alcohol and Related Conditions. *Psychosomatic Medicine, 73,* 697–707. http://dx.doi.org/10.1097/PSY.0b013e3182303775

Pietrzak, R. H., Van Ness, P. H., Fried, T. R., Galea, S., & Norris, F. H. (2013). Trajectories of posttraumatic stress symptomatology in older persons affected by a large-magnitude disaster. *Journal of Psychiatric Research, 47,* 520–526. http://dx.doi.org/10.1016/j.jpsychires.2012.12.005

Plante, T. G. (2007). Integrating spirituality and psychotherapy: Ethical issues and principles to consider. *Journal of Clinical Psychology, 63,* 891–902. http://dx.doi.org/10.1002/jclp.20383

Pole, N., Gone, J. P., & Kulkarni, M. (2008). Posttraumatic stress disorder among ethnoracial minorities in the United States. *Clinical Psychology: Science and Practice, 15,* 35–61. http://dx.doi.org/10.1111/j.1468-2850.2008.00109.x

Ponniah, K., & Hollon, S. D. (2009). Empirically supported psychological treatments for adult acute stress disorder and posttraumatic stress disorder: A review. *Depression and Anxiety, 26,* 1086–1109. http://dx.doi.org/10.1002/da.20635

Powers, M. B., Halpern, J. M., Ferenschak, M. P., Gillihan, S. J., & Foa, E. B. (2010). A meta-analytic review of prolonged exposure for posttraumatic stress disorder. *Clinical Psychology Review, 30,* 635–641. http://dx.doi.org/10.1016/j.cpr.2010.04.007

Presidential Task Force on Posttraumatic Stress Disorder and Trauma in Children and Adolescents. (2008). *Children and trauma: Update for mental health professionals.* Retrieved from American Psychological Association website: http://www.apa.org/pi/families/resources/children-trauma-update.aspx

Pritt, A. F. (1998). Spiritual correlates of reported sexual abuse among Mormon women. *Journal for the Scientific Study of Religion, 37,* 273–285. http://dx.doi.org/10.2307/1387527

Propst, L. R., Ostrom, R., Watkins, P., Dean, T., & Mashburn, D. (1992). Comparative efficacy of religious and nonreligious cognitive–behavioral therapy for the treatment of clinical depression in religious individuals. *Journal of Consulting and Clinical Psychology, 60,* 94–103. http://dx.doi.org/10.1037/0022-006X.60.1.94

Pyszczynski, T., & Kesebir, P. (2011). Anxiety buffer disruption theory: A terror management account of posttraumatic stress disorder. *Anxiety, Stress, & Coping, 24*, 3–26. http://dx.doi.org/10.1080/10615806.2010.517524

Qureshi, S. U., Pyne, J. M., Magruder, K. M., Schulz, P. E., & Kunik, M. E. (2009). The link between post-traumatic stress disorder and physical comorbidities: A systematic review. *Psychiatric Quarterly, 80*, 87–97. http://dx.doi.org/10.1007/s11126-009-9096-4

Raue, P. J., Weinberger, M. I., Sirey, J. A., Meyers, B. S., & Bruce, M. L. (2011). Preferences for depression treatment among elderly home health care patients. *Psychiatric Services, 62*, 532–537. http://dx.doi.org/10.1176/ps.62.5.pss6205_0532

Reed, G. L., & Enright, R. D. (2006). The effects of forgiveness therapy on depression, anxiety, and posttraumatic stress for women after spousal emotional abuse. *Journal of Consulting and Clinical Psychology, 74*, 920–929. http://dx.doi.org/10.1037/0022-006X.74.5.920

Rees, B. (2011). Overview of outcome data of potential meditation training for soldier resilience. *Military Medicine, 176*, 1232–1242. http://dx.doi.org/10.7205/MILMED-D-11-00067

Resick, P. A. (2001). *Stress and trauma.* New York, NY: Taylor & Francis.

Resick, P. A., Monson, C. M., & Chard, K. M. (2008). *Cognitive processing therapy: Veteran/military version.* Washington, DC: Department of Veterans Affairs.

Resick, P. A., Monson, C. M., & Gutner, C. (2007). Psychosocial treatments for PTSD. In M. J. Friedman, T. M. Keane, & P. A. Resick (Eds.), *Handbook of PTSD: Science and Practice* (pp. 330–358). New York, NY: Guilford Press.

Resick, P. A., & Schnicke, M. K. (1993). *Cognitive processing therapy for rape victims: A treatment manual.* Newbury Park, CA: Sage.

Richards, P. S., & Bergin, A. E. (Eds.). (2014). *Handbook of psychotherapy and religious diversity* (2nd ed.). Washington, DC: American Psychological Association. http://dx.doi.org/10.1037/14371-000

Riggs, D. S., Cahill, S. P., & Foa, E. B. (2006). Prolonged exposure treatment of posttraumatic stress disorder. In V. M. Follette & J. I. Ruzek (Eds.), *Cognitive–behavioral therapies for trauma* (2nd ed., pp. 65–95). New York, NY: Guilford Press.

Riggs, D. S., Monson, C. M., Glynn, S. M., & Canterino, J. (2009). Couple and family therapy for adults. In E. B. Foa, T. M. Keane, M. J. Friedman, & J. A. Cohen (Eds.), *Effective treatments for PTSD: Practice guidelines from the International Society for Traumatic Stress Studies* (2nd ed., pp. 458–478). New York, NY: Guilford Press.

Robjant, K., & Fazel, M. (2010). The emerging evidence for narrative exposure therapy: A review. *Clinical Psychology Review, 30*, 1030–1039. http://dx.doi.org/10.1016/j.cpr.2010.07.004

Roesch, S. C., & Ano, G. (2003). Testing an attribution and coping model of stress: Religion as an orienting system. *Journal of Psychology and Christianity, 22*, 197–209.

Rosenfeld, G. W. (2011). Contributions from ethics and research that guide integrating religion into psychotherapy. *Professional Psychology: Research and Practice*, *42*, 192–199. http://dx.doi.org/10.1037/a0022742

Rothbaum, B. O., Gerardi, M., Bradley, B., & Friedman, M. J. (2011). Evidence-based treatments for posttraumatic stress disorder in Operation Enduring Freedom and Operation Iraqi Freedom military personnel. In J. I. Ruzek, P. P. Schnurr, J. J. Vasterling, & M. J. Friedman (Eds.), *Caring for veterans with deployment-related stress disorders* (pp. 215–239). Washington, DC: American Psychological Association. http://dx.doi.org/10.1037/12323-010

Rothbaum, F., Weisz, J. R., & Snyder, S. S. (1982). Changing the world and changing the self: A two-process model of perceived control. *Journal of Personality and Social Psychology*, *42*, 5–37. http://dx.doi.org/10.1037/0022-3514.42.1.5

Russell, S. R., & Yarhouse, M. A. (2006). Training in religion/spirituality within APA-accredited psychology predoctoral internships. *Professional Psychology: Research and Practice*, *37*, 430–436. http://dx.doi.org/10.1037/0735-7028.37.4.430

Rye, M. S., Pargament, K. I., Ali, M. A., Beck, G. L., Dorff, E. N., Hallisey, C., . . . Williams, J. G. (2000). Religious perspectives on forgiveness. *Forgiveness: Theory, research, and practice* (pp. 17–40). New York, NY: Guilford Press.

Saakvitne, K. W. (2002). Shared trauma: The therapist's increased vulnerability. *Psychoanalytic Dialogues*, *12*, 443–449. http://dx.doi.org/10.1080/10481881209348678

Saakvitne, K. W., Gamble, S. G., Pearlman, L. A., & Lev, B. L. (2000). *Risking Connection: A training curriculum for working with survivors of childhood abuse*. Lutherville, MD: Sidran Press.

Sabin-Farrell, R., & Turpin, G. (2003). Vicarious traumatization: Implications for the mental health of health workers? *Clinical Psychology Review*, *23*, 449–480. http://dx.doi.org/10.1016/S0272-7358(03)00030-8

Safran, J. D., & Muran, J. C. (2000). *Negotiating the therapeutic alliance: A relational treatment guide*. New York, NY: Guilford Press.

Sakuma, Y., Sasaki-Otomaru, A., Ishida, S., Kanoya, Y., Arakawa, C., Mochizuki, Y., . . . Sato, C. (2012). Effect of a home-based simple yoga program in child-care workers: A randomized controlled trial. *The Journal of Alternative and Complementary Medicine*, *18*, 769–776. http://dx.doi.org/10.1089/acm.2011.0080

Saroglou, V. (2002). Religion and the five factors of personality: A meta-analytic review. *Personality and Individual Differences*, *32*, 15–25. http://dx.doi.org/10.1016/S0191-8869(00)00233-6

Saroglou, V., & Cohen, A. B. (2013). Cultural and cross-cultural psychology of religion. In R. F. Paloutzian & C. L. Park (Eds.), *Handbook of the psychology of religion and spirituality* (2nd ed., pp. 330–354). New York, NY: Guilford Press.

Saunders, S. M., Miller, M. S., & Bright, M. M. (2010). Spiritually conscious psychological care. *Professional Psychology: Research and Practice*, *41*, 355–362. http://dx.doi.org/10.1037/a0020953

Schafer, R. M., Handal, P. J., Brawer, P. A., & Ubinger, M. (2011). Training and education in religion/spirituality within APA-accredited clinical psychology pro-

grams: 8 years later. *Journal of Religion and Health, 50*, 232–239. http://dx.doi.org/
10.1007/s10943-009-9272-8

Schauben, L., & Frazier, P. (1995). Vicarious trauma: The effects on female counselors of working with sexual violence survivors. *Psychology of Women Quarterly, 19*, 49–64. http://dx.doi.org/10.1111/j.1471-6402.1995.tb00278.x

Schauer, M., Neuner, F., & Elbert, T. (2011). *Narrative exposure therapy: Short-term treatment for traumatic stress disorders.* Cambridge, MA: Hogrefe.

Schnitker, S. A., & Emmons, R. H. (2013). Spiritual striving and seeking the sacred: Religion and meaningful goal-directed behavior. *International Journal for the Psychology of Religion, 23*, 315–324. http://dx.doi.org/10.1080/10508619.2013.795822

Schure, M. B., Christopher, J., & Christopher, S. (2008). Mind–body medicine and the art of self-care: Teaching mindfulness to counseling students through yoga, meditation and QiGong. *Journal of Counseling & Development, 86*, 47–56. http://dx.doi.org/10.1002/j.1556-6678.2008.tb00625.x

Schwartz, S. H., & Bilsky, W. (1990). Toward a theory of the universal content and structure of values: Extensions and cross-cultural replications. *Journal of Personality and Social Psychology, 58*, 878–891. http://dx.doi.org/10.1037/0022-3514.58.5.878

Sedikides, C., & Gebauer, J. E. (2010). Religiosity as self-enhancement: A meta-analysis of the relation between socially desirable responding and religiosity. *Personality and Social Psychology Review, 14*, 17–36. http://dx.doi.org/10.1177/1088868309351002

Segerstrom, S. C., Stanton, A. L., Alden, L. E., & Shortridge, B. E. (2003). A multidimensional structure for repetitive thought: What's on your mind, and how, and how much? *Journal of Personality and Social Psychology, 85*, 909–921.

Seirmarco, G., Neria, Y., Insel, B., Kiper, D., Doruk, A., Gross, R., & Litz, B. (2012). Religiosity and mental health: Changes in religious beliefs, complicated grief, posttraumatic stress disorder, and major depression following the September 11, 2001 Attacks. *Psychology of Religion and Spirituality, 4*, 10–18. http://dx.doi.org/10.1037/a0023479

Shafranske, E. P., & Cummings, J. P. (2013). Religious and spiritual beliefs, affiliations, and practices of psychologists. In K. I. Pargament, A. Mahoney, & E. Shafranske (Eds.), *Religious and spiritual beliefs, affiliations, and practices of psychologists* (Vol. II, pp. 23–41). Washington, DC: American Psychological Association. http://dx.doi.org/10.1037/14046-002

Shafranske, E. P., & Malony, H. N. (1990). Clinical psychologists' religious and spiritual orientations and their practice of psychotherapy. *Psychotherapy: Theory, Research, Practice, Training, 27*, 72–78. http://dx.doi.org/10.1037/0033-3204.27.1.72

Shaw, A., Joseph, S., & Linley, A. (2005). Religion, spirituality, and posttraumatic growth: A systematic review. *Mental Health, Religion & Culture, 8*, 1–11. http://dx.doi.org/10.1080/1367467032000157981

Shubs, C. (2008). Countertransference issues in the assessment and treatment of trauma recovery with victims of violent crime. *Psychoanalytic Psychology, 25*, 156–180. http://dx.doi.org/10.1037/0736-9735.25.1.156

Shuman, J. J., & Meador, K. G. (2003). *Heal thyself: Spirituality, medicine, and the distortion of Christianity.* New York, NY: Oxford University Press. http://dx.doi.org/10.1093/019515469X.001.0001

Silton, N. R., Flannelly, K. J., Galek, K., & Ellison, C. G. (2014). Beliefs about God and mental health among American adults. *Journal of Religion and Health, 53,* 1285–1296. http://dx.doi.org/10.1007/s10943-013-9712-3

Slattery, J. M., & Park, C. L. (2011a). *Empathic counseling: Meaning, context, ethics, and skill.* Pacific Grove, CA: Brooks/Cole.

Slattery, J. M., & Park, C. L. (2011b). Meaning making and spiritually oriented interventions. In J. D. Aten, M. R. McMinn, & E. L. Worthington, Jr. (Eds.), *Spiritually oriented interventions for counseling and psychotherapy* (pp. 15–40). Washington, DC: American Psychological Association. http://dx.doi.org/10.1037/12313-001

Slattery, J. M., & Park, C. L. (2012a). Clinical approaches to discrepancies in meaning: Conceptualization, assessment, and treatment. In P. T. P. Wong (Ed.), *Human quest for meaning* (2nd ed., pp. 493–516). New York, NY: Routledge.

Slattery, J. M., & Park, C. L. (2012b). Religious and spiritual beliefs in psychotherapy: A meaning perspective. In J. Aten, K. O'Grady, & E. V. Worthington (Eds.), *The psychology of religion and spirituality for clinicians: Using research in your practice* (pp. 189–215). New York, NY: Routledge.

Slattery, J. M., & Park, C. L. (2015). Spirituality and making meaning: Implications for therapy with trauma survivors. In D. F. Walker, C. A. Courtois, & J. D. Aten (Eds.), *Spiritually oriented trauma psychotherapy* (pp. 127–146). Washington, DC: American Psychological Association. http://dx.doi.org/10.1037/14500-007

Slattery, J. M., Park, C. L., & Snavely, A. (2014, August). *Links between trauma and spirituality: A systematic review.* Paper presented at the meeting of the American Psychological Association, Washington, DC.

Slife, B. D., & Reber, J. S. (2009). Is there a pervasive implicit bias against theism in psychology? *Journal of Theoretical and Philosophical Psychology, 29,* 63–79. http://dx.doi.org/10.1037/a0016985

Smith, B. W., Ortiz, J. A., Steffen, L. E., Tooley, E. M., Wiggins, K. T., Yeater, E. A., . . . Bernard, M. L. (2011). Mindfulness is associated with fewer PTSD symptoms, depressive symptoms, physical symptoms, and alcohol problems in urban firefighters. *Journal of Consulting and Clinical Psychology, 79,* 613–617. http://dx.doi.org/10.1037/a0025189

Smith, B. W., Pargament, K. I., Brant, C., & Oliver, J. M. (2000). Noah revisited: Religious coping by church members and the impact of the 1993 Midwest flood. *Journal of Community Psychology, 28,* 169–186. http://dx.doi.org/10.1002/(SICI)1520-6629(200003)28:2<169::AID-JCOP5>3.0.CO;2-I

Smith, S. (2004). Exploring the interaction of trauma and spirituality. *Traumatology, 10,* 231–243. http://dx.doi.org/10.1177/153476560401000403

Solomon, Z., & Dekel, R. (2007). Posttraumatic stress disorder and posttraumatic growth among Israeli ex-POWs. *Journal of Traumatic Stress, 20*, 303–312. http://dx.doi.org/10.1002/jts.20216

Solomon, Z., Horesh, D., Ein-Dor, T., & Ohry, A. (2012). Predictors of PTSD trajectories following captivity: A 35-year longitudinal study. *Psychiatry Research, 199*, 188–194. http://dx.doi.org/10.1016/j.psychres.2012.03.035

Sperry, L. (2005). Integrative spiritually oriented psychotherapy. In L. Sperry & E. P. Shafranske (Eds.), *Spiritually oriented psychotherapy* (pp. 307–329). Washington, DC: American Psychological Association. http://dx.doi.org/10.1037/10886-013

Sperry, L. (2012). *Spirituality in clinical practice: Theory and practice of spiritually oriented psychotherapy* (2nd ed.). New York, NY: Routledge.

Sperry, L., & Shafranske, E. P. (Eds.). (2005). *Spiritually oriented psychotherapy.* Washington, DC: American Psychological Association. http://dx.doi.org/10.1037/10886-000

Spilka, B., Hood, R. W., Hunsberger, B., & Gorsuch, R. (2003). *The psychology of religion: An empirical approach* (3rd ed.). New York, NY: Guilford Press.

Spilka, B., Shaver, P., & Kirkpatrick, L. (1985). A general attribution theory for the psychology of religion. *Journal for the Scientific Study of Religion, 24*, 1–20. http://dx.doi.org/10.2307/1386272

Staples, J. K., Hamilton, M. F., & Uddo, M. (2013). A yoga program for the symptoms of post-traumatic stress disorder in veterans. *Military Medicine, 178*, 854–860. http://dx.doi.org/10.7205/MILMED-D-12-00536

Steenkamp, M. M., Litz, B. T., Gray, M. J., Lebowitz, L., Nash, W., Conoscenti, L., . . . Lang, A. (2011). A brief exposure-based intervention for service members with PTSD. *Cognitive and Behavioral Practice, 18*, 98–107. http://dx.doi.org/10.1016/j.cbpra.2009.08.006

Steger, M. F. (2009). Meaning in life. In S. J. Lopez & C. R. Snyder (Eds.), *Oxford handbook of positive psychology* (2nd ed., pp. 679–687). New York, NY: Oxford University Press.

Steger, M. F., & Frazier, P. (2005). Meaning in life: One link in the chain from religiousness to well-being. *Journal of Counseling Psychology, 52*, 574–582. http://dx.doi.org/10.1037/0022-0167.52.4.574

Steger, M. F., Frazier, P., Oishi, S., & Kaler, M. (2006). The Meaning in Life Questionnaire: Assessing the presence of and search for meaning in life. *Journal of Counseling Psychology, 53*, 80–93.

Steger, M. F., Owens, G. P., & Park, C. L. (2015). Violations of war: Testing the meaning-making model among Vietnam veterans. *Journal of Clinical Psychology, 71*, 105–116. http://dx.doi.org/10.1002/jclp.22121

Stein, C. H., Abraham, K. M., Bonar, E. E., McAuliffe, C. E., Fogo, W. R., Faigin, D. A., . . . Potokar, D. N. (2009). Making meaning from personal loss: Religious, benefit finding, and goal-oriented attributions. *Journal of Loss and Trauma, 14,* 83–100. http://dx.doi.org/10.1080/15325020802173819

Stein, N. R., Mills, M. A., Arditte, K., Mendoza, C., Borah, A. M., Resick, P. A., . . . Wright, E., & the STRONG STAR Consortium. (2012). A scheme for categorizing traumatic military events. *Behavior Modification, 36,* 787–807. http://dx.doi.org/10.1177/0145445512446945

Steinhardt, M., & Dolbier, C. (2008). Evaluation of a resilience intervention to enhance coping strategies and protective factors and decrease symptomatology. *Journal of American College Health, 56,* 445–453. http://dx.doi.org/10.3200/JACH.56.44.445-454

Streeter, C. C., Gerbarg, P. L., Saper, R. B., Ciraulo, D. A., & Brown, R. P. (2012). Effects of yoga on the autonomic nervous system, gamma-aminobutyric-acid, and allostasis in epilepsy, depression, and post-traumatic stress disorder. *Medical Hypotheses, 78,* 571–579. http://dx.doi.org/10.1016/j.mehy.2012.01.021

Sturgeon, J. A., & Zautra, A. J. (2010). Resilience: A new paradigm for adaptation to chronic pain. *Current Pain and Headache Reports, 14,* 105–112. http://dx.doi.org/10.1007/s11916-010-0095-9

Taylor, R. J., Chatters, L. M., & Jackson, J. S. (2007). Religious and spiritual involvement among older African Americans, Caribbean Blacks, and non-Hispanic Whites: Findings from the national survey of American life. *The Journals of Gerontology: Series B: Psychological Sciences and Social Sciences, 62,* S238–S250. http://dx.doi.org/10.1093/geronb/62.4.S238

Teasdale, J. D., Scott, J., Moore, R. G., Hayhurst, H., Pope, M., & Paykel, E. S. (2001). How does cognitive therapy prevent relapse in residual depression? Evidence from a controlled trial. *Journal of Consulting and Clinical Psychology, 69,* 347–357. http://dx.doi.org/10.1037/0022-006X.69.3.347

Tedeschi, R. G., & Calhoun, L. G. (2004). Posttraumatic growth: Conceptual foundations and empirical evidence. *Psychological Inquiry, 15,* 1–18. http://dx.doi.org/10.1207/s15327965pli1501_01

Telles, S., Singh, N., Joshi, M., & Balkrishna, A. (2010). Post traumatic stress symptoms and heart rate variability in Bihar flood survivors following yoga: A randomized controlled study. *BMC Psychiatry, 10.* http://dx.doi.org/10.1186/1471-244X-10-18

Thielman, S. B. (2011). Religion and spirituality in the description of post-traumatic stress disorder. In S. B. Thielman, J. R. Peteet, F. G. Lu, & W. E. Narrow (Eds.), *Religious and spiritual issues in psychiatric diagnosis: A research agenda for* DSM–V (pp. 105–114). Arlington, VA: American Psychiatric Association.

Thompson, S. C., & Janigian, A. S. (1988). Life schemes: A framework for understanding the search for meaning. *Journal of Social and Clinical Psychology, 7,* 260–280. http://dx.doi.org/10.1521/jscp.1988.7.2-3.260

Tjeltveit, A. C. (2006). To what ends? Psychotherapy goals and outcomes, the good life, and the principle of beneficence. *Psychotherapy: Theory, Research, Practice, Training, 43,* 186–200. http://dx.doi.org/10.1037/0033-3204.43.2.186

Tomer, A., & Eliason, G. (2000). Beliefs about self, life, and death: Testing aspects of a comprehensive model of death anxiety and death attitudes. In A. Tomer (Ed.), *Death attitudes and the older adult: Theories, concepts, and applications* (pp. 137–153). New York, NY: Brunner-Routledge.

Tomich, P. L., & Helgeson, V. S. (2012). Posttraumatic growth following cancer: Links to quality of life. *Journal of Traumatic Stress, 25*, 567–573. http://dx.doi.org/10.1002/jts.21738

Trippany, R. L., White Kress, V. E., & Wilcoxon, S. A. (2004). Preventing vicarious trauma: What counselors should know when working with trauma survivors. *Journal of Counseling & Development, 82*, 31–37. http://dx.doi.org/10.1002/j.1556-6678.2004.tb00283.x

Tuval-Mashiach, R., & Dekel, R. (2014). Religious meaning-making at the community level: The forced relocation from the Gaza Strip. *Psychology of Religion and Spirituality, 6*, 64–71. http://dx.doi.org/10.1037/a0033917

Uecker, J. E. (2008). Religious and spiritual responses to 9/11: Evidence from the Add Health Study. *Sociological Spectrum, 28*, 477–509. http://dx.doi.org/10.1080/02732170802206047

U.S. Department of Veterans Affairs. (2015). *National Center for PTSD: Professionals.* Retrieved from http://www.ptsd.va.gov/professional/index.asp

van der Kolk, B. A. (2007). The history of PTSD in psychiatry. In M. J. Friedman, T. M. Keane, & P. A. Resick (Eds.), *Handbook of PTSD: Science and practice* (pp. 3–18). New York, NY: Guilford Press.

van der Kolk, B. A., MacFarlane, A. C., & van der Hart, O. (1996). A general approach to treatment of posttraumatic stress disorder. In B. A. van der Kolk, A. C. MacFarlane, & L. Weisaet (Eds.), *Traumatic stress: The effects of overwhelming experience on mind, body, and society* (pp. 417–440). New York, NY: Guilford Press.

van der Kolk, B. A., Roth, S., Pelcovitz, D., Sunday, S., & Spinazzola, J. (2005). Disorders of extreme stress: The empirical foundation of a complex adaptation to trauma. *Journal of Traumatic Stress, 18*, 389–399. http://dx.doi.org/10.1002/jts.20047

van der Kolk, B. A., Stone, L., West, J., Rhodes, A., Emerson, D., Suvak, M., & Spinazzola, J. (2014). Yoga as an adjunctive treatment for posttraumatic stress disorder: A randomized controlled trial. *Journal of Clinical Psychiatry, 75*, e559–e565. http://dx.doi.org/10.4088/JCP.13m08561

Van Eenwyk, J. R. (1996). Switching tracks: Parallel paradigms in psychology and religion. In E. P. Shafranske (Ed.), *Religion and the clinical practice of psychology* (pp. 461–482). Washington, DC: American Psychological Association. http://dx.doi.org/10.1037/10199-017

Van Hooff, M., McFarlane, A. C., Baur, J., Abraham, M., & Barnes, D. J. (2009). The stressor Criterion-A1 and PTSD: A matter of opinion? *Journal of Anxiety Disorders, 23*, 77–86. http://dx.doi.org/10.1016/j.janxdis.2008.04.001

Van Tongeren, D. R., Burnette, J. L., O'Boyle, E. O., Worthington, E. L., Jr., & Forsyth, D. (2014). A meta-analysis of intergroup forgiveness. *The Journal of Positive Psychology, 9,* 81–95. http://dx.doi.org/10.1080/17439760.2013.844268

Vargas, A. F., Hanson, T., Kraus, D., Drescher, K., & Foy, D. (2013). Moral injury themes in combat veterans' narrative responses from the National Vietnam Veterans' Readjustment Study. *Traumatology, 19,* 243–250. http://dx.doi.org/10.1177/1534765613476099

Verbeck, E. G., Arzoumanian, M. A., Estrellado, J. E., DeLorme, J., Dahlin, K., Hennrich, E., . . . Dalenberg, C. (2015). Religion, spirituality, and the working alliance with trauma survivors. In D. F. Walker, C. A. Courtois, & J. D. Aten (Eds.), *Spiritually oriented trauma psychotherapy* (pp. 103–126). Washington, DC: American Psychological Association. http://dx.doi.org/10.1037/14500-006

Vieten, C., Scammell, S., Pilato, R., Ammondson, I., Pargament, K. I., & Lukoff, D. (2013). Spiritual and religious competencies for psychologists. *Psychology of Religion and Spirituality, 5,* 129–144. http://dx.doi.org/10.1037/a0032699

Vieweg, W. V. R., Julius, D. A., Fernandez, A., Beatty-Brooks, M., Hettema, J. M., & Pandurangi, A. K. (2006). Posttraumatic stress disorder: Clinical features, pathophysiology, and treatment. *The American Journal of Medicine, 119,* 383–390. http://dx.doi.org/10.1016/j.amjmed.2005.09.027

Vis, J.-A., & Boynton, H. M. (2008). Spirituality and transcendent meaning making: Possibilities for enhancing posttraumatic growth. *Journal of Religion & Spirituality in Social Work: Social Thought, 27,* 69–86. http://dx.doi.org/10.1080/15426430802113814

Vogel, M. J., McMinn, M. R., Peterson, M. A., & Gathercoal, K. A. (2013). Examining religion and spirituality as diversity training: A multidimensional look at training in the American Psychological Association. *Professional Psychology: Research and Practice, 44,* 158–167. http://dx.doi.org/10.1037/a0032472

Volkert, J., Schulz, H., Brutt, A. L., & Andreas, S. (2014). Meaning in life: Relationships to clinical diagnoses and psychotherapy outcomes. *Journal of Clinical Psychology, 70,* 528–535. http://dx.doi.org/10.1002/jclp.22053

Wade, N. G., Hoyt, W. T., Kidwell, J. E. M., & Worthington, E. L., Jr. (2014). Efficacy of psychotherapeutic interventions to promote forgiveness: A meta-analysis. *Journal of Consulting and Clinical Psychology, 82,* 154–170. http://dx.doi.org/10.1037/a0035268

Wade, N. G., Johnson, C. V., & Meyer, J. E. (2008). Understanding concerns about interventions to promote forgiveness: A review of the literature. *Psychotherapy: Theory, Research, Practice, Training, 45,* 88–102. http://dx.doi.org/10.1037/0033-3204.45.1.88

Walker, D. F., Courtois, C. A., & Aten, J. D. (Eds.). (2015). *Spiritually oriented psychotherapy for trauma.* Washington, DC: American Psychological Association. http://dx.doi.org/10.1037/14500-000

Walker, D. F., Gorsuch, R. L., & Tan, S.-Y. (2004). Therapists' integration of religion and spirituality in counseling: A meta-analysis. *Counseling and Values, 49,* 69–80. http://dx.doi.org/10.1002/j.2161-007X.2004.tb00254.x

Walker, D. F., Gorsuch, R. L., & Tan, S.-Y. (2005). Therapists' use of religious and spiritual interventions in Christian counseling: A preliminary report. *Counseling and Values, 49*, 107–119. http://dx.doi.org/10.1002/j.2161-007X.2005.tb00257.x

Walker, D. F., Reid, H. R., O'Neill, T., & Brown, L. (2009). Changes in personal religion/spirituality during and after childhood abuse: A review and synthesis. *Psychological Trauma: Theory, Research, Practice, and Policy, 1*, 130–145. http://dx.doi.org/10.1037/a0016211

Walser, R. D., & Westrup, D. (2007). *Acceptance and commitment therapy for the treatment of post-traumatic stress disorder and trauma-related problems*. Oakland, CA: New Harbinger.

Way, I., VanDeusen, K. M., Martin, G., Applegate, B., & Jandle, D. (2004). Vicarious trauma: A comparison of clinicians who treat survivors of sexual abuse and sexual offenders. *Journal of Interpersonal Violence, 19*, 49–71. http://dx.doi.org/10.1177/0886260503259050

Weathers, F., & Ford, J. (1996). Psychometric properties of the PTSD Checklist (PCL–C, PCL–S, PCL–M, PCL–PR). In B. H. Stamm (Ed.), *Measurement of stress, trauma, and adaptation* (pp. 250–252). Lutherville, MD: Sidran Press.

Wechsler, D. (2003). *Wechsler Intelligence Scale for Children—Fourth Edition (WISC–IV)*. San Antonio, TX: Pearson.

Weeks, M., & Lupfer, M. B. (2000). Religious attributions and proximity of influence: An investigation of direct interventions and distal explanations. *Journal for the Scientific Study of Religion, 39*, 348–362. http://dx.doi.org/10.1111/0021-8294.00029

White, B., Driver, S., & Warren, A. M. (2010). Resilience and indicators of adjustment during rehabilitation from a spinal cord injury. *Rehabilitation Psychology, 55*, 23–32. http://dx.doi.org/10.1037/a0018451

Wilson, J. P., & Moran, T. A. (1998). Psychological trauma: Posttraumatic stress disorder and spirituality. *Journal of Psychology and Theology, 26*, 168–178.

Witvliet, C. V. O., Phipps, K. A., Feldman, M. E., & Beckham, J. C. (2004). Posttraumatic mental and physical health correlates of forgiveness and religious coping in military veterans. *Journal of Traumatic Stress, 17*, 269–273. http://dx.doi.org/10.1023/B:JOTS.0000029270.47848.e5

Wong, P. T. P. (1998). Academic values and achievement motivation. In P. T. P. Wong & P. S. Prem (Eds.), *The human quest for meaning: A handbook of psychological research and clinical applications* (pp. 261–292). Mahwah, NJ: Erlbaum.

Wood, B. T., Worthington, E. L., Jr., Exline, J. J., Yali, A. M., Aten, J. D., & McMinn, M. R. (2010). Development, refinement, and psychometric properties of the Attitudes Toward God Scale (ATGS–9). *Psychology of Religion and Spirituality, 2*, 148–167. http://dx.doi.org/10.1037/a0018753

World Health Organization. (2016). *International statistical classification of diseases and related health problems* (10th rev.). Retrieved from http://apps.who.int/classifications/icd10/browse/2016/en

Worthington, E. L., Davis, D. E., Hook, J. N., Van Tongeren, D. R., Gartner, A. L., Jennings, D. R., . . . Lin, Y. (2013). Religion and spirituality and forgiveness. In R. Paloutzian & C. L. Park (Eds.), *Handbook of the psychology of religion and spirituality* (2nd ed., pp. 476–497). New York, NY: Guilford Press.

Worthington, E. L., Johnson, E. L., Hook, J. N., & Aten, J. D. (2013). *Evidence-based practices for Christian counseling and psychotherapy.* Downers Grove, IL: Intervarsity Press.

Worthington, E. L., & Langberg, D. (2012). Religious considerations and self-forgiveness in treating complex trauma and moral injury in present and former soldiers. *Journal of Psychology and Theology, 40,* 274–288.

Worthington, E. L., Wade, N. E., Hight, T. L., Ripley, J. S., McCullough, M. E., Berry, J. W., . . . O'Connor, L. (2003). The Religious Commitment Inventory–10: Development, refinement and validation of a brief scale for research and counseling. *Journal of Counseling Psychology, 50,* 84–96. http://dx.doi.org/10.1037/0022-0167.50.1.84

Wortmann, J. H., Park, C. L., & Edmondson, D. (2011). Trauma and PTSD symptoms: Does spiritual struggle mediate the link? *Psychological Trauma: Theory, Research, Practice and Policy, 3,* 442–452. http://dx.doi.org/10.1037/a0021413

Wrosch, C., Scheier, M. F., Miller, G. E., Schulz, R., & Carver, C. S. (2003). Adaptive self-regulation of unattainable goals: Goal disengagement, goal reengagement, and subjective well-being. *Personality and Social Psychology Bulletin, 29,* 1494–1508. http://dx.doi.org/10.1177/0146167203256921

Yakushko, O., Davidson, M. M., & Williams, E. N. (2009). Identity salience model: A paradigm for integrating multiple identities in clinical practice. *Psychotherapy: Theory, Research, Practice, Training, 46,* 180–192. http://dx.doi.org/10.1037/a0016080

Yalom, I. D. (1980). *Existential psychotherapy.* New York, NY: Basic Books.

Yanez, B., Edmondson, D., Stanton, A. L., Park, C. L., Kwan, L., Ganz, P. A., & Blank, T. O. (2009). Facets of spirituality as predictors of adjustment to cancer: Relative contributions of having faith and finding meaning. *Journal of Consulting and Clinical Psychology, 77,* 730–741. http://dx.doi.org/10.1037/a0015820

Yarhouse, M. A., & Johnson, V. (2013). Value and ethical issues: The interface between psychology and religion. In K. I., Pargament, A., Mahoney, & E. Shafranske (Eds.), *APA handbook of psychology, religion, and spirituality: Vol. 2. An applied psychology of religion and spirituality* (pp. 43–70). Washington, DC: American Psychological Association. http://dx.doi.org/10.1037/14046-003

Young, J. C., Dowdle, S., & Flowers, L. (2009). How spirituality can affect the therapeutic alliance. In J. D. Aten & M. M. Leach (Eds.), *Spirituality and the therapeutic process* (pp. 167–192). Washington, DC: American Psychological Association. http://dx.doi.org/10.1037/11853-008

Young, M. J., & Morris, M. W. (2004). Existential meanings and cultural models: The interplay of personal and supernatural agency in American and Hindu ways of responding to uncertainty. In J. Greenberg, S. L. Koole, & T. Pyszczynski

(Eds.), *Handbook of experimental existential psychology* (pp. 215–230). New York, NY: Guilford Press.

Ysseldyk, R., Matheson, K., & Anisman, H. (2010). Religiosity as identity: Toward an understanding of religion from a social identity perspective. *Personality and Social Psychology Review, 14*, 60–71.

Yuan, J., Ding, N., Liu, Y., & Yang, J. (2015). Unconscious emotion regulation: Nonconscious reappraisal decreases emotion-related physiological reactivity during frustration. *Cognition and Emotion, 29*, 1042–1053.

Zell, A. L., & Baumeister, R. F. (2013). How religion can support self-control and moral behavior. In R. Paloutzian & C. L. Park (Eds.), *Handbook of the psychology of religion and spirituality* (2nd ed., pp. 498–516). New York, NY: Guilford Press.

Zenner, C., Herrnleben-Kurz, S., & Walach, H. (2014). Mindfulness-based interventions in schools—A systematic review and meta-analysis. *Frontiers in Psychology, 5*, 603. http://dx.doi.org/10.3389/fpsyg.2014.00603

Zimbardo, P. G., & Boyd, J. N. (1999). Putting time in perspective: A valid, reliable individual-differences metric. *Journal of Personality and Social Psychology, 77*, 1271–1288. http://dx.doi.org/10.1037/0022-3514.77.6.1271

Zinnbauer, B. J., & Pargament, K. I. (1998). Spiritual conversion: A study of religious change among college students. *Journal for the Scientific Study of Religion, 37*, 161–180. http://dx.doi.org/10.2307/1388035

Zinnbauer, B. J., & Pargament, K. I. (2005). Religiousness and spirituality. In R. F. Paloutzian & C. L. Park (Eds.), *Handbook of the psychology of religion and spirituality* (pp. 121–142). New York, NY: Guilford Press.

INDEX

Bordin, E., 120, 121
Brenner, P. S., 106
Breuer, J., 65
Brief RCOPE, 110, 240
Briere, J., 5, 9
Brown, L., 88
BSS (Building Spiritual Strength),
179–181
Buckwalter, G., 220
Buddhism
global beliefs of, 22–25
within-group differences in, 97
Building Spiritual Strength (BSS),
179–181
Burnout, therapist, 149

Cai, W., 138
Calhoun, L. G., 71, 92
Cancer, 52, 71, 178
Carey, M. P., 87
Catholicism
and psychologist religious identity,
210
reconciliation and forgiveness in,
142
within-group differences in, 97
Causal attributions, 32, 37, 43
CBT. See Cognitive behavior therapy
Childhood sexual abuse
myths about, 145
processing memories of, 65–66
research on spirituality following, 52
Chisty, K., 112
Christianity. See also Catholicism
beliefs about good and evil in, 28
Evangelical, 97
global beliefs of, 22–25
mainstream focus on, 5
and psychologist religious identity,
210
and Western culture, 178
within-group differences in, 97
Chronic pain, 186
Churches, 86
Clergy, 155–156
Cognition
dialectical process between affect
and, 127
with posttraumatic stress disorder, 58

Cognitive behavior therapy (CBT),
120, 130, 174
Cognitive complexity, 148
Cognitive processing therapy (CPT),
66–67, 120
Coherence, 21
Comfort, religious, 111
Communities, spiritual
reliance on, 152
and resilience, 192–193
social support from, 165–166
and spiritual assessment, 101, 102,
104
Comorbidity, 59
Compassion fatigue, 147
Competence in addressing spirituality,
207–212, 231–232
Complicated grief, 47
Confidentiality, 217
Connection, 51
Contamination stories, 154–155
Control
global beliefs surrounding, 20, 21
secondary, 28
Conversion, religious, 52, 91
Coping
forms of spiritual, 46–47, 99, 110
problem-focused, 34
and reciprocal meaning-making
model, 82, 84
research on spirituality as factor in, 5
strategies for, 151–152
with vicarious trauma, 148
Corrective emotional experiences, 141
Countertransference, 146–147
Couples therapy, 70
Courage, 101–103
Courtois, C. A., 6
CPT (cognitive processing therapy),
66–67, 120
Culture, 60–61, 155–156, 231
Currier, J. M., 112
Cynicism, 40

Davis, D. E., 50
DBT (dialectical behavior therapy), 65
Decker, L. R., 51
Denton, R. T., 180
Deservedness, 43

therapist role in. *See* Therapist role in reciprocal meaning-making model
and trauma treatment, 56, 69, 164
Recovery. *see* Phase-based model of recovery
Re-Creating Your Life intervention, 178–179
Redemption stories, 154
Re-experiencing symptoms, 61
Reid, H. R., 88
Relationship(s)
    global meaning and restoring, 61, 68–72
    posttrauma, 137–141
    therapeutic, 141–146. *See also* Therapeutic alliance
Religion, 8. *See also specific headings*
Religious and Spiritual Struggles Scale, 110, 241
Religious bias, 141, 203–207
Religious comfort, 111
Religious Comfort and Strains Scale, 114
Religious Commitment Inventory–10, 106, 237
Religious conversion, 52, 91
Religious identity
    assessment of, 105–106
    and global beliefs, 20–21
    of psychologists, 210
Religious leaders, 192–194, 215–217, 232
Religiousness, 6
Religious nones, 6
Religious rituals. *See* Spiritual behaviors and religious rituals
Resick, P. A., 66
Resilience, 185–199
    and adaptive assimilation, 78
    case examples, 187, 188, 196–197
    definitions of, 186–187
    future directions for research and clinical focus on, 229, 232
    in global meaning systems, 129
    and primary prevention, 187, 189–192
    research on spirituality as factor in, 5
    resources associated with greater, 188
    and secondary prevention, 187, 192–196

subsequent to initial traumas, 197–198
Respect, 204, 212
Responsibility, 43
Restorying techniques, 158–159
Risking Connection (treatment protocol), 148
Rituals. *See* Spiritual behaviors and religious rituals
Rothbaum, B. O., 90
Rumination, 124

Safety
    in phase-based model of recovery, 61, 64–65
    in posttrauma relationships, 138
    in secondary prevention strategies, 195
    and therapeutic alliance, 120–124
Salvation, 29
Sanctification, 29
Saunders, S. M., 211
Schemas. *See* Global meaning
Schnick, M. K., 66
School-based interventions, 191
Scott, C., 5
Secondary control, 28
Secondary prevention, 187, 192–196
Secondary traumatic stress, 147
Secular meaning, 226
Seeking Safety (SS) model, 64–65
Self-awareness, 148, 203–207
Self-blame, 162
Self-care, 64, 77, 125, 148
Self-esteem, 20, 106, 147, 165, 191
Selfhood, 48
Self-surrender, 21
September 11th terrorist attacks, 71, 194, 195
7×7 model of spiritual assessment, 101–104
Sexism, 145
Sexual abuse
    childhood. *See* Childhood sexual abuse
    manualized intervention for survivors of, 179
    and reciprocal meaning-making model, 89
Shame, 40, 156

SS (Seeking Safety) model, 64–65
Stein, N. R., 128
Stigma, 122
Struggle, spiritual. *See* Spiritual
  struggle
Substance abuse, 64, 65
Suffering
  assessing client's beliefs about, 104,
    107
  explanations for, 21, 28
  and reciprocal meaning-making
    model, 81
  and spiritual growth, 49
  ubiquitous realities of, 218
Suicidality, 64
Superiority, moral, 20
Support. *See* Social support

Tarakeshwar, N., 88
Tedeschi, R. G., 71, 92
Theodicy
  assessment of, 107
  in case example, 46
  defined, 21
  inadequate explanations for trauma
    in, 170
  and primary prevention, 187
  and reciprocal meaning-making
    model, 81
  and responses to traumatic events, 28
Theology, 182
Therapeutic alliance
  development of, 120–124
  and informed consent, 214
  and trust, 60
Therapist role in reciprocal meaning-
    making model, 135–150
  case example, 136, 139–144, 147
  and impact on meaning, 146–150
  and posttrauma relationships,
    137–141
  and therapeutic relationship,
    141–146
Training, clinician, 207–208, 231–232
Transcendence, 29
Transference, 140, 174
Transgression-Related Interpersonal
    Motivations Scale—12
    (TRIM–12), 113, 245

Trauma
  definitions of, 9–10
  increase in research on, 5
  resilience subsequent to initial,
    197–198
  and spirituality, 3–13. *See also*
    specific headings
  Type I, 59–60
  Type II, 59–60
  vicarious, 147–148
Trauma treatment, 55–73, 151–166
  assessing maladaptive meanings in,
    158–162
  case studies, 56–60, 64, 68–72,
    152–153, 155–166
  challenging maladaptive appraisals
    in, 164–165
  client's sense of the past in, 153,
    158–162
  clinical concerns in, 58–63
  future directions for, 230
  increased research on, 55–56
  mainstream approaches to, 5
  processing traumatic memories and
    situational meanings in, 61,
    65–68
  promoting safety in, 61, 64–65
  responding to spiritual barriers to,
    155–157
  restoring relationships and global
    meaning in, 61, 68–72
  setting stage for, 158
  and spiritually relevant social
    support, 165–166
  telling adaptive stories in,
    154–155
  working with moral injury in,
    162–163
TRIM–12 (Transgression-Related
    Interpersonal Motivations
    Scale—12), 113, 245
Trust
  posttraumatic loss of, 51
  and therapeutic alliance, 60, 120
  trauma as violation of, 39–40
Type II trauma, 59–60
Type I trauma, 59–60

U.S. Army, 192

Values
    defined, 29
    function of, 29–30
    global, 220
Veterans Administration (VA) system,
        112, 118
Vicarious trauma, 147–148
Vieten, C., 211, 212
Vietnam War veterans, 5, 44, 84
Views of Suffering Scale, 107, 238
Violations, 44–45
    consequences of, 124
    and posttraumatic growth, 71

and situational meaning, 32–33
    of therapist meaning systems, 218
Vocation, 101–103
Vulnerability
    global beliefs surrounding, 20, 21
    in spiritual meaning systems, 43

Walker, D. F., 6, 88
Westwood, M. J., 150
Worldviews. *See* Global beliefs
Worthington, E. L., 50, 113, 180

Yoga, 176–177

ABOUT THE AUTHORS

Crystal L. Park, PhD, is a professor of clinical psychology at the University of Connecticut. Her research focuses on multiple aspects of coping with stressful events, including the roles of religious beliefs and religious coping, the phenomenon of stress-related growth, and the making of meaning in the context of bereavement, traumatic events, and life-threatening illnesses. Her recent work has focused on integrative approaches to health, especially yoga. She is coeditor of *The Handbook of the Psychology of Religion and Spirituality* (2nd ed.; 2013) and *Medical Illness and Positive Life Change: Can Crisis Lead to Personal Transformation?* (2009).

Joseph M. Currier, PhD, is an assistant professor and director of clinical training in the combined Clinical and Counseling Psychology Doctoral Program at the University of South Alabama. His research focuses on psychological, spiritual/existential, and physical health consequences of military trauma and other stressful life events (e.g., bereavement, community violence) and on enhancing clinical interventions and assessment practices for individuals and families dealing with these issues. Many of his recent projects have focused on testing and validating the construct of moral injury as it relates to military populations and on illumining ways in which religion and spirituality can help and hinder recovery from trauma.

J. Irene Harris, PhD, LP, is an assistant professor at the University of Minnesota Departments of Psychiatry and Counseling Psychology, as well as a clinician investigator at the Minneapolis VA Health Care System. Her research focuses on the intersection and clinical applications of relationships between spiritual/religious functioning and mental health, with an emphasis on trauma and posttraumatic stress disorder (PTSD). Her recent work has focused on clinical approaches to the treatment of moral injury and spiritually integrated approaches to the treatment of PTSD.

Jeanne M. Slattery, PhD, is professor of psychology at Clarion University. She has written *Empathic Counseling: Meaning, Context, Ethics, and Skill* (with Crystal Park; 2011) and *Counseling Diverse Clients: Bringing Context Into Therapy* (2003). She has a small private practice working with adults and children with mood and anxiety disorders, especially subsequent to a history of trauma.